CoNLL SIGMORPHON 2018 Shared Task: Universal Morphological Reinflection

Brussels, Belgium
31 October 2018

ISBN: 978-1-5108-7415-2

CoNLL 2018

Proceedings of the

CoNLL–SIGMORPHON 2018 Shared Task: Universal Morphological Reinflection

October 31, 2018
Brussels, Belgium

© 2018 The Association for Computational Linguistics

Order copies of this and other ACL proceedings from:

Association for Computational Linguistics (ACL)
209 N. Eighth Street
Stroudsburg, PA 18360
USA
Tel: +1-570-476-8006
Fax: +1-570-476-0860
acl@aclweb.org

Preface

This volume contains the system description papers associated with the CoNLL-SIGMORPHON shared task in morphological reinflection held at CoNLL 2018, in Brussels, Belgium. This is the second in a two-year series of shared tasks that address supervised learning of morphology. The origin of these two tasks was the SIGMORPHON shared task in 2016, which was subsequently expanded in both 2017 and 2018, called the CoNLL-SIGMORPHON shared tasks. While the first two iterations focused on learning inflectional patterns from examples, we this year introduced a new task similar to a cloze test—a format familiar from L2-learner exams—where participants we asked to inflect words in their sentential context in a morphosyntactically appropriate way.

To support the inflection task 1 this year, we collected and curated inflection table data from 103 languages, representing a typologically and genealogically diverse data set against which to evaluate performance of the systems. We evaluated the ability to learn to inflect nouns, andjectives, and verbs from their lemmata (citation forms) into a desired target form.

For task 2, we collected annotated text data for 7 languages from the Universal Dependencies resources, and matched tokens to their UniMorph inflection tables, so that each word form would be associated with an inflection table representing all the possible forms of that word. Following this, we annotated the target words to be completed by learning algorithms with all their plausible grammatically well-formed variants for fine-grained evaluation.

Both tasks were evaluated under three different training data conditions: low, medium, and high.

A total of 15 teams with members from 17 institutions participated in the shared task with a total of 33 system submissions. Task 1 received 27 submissions and task 2 received 6. Consistent with previous SIGMORPHON and CoNLL-SIGMORPHON shared task results, neural network models performed very well in each data condition, including with a very low-resource training set.

The creation of several components in the shared task received support from DARPA I20 in the program Low Resource Languages for Emergent Incidents (LORELEI). We wish to thank the organizers of CoNLL 2018 and the parallel Universal Dependencies CoNLL shared task (Multilingual Parsing from Raw Text to Universal Dependencies) for their support and help. We also want to thank the participants and other members of the community who actively participated by providing useful commentary, advice, and feedback on the organization and structure of the tasks.

We hope the data sets, which are now available, will serve as a useful resource to develop further techniques and research to address various challenges in the learning of morphology.

MANS HULDEN & RYAN COTTERELL, on behalf of the shared task organizers
September 2018

Organizers:

Mans Hulden (co-chair)	University of Colorado
Ryan Cotterell (co-chair)	Johns Hopkins University
Jason Eisner	Johns Hopkins University
Katharina Kann	New York University
Christo Kirov	Johns Hopkins University
Arya D. McCarthy	Johns Hopkins University
Sebastian Mielke	Johns Hopkins University
Garrett Nicolai	Johns Hopkins University
Miikka Silfverberg	University of Colorado / University of Helsinki
John Sylak-Glassman	Johns Hopkins University
Ekaterina Vylomova	University of Melbourne
Géraldine Walther	University of Zurich
David Yarowsky	Johns Hopkins University

Table of Contents

Conference Program

Wednesday, October 31st, 2018

11:00–11:30   *The CoNLL–SIGMORPHON 2018 Shared Task: Universal Morphological Reinflection*
Ryan Cotterell, Christo Kirov, John Sylak-Glassman, Géraldine Walther, Ekaterina Vylomova, Arya D. McCarthy, Katharina Kann, Sebastian Mielke, Garrett Nicolai, Miikka Silfverberg, David Yarowsky, Jason Eisner and Mans Hulden

11:30–12:30: Poster session: shared task systems

KU-CST at CoNLLSIGMORPHON 2018 Shared Task: a Tridirectional Model
Manex Agirrezabal

IPS-WASEDA system at CoNLL-SIGMORPHON 2018 Shared Task on morphological inflection
Rashel Fam and Yves Lepage

AX Semantics' Submission to the CoNLL-SIGMORPHON 2018 Shared Task
Andreas Madsack, Alessia Cavallo, Johanna Heininger and Robert Weißgraeber

Experiments on Morphological Reinflection: CoNLL-2018 Shared Task
Rishabh Jain and Anil Kumar Singh

The NYU System for the CoNLL–SIGMORPHON 2018 Shared Task on Universal Morphological Reinflection
Katharina Kann, Stanislas Lauly and Kyunghyun Cho

Attention-free encoder decoder for morphological processing
Stefan Daniel Dumitrescu and Tiberiu Boros

UZH at CoNLL-SIGMORPHON 2018 Shared Task on Universal Morphological Reinflection
Peter Makarov and Simon Clematide

Finding the way from ä to a: Sub-character morphological inflection for the SIGMORPHON 2018 shared task
Fynn Schröder, Marcel Kamlot, Gregor Billing and Arne Köhn

Morphological Reinflection in Context: CU Boulder's Submission to CoNLL-SIGMORPHON 2018 Shared Task
Ling Liu, Ilamvazhuthy Subbiah, Adam Wiemerslage, Jonathan Lilley and Sarah Moeller

Copenhagen at CoNLL–SIGMORPHON 2018: Multilingual Inflection in Context with Explicit Morphosyntactic Decoding
Yova Kementchedjhieva, Johannes Bjerva and Isabelle Augenstein

The CoNLL–SIGMORPHON 2018 Shared Task: Universal Morphological Reinflection

Ryan Cotterell[1] and **Christo Kirov**[1] and **John Sylak-Glassman**[1] and
Géraldine Walther[2] and **Ekaterina Vylomova**[3] and **Arya D. McCarthy**[1] and
Katharina Kann[4] and **Sebastian Mielke**[1] and **Garrett Nicolai**[1] and
Miikka Silfverberg[5,6] and **David Yarowsky**[1] and **Jason Eisner**[1] and **Mans Hulden**[5]
Johns Hopkins University[1]   University of Zurich[2]   University of Melbourne[3]
NYU[4]   University of Colorado[5]   University of Helsinki[6]

Abstract

The CoNLL-SIGMORPHON 2018 shared task on supervised learning of morphological generation featured data sets from 103 typologically diverse languages. Apart from extending the number of languages involved in earlier supervised tasks of generating inflected forms, this year the shared task also featured a new second task which asked participants to inflect words in sentential context, similar to a cloze task. This second task featured seven languages. Task 1 received 27 submissions and task 2 received 6 submissions. Both tasks featured a low, medium, and high data condition. Nearly all submissions featured a neural component and built on highly-ranked systems from the earlier 2017 shared task. In the inflection task (task 1), 41 of the 52 languages present in last year's inflection task showed improvement by the best systems in the low-resource setting. The cloze task (task 2) proved to be difficult, and few submissions managed to consistently improve upon both a simple neural baseline system and a lemma-repeating baseline.

1 Introduction

Some of a word's syntactic and semantic properties are expressed on the word form through a process termed morphological inflection. For example, each English count noun has both singular and plural forms (`robot/robots`, `process/processes`), known as the inflected forms of the noun. Some languages display little inflection, while others possess a proliferation of forms. A Polish verb can have nearly 100 inflected forms and an Archi verb has thousands (Kibrik, 1998).

Natural language processing systems must be able to analyze and generate these inflected forms. Fortunately, inflected forms tend to be systematically related to one another. This is why English

Lang	Lemma	Inflection	Inflected form
en	hug	V;PST	hugged
	spark	V;V.PTCP;PRS	sparking
es	liberar	V;IND;FUT;2;SG	liberarás
	descomponer	V;NEG;IMP;2;PL	no descompongáis
de	aufbauen	V;IND;PRS;2;SG	baust auf
	Ärztin	N;DAT;PL	Ärztinnen

Table 1: Example training data from task 1. Each training example maps a *lemma* and *inflection* to an *inflected form*, The inflection is a bundle of *morphosyntactic features*. Note that inflected forms (and lemmata) can encompass multiple words. In the test data, the last column (the inflected form) must be predicted by the system.

speakers can usually predict the singular form from the plural and vice versa, even for words they have never seen before: given a novel noun `wug`, an English speaker knows that the plural is `wugs`.

We conducted a competition on generating inflected forms. This "shared task" consisted of two separate scenarios. In Task 1, participating systems must inflect word forms based on labeled examples. In English, an example of inflection is the conversion of a citation form[1] `run` to its present participle, `running`. The system is provided with the source form and the morphosyntactic description (MSD) of the target form, and must generate the actual target form. Task 2 is a harder version of Task 1, where the system must infer the appropriate MSD from a sentential context. This is essentially a cloze task, asking participants to provide the correct form of a lemma in context.

2 Tasks and Evaluation

2.1 Task 1: Inflection

The first task was identical to sub-task 1 from the CoNLL-SIGMORPHON 2017 shared task (Cotterell et al., 2017), but the language selection was extended from 52 languages to 103. The data

---

[1]In this work we use the terms *citation form* and *lemma* interchangeably.

1

Proceedings of the CoNLL–SIGMORPHON 2018 Shared Task: Universal Morphological Reinflection, pages 1–27,
Brussels, Belgium, October 31, 2018. ©2018 Association for Computational Linguistics

sets for the overlapping languages between 2017 and 2018 were also resampled and are not identical. The task consists of morphological generation with sparse training data, something that can be practically useful for MT and other downstream tasks in NLP. Here, participants were given examples of inflected forms as shown in Table 1. Each test example asked participants to produce some other inflected form when given a lemma and a bundle of morphosyntactic features as input.

The training data was sparse in the sense that it included only a few inflected forms from each lemma. That is, as in human L1 learning, the learner does not necessarily observe any complete paradigms in a language where the paradigms are large (e.g., dozens of inflected forms per lemma).[2]

Key points:

1. The task is inflection: Given an input lemma and desired output tags, participants had to generate the correct output inflected form (a string).

2. The supervised training data consisted of individual forms (see Table 1) that were sparsely sampled from a large number of paradigms.

3. Forms that are empirically more frequent were more likely to appear in both training and test data (see §3 for details).

4. Systems were evaluated after training on 10^2 (low), 10^3 (medium), and 10^4 (high) lemma/MSD/inflected form triplets.

2.2 Task 2: Inflection in Context

The cloze test is a common exercise in an L2 instruction setting. In the cloze test, a number of words are deleted from a text and students are required to fill in the gaps with contextually plausible forms, often working from the knowledge about which lemma should be inflected. The second task of the morphology shared task presents two variations of this traditional cloze test in two tracks specifically aimed at data-driven morphology learning.

---

² Of course, human L1 learners do not get to observe explicit morphological feature bundles for the types that they observe. Rather, they analyze inflected tokens in context to discover both morphological features (including *inherent* features such as noun gender (Arnon and Ramscar, 2012)) and paradigmatic structure (number of forms per lemma, number of expressed featural contrasts such as tense, number, person...).

Solving a cloze test well requires integration of many types of evidence beyond the pure capacity to inflect a word on demand. Since our training sets were gathered from actual textual resources, a good solver that accurately determines the most plausible form must implicitly combine knowledge of morphology, morphosyntax, semantics, and pragmatics. Potentially, even textual register and genre may affect the choice of correct form. Hence, the task is both intrinsically interesting from a linguistic point of view and carries potential to support many downstream NLP applications.

TRACK 1:

The ___ are barking
the/DT dog be/AUX+PRES+3PL bark/V+V.PTCP

TRACK 2:

The ___ are barking.
dog

Figure 1: Test examples for tracks 1 and 2 in the cloze task. The objective is to inflect the target lemma dog in a contextually appropriate form, which in this case is dogs. Competitors observe context word forms, their lemmata and MSDs in track 1, whereas they only observe the context word forms in track 2.

As shown in Figure 1, both tracks supply the lemma of the omitted target word form and ask the competitors to inflect the lemma in a contextually appropriate way. In the first track, the competitors additionally see the lemmata and MSDs for all context words, whereas in the second track only the context words are available. In contrast to task 1, the MSD for the target lemma is never observed in either the first or the second track. This means that successful inflection requires the competitors to identify relevant contextual cues.

TRACK 1:

The dogs are barking
the/DT dog/N+PL be/AUX+PRES+3PL bark/V+V.PTCP

TRACK 2:

The dogs are barking.
dog

Figure 2: Training examples for tracks 1 and 2 in the cloze task. Track 1 supplies a full morphosyntactically annotated corpus as training data, whereas track 2 only supplies lemmata for a number of selected training tokens. Remaining tokens lack annotation altogether.

As training data, the first track supplies a

full morphosyntactically annotated corpus of sentences: every token is annotated with a lemma and MSD as shown in Figure 2. In the second track, the training data identifies a number of target tokens. Lemmata are supplied for these tokens but the remaining tokens receive no MSD annotation.

Similarly to task 1, both tracks in task 2 provide three different training data settings providing varying amounts of data: low (ca. 10^3 tokens), medium (ca. 10^4 tokens) and high (ca. 10^5 tokens). The token counts refer to the total number of tokens in the training sets. In the first track, this allows competitors to train their systems on all available tokens. In the second track, however, only a number of tokens supply the input lemma as explained above. Thus, the effective number of training examples is smaller in the second track than in the first track. In both tracks, competitors were restricted to using only the provided training sets. For example, semi-supervised training using external data was forbidden.

Key points:

1. The task is inflection in context. Given an input lemma in sentential context, participants generate the correct inflected output form.

2. Two degrees of supervision are provided. In track 1, participants see context word forms and their lemmata, as well as their MSDs. In track 2, participants only witness context word forms.

3. The supervised training data, the development data, and the test data consist of sampled sentences from Universal Dependencies (UD) treebanks (Nivre et al., 2017) together with UD-provided lemmata as well as MSDs, which were converted to the UniMorph format, in track 1.

3 Data

3.1 Data for Task 1

Languages The data for the shared task was highly multilingual, comprising 103 unique languages. Of these, 52 were shared with the 2017 shared task (Cotterell et al., 2017). As with all but 5 of the 2017 languages (Khaling, Kurmanji Kurdish, Sorani Kurdish, Haida, and Basque), the 34 remaining 2018 languages were sourced from the English edition of Wiktionary, a large multilingual crowd-sourced dictionary containing morphological paradigms for many lemmata.[3]

The shared task language set is genealogically diverse, including languages from ∼20 language stocks. Although the majority of the languages are Indo-European, we also include two language isolates (Haida and Basque) along with languages from Athabaskan (Navajo), Kartvelian (Georgian), Quechua, Semitic (Arabic, Hebrew), Sino-Tibetan (Khaling), Turkic (Turkish), and Uralic (Estonian, Finnish, Hungarian, and Northern Sami) language families. The shared task language set is also diverse in terms of morphological structure, with languages which use primarily prefixes (Navajo), suffixes (Quechua and Turkish), and a mix, with Spanish exhibiting internal vowel variations along with suffixes and Georgian using both infixes and suffixes. The language set also exhibits features such as templatic morphology (Arabic, Hebrew), vowel harmony (Turkish, Finnish, Hungarian), and consonant harmony (Navajo) which require systems to learn non-local alternations. Finally, the resource level of the languages in the shared task set varies greatly, from major world languages (e.g. Arabic, English, French, Spanish, Russian) to languages with few speakers (e.g. Haida, Khaling). Typologically, the majority of the languages are agglutinating or fusional, with three polysynthetic languages; Haida, Greenlandic, and Navajo.[4]

Data Format For each language, the basic data consists of triples of the form (lemma, feature bundle, inflected form), as in Table 1. The first feature in the bundle always specifies the core part of speech (e.g., verb).

All features in the bundle are coded according to the UniMorph Schema, a cross-linguistically consistent universal morphological feature set (Sylak-Glassman et al., 2015a,b).

Extraction from Wiktionary For each of the Wiktionary languages, Wiktionary provides a number of tables, each of which specifies the full inflectional paradigm for a particular lemma. These tables were extracted using a template annotation procedure described in (Kirov et al., 2018).

Within a language, different paradigms may

---

[3] https://en.wiktionary.org/ (08-2016 snapshot)

[4] Although, some linguists (Baker, 1996) would exclude Navajo from the polysynthetic languages due to its lack of noun incorporation.

have different shapes. To prepare the shared task data, each language's parsed tables from Wiktionary were grouped according to their tabular structure and number of cells. Each group represents a different type of paradigm (e.g., verb). We used only groups with a large number of lemmata, relative to the number of lemmata available for the language as a whole. For each group, we associated a feature bundle with each cell position in the table, by manually replacing the prose labels describing grammatical features (e.g. "accusative case") with UniMorph features (e.g. ACC). This allowed us to extract triples as described in the previous section. The dataset produced by this process was sampled to create appropriately-sized data for the shared task, as described in §3.1.[5] The dataset sizes by language are given in Table 2 and Table 3.

Sampling the Train-Dev-Test Splits. From each language's collection of paradigms, we sampled the training, development, and test sets as follows.[6]

Our first step was to construct probability distributions over the (lemma, feature bundle, inflected form) triples in our full dataset. For each triple, we counted how many tokens the inflected form has in the February 2017 dump of Wikipedia for that language. To distribute the counts of an observed form over all the triples that have this token as its form, we use the syncretism resolution method of Cotterell et al. (2018), training a neural network on unambiguous forms to estimate the distribution over all, even ambiguous, forms. We then sampled 12,000 triples without replacement from this distribution. The first 100 were taken as the low-resource training set for sub-task 1, the first 1,000 as the medium-resource training set, and the first 10,000 as the high-resource training set. Note that these training sets are nested, and that the highest-count triples tend to appear in the smaller training sets.

The final 2,000 triples were randomly shuffled and then split in half to obtain development and test sets of 1,000 forms each. The final shuffling was performed to ensure that the development set is similar to the test set. By contrast, the development and test sets tend to contain lower-count

triples than the training set.[7] Note that for languages that do not have enough triples for this process, we settle for omitting the higher-resource training regimes and scale down the other sizes. Details for all languages are found in Tables 2 and 3.

3.2 Data for Task 2

All task 2 data sets are based on Universal Dependencies (UD) v2 treebanks (Nivre et al., 2017). We used the data sets aimed for the 2017 CoNLL shared task on Multilingual Dependency Parsing (Zeman et al., 2017) because those were available before the official UD v2 data sets.[8] For contextual inflection data sets, we retained only word forms, lemmata, part-of-speech tags and morphosyntactic feature descriptions. Dependency trees were discarded along with all other annotations present in the treebanks.

Task 2 submissions are evaluated with regard to two distinct criteria: (1) the ability of the system to reconstruct the *original* word form in the UD test set and (2) the ability of the system to find a *contextually plausible* form even if the form differs from the original one. Evaluation on plausible forms is based on manually identifying the set of contextually plausible forms for each test example. Because of the need for manual annotation, task 2 covers a more limited set of languages than task 1. In total, there are seven languages: English, Finnish, French, German, Russian, Spanish and Swedish. Token counts for the training, development and test sets are given in Table 4.

Data Conversion Some of the UD treebanks required slight modifications in order to be suitable for reinflection. In the Finnish data sets, lemmata for compound words included morpheme boundaries, for example `muisti#kapasiteetti` 'memory capacity'. The morpheme boundary symbols were deleted. In the Russian treebanks,

---

[5]Full, unsampled Wiktionary parses are made available at `unimorph.org` on a rolling basis.

[6]These datasets can be obtained from `https://sigmorphon.github.io/sharedtasks/2018/`

[7]This is a realistic setting, since supervised training is usually employed to generalize from frequent words that appear in annotated resources to less frequent words that do not. Unsupervised learning methods also tend to generalize from more frequent words (which can be analyzed more easily by combining information from many contexts) to less frequent ones.

[8]The German 2017 CoNLL UD shared task data set is problematic: (1) there are many sentence fragments, (2) some words have complete MSDs while others are lacking MSD altogether. Therefore, we eventually decided to use the official v2 UD data sets for the German test data. These problems are not present in the official UD distribution.

Language	Family	Lemmata / Forms	High	Medium	Low	Dev	Test
Adyghe	Caucasian	1666 / 20475	1664/10000	760/1000	99/100	763/1000	749/1000
Albanian	Indo-European	589 / 33483	588/10000	375/1000	84/100	377/1000	373/1000
Arabic	Semitic	4134 / 140003	3204/10000	832/1000	99/100	807/1000	813/1000
Armenian	Indo-European	7033 / 338750	4658/10000	903/1000	98/100	880/1000	900/1000
Asturian	Romance	436 / 29797	432/10000	361/1000	90/100	368/1000	365/1000
Azeri	Iranian	340 / 8004	340/6488	290/1000	79/100	73/100	81/100
Bashkir	Turkic	1084 / 12168	1084/10000	662/1000	94/100	657/1000	651/1000
Basque	Isolate	45 / 12663	45/10000	42/1000	24/100	41/1000	43/1000
Belarusian	Slavic	1027 / 16113	1027/10000	616/1000	98/100	628/1000	630/1000
Bengali	Indo-Aryan	136 / 4443	136/4243	134/1000	65/100	65/100	68/100
Breton	Celtic	44 / 2294	44/1983	44/1000	40/100	38/100	39/100
Bulgarian	Slavic	2468 / 55730	2133/10000	716/1000	98/100	742/1000	744/1000
Catalan	Romance	1547 / 81576	1545/10000	746/1000	95/100	738/1000	738/1000
Classical-Syriac	Semitic	160 / 3652	160/2396	160/1000	74/100	70/100	73/100
Cornish	Celtic	9 / 469	—	9/346	9/100	9/50	9/50
Crimean-Tatar	Turkic	1230 / 7514	1230/7314	704/1000	94/100	95/100	95/100
Czech	Slavic	5125 / 134527	3908/10000	848/1000	97/100	848/1000	849/1000
Danish	Germanic	3193 / 25508	3137/10000	877/1000	100/100	866/1000	853/1000
Dutch	Germanic	4993 / 55467	4161/10000	913/1000	100/100	898/1000	894/1000
English	Germanic	22765 / 120004	8367/10000	989/1000	100/100	985/1000	984/1000
Estonian	Uralic	886 / 38215	886/10000	587/1000	94/100	553/1000	577/1000
Faroese	Germanic	3077 / 45474	2959/10000	857/1000	99/100	852/1000	865/1000
Finnish	Uralic	57642 / 2490377	8643/10000	985/1000	100/100	983/1000	987/1000
French	Romance	7535 / 367732	5592/10000	936/1000	98/100	948/1000	941/1000
Friulian	Romance	168 / 8071	168/7871	168/1000	76/100	79/100	79/100
Galician	Romance	486 / 36801	486/10000	421/1000	91/100	421/1000	423/1000
Georgian	Kartvelian	3782 / 74412	3537/10000	861/1000	100/100	872/1000	874/1000
German	Germanic	15060 / 179339	6797/10000	961/1000	100/100	945/1000	962/1000
Greek	Hellenic	10581 / 186663	5130/10000	897/1000	98/100	915/1000	908/1000
Greenlandic	Inuit	23 / 368	—	23/268	23/100	21/50	21/50
Haida	Isolate	41 / 7040	41/6840	41/1000	40/100	34/100	38/100
Hebrew	Semitic	510 / 13818	510/10000	470/1000	95/100	431/1000	453/1000
Hindi	Indo-Aryan	258 / 54438	258/10000	252/1000	85/100	254/1000	255/1000
Hungarian	Uralic	13989 / 503042	7123/10000	963/1000	100/100	973/1000	978/1000
Icelandic	Germanic	4775 / 76945	4115/10000	894/1000	100/100	898/1000	906/1000
Ingrian	Uralic	50 / 1099	—	50/999	45/100	30/50	31/50
Irish	Celtic	7464 / 107298	5040/10000	906/1000	99/100	913/1000	893/1000
Italian	Romance	10009 / 509574	6389/10000	948/1000	100/100	942/1000	944/1000
Kabardian	Caucasian	250 / 3092	250/2892	246/1000	81/100	82/100	81/100
Kannada	Dravidian	159 / 6402	159/4383	147/1000	54/100	53/100	59/100
Karelian	Uralic	20 / 682	—	20/582	20/100	17/50	18/50
Kashubian	Slavic	37 / 509	—	37/402	34/100	27/50	28/50
Kazakh	Turkic	26 / 357	—	26/257	26/100	22/50	25/50
Khakas	Turkic	75 / 1200	—	52/732	44/100	31/50	32/50
Khaling	Sino-TIbetan	591 / 156097	584/10000	426/1000	92/100	411/1000	422/1000
Kurmanji	Iranian	15083 / 216370	7046/10000	945/1000	100/100	949/1000	958/1000
Ladin	Romance	180 / 7656	180/7456	179/1000	80/100	81/100	75/100
Latin	Romance	17214 / 509182	6517/10000	943/1000	100/100	939/1000	945/1000

Table 2: Total number of lemmata and forms available for sampling, and number of distinct lemmata and forms present in each data condition in Task 1. Data permitting, there were 10000,1000, and 100 forms in the High, Medium, and Low conditions, respectively, and 1000 forms in each Dev and Test set.

Language	Family	Lemmata / Forms	High	Medium	Low	Dev	Test
Latvian	Baltic	7548 / 136998	5268/10000	930/1000	99/100	922/1000	923/1000
Lithuanian	Baltic	1458 / 34130	1443/10000	632/1000	96/100	664/1000	639/1000
Livonian	Uralic	203 / 3987	203/3787	203/1000	71/100	70/100	70/100
Lower-Sorbian	Slavic	994 / 20121	993/10000	616/1000	96/100	621/1000	631/1000
Macedonian	Slavic	10313 / 168057	6107/10000	951/1000	99/100	943/1000	956/1000
Maltese	Semitic	112 / 3584	112/1560	112/1000	68/100	71/100	69/100
Mapudungun	Araucanian	26 / 783	—	26/602	26/100	22/50	23/50
Middle-French	Romance	603 / 36970	603/10000	480/1000	92/100	491/1000	505/1000
Middle-High-German	Germanic	29 / 708	—	29/594	27/100	19/50	22/50
Middle-Low-German	Germanic	52 / 1513	—	52/988	43/100	30/50	34/50
Murrinhpatha	Australian	29 / 1110	—	29/973	28/100	24/50	24/50
Navajo	Athabaskan	674 / 12354	674/10000	489/1000	92/100	491/1000	494/1000
Neapolitan	Romance	40 / 1808	40/1568	40/1000	36/100	38/100	37/100
Norman	Romance	5 / 280	—	5/100	5/100	5/50	5/50
North-Frisian	Germanic	51 / 3204	51/2256	51/1000	42/100	43/100	44/100
Northern-Sami	Uralic	2103 / 62677	1977/10000	750/1000	97/100	717/1000	730/1000
Norwegian-Bokmaal	Germanic	5527 / 19238	5041/10000	925/1000	100/100	928/1000	930/1000
Norwegian-Nynorsk	Germanic	4689 / 16563	4420/10000	922/1000	99/100	903/1000	912/1000
Occitan	Romance	174 / 8316	174/8116	173/1000	76/100	81/100	75/100
Old-Armenian	Indo-European	4300 / 93085	3413/10000	837/1000	100/100	802/1000	822/1000
Old-Church-Slavonic	Slavic	152 / 4148	152/2961	151/1000	78/100	70/100	76/100
Old-English	Germanic	1867 / 42425	1795/10000	688/1000	96/100	708/1000	701/1000
Old-French	Romance	1700 / 123374	1666/10000	745/1000	96/100	769/1000	722/1000
Old-Irish	Celtic	49 / 1078	—	49/851	38/100	27/50	26/50
Old-Saxon	Germanic	863 / 22287	861/10000	514/1000	85/100	535/1000	494/1000
Pashto	Iranian	395 / 6945	395/6340	289/1000	82/100	77/100	78/100
Persian	Iranian	273 / 37128	273/10000	269/1000	82/100	268/1000	267/1000
Polish	Slavic	10185 / 201024	5922/10000	935/1000	99/100	938/1000	942/1000
Portuguese	Romance	4001 / 305961	3657/10000	905/1000	98/100	868/1000	865/1000
Quechua	Quechuan	1006 / 180004	957/10000	515/1000	91/100	492/1000	506/1000
Romanian	Romance	4405 / 80266	3351/10000	858/1000	99/100	854/1000	828/1000
Russian	Slavic	28068 / 473481	8241/10000	973/1000	100/100	985/1000	977/1000
Sanskrit	Indo-Aryan	917 / 33847	917/10000	548/1000	91/100	585/1000	558/1000
Scottish-Gaelic	Celtic	73 / 781	—	73/681	57/100	36/50	39/50
Serbo-Croatian	Slavic	24419 / 840799	6726/10000	963/1000	99/100	965/1000	945/1000
Slovak	Slavic	1046 / 14796	1046/10000	625/1000	95/100	590/1000	633/1000
Slovene	Slavic	2535 / 60110	2368/10000	757/1000	99/100	760/1000	793/1000
Sorani	Iranian	274 / 22990	263/10000	197/1000	74/100	198/1000	199/1000
Spanish	Romance	5460 / 383390	4621/10000	906/1000	99/100	902/1000	922/1000
Swahili	Bantu	100 / 10092	100/8800	88/1000	49/100	50/100	42/100
Swedish	Germanic	10552 / 78407	6508/10000	952/1000	100/100	954/1000	970/1000
Tatar	Turkic	1283 / 7832	1283/7632	736/1000	98/100	95/100	95/100
Telugu	Dravidian	127 / 1548	—	—	18/61	16/50	16/50
Tibetan	Sino-Tibetan	65 / 353	—	63/158	56/100	38/50	38/50
Turkish	Turkic	3579 / 275460	2876/10000	821/1000	98/100	849/1000	840/1000
Turkmen	Turkic	68 / 810	—	68/710	51/100	35/50	35/50
Ukrainian	Slavic	1493 / 20904	1491/10000	722/1000	99/100	745/1000	736/1000
Urdu	Indo-Aryan	182 / 12572	182/10000	113/1000	53/100	105/1000	107/1000
Uzbek	Turkic	15 / 1260	15/1060	15/1000	15/100	15/100	15/100
Venetian	Romance	368 / 18227	368/10000	339/1000	88/100	341/1000	340/1000
Votic	Uralic	55 / 1430	55/1230	55/1000	50/100	48/100	47/100
Welsh	Celtic	183 / 10641	183/10000	181/1000	78/100	76/100	80/100
West-Frisian	Germanic	85 / 1429	85/1078	85/1000	53/100	62/100	61/100
Yiddish	Germanic	803 / 7986	803/7356	581/1000	96/100	90/100	93/100
Zulu	Bantu	566 / 39607	566/10000	450/1000	90/100	449/1000	443/1000

Table 3: Total number of lemmata and forms available for sampling, and number of distinct lemmata and forms present in each data condition in Task 1. Data permitting, there were 10000,1000, and 100 forms in the High, Medium, and Low conditions, respectively, and 1000 forms in each Dev and Test set.

Language	Train			Dev	Test
	low	medium	high		
English	1,009	10,016	100,031	22,509	22,765
Finnish	1,001	10,009	100,003	16,543	15,452
French	1,016	10,004	100,001	28,304	14,992
German	1,005	10,001	79,439	3,752	22,903
Russian	1,003	10,020	75,964	11,292	27,935
Spanish	1,017	10,035	100,000	35,209	27,807
Swedish	1,007	10,009	66,645	7,999	20,808

Table 4: Token counts of the training, development and test sets for task 2.

Language	Dev	Test
English	2,489	993
Finnish	1,881	787
French	1,655	491
German	333	989
Russian	1,181	996
Spanish	2,268	713
Swedish	573	940

Table 5: Counts of target lemmata to be inflected in the development and test sets for task 2.

all lemmata were written completely in upper case letters. These were converted to lower case.[9]

Manual annotation To produce the complete list of "plausible forms" annotators were given complete UniMorph inflection tables for the center lemma for each sentence and were asked to check off all forms that are "grammatically plausible" in the particular context. For example, given an original sentence **We saw the dog**, the form **dogs** would be contextually plausible and would be annotated into the test set. For pro-drop languages and short sentences, it is sometimes the case that all or most indicative, conditional, and future forms of a verb are acceptable when the subject is omitted and agreement is unknown. For example, consider the Spanish sentence from the test data:

	la	mejor	de	Primera
ser				
'to be'	'the'	'best'	'of'	'premier (league)'

Obviously, almost any person, tense, and aspect of the verb 'to be' will be appropriate for this limited context (sería 'I would be', fue 'he/she/it was', eres 'you are', ...). Of course, depending on the genre of the text, some would be highly

---

[9]We used the Python3 function string.lower.

implausible, but the annotation intends to capture morphosyntactic rather than semantic and pragmatic felicity.

We had one annotator for each test set, with the exception of French, in which, due to practical difficulties in finding a native speaker annotator, we did not annotate the plausible forms and instead used the original sentences.

When forming the final test sets, all test examples with more than 5 contextually plausible word form alternatives were filtered out. This was done because a large number of plausible word forms was deemed to raise the risk of annotation errors. A threshold of 5 plausible forms was chosen because it means that all languages have test sets greater than 700 examples. The test set for French is smaller but this is not due to manual annotations.

UD:

So	what	happened	?
ADV	PRON	VERB Mood=Ind Tense=Past VerbForm=Fin	PUNCT

UniMorph:

So	what	happened	?
ADV	PRO	V IND PST FIN	PUNCT

Figure 3: A morphosyntactically annotated sentence from the original UD treebank for English and the result of an automatic conversion into the UniMorph annotation schema.

Sampling examples The data sets for each language are based on UD treebanks for the given language. We preserved UD splits into training, development and test data.

For each UD treebank, we first formed sets of training, development and test candidate sentences. A sentence was a candidate for the shared task data set if it contained a token found in the UniMorph resource for the relevant language; or more precisely, a token whose word form, lemma and MSD occur in a same UniMorph inflection table.

We limited target tokens to tokens present in the UniMorph resource in order to facilitate manual annotation of data sets. In particular, we limited the set of possible target MSDs to MSDs which occur in the Unimorph resource. This was necessary to avoid a prohibitively large number of contextually plausible inflections in certain languages. For example, Finnish includes a number of clitics (ko/kä, kin, han/hän, pa/pä, s, kaan/kään) which can be appended relatively freely to word forms. Combinations of clitics are also possible. This easily leads to hundreds of word forms which can be contextually plausible. Restricting the MSDs of a possible output form to the more limited set of MSDs occurring in the UniMorph resource made the selection of plausible forms far more manageable from an annotation perspective.

Training data sets were formed from candidate sentences simply by sampling a suitable number of sentences from the candidate sets in order to achieve the desired token counts 10^3, 10^4, and 10^5 for the low, medium, and high data settings, respectively. For German and Russian, all candidate sentences were used in the high data setting, although this was not sufficient to create a training set of 10^4 tokens. The training sets for German and Russian are, therefore, smaller than those for the other languages. For the development sets, we used all available candidate sentences for all of the languages.

For the test data, we first formed a set of candidate sentences so that the combined number of target tokens in the test sets was 1,000.[10] Target tokens in these initial test sets were then manually annotated with additional contextually plausible word forms.

MSD conversion Sampling of training, development and test examples was based on comparing UD word forms, lemmata and MSDs to equivalents in UniMorph paradigms. Therefore, it was necessary to convert the morphosyntactic annotation in the UD data sets into UniMorph morphosyntactic annotation. We used deterministic tag conversion rules to accomplish this. An example of a source UD sentence and a target UniMorph sentence is shown in Figure 3.

Since the selection of languages in task 2 is small and we do not attempt to correct annotation errors in the UD source materials, conversion between UD and UniMorph morphosyntactic descriptions is generally straightforward.[11] However, UD descriptions are more fine-grained than

---

their UniMorph equivalents. For example, UD denotes lexical features such as noun gender which are inherent features of a lexeme possessed by all of its word forms. Such inherent features are missing from UniMorph which exclusively annotates inflectional morphology (McCarthy et al., 2018). Therefore, UD features which lack correspondents in the UniMorph tagging schema were simply dropped during conversion.

4 Baselines

4.1 Task 1 Baseline

The baseline system provided for task 1 was based on the observation that, for a large number of languages, producing an inflected form from an input citation form can often be done by memorizing the suffix changes that occur in doing so, assuming enough examples are seen (Liu and Mao, 2016). For example, in witnessing a Finnish inflection of the noun koti 'home' in the singular elative case as kodista, a number of transformation rules can be extracted that may apply to previously unseen nouns:

```
$koti$
$kodista$   N;IN+ABL;SG
```

In this example, the following transformation rules are extracted:

```
$ → sta$          i$ → ista$
ti$ → dista$      oti$ → odista$
koti$ → kodista$
```

Such rules are then extracted from each example inflection in the training data. At generation time, the longest matching left hand side of a rule is identified and applied to the citation form. For example, if the Finnish noun luoti 'bullet' were to be inflected in the elative (N;IN+ABL;SG) using only the extracted rules given above, the transformation oti$ → odista$ would be triggered, producing the output luodista. In case there are multiple candidate rules of equally long left hand sides that all match, ties are broken by frequency—i.e. the rule that has been witnessed most times in the training data applies.

Since languages may also use prefixation as an inflectional strategy, a similar process is applied to any identified prefix changes. Identifying which parts of a change in a word form correspond to a prefix and which are considered suffixes requires alignment of the citation form and the output form, which is performed as a preliminary step. We refer the reader to Cotterell et al. (2017) for a detailed description of the baseline system.

4.2 Task 2 Baseline

Neural Baseline The neural baseline system is an encoder-decoder reinflection system with attention inspired by Kann and Schütze (2016). The crucial difference is that the reinflection is conditioned on sentence context. This is accomplished by conditioning the encoder on embeddings of context words in track 2 and context words, their lemmata and their MSDs in track 1.

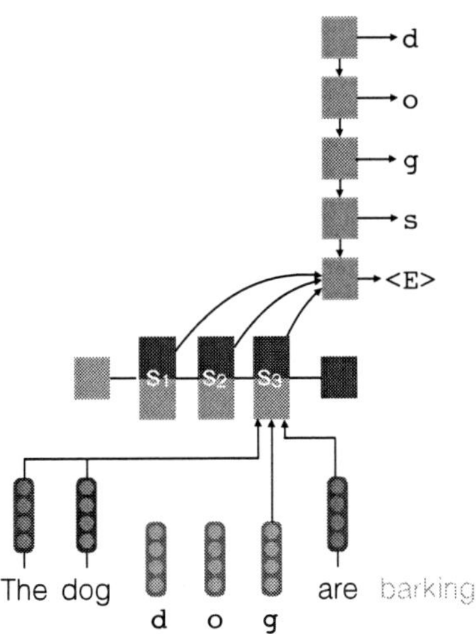

Figure 4: The neural baseline system for track 2 of task 2: A bidirectional LSTM encoder, conditioned on embeddings of the left context word **The**, right context word **are** and a whole token embedding of the lemma **dog**, is used to encode the character sequence (**d**, **o**, **g**) into representation vectors s_1, s_2 and s_3. An LSTM decoder with an attention mechanism generates the contextually appropriate output word form **dogs**. The neural baseline system for track 1 is very similar but the encoder is conditioned on embeddings of the context words, context lemmata and context MSDs.

The neural baseline system takes as input

1. A lemma $l = l_1, ..., l_m$,

2. a left and right context word form w_L and w_R, respectively.

3. a left and right context lemma l_L and l_R, respectively (only in track 1) and

4. a left and right context MSD m_L and m_R, respectively (only in track 1).

The neural baseline system produces an inflected form $w = w_1, ..., w_n$ of the lemma as output.

The input characters l_i are first embedded: $l_i \mapsto \mathrm{E}(l_i)$. Then, context words ($w_L$ and w_R) for both tracks, as well as context lemmata (l_L and l_R) and MSDs (m_L and m_R) for track 1 are also embedded: $w_X \mapsto \mathrm{E}(w_X)$, $l_X \mapsto \mathrm{E}(l_X)$ and $m_X \mapsto \mathrm{E}(m_X)$. The system also a uses the whole token embedding of the input lemma l: $l \mapsto \mathrm{E}(l)$.

A bidirectional LSTM encoder is used to encode the lemma into representation vectors. In order to condition the encoder on the sentence context of the lemma, the encoder input vector e_i for character l_i is

1. a concatenation of embeddings for the context word forms, context lemmata, context MSDs, input lemma and input character: $e_i = [\mathrm{E}(w_L); \mathrm{E}(l_L); \mathrm{E}(m_L); \mathrm{E}(l); \mathrm{E}(w_R); \mathrm{E}(l_R); \mathrm{E}(m_R); \mathrm{E}(l_i)]$ for track 1, and

2. a concatenation of embeddings for the context word forms, input lemma and input character: $e_i = [\mathrm{E}(w_L); \mathrm{E}(l); \mathrm{E}(w_R); \mathrm{E}(l_i)]$ for track 2.

The input vectors $e_1, ..., e_m$ are then encoded into representations $s_1, ..., s_m$ by a bidirectional LSTM encoder. Finally, a decoder with additive attention (Vaswani et al., 2017) is used for generating the output word form $w = w_1, ..., w_n$ based on the representations $s_1, ..., s_m$.

The baseline system uses 100-dimensional embeddings and the LSTM hidden dimension for both the encoder and decoder is of size 100. Both encoder and decoder LSTM networks are single layer networks. The additive attention network is a 2-layer feed-forward network with hidden dimension 100 and tanh nonlinearity.

The baseline system is trained for 20 epochs in both tracks and under all data settings using Adam (Kingma and Ba, 2014). During training, 30% dropout is applied on all input and recurrent connections in the encoder and decoder LSTM networks. Whole token embeddings for the input lemma, context word forms, lemmata and MSDs are dropped with a probability of 10%.

Copy Baseline The second baseline is very straightforward. It simply copies the input lemma into the output. The system is based on the observation that in many languages the lemma form is quite common. In some languages, such as English, this baseline is in fact quite difficult to beat when the training set is small.

5 Results

The CoNLL-SIGMORPHON 2018 shared task received submissions from 15 teams with members from 17 universities or institutes (Table 7). Many of the teams submitted more than one system, yielding a total of 33 unique systems entered—27 for task 1, and 6 for task 2. In addition, baseline systems provided by the organizers for both tasks were also evaluated.

5.1 Task 1 Results

The relative system performance is described in Table 8, which show the average per-language accuracy of each system by resource condition. The table reflects the fact that some teams submitted more than one system (e.g. UZH-1 & UZH-2 in the table). Learning curves for each language across conditions are shown in Tables 9 and 10, which indicates the best per-form accuracy achieved by a submitted system. Full results can be found in Appendix A. Newer approaches led to better overall results in 2018 compared to 2017. In the low-resource condition, 41 (80%) of the 52 languages shared across years saw improvement in top system performance.

In the lower data conditions, encoder-decoder models are known to perform worse than the baseline model due to data sparsity. One way to work around this weakness is to learn sequences of edit operations instead of a standard string-to-string transductions, a strategy which was used by teams last year and this year (AX SEMANTICS, UZH, UHH, MSU, RACAI). Another strategy is to create artificial training data that biases the neural model toward copying (Kann and Schütze, 2017; Bergmanis et al., 2017; Silfverberg et al., 2017; Zhou and Neubig, 2017; Nicolai et al., 2017), which was also employed this year (TUEBINGEN-OSLO, WASEDA). Learning edit sequences requires input/output alignment, often as a preliminary step. The UZH submissions, which attained the highest average accuracy on the higher data conditions, built upon ideas in their last year's submission (Makarov et al., 2017), which had used such a separate alignment step followed by the application of an edit sequence. Their 2018 submission included edit distance alignment as part of the training loss function in the model, producing an end-to-end model. Another alternative to the edit sequence model is to use pointer generator networks, introduced by (See et al., 2017) for text summarization, which also allow for copying parts of the input. This was employed by IITBHU. BME used a modified attention model that attended to both the lemma sequence and the tag sequence, which worked well in the high data condition, but, being without models of data augmentation or edit sequences, it suffered in the low data setting. In general, systems that included edit sequence generation or data augmentation fared significantly better in the low data settings. The HAMBURG submission attempted to learn similarities between characters based on rendering them visually using a font, with the intent to discover similarities such as those between **a** and **ä**, where the former is usually a low back vowel, and the latter a fronted version. Ensembling was also a popular choice to improve system performance. The UA system combined multiple models, both neural and non-neural, and focused on performance in the low data setting.

Even though the top-ranked systems used some form of ensembling to improve performance, different teams relied on different overall approaches. As a result, submissions may contain some amount of complementary information, so that a global ensemble may improve accuracy. As in 2017, we present an upper bound on the possible performance of such an ensemble. Table 8 includes an "Ensemble Oracle" system (oracle-e) that gives the correct answer if *any* of the submitted systems is correct. The oracle performs significantly better than any one system in both the Medium ($\sim$10%) and Low ($\sim$25%) conditions. This suggests that the different strategies used by teams to "bias" their systems in an effort to make up for sparse data lead to substantially different generalization patterns.

As in 2017, we also present a second "Feature Combination" Oracle (oracle-fc) that gives the correct answer for a given test triple iff its feature bundle appeared in training (with any lemma). Thus, oracle-fc provides an upper bound on the performance of systems that treat a feature bundle such as V;SBJV;FUT;3;PL as atomic. In the low-data condition, this upper bound was 77%, meaning that 23% of the test bundles had never been seen in training data. Nonetheless, systems should

	predict MSD	subword context	context RNN	context attention	multilingual	beam search
BME-HAS (Ács, 2018)	...	✓	✓	...	...	...
COPENHAGEN (Kementchedjhieva et al., 2018)	✓	...	✓	...	✓	...
CUBoulder (Liu et al., 2018)	✓	...	...	...	...	...
NYU (Kann et al., 2018)	–	✓	✓	✓	–	–
UZH (Makarov and Clematide, 2018)	...	✓	...	...	...	✓

Table 6: Features of Task 2 systems.

Team	Institute(s)	System Description Paper
AXSEMANTICS[1]	AX Semantics	Madsack et al. (2018)
BME[1]/BME-HAS[2]	Budapest University of Technology and Economics / Hungarian Academy of Sciences	Ács (2018)
COPENHAGEN[2]	University of Copenhagen	Kementchedjhieva et al. (2018)
CUBoulder[2]	University of Colorado, Boulder	Liu et al. (2018)
HAMBURG[1]	Universität Hamburg	Schröder et al. (2018)
IITBHU[1]	IIT (BHU) Varanasi / IIIT Hyderabad	Sharma et al. (2018)
IIT-VARANASI[1]	Indian Institute of Technology (BHU) Varanasi	Jain and Singh (2018)
KUCST[1]	University of Copenhagen, Centre for Language Technology	Agirrezabal (2018)
MSU[1]	Moscow State University	Sorokin (2018)
NYU[2]	New York University	Kann et al. (2018)
RACAI[1]	Romanian Academy	Dumitrescu and Boros (2018)
TUEBINGEN-OSLO[1]	University of Oslo / University of Tübingen	Rama and Çöltekin (2018)
UA[1]	University of Alberta	Najafi et al. (2018)
UZH[1,2]	University of Zurich	Makarov and Clematide (2018)
WASEDA[1]	Waseda University	Fam and Lepage (2018)

Table 7: Participating teams, member institutes, and the corresponding system description papers. In the results and the main text, team submissions have an additional integer index to distinguish between multiple submissions by one team. The numbers at each abbreviated team name show whether teams participated in task 1, task 2, or both.

be able to make some accurate predictions on this 23% by decomposing each test bundle into individual morphological features such as FUT (future) and PL (plural), and generalizing from training examples that involve those features. For example, a particular feature or sub-bundle might be realized as a particular affix. For systems to succeed at this type of generalization, they must treat each individual feature separately, rather than treating feature bundles as holistic. In the medium data condition for some languages, some submissions far surpassed oracle-fc. As in 2017, the most notable example of this is Basque, where oracle-fc produced a 44% accuracy while six of the submitted systems produced an accuracy of 80% or above. Basque is an extreme example with very large paradigms for the few verbs that inflect in the language, so the problem of generalizing correctly to unseen feature combinations is amplified.

5.2 Task 2 Results

All systems submitted for task 2 were neural systems. All but one of the systems were encoder-decoder systems reminiscent of Kann and Schütze (2016). The exception, Makarov and Clematide (2018), used a neural transition-based transducer with a designated copy action, which edits the input lemma into an output form. Table 6 details some of the design features in task 2 systems.

Predict MSD systems predicted the MSD of the target word form based on contextual cues and used the MSD to improve performance. The system by Kementchedjhieva et al. (2018) used MSD prediction as an auxiliary task. The system by Liu et al. (2018) instead converted the contextual reinflection problem into ordinary morphological reinflection. They first predicted the MSD of the target word form based on sentence context and then generated the target word form using the input lemma and the predicted MSD.

Several systems improved upon the context model in the neural baseline system. Three systems (BME-HAS, NYU, and ZHU) used *subword context* models, for example, character-level models to encode context word forms, lemmata and MSDs. Many systems (Ács, 2018; Kementchedjhieva et al., 2018; Kann et al., 2018) also used a *context RNN* for encoding sentence context exceeding the immediate neighboring words. Kann et al. (2018) used *context attention* which refers to an attention mechanisms directed at contextual information.

The system by Kementchedjhieva et al. (2018) was *multilingual* in the sense that it combined training data for all task 2 languages. Finally, the system by Makarov and Clematide (2018) used *beam search* for decoding.

	High	Medium	Low
uzh-01	**96.00 / 0.08**	**86.64 / 0.26**	57.18 / 1.00
uzh-02	95.97 / 0.08	86.38 / 0.27	**57.21 / 1.02**
bme-02	94.66 / 0.11	67.26 / 0.88	2.43 / 6.91
iitbhu-iiith-01	94.43 / 0.11	82.90 / 0.34	49.79 / 1.18
iitbhu-iiith-02	94.43 / 0.11	84.19 / 0.32	52.60 / 1.10
bme-03	93.97 / 0.12	67.36 / 0.75	3.63 / 6.75
bme-01	93.88 / 0.12	67.43 / 0.75	3.74 / 6.72
msu-04	91.87 / 0.23	76.40 / 0.55	31.40 / 2.16
iit-varanasi-01	91.73 / 0.16	70.17 / 0.66	23.33 / 2.40
waseda-01	91.12 / 0.19	77.38 / 0.67	44.09 / 1.68
msu-03	90.52 / 0.25	75.74 / 0.55	25.86 / 2.38
axsemantics-01	84.19 / 0.40	*58.00 / 1.10*	*72.00 / 0.96*
msu-02	82.68 / 0.41	69.45 / 0.79	41.61 / 1.86
racai-01	*79.93 / 0.43*	*— / —*	*— / —*
hamburg-01	77.53 / 0.44	74.03 / 0.54	40.28 / 1.45
axsemantics-02	74.77 / 0.68	60.00 / 1.03	*14.89 / 3.89*
msu-01	74.33 / 0.78	*64.57 / 0.93*	*— / —*
tuebingen-oslo-03	63.05 / 1.15	30.98 / 2.25	1.39 / 5.70
tuebingen-oslo-02	56.60 / 1.34	29.72 / 2.36	4.43 / 5.06
kucst-01	*54.37 / 1.57*	*32.28 / 2.23*	*2.79 / 5.28*
tuebingen-oslo-01	49.52 / 1.67	20.97 / 2.81	0.00 / 7.94
ua-08	*— / —*	*— / —*	53.22 / 1.35
ua-05	*— / —*	*— / —*	50.53 / 1.34
ua-06	*— / —*	*— / —*	49.73 / 1.46
ua-03	*— / —*	*— / —*	44.82 / 1.45
ua-02	*— / —*	*— / —*	*41.61 / 2.47*
ua-07	*— / —*	*— / —*	*39.52 / 1.76*
ua-01	*— / —*	*— / —*	38.22 / 2.02
ua-04	*— / —*	*— / —*	21.25 / 3.43
baseline	77.42 / 0.51	63.53 / 0.90	38.89 / 1.88
oracle-fc	99.87 / ...	98.27 / ...	77.23 / ...
oracle-e	98.90 / ...	93.74 / ...	74.88 / ...

Table 8: Task 1 results: Per-form accuracy (in percentage points) and average Levenshtein distance from the correct form (in characters), averaged across the 103 languages with all languages weighted equally. The columns represent the different training size conditions. Rows are sorted by accuracy under the "High" condition. Numbers in bold are the best accuracy in their category. Greyed-out cells represent partial submissions that did not provide output for every language, and thus do not have comparable mean scores. The per-language performance of these systems can be found in the Appendix.

Overall performance for all data settings in tracks 1 and 2 of task 2 is described in Table 11. For evaluation with regard to original forms, the evaluation criterion is accuracy; that is, how often a system correctly predicted the original UD form. For evaluation with regard to plausible forms, the evaluation criterion is relaxed accuracy given the set of contextually plausible forms. In other words, we measure how often the prediction was one of the variants in the set of plausible forms.

In track 1, the COPENHAGEN system is the clear winner in the high and medium data settings, wherea, the UZH system is the clear winner in the low data setting. In fact, UZH is the only system which can beat the lemma copying

baseline COPY-BL in the low setting. In track 2, the COPENHAGEN system and the neural baseline system NEURAL-BL deliver comparable performance in the high data setting. In the medium and low setting, the UZH system is the clear winner. Once again, the UZH system is the only system which can beat the lemma copying baseline COPY-BL in the low setting.

Table 11 shows that the best track 1 system outperforms the best track 2 system for every data setting, meaning that the additional supervision offered by context lemmata and MSDs is useful. Moreover, this effect seems to strengthen with increasing amounts of training data: the difference in performance between the best track 1 and track 2 systems for original forms in the low data setting is 3.8%-points, in the medium setting 7.8%-points, and in the high setting 13.6%-points. A further observation is that it seems to be more difficult to deliver improvements over the neural baseline system NEURAL-BL in the high setting in track 2, where NEURAL-BL in fact is one of the top two systems. This may be a result of the relatively small training sets: even in the high data setting, the training sets only contain approximately 10^5 tokens.

The results on original and plausible forms show strong agreement. In all but one case, the same systems deliver the strongest performance for both evaluation criteria. The only exception is the Track 2 high setting where COPENHAGEN is the top system with regard to original forms and NEURAL-BL with regard to plausible forms. However, the performance of these systems is very similar. This strong agreement indicates that evaluation on plausible forms might not be necessary.

The best-performing systems for each language, track, and data setting in task 2 are given in Table 12. In track 1, COPENHAGEN achieves the strongest results for most languages in the high and medium data settings, whereas UZH delivers the best performance on all languages in the low setting. In track 2, COPENHAGEN and NEURAL-BL deliver the best performance on an equal number of languages in the high setting, whereas UZH delivers best performance for most languages in the low and medium settings, and COPENHAGEN performs best for the remaining languages.

| | Task 1 - Part 1 | | |
	High	Medium	Low
Adyghe	100.00(uzh-2)	94.40(uzh-1)	90.60(ua-8)
Albanian	98.90(bme-2)	88.80(iitbhu-iiith-2)	36.40(uzh-1)
Arabic	93.70(uzh-1)	79.40(uzh-1)	45.20(uzh-1)
Armenian	96.90(bme-2)	92.80(uzh-1)	64.90(uzh-1)
Asturian	98.70(uzh-1)	92.40(iitbhu-iiith-2)	74.60(uzh-2)
Azeri	100.00(axsemantics-2)	96.00(iitbhu-iiith-2)	65.00(iitbhu-iiith-2)
Bashkir	99.90(uzh-2)	97.30(uzh-2)	77.80(iitbhu-iiith-1)
Basque	98.90(bme-2)	88.10(iitbhu-iiith-2)	13.30(uzh-1)
Belarusian	94.90(uzh-1)	70.40(uzh-1)	33.40(ua-8)
Bengali	99.00(bme-3)	99.00(uzh-2)	72.00(uzh-2)
Breton	100.00(waseda-1)	96.00(uzh-2)	72.00(uzh-1)
Bulgarian	98.30(uzh-2)	83.80(uzh-2)	62.90(ua-8)
Catalan	98.90(uzh-2)	92.80(waseda-1)	72.50(ua-8)
Classical-syriac	100.00(axsemantics-1)	100.00(axsemantics-2)	96.00(uzh-2)
Cornish	—	70.00(uzh-1)	40.00(ua-4)
Crimean-tatar	100.00(iit-varanasi-1)	98.00(uzh-2)	91.00(iitbhu-iiith-2)
Czech	94.70(uzh-1)	87.20(uzh-1)	46.50(uzh-2)
Danish	95.50(uzh-1)	80.40(uzh-1)	87.70(ua-6)
Dutch	97.90(uzh-1)	85.70(uzh-1)	69.30(ua-6)
English	97.10(uzh-2)	94.50(uzh-1)	91.80(ua-8)
Estonian	98.40(uzh-2)	81.60(uzh-1)	35.20(uzh-1)
Faroese	87.10(bme-2)	72.60(uzh-1)	49.80(ua-8)
Finnish	95.40(uzh-1)	82.80(uzh-1)	25.70(uzh-1)
French	90.40(uzh-2)	80.90(uzh-2)	66.60(uzh-2)
Friulian	99.00(axsemantics-2)	97.00(iitbhu-iiith-1)	79.00(uzh-2)
Galician	99.50(uzh-1)	90.80(uzh-1)	61.10(uzh-2)
Georgian	99.10(uzh-1)	94.00(uzh-2)	88.20(ua-8)
German	90.20(uzh-2)	80.10(uzh-1)	67.10(ua-3)
Greek	91.70(uzh-1)	75.50(uzh-2)	32.30(uzh-1)
Greenlandic	—	98.00(uzh-2)	80.00(iitbhu-iiith-1)
Haida	100.00(axsemantics-2)	94.00(uzh-2)	63.00(uzh-2)
Hebrew	99.50(uzh-1)	85.40(uzh-1)	56.70(ua-8)
Hindi	100.00(axsemantics-1)	97.60(uzh-2)	78.00(uzh-2)
Hungarian	87.20(uzh-1)	74.50(iitbhu-iiith-2)	48.20(ua-8)
Icelandic	91.30(uzh-1)	73.80(uzh-1)	56.20(ua-8)
Ingrian	—	92.00(uzh-2)	46.00(iitbhu-iiith-2)
Irish	91.50(uzh-2)	77.10(uzh-1)	37.70(uzh-1)
Italian	98.00(uzh-2)	95.10(uzh-2)	57.40(uzh-2)
Kabardian	100.00(hamburg-1)	100.00(bme-2)	92.00(uzh-1)
Kannada	100.00(bme-3)	94.00(uzh-2)	61.00(uzh-1)
Karelian	—	100.00(uzh-2)	94.00(ua-5)
Kashubian	—	88.00(bme-2)	68.00(ua-5)
Kazakh	—	88.00(iitbhu-iiith-2)	86.00(uzh-2)
Khakas	—	98.00(bme-3)	86.00(iitbhu-iiith-2)
Khaling	99.70(uzh-1)	86.00(iitbhu-iiith-1)	33.80(ua-8)
Kurmanji	94.60(uzh-1)	93.20(uzh-1)	87.40(uzh-2)
Ladin	99.00(uzh-2)	95.00(uzh-2)	72.00(uzh-1)
Latin	78.90(bme-2)	53.30(uzh-1)	33.10(ua-6)

Table 9: Best per-form accuracy (and corresponding system) by language. First 50 languages.

	Task 1 - Part 2		
	High	Medium	Low
Latvian	98.20(uzh-2)	90.60(uzh-1)	57.30(ua-6)
Lithuanian	95.50(uzh-2)	63.90(uzh-1)	32.60(ua-6)
Livonian	100.00(uzh-2)	82.00(uzh-1)	35.00(ua-8)
Lower-sorbian	97.80(uzh-1)	85.10(uzh-1)	54.30(ua-6)
Macedonian	97.40(uzh-1)	91.60(uzh-1)	68.80(ua-6)
Maltese	97.00(uzh-2)	95.00(uzh-1)	49.00(ua-6)
Mapudungun	—	100.00(uzh-2)	86.00(ua-4)
Middle-french	99.30(uzh-2)	94.50(uzh-2)	84.50(uzh-2)
Middle-high-german	—	100.00(uzh-2)	84.00(uzh-2)
Middle-low-german	—	100.00(iitbhu-iiith-1)	54.00(uzh-1)
Murrinhpatha	—	96.00(uzh-2)	38.00(ua-8)
Navajo	91.00(bme-2)	54.30(uzh-1)	20.80(uzh-1)
Neapolitan	99.00(uzh-2)	99.00(uzh-2)	89.00(uzh-2)
Norman	—	88.00(iitbhu-iiith-1)	66.00(ua-4)
North-frisian	96.00(bme-1)	91.00(uzh-1)	45.00(iitbhu-iiith-2)
Northern-sami	98.30(uzh-1)	76.10(uzh-1)	35.80(ua-8)
Norwegian-bokmaal	92.10(uzh-2)	84.10(uzh-1)	90.10(ua-6)
Norwegian-nynorsk	94.90(uzh-2)	67.10(uzh-1)	83.60(ua-8)
Occitan	99.00(bme-2)	96.00(waseda-1)	77.00(uzh-2)
Old-armenian	90.40(uzh-2)	80.20(uzh-1)	42.00(uzh-2)
Old-church-slavonic	97.00(uzh-2)	93.00(uzh-2)	53.00(iitbhu-iiith-2)
Old-english	88.70(uzh-1)	65.60(uzh-1)	46.50(ua-8)
Old-french	92.40(uzh-1)	79.30(uzh-1)	46.20(uzh-2)
Old-irish	—	40.00(uzh-1)	8.00(baseline)
Old-saxon	98.30(uzh-1)	80.90(uzh-2)	46.60(ua-6)
Pashto	100.00(waseda-1)	85.00(uzh-1)	48.00(uzh-2)
Persian	99.90(bme-2)	93.40(uzh-2)	67.60(uzh-2)
Polish	93.40(uzh-2)	82.40(uzh-2)	49.40(ua-6)
Portuguese	98.60(uzh-2)	94.80(uzh-2)	75.80(uzh-2)
Quechua	99.90(uzh-2)	98.90(uzh-1)	70.20(uzh-2)
Romanian	89.00(uzh-2)	77.60(uzh-1)	46.20(uzh-1)
Russian	94.40(uzh-2)	86.90(uzh-1)	53.50(uzh-1)
Sanskrit	96.50(uzh-1)	85.90(uzh-2)	58.00(uzh-1)
Scottish-gaelic	—	94.00(iitbhu-iiith-1)	74.00(iitbhu-iiith-2)
Serbo-croatian	92.40(uzh-2)	86.10(uzh-1)	44.80(ua-3)
Slovak	97.10(uzh-1)	78.60(uzh-1)	51.80(uzh-2)
Slovene	97.40(uzh-1)	86.20(uzh-1)	58.00(uzh-2)
Sorani	90.60(uzh-2)	80.20(iitbhu-iiith-2)	40.10(uzh-1)
Spanish	98.10(uzh-2)	92.00(iitbhu-iiith-2)	73.20(ua-8)
Swahili	100.00(bme-3)	99.00(uzh-2)	72.00(iitbhu-iiith-2)
Swedish	93.30(uzh-1)	79.80(uzh-1)	79.00(ua-8)
Tatar	99.00(axsemantics-1)	98.00(uzh-2)	90.00(ua-8)
Telugu	—	—	96.00(ua-8)
Tibetan	—	56.00(uzh-2)	58.00(iitbhu-iiith-1)
Turkish	98.50(uzh-2)	90.70(uzh-1)	39.50(iitbhu-iiith-2)
Turkmen	—	98.00(iitbhu-iiith-1)	90.00(uzh-2)
Ukrainian	96.20(uzh-2)	81.40(uzh-1)	57.10(ua-6)
Urdu	100.00(iitbhu-iiith-1)	96.80(uzh-2)	72.50(uzh-2)
Uzbek	100.00(axsemantics-1)	100.00(axsemantics-2)	92.00(uzh-1)
Venetian	99.20(uzh-2)	95.10(uzh-2)	78.80(uzh-2)
Votic	90.00(uzh-2)	88.00(uzh-2)	34.00(ua-7)
Welsh	95.00(bme-3)	85.00(bme-2)	55.00(uzh-2)
West-frisian	99.00(uzh-1)	98.00(uzh-2)	56.00(uzh-1)
Yiddish	100.00(uzh-2)	94.00(uzh-2)	87.00(ua-8)
Zulu	99.80(uzh-1)	87.30(uzh-2)	33.00(uzh-1)

Table 10: Best per-form accuracy (and corresponding system) by language. Remaining 53 languages.

	Track 1						Track 2					
	Original			Plausible			Original			Plausible		
	High	Medium	Low	High	Medium	Low	High	Medium	Low	High	Medium	Low
BME-HAS	65.69	45.71	29.34	73.21	51.28	32.98	51.83	36.82	24.71	60.15	43.80	31.18
COPENHAGEN	**68.51**	**56.70**	24.40	**76.10**	**63.24**	26.24	**54.93**	45.18	29.38	60.50	51.36	33.77
CUBoulder–1	59.73	46.27	23.16	66.22	52.52	25.59	48.97	38.29	23.76	55.63	43.33	26.83
CUBoulder–2	50.32	42.08	29.86	53.89	46.85	34.85	-	-	-	-	-	-
NYU	-	-	-	-	-	-	-	-	33.38	-	-	38.62
UZH	-	53.02	**42.42**	-	61.02	**48.49**	-	**48.88**	**38.60**	-	**55.67**	**45.09**
NEURAL-BL	62.41	44.09	1.85	69.53	48.81	2.63	54.48	38.56	2.19	**60.79**	46.74	3.11
COPY-BL	36.62	36.62	36.62	42.00	42.00	42.00	36.62	36.62	36.62	42.00	42.00	42.00

Table 11: Overall accuracies (in %-points) for Tracks 1 and 2 in Task 2 for different training data settings. Results are presented separately with regard to the original forms in the UD test data sets and the manually annotated sets of plausible forms. NEURAL-BL refers to the baseline encoder-decoder system and COPY-BL to the "lemma copying" baseline system. Note that the output of the COPY-BL is independent of the training data and therefore results for the high, medium and low data setting are the same.

	Track 1					
	Original			Plausible		
	High	Medium	Low	High	Medium	Low
de	73.21 (BME-HAS)	63.90 (UZH)	60.06 (UZH)	77.55 (BME-HAS)	67.34 (UZH)	62.39 (UZH)
en	77.84 (CPH)	68.08 (CBL)	68.08 (UZH)	86.81 (CPH)	76.23 (CPH)	74.02 (UZH)
es	56.24 (CPH)	51.33 (CPH)	34.78 (UZH)	67.88 (CPH)	60.59 (CPH)	42.08 (UZH)
fi	55.27 (CPH)	35.71 (CPH)	24.90 (UZH)	63.02 (CPH)	43.07 (CPH)	28.97 (UZH)
fr	70.67 (CPH)	60.29 (CPH)	35.03 (UZH)	-	-	-
ru	77.91 (CPH)	63.05 (CPH)	40.76 (UZH)	81.53 (CPH)	66.57 (CPH)	43.47 (UZH)
sv	69.26 (CPH)	57.66 (CPH)	33.30 (UZH)	80.32 (CPH)	67.23 (CPH)	40.00 (UZH)

	Track 2					
	Original			Plausible		
	High	Medium	Low	High	Medium	Low
de	65.72 (NBL)	60.26 (UZH)	59.15 (UZH)	69.97 (NBL)	64.21 (UZH)	61.38 (UZH)
en	71.90 (CPH)	68.08 (UZH)	68.08 (UZH)	79.86 (CPH)	75.63 (CPH)	74.02 (UZH)
es	51.05 (NBL)	42.50 (CPH)	32.68 (UZH)	59.19 (NBL)	51.75 (CPH)	37.31 (CPH)
fi	34.82 (NBL)	27.06 (UZH)	24.40 (UZH)	41.17 (NBL)	31.89 (UZH)	28.21 (UZH)
fr	61.51 (CPH)	45.62 (CPH)	29.53 (CPH)	-	-	-
ru	56.73 (BME-HAS)	54.02 (UZH)	28.11 (UZH)	60.04 (BME-HAS)	56.53 (UZH)	30.42 (UZH)
sv	55.96 (CPH)	47.87 (UZH)	32.77 (UZH)	66.06 (CPH)	56.17 (UZH)	39.36 (UZH)

Table 12: Best accuracies (in %-points) and the for all tracks, settings and languages in task 2. The best performing system is given in parentheses. "CPH" refers to "COPENHAGEN", "NBL" to the neural baseline system and "CBL" to the "lemma copying" baseline system. Note, that there are no results for French with regard to plausible forms because this gold standard data set was not annotated for plausible forms (see Section 3.2).

6 Future Directions

In the case of inflection an interesting future topic could involve departing from orthographic representation and using more IPA-like representations, i.e. transductions over pronunciations. Different languages, in particular those with idiosyncratic orthographies, may offer new challenges in this respect.[12]

Neither task this year included unannotated monolingual corpora. Using such data is well-motivated from an L1-learning point of view, and may affect the performance of low-resource data settings, especially for the cloze task. In the inflection task, some results from last year (Zhou and Neubig, 2017) did not see significant gains by using extra data.

Only one team tried to learn inflection in a multilingual setting—i.e. to use all training data to train one model. Such transfer learning is an interesting avenue of future research, but evaluation could be difficult. Whether any cross-language transfer is actually being learned vs. whether having more data better biases the networks to copy strings is an evaluation step to disentangle.[13]

Creating new data sets that accurately reflect learner exposure (whether L1 or L2) is also an important consideration in the design of future shared tasks.

The results for task 2 show that evaluation against the original test form versus against set of plausible forms results in a very similar ranking of systems, justifying the use of the former, much simpler, method for future shared tasks. No manual annotation would then be required for the creation of test sets, allowing the inclusion of a wider variety of languages.

In track 2 of task 2, it turned out to be difficult to achieve clear improvements over the neural baseline system. This may be a consequence of the limited amount of training data. Increasing the amount of training data is an obvious solution, but encouraging the use of external datasets for semi-supervised learning could also be an interesting direction to pursue. Such semi-supervised methods could take the form of pretrained embeddings from monolingual corpora or more expressive models dedicated to improving morphological inflection, e.g., Wolf-Sonkin et al. (2018).

7 Conclusion

The CoNLL-SIGMORPHON 2018 shared task introduced a new cloze-test task with data sets for 7 languages, as well as extended the existing inflection task to include 103 languages. In task 1 (inflection) 27 systems were submitted, while 6 systems were submitted in task 2 (cloze test). Neural network models prevailed in both, although significant modifications to standard architectures were required to beat a simple baseline in the low data settings in both tasks.

As in previous years, we compared inflection system performance to oracle ensembles, showing that systems possessed complementary strengths. We released the training, development, and test sets for each task, and expect these to be useful for future endeavors in morphological learning, both in sentential context and in the case of isolated word inflection.

Acknowledgements

The first author would like to acknowledge the support of an NDSEG fellowship. MS was supported by a grant from the Society of Swedish Literature in Finland (SLS). Several authors (CK, DY, JSG, MH) were supported in part by the Defense Advanced Research Projects Agency (DARPA) in the program Low Resource Languages for Emergent Incidents (LORELEI) under contract No. HR0011-15-C-0113. Any opinions, findings and conclusions or recommendations expressed in this material are those of the authors and do not necessarily reflect the views of the Defense Advanced Research Projects Agency (DARPA). NVIDIA Corp. donated a Titan Xp GPU used for this research.

References

Judit Ács. 2018. BME-HAS system for CoNLL–SIGMORPHON 2018 shared task: Universal morphological reinflection. In *Proceedings of the CoNLL SIGMORPHON 2018 Shared Task: Universal Morphological Reinflection*, Brussels. Association for Computational Linguistics.

Manex Agirrezabal. 2018. KU-CST at CoNLL-SIGMORPHON 2018 shared task: a tridirectional model. In *Proceedings of the CoNLL SIGMOR-PHON 2018 Shared Task: Universal Morphologi-*

---

[12]Although some recent research suggests that working with IPA or phonological distinctive features in this context yields very similar results to working with graphemes (Wiemerslage et al., 2018).

[13]This has been recently addressed by Jin and Kann (2017).

cal Reinflection, Brussels. Association for Computational Linguistics.

Inbal Arnon and Michael Ramscar. 2012. Granularity and the acquisition of grammatical gender: How order-of-acquisition affects what gets learned. *Cognition*, 122:292–305.

Mark C Baker. 1996. *The polysynthesis parameter*. Oxford University Press.

Toms Bergmanis, Katharina Kann, Hinrich Schütze, and Sharon Goldwater. 2017. Training data augmentation for low-resource morphological inflection. In *Proceedings of the CoNLL SIGMORPHON 2017 Shared Task: Universal Morphological Reinflection*, pages 31–39, Vancouver. Association for Computational Linguistics.

Ryan Cotterell, Christo Kirov, Sebastian J. Mielke, and Jason Eisner. 2018. Unsupervised disambiguation of syncretism in inflected lexicons. In *Proceedings of the 2018 Conference of the North American Chapter of the Association for Computational Linguistics: Human Language Technologies, Volume 2 (Short Papers)*, pages 548–553, New Orleans, Louisiana. Association for Computational Linguistics.

Ryan Cotterell, Christo Kirov, John Sylak-Glassman, Géraldine Walther, Ekaterina Vylomova, Patrick Xia, Manaal Faruqui, Sandra Kübler, David Yarowsky, Jason Eisner, and Mans Hulden. 2017. The CoNLL-SIGMORPHON 2017 shared task: Universal morphological reinflection in 52 languages. In *Proceedings of the CoNLL-SIGMORPHON 2017 Shared Task: Universal Morphological Reinflection*, Vancouver, Canada. Association for Computational Linguistics.

Stefan Daniel Dumitrescu and Tiberiu Boros. 2018. Attention-free encoder decoder for morphological processing. In *Proceedings of the CoNLL SIGMORPHON 2018 Shared Task: Universal Morphological Reinflection*, Brussels. Association for Computational Linguistics.

Rashel Fam and Yves Lepage. 2018. IPS-WASEDA system at CoNLL-SIGMORPHON 2018 shared task on morphological inflection. In *Proceedings of the CoNLL SIGMORPHON 2018 Shared Task: Universal Morphological Reinflection*, Brussels. Association for Computational Linguistics.

Rishabh Jain and Anil Kumar Singh. 2018. Experiments on morphological reinflection: CoNLL-2018 shared task. In *Proceedings of the CoNLL SIGMORPHON 2018 Shared Task: Universal Morphological Reinflection*, Brussels. Association for Computational Linguistics.

Huiming Jin and Katharina Kann. 2017. Exploring cross-lingual transfer of morphological knowledge in sequence-to-sequence models. In *Proceedings of the First Workshop on Subword and Character Level Models in NLP*, pages 70–75.

Katharina Kann, Stanislas Lauly, and Kyunghyun Cho. 2018. The NYU system for the CoNLL–SIGMORPHON 2018 shared task on universal morphological reinflection. In *Proceedings of the CoNLL SIGMORPHON 2018 Shared Task: Universal Morphological Reinflection*, Brussels. Association for Computational Linguistics.

Katharina Kann and Hinrich Schütze. 2016. Single-model encoder-decoder with explicit morphological representation for reinflection. In *Proceedings of the 54th Annual Meeting of the Association for Computational Linguistics (Volume 2: Short Papers)*, pages 555–560, Berlin, Germany. Association for Computational Linguistics.

Katharina Kann and Hinrich Schütze. 2017. The lmu system for the conll-sigmorphon 2017 shared task on universal morphological reinflection. In *Proceedings of the CoNLL SIGMORPHON 2017 Shared Task: Universal Morphological Reinflection*, pages 40–48, Vancouver. Association for Computational Linguistics.

Yova Kementchedjhieva, Johannes Bjerva, and Isabelle Augenstein. 2018. Copenhagen at CoNLL–SIGMORPHON 2018: Multilingual inflection in context with explicit morphosyntactic decoding. In *Proceedings of the CoNLL SIGMORPHON 2018 Shared Task: Universal Morphological Reinflection*, Brussels. Association for Computational Linguistics.

Aleksandr E. Kibrik. 1998. Archi. In Andrew Spencer and Arnold M. Zwicky, editors, *The Handbook of Morphology*, pages 455–476. Oxford: Blackwell Publishers.

Diederik P. Kingma and Jimmy Ba. 2014. Adam: A method for stochastic optimization. *CoRR*, abs/1412.6980.

Christo Kirov, Ryan Cotterell, John Sylak-Glassman, Graldine Walther, Ekaterina Vylomova, Patrick Xia, Manaal Faruqui, Sebastian Mielke, Arya D. McCarthy, Sandra Kbler, David Yarowsky, Jason Eisner, and Mans Hulden. 2018. UniMorph 2.0: Universal Morphology. In *Proceedings of the Eleventh International Conference on Language Resources and Evaluation (LREC 2018)*, Miyazaki, Japan. European Language Resources Association (ELRA).

Ling Liu and Lingshuang Jack Mao. 2016. Morphological reinflection with conditional random fields and unsupervised features. In *Proceedings of the 2016 Meeting of SIGMORPHON*, Berlin, Germany. Association for Computational Linguistics.

Ling Liu, Ilamvazhuthy Subbiah, Adam Wiemerslage, Jonathan Lilley, and Sarah Moeller. 2018. Morphological reinflection in context: CU Boulder's submission to CoNLL-SIGMORPHON 2018 shared task. In *Proceedings of the CoNLL SIGMORPHON 2018 Shared Task: Universal Morphological Reinflection*, Brussels. Association for Computational Linguistics.

Andreas Madsack, Alessia Cavallo, Johanna Heininger, and Robert Weißgraeber. 2018. AX Semantics' submission to the CoNLL-SIGMORPHON 2018 shared task. In *Proceedings of the CoNLL SIGMORPHON 2018 Shared Task: Universal Morphological Reinflection*, Brussels. Association for Computational Linguistics.

Peter Makarov and Simon Clematide. 2018. UZH at CoNLL-SIGMORPHON 2018 shared task on universal morphological reinflection. In *Proceedings of the CoNLL SIGMORPHON 2018 Shared Task: Universal Morphological Reinflection*, Brussels. Association for Computational Linguistics.

Peter Makarov, Tatiana Ruzsics, and Simon Clematide. 2017. Align and copy: UZH at SIGMORPHON 2017 shared task for morphological reinflection. In *Proceedings of the CoNLL SIGMORPHON 2017 Shared Task: Universal Morphological Reinflection*, pages 49–57, Vancouver. Association for Computational Linguistics.

Arya D. McCarthy, Miikka Silfverberg, Mans Hulden, David Yarowsky, and Ryan Cotterell. 2018. Marrying universal dependencies and universal morphology. In *Proceedings of the Workshop on Universal Dependencies (UDW'18)*.

Saeed Najafi, Bradley Hauer, Rashed Ruby Riyadh, Leyuan Yu, and Grzegorz Kondrak. 2018. Combining neural and non-neural methods for low-resource morphological reinflection. In *Proceedings of the CoNLL SIGMORPHON 2018 Shared Task: Universal Morphological Reinflection*, Brussels. Association for Computational Linguistics.

Garrett Nicolai, Bradley Hauer, Mohammad Motallebi, Saeed Najafi, and Grzegorz Kondrak. 2017. If you can't beat them, join them: the university of alberta system description. In *Proceedings of the CoNLL SIGMORPHON 2017 Shared Task: Universal Morphological Reinflection*, pages 79–84, Vancouver. Association for Computational Linguistics.

Joakim Nivre, Željko Agić, Lars Ahrenberg, Lene Antonsen, Maria Jesus Aranzabe, Masayuki Asahara, Luma Ateyah, Mohammed Attia, Aitziber Atutxa, Liesbeth Augustinus, et al. 2017. Universal dependencies 2.1. LINDAT/CLARIN digital library at the Institute of Formal and Applied Linguistics (ÚFAL), Faculty of Mathematics and Physics, Charles University.

Taraka Rama and Çağrı Çöltekin. 2018. Tbingen-Oslo system at SIGMORPHON shared task on morphological inflection. a multi-tasking multilingual sequence to sequence model. In *Proceedings of the CoNLL SIGMORPHON 2018 Shared Task: Universal Morphological Reinflection*, Brussels. Association for Computational Linguistics.

Fynn Schröder, Marcel Kamlot, Gregor Billing, and Arne Köhn. 2018. Finding the way from ä to a:

Sub-character morphological inflection for the SIGMORPHON 2018 shared task. In *Proceedings of the CoNLL SIGMORPHON 2018 Shared Task: Universal Morphological Reinflection*, Brussels. Association for Computational Linguistics.

Abigail See, Peter J. Liu, and Christopher D. Manning. 2017. Get to the point: Summarization with pointer-generator networks. *arXiv preprint arXiv:1704.04368*.

Abhishek Sharma, Ganesh Katrapati, and Dipti Misra Sharma. 2018. IIT(BHU)IIITH at CoNLL–SIGMORPHON 2018 shared task on universal morphological reinflection. In *Proceedings of the CoNLL SIGMORPHON 2018 Shared Task: Universal Morphological Reinflection*, Brussels. Association for Computational Linguistics.

Miikka Silfverberg, Adam Wiemerslage, Ling Liu, and Lingshuang Jack Mao. 2017. Data augmentation for morphological reinflection. In *Proceedings of the CoNLL SIGMORPHON 2017 Shared Task: Universal Morphological Reinflection*, pages 90–99, Vancouver. Association for Computational Linguistics.

Alexey Sorokin. 2018. What can we gain from language models for morphological inflection? In *Proceedings of the CoNLL SIGMORPHON 2018 Shared Task: Universal Morphological Reinflection*, Brussels. Association for Computational Linguistics.

John Sylak-Glassman, Christo Kirov, Matt Post, Roger Que, and David Yarowsky. 2015a. A universal feature schema for rich morphological annotation and fine-grained cross-lingual part-of-speech tagging. In Cerstin Mahlow and Michael Piotrowski, editors, *Proceedings of the 4th Workshop on Systems and Frameworks for Computational Morphology (SFCM)*, Communications in Computer and Information Science, pages 72–93. Springer, Berlin.

John Sylak-Glassman, Christo Kirov, David Yarowsky, and Roger Que. 2015b. A language-independent feature schema for inflectional morphology. In *Proceedings of the 53rd Annual Meeting of the Association for Computational Linguistics and the 7th International Joint Conference on Natural Language Processing (Volume 2: Short Papers)*, pages 674–680, Beijing, China. Association for Computational Linguistics.

Ashish Vaswani, Noam Shazeer, Niki Parmar, Jakob Uszkoreit, Llion Jones, Aidan N Gomez, Łukasz Kaiser, and Illia Polosukhin. 2017. Attention is all you need. In *Advances in Neural Information Processing Systems*, pages 5998–6008.

Adam Wiemerslage, Miikka Silfverberg, and Mans Hulden. 2018. Phonological features for morphological inflection. In *Proceedings of the Fifteenth Workshop on Computational Research in Phonetics, Phonology, and Morphology*, pages 161–166, Brussels, Belgium. Association for Computational Linguistics.

Lawrence Wolf-Sonkin, Jason Naradowsky, Sebastian J. Mielke, and Ryan Cotterell. 2018. A structured variational autoencoder for contextual morphological inflection. In *Proceedings of the 56th Annual Meeting of the Association for Computational Linguistics (Volume 1: Long Papers)*, pages 2631–2641, Melbourne, Australia. Association for Computational Linguistics.

Daniel Zeman, Martin Popel, Milan Straka, Jan Hajic, Joakim Nivre, Filip Ginter, Juhani Luotolahti, Sampo Pyysalo, Slav Petrov, Martin Potthast, Francis Tyers, Elena Badmaeva, Memduh Gokirmak, Anna Nedoluzhko, Silvie Cinkova, Jan Hajic jr., Jaroslava Hlavacova, Václava Kettnerová, Zdenka Uresova, Jenna Kanerva, Stina Ojala, Anna Missilä, Christopher D. Manning, Sebastian Schuster, Siva Reddy, Dima Taji, Nizar Habash, Herman Leung, Marie-Catherine de Marneffe, Manuela Sanguinetti, Maria Simi, Hiroshi Kanayama, Valeria dePaiva, Kira Droganova, Héctor Martínez Alonso, Çağr Çöltekin, Umut Sulubacak, Hans Uszkoreit, Vivien Macketanz, Aljoscha Burchardt, Kim Harris, Katrin Marheinecke, Georg Rehm, Tolga Kayadelen, Mohammed Attia, Ali Elkahky, Zhuoran Yu, Emily Pitler, Saran Lertpradit, Michael Mandl, Jesse Kirchner, Hector Fernandez Alcalde, Jana Strnadová, Esha Banerjee, Ruli Manurung, Antonio Stella, Atsuko Shimada, Sookyoung Kwak, Gustavo Mendonca, Tatiana Lando, Rattima Nitisaroj, and Josie Li. 2017. Conll 2017 shared task: Multilingual parsing from raw text to universal dependencies. In *Proceedings of the CoNLL 2017 Shared Task: Multilingual Parsing from Raw Text to Universal Dependencies*, pages 1–19, Vancouver, Canada. Association for Computational Linguistics.

Chunting Zhou and Graham Neubig. 2017. Morphological inflection generation with multi-space variational encoder-decoders. In *Proceedings of the CoNLL SIGMORPHON 2017 Shared Task: Universal Morphological Reinflection*, pages 58–65, Vancouver. Association for Computational Linguistics.

A   Detailed Task 1 Results

This section contains detailed results for each submitted system on each language. Systems are ordered by average per-form accuracy for each sub-task and data condition. Three metrics are presented for each system/language combination.

1. Per-Form Accuracy: Percentage of test forms inflected correctly.

2. Levenshtein Distance: Average Levenshtein distance of system-predicted form from gold inflected form.

Scores in bold include the highest scoring non-oracle system for each language as well as any other systems that did not differ significantly in terms of per-form accuracy according to a sign test ($p >= 0.05$). Scores marked with a † indicate submissions that were significantly better than the feature combination oracle ($p < 0.05$), showing per-feature generalization. Scores marked with ‡ did not differ significantly from the ensemble oracle, suggesting minimal complementary information across systems.

	oracle-fc	oracle-e	uzh-01	uzh-02	bme-02	iitbhu-iiith-01	iitbhu-iiith-02	bme-03	bme-01	msu-04	iit-varanasi-01	waseda-01
Adyghe	100.00/*	100.00/*	100.00/0.00‡	100.00/0.00‡	97.90/0.02	99.90/0.00‡	99.90/0.00‡	99.40/0.01	99.20/0.01	99.30/0.01	99.80/0.00‡	95.00/0.07
Albanian	100.00/*	99.60/*	97.70/0.08	96.50/0.12	98.90/0.02	98.00/0.04	98.00/0.04	97.50/0.05	97.50/0.05	95.00/0.14	96.50/0.05	88.80/0.41
Arabic	100.00/*	97.40/*	93.70/0.28	93.50/0.28	92.20/0.30	93.30/0.26	93.30/0.26	90.30/0.32	90.60/0.37	0.00/9.16	84.40/0.45	90.20/0.34
Armenian	100.00/*	99.60/*	96.40/0.07	96.80/0.05	96.90/0.05	96.10/0.07	96.10/0.07	94.70/0.09	94.70/0.09	94.90/0.12	93.70/0.10	94.30/0.10
Asturian	99.20/*	99.80/*	98.70/0.02	98.50/0.03	98.00/0.04	98.60/0.03	98.60/0.03	97.80/0.04	97.80/0.04	98.40/0.03	98.50/0.03	98.40/0.03
Azeri	100.00/*	100.00/*	98.00/0.02‡	98.00/0.02‡	97.00/0.05‡	99.00/0.01‡	99.00/0.01‡	98.00/0.02‡	98.00/0.02‡	98.00/0.02‡	99.00/0.02‡	93.00/0.10
Bashkir	100.00/*	100.00/*	99.90/0.00†	99.90/0.00†	99.80/0.00‡	99.80/0.00‡	99.80/0.00‡	99.80/0.00‡	99.80/0.00‡	99.80/0.00‡	99.70/0.01‡	93.20/0.11
Basque	99.00/*	99.70/*	98.90/0.02	98.70/0.03	98.90/0.02	98.60/0.03	98.60/0.03	98.30/0.03	98.10/0.07	95.10/0.09	98.00/0.04	97.20/0.06
Belarusian	100.00/*	98.90/*	94.90/0.09	94.70/0.09	93.10/0.14	92.10/0.14	92.10/0.14	92.90/0.12	92.60/0.12	92.70/0.14	88.40/0.20	85.60/0.31
Bengali	100.00/*	99.00/*	99.00/0.03‡	99.00/0.03‡	99.00/0.05‡	99.00/0.02‡	99.00/0.02‡	99.00/0.05‡	99.00/0.05‡	98.00/0.06‡	99.00/0.05‡	98.00/0.06‡
Breton	94.00/*	100.00/*	97.00/0.05‡	98.00/0.06‡	92.00/0.22	99.00/0.03‡	99.00/0.03‡	93.00/0.17	93.00/0.17	96.00/0.08‡	93.00/0.17	100.00/0.00†‡
Bulgarian	100.00/*	99.40/*	98.10/0.04	98.30/0.04	96.40/0.06	96.80/0.05	96.80/0.05	95.40/0.08	94.90/0.08	96.20/0.06	94.50/0.10	91.90/0.21
Catalan	100.00/*	99.60/*	98.70/0.04	98.90/0.03	98.40/0.04	97.70/0.04	97.70/0.04	98.20/0.05	98.20/0.05	98.40/0.04	98.00/0.05	98.50/0.04
Classical-syriac	100.00/*	100.00/*	100.00/0.00‡	100.00/0.00‡	99.00/0.01‡	99.00/0.01‡	99.00/0.01‡	98.00/0.02‡	97.00/0.04‡	100.00/0.00‡	100.00/0.00‡	98.00/0.02‡
Crimean-tatar	100.00/*	100.00/*	98.00/0.04‡	98.00/0.04‡	99.00/0.03‡	99.00/0.03‡	99.00/0.03‡	99.00/0.03‡	99.00/0.03‡	99.00/0.03‡	100.00/0.00‡	97.00/0.05‡
Czech	99.80/*	97.90/*	94.70/0.10	94.50/0.11	93.20/0.12	91.10/0.16	91.10/0.16	92.00/0.14	92.00/0.14	93.10/0.12	88.00/0.23	90.70/0.21
Danish	100.00/*	98.50/*	95.50/0.07	94.60/0.08	90.40/0.16	91.50/0.13	91.50/0.13	89.40/0.17	89.40/0.17	91.80/0.12	91.30/0.13	90.70/0.15
Dutch	100.00/*	99.20/*	97.90/0.03	97.70/0.04	96.80/0.05	95.30/0.09	95.30/0.09	94.60/0.08	94.60/0.08	96.00/0.06	93.10/0.12	95.60/0.07
English	100.00/*	99.20/*	97.00/0.06	97.10/0.06	96.70/0.06	96.30/0.07	96.30/0.07	96.10/0.07	95.80/0.08	94.30/0.11	95.80/0.07	95.40/0.08
Estonian	100.00/*	99.60/*	98.30/0.05	98.40/0.05	97.00/0.07	97.30/0.06	97.30/0.06	96.90/0.07	96.90/0.07	94.40/0.11	95.90/0.09	91.50/0.21
Faroese	100.00/*	97.50/*	85.60/0.29	86.40/0.26	87.10/0.26	83.90/0.33	83.90/0.33	83.80/0.33	85.30/0.27	84.80/0.33	81.10/0.37	81.30/0.37
Finnish	100.00/*	98.90/*	95.40/0.09	94.90/0.09	93.30/0.11	92.30/0.15	92.30/0.15	92.00/0.15	92.00/0.15	89.80/0.19	76.40/0.47	84.40/0.36
French	100.00/*	96.60/*	90.20/0.16	90.40/0.16	88.10/0.19	87.60/0.21	87.60/0.21	86.40/0.22	86.40/0.22	88.50/0.20	81.10/0.32	84.80/0.25
Friulian	100.00/*	99.00/*	99.00/0.03‡	99.00/0.03‡	99.00/0.03‡	99.00/0.03‡	99.00/0.03‡	99.00/0.03‡	99.00/0.03‡	99.00/0.03‡	99.00/0.03‡	99.00/0.03‡
Galician	100.00/*	99.80/*	99.50/0.01‡	99.30/0.01‡	99.30/0.01‡	98.90/0.01	98.90/0.01	99.20/0.01	99.20/0.01	97.90/0.04	98.70/0.02	98.60/0.03
Georgian	100.00/*	99.60/*	99.10/0.01‡	98.80/0.01	98.00/0.05	98.10/0.02	98.10/0.02	97.10/0.05	96.60/0.05	97.50/0.04	97.30/0.04	97.80/0.04
German	100.00/*	96.70/*	89.70/0.25	90.20/0.23	88.50/0.27	87.60/0.26	87.60/0.26	86.20/0.29	86.20/0.29	88.30/0.24	83.70/0.33	87.50/0.27
Greek	100.00/*	97.30/*	91.70/0.16	91.00/0.17	89.10/0.24	88.20/0.23	88.20/0.23	86.60/0.26	86.60/0.26	88.60/0.22	80.80/0.38	83.70/0.31
Haida	100.00/*	100.00/*	99.00/0.02‡	99.00/0.02‡	99.00/0.02‡	93.00/0.23	93.00/0.23	100.00/0.00‡	100.00/0.00‡	99.00/0.02‡	100.00/0.00‡	66.00/0.73
Hebrew	100.00/*	99.70/*	99.50/0.01‡	99.30/0.01‡	99.30/0.01‡	98.80/0.02	98.80/0.02	98.50/0.02	98.50/0.02	98.20/0.02	97.30/0.03	98.40/0.02
Hindi	100.00/*	100.00/*	100.00/0.00‡	100.00/0.00‡	100.00/0.00‡	99.70/0.01‡	99.70/0.01‡	99.90/0.00‡	100.00/0.00‡	99.90/0.00†	99.40/0.01	73.60/0.71
Hungarian	100.00/*	94.30/*	87.20/0.31	86.60/0.31	85.50/0.34	85.90/0.34	85.90/0.34	83.70/0.38	83.70/0.38	84.30/0.36	82.30/0.41	79.60/0.47
Icelandic	100.00/*	96.90/*	91.30/0.18	91.10/0.18	87.00/0.27	85.00/0.29	85.00/0.29	86.00/0.27	86.00/0.27	86.10/0.30	83.90/0.32	81.90/0.34
Irish	100.00/*	96.90/*	91.40/0.28	91.50/0.27	91.10/0.27	87.60/0.39	87.60/0.39	87.70/0.37	88.80/0.33	87.20/0.36	67.20/0.99	77.80/0.72
Italian	100.00/*	98.80/*	98.00/0.04	98.00/0.04	97.40/0.04	97.50/0.06	97.50/0.06	96.30/0.07	96.70/0.06	97.40/0.04	95.70/0.08	97.40/0.04
Kabardian	100.00/*	100.00/*	99.00/0.01‡	96.00/0.04‡	99.00/0.01‡	99.00/0.01‡	99.00/0.01‡	98.00/0.02‡	98.00/0.02‡	97.00/0.03‡	99.00/0.01‡	95.00/0.09‡
Kannada	100.00/*	100.00/*	100.00/0.00‡	100.00/0.00‡	100.00/0.00‡	98.00/0.02‡	98.00/0.02‡	100.00/0.00‡	99.00/0.01‡	99.00/0.01‡	100.00/0.00‡	99.00/0.02‡
Khaling	100.00/*	100.00/*	99.70/0.01‡	99.60/0.01‡	99.60/0.00‡	99.50/0.01‡	99.50/0.01‡	99.00/0.02	99.60/0.01‡	93.90/0.08	98.40/0.03	99.40/0.01
Kurmanji	100.00/*	98.90/*	94.60/0.06	94.40/0.07	93.60/0.12	93.80/0.11	93.80/0.11	92.80/0.11	92.80/0.11	93.40/0.08	93.50/0.08	89.60/0.21
Ladin	100.00/*	100.00/*	98.00/0.03‡	99.00/0.01‡	97.00/0.06‡	98.00/0.03‡	98.00/0.03‡	97.00/0.07‡	94.00/0.10	97.00/0.07‡	98.00/0.03‡	98.00/0.05‡
Latin	100.00/*	94.40/*	75.90/0.35	74.60/0.39	78.90/0.32	73.70/0.42	73.70/0.42	77.40/0.37	77.40/0.37	72.40/0.42	61.50/0.60	65.40/0.55
Latvian	100.00/*	99.70/*	97.70/0.03	98.20/0.02	96.00/0.07	96.10/0.07	96.10/0.07	94.00/0.12	94.00/0.12	95.80/0.07	92.80/0.16	94.90/0.09
Lithuanian	100.00/*	98.90/*	95.40/0.07	95.50/0.07	91.60/0.13	91.80/0.15	91.80/0.15	87.50/0.19	90.90/0.14	88.90/0.16	88.10/0.19	88.10/0.23
Livonian	100.00/*	100.00/*	98.00/0.03‡	100.00/0.00‡	87.00/0.24	98.00/0.03‡	98.00/0.03‡	92.00/0.15	92.00/0.15	92.00/0.12	97.00/0.06‡	94.00/0.11
Lower-sorbian	100.00/*	99.30/*	97.80/0.05	97.50/0.06	96.60/0.07	96.30/0.07	96.30/0.07	96.40/0.06	96.40/0.06	95.60/0.09	94.30/0.11	95.40/0.10
Macedonian	100.00/*	99.00/*	97.10/0.04	97.10/0.04	95.30/0.07	96.50/0.06	96.50/0.06	94.40/0.10	94.30/0.10	95.30/0.07	94.60/0.08	88.30/0.16
Maltese	99.00/*	98.00/*	96.00/0.09‡	97.00/0.07‡	94.00/0.08‡	95.00/0.10‡	95.00/0.10‡	90.00/0.15	88.00/0.15	83.00/0.27	69.00/0.56	95.00/0.08‡
Middle-french	99.90/*	99.80/*	99.20/0.01	99.30/0.02‡	99.00/0.02	98.70/0.02	98.70/0.02	98.60/0.03	98.60/0.03	99.00/0.02	96.70/0.08	98.70/0.03
Navajo	100.00/*	97.00/*	88.10/0.29	87.40/0.33	91.00/0.21	83.50/0.44	83.50/0.44	86.70/0.32	86.70/0.32	87.00/0.35	75.30/0.53	83.70/0.39
Neapolitan	99.00/*	99.00/*	99.00/0.02‡	99.00/0.02‡	99.00/0.06‡	97.00/0.06‡	97.00/0.06‡	97.00/0.09‡	97.00/0.09‡	97.00/0.04‡	97.00/0.06‡	95.00/0.13‡
North-frisian	100.00/*	99.00/*	94.00/0.15‡	95.00/0.14‡	95.00/0.10‡	96.00/0.05‡	96.00/0.05‡	94.00/0.15‡	95.00/0.15	96.00/0.06‡	92.00/0.14	92.00/0.14
Northern-sami	100.00/*	99.10/*	98.30/0.04	98.10/0.05	96.20/0.07	96.90/0.06	96.90/0.06	95.20/0.10	95.80/0.08	96.10/0.07	92.60/0.12	94.50/0.11
Norwegian-bokmaal	99.90/*	98.60/*	92.00/0.13	92.10/0.13	88.30/0.19	89.00/0.18	89.00/0.18	88.20/0.19	88.20/0.19	88.60/0.18	89.00/0.17	90.50/0.17
Norwegian-nynorsk	100.00/*	98.90/*	94.60/0.09	94.90/0.08	85.30/0.26	84.60/0.26	84.60/0.26	90.80/0.15	90.80/0.15	82.60/0.29	83.40/0.28	[illegible]
Occitan	100.00/*	99.00/*	99.00/0.01‡	99.00/0.01‡	99.00/0.01‡	98.00/0.03‡	98.00/0.03‡	97.00/0.04‡	97.00/0.04‡	99.00/0.01‡	99.00/0.01‡	98.00/0.02‡
Old-armenian	99.80/*	97.50/*	90.40/0.19	90.40/0.19	89.30/0.21	89.10/0.21	89.10/0.21	87.70/0.23	87.70/0.23	88.60/0.20	87.30/0.25	88.80/0.22
Old-church-slavonic	100.00/*	99.00/*	97.00/0.04‡	97.00/0.04‡	94.00/0.10	96.00/0.07‡	96.00/0.07‡	94.00/0.10	93.00/0.11	97.00/0.04‡	93.00/0.12	97.00/0.04‡
Old-english	100.00/*	97.20/*	88.70/0.20	87.90/0.22	88.20/0.23	86.00/0.25	86.00/0.25	87.10/0.23	87.10/0.23	84.50/0.27	83.40/0.30	83.70/0.28
Old-french	99.60/*	98.00/*	92.40/0.13	91.70/0.16	91.40/0.17	89.90/0.20	89.90/0.20	91.50/0.15	91.50/0.16	90.30/0.18	86.50/0.25	88.40/0.22
Old-saxon	100.00/*	99.60/*	98.30/0.03	97.80/0.04	97.20/0.05	97.00/0.06	97.00/0.06	96.10/0.07	96.30/0.06	95.40/0.07	96.30/0.06	95.10/0.08
Pashto	100.00/*	100.00/*	98.00/0.04‡	97.00/0.05‡	98.00/0.03‡	99.00/0.01‡	99.00/0.01‡	94.00/0.09	93.00/0.14	97.00/0.07‡	100.00/0.00‡	100.00/0.00†
Persian	100.00/*	100.00/*	99.80/0.00‡	99.80/0.00‡	99.80/0.00‡	99.70/0.00‡	99.70/0.00‡	99.60/0.01‡	99.60/0.01‡	98.60/0.02	99.80/0.01‡	62.90/1.14
Polish	100.00/*	97.80/*	93.00/0.16	93.40/0.14	90.80/0.25	88.70/0.26	88.70/0.26	89.30/0.25	89.30/0.25	87.30/0.25	82.80/0.40	89.30/0.24
Portuguese	100.00/*	99.40/*	98.60/0.02	98.60/0.02	98.20/0.03	98.00/0.04	98.00/0.04	97.90/0.03	97.90/0.03	99.30/0.01	99.40/0.01‡	95.10/0.10
Quechua	100.00/*	99.90/*	99.90/0.00‡	99.90/0.00‡	99.50/0.01‡	99.50/0.01‡	99.50/0.01‡	99.30/0.01	99.30/0.01	99.30/0.01	99.40/0.01‡	97.90/0.04
Romanian	100.00/*	96.80/*	88.30/0.35	89.00/0.34	87.90/0.39	85.80/0.40	85.80/0.40	84.10/0.50	85.20/0.46	84.60/0.42	79.00/0.58	83.20/0.52
Russian	100.00/*	97.90/*	94.00/0.15	94.40/0.13	92.00/0.28	91.00/0.27	91.00/0.27	90.40/0.27	90.40/0.27	92.00/0.21	85.40/0.35	88.40/0.34
Sanskrit	100.00/*	99.30/*	96.50/0.05	96.30/0.06	93.00/0.12	94.40/0.09	94.40/0.09	93.80/0.10	93.80/0.10	93.50/0.10	92.10/0.12	87.10/0.20
Serbo-croatian	100.00/*	96.80/*	92.10/0.16	92.40/0.15	91.30/0.17	91.30/0.18	91.30/0.18	90.00/0.18	90.00/0.18	87.80/0.25	84.10/0.36	85.50/0.28
Slovak	100.00/*	99.70/*	97.10/0.04	96.90/0.04	94.20/0.09	92.50/0.14	92.50/0.14	93.30/0.10	93.30/0.10	93.10/0.12	92.80/0.13	90.80/0.16
Slovene	100.00/*	99.60/*	97.40/0.05	97.30/0.05	94.90/0.10	94.80/0.08	94.80/0.08	94.10/0.11	94.90/0.10	33.30/0.77	95.30/0.08	95.60/0.07
Sorani	100.00/*	99.30/*	90.60/0.11	90.60/0.11	88.90/0.13	89.50/0.13	89.50/0.13	89.50/0.14	89.50/0.14	89.30/0.13	89.00/0.13	88.30/0.14
Spanish	100.00/*	99.90/*	97.90/0.03	98.10/0.02	97.90/0.03	97.70/0.03	97.70/0.03	96.20/0.06	96.20/0.06	97.70/0.03	93.40/0.13	97.20/0.04
Swahili	100.00/*	100.00/*	99.00/0.01‡	99.00/0.01‡	100.00/0.00‡	99.00/0.01‡	99.00/0.01‡	100.00/0.00‡	99.00/0.01‡	98.00/0.02‡	100.00/0.00‡	98.00/0.02‡
Swedish	100.00/*	98.50/*	93.30/0.12	93.10/0.12	89.30/0.19	88.10/0.23	88.10/0.23	88.40/0.21	88.40/0.21	89.10/0.20	87.20/0.21	88.10/0.22
Tatar	100.00/*	99.00/*	98.00/0.02‡	98.00/0.02‡	98.00/0.02‡	99.00/0.01‡	99.00/0.01‡	99.00/0.01‡	99.00/0.01‡	99.00/0.01‡	99.00/0.01‡	96.00/0.04‡
Turkish	100.00/*	99.40/*	98.10/0.03	98.50/0.02	97.80/0.03	97.10/0.07	97.10/0.07	97.30/0.04	97.30/0.04	97.40/0.04	97.30/0.04	89.50/0.21
Ukrainian	100.00/*	98.70/*	96.00/0.06	96.20/0.06	91.40/0.16	92.80/0.14	92.80/0.14	91.60/0.14	91.70/0.16	93.40/0.12	92.50/0.13	89.10/0.18
Urdu	100.00/*	100.00/*	99.50/0.01‡	99.50/0.01‡	99.30/0.01	100.00/0.00‡	100.00/0.00‡	99.20/0.01	99.40/0.01	99.20/0.01	99.70/0.01‡	97.30/0.04
Uzbek	100.00/*	100.00/*	100.00/0.00‡	100.00/0.00‡	100.00/0.00‡	100.00/0.00‡	100.00/0.00‡	100.00/0.00‡	100.00/0.00‡	100.00/0.00‡	98.00/0.03‡	93.00/0.28
Venetian	99.60/*	99.50/*	99.00/0.02‡	99.20/0.01‡	98.80/0.02	98.80/0.02	98.80/0.02	98.40/0.03	98.70/0.02	99.00/0.02‡	99.10/0.02‡	99.00/0.02‡
Votic	100.00/*	97.00/*	88.00/0.15	90.00/0.13	84.00/0.29	82.00/0.26	82.00/0.26	85.00/0.25	79.00/0.48	84.00/0.23	66.00/0.53	80.00/0.31
Welsh	100.00/*	98.00/*	94.00/0.10‡	93.00/0.11‡	94.00/0.10‡	94.00/0.09‡	94.00/0.09‡	95.00/0.10‡	95.00/0.10‡	95.00/0.06‡	94.00/0.09‡	90.00/0.19
West-frisian	100.00/*	100.00/*	99.00/0.01‡	98.00/0.02‡	91.00/0.26	91.00/0.23	91.00/0.23	93.00/0.22	93.00/0.22	89.00/0.23	74.00/0.55	92.00/0.18
Yiddish	100.00/*	100.00/*	100.00/0.00‡	100.00/0.00‡	99.00/0.01‡	100.00/0.00‡	100.00/0.00‡	99.00/0.01‡	98.00/0.02‡	97.00/0.04‡	99.00/0.06‡	98.00/0.04‡
Zulu	99.90/*	99.90/*	99.80/0.00‡	99.70/0.01‡	99.00/0.02	99.30/0.01	99.30/0.01	99.20/0.02	98.10/0.04	96.00/0.08	97.20/0.05	98.90/0.01

Table 13: Task 1 High Condition Part 1.

	msu-03	axsemantics-01	msu-02	racai-01	hamburg-01	baseline	axsemantics-02	msu-01	tuebingen-oslo-03	tuebingen-oslo-02	kucst-01	tuebingen-oslo-01
Adyghe	96.70/0.03	99.00/0.01	99.00/0.01	92.00/0.08	93.90/0.07	91.60/0.08	**99.60/0.00**‡	95.40/0.05	97.40/0.04	88.20/0.16	98.30/0.02	88.90/0.24
Albanian	92.70/0.17	88.90/0.53	92.40/0.20	95.60/0.11	79.90/0.54	79.60/0.69	40.90/2.66	83.80/0.60	17.90/5.12	10.20/5.87	13.80/3.68	11.60/5.88
Arabic	0.00/9.25	58.20/1.38	0.00/4.70	88.50/0.40	74.70/0.76	47.10/1.49	34.00/2.42	0.00/7.79	79.40/0.67	68.70/1.05	0.00/10.78	0.10/7.55
Armenian	95.40/0.08	90.30/0.17	91.30/0.15	—	87.60/0.20	86.70/0.25	73.40/0.84	90.10/0.15	52.70/1.85	47.10/2.06	47.60/1.36	33.60/2.38
Asturian	**98.60/0.03**	95.30/0.11	94.60/0.12	95.40/0.13	96.20/0.07	95.10/0.11	91.10/0.13	97.00/0.07	84.20/0.24	82.70/0.34	88.80/0.26	69.70/0.56
Azeri	**98.00/0.06**‡	94.00/0.15	**95.00/0.05**‡	90.00/0.19	88.00/0.24	71.00/0.86	**100.00/0.00**‡	66.00/0.76	91.00/0.14	88.00/0.24	47.00/1.07	79.00/0.50
Bashkir	98.90/0.03	**99.80/0.00**‡	99.10/0.02	—	99.10/0.01	90.50/0.26	**99.80/0.00**‡	96.50/0.11	97.10/0.05	90.90/0.17	62.80/0.72	91.60/0.18
Basque	94.50/0.10	8.20/2.45	13.40/3.17	86.80/0.35	46.90/1.24	7.60/3.37	5.40/2.28	24.30/2.85	6.20/2.85	9.60/2.58	73.20/0.51	8.10/2.58
Belarusian	86.40/0.24	47.30/1.25	81.60/0.62	3.80/2.73	57.20/1.28	40.80/1.56	52.80/1.23	68.20/1.66	69.00/1.22	53.30/1.68	62.60/0.78	57.40/1.61
Bengali	**99.00/0.05**‡	**96.00/0.12**‡	**96.00/0.09**‡	**99.00/0.03**‡	93.00/0.14	81.00/0.26	78.00/0.27	90.00/0.23	55.00/0.75	72.00/0.52	82.00/0.48	65.00/0.60
Breton	**95.00/0.14**‡	80.00/0.55	79.00/0.68	—	91.00/0.17	73.00/0.85	85.00/0.22	82.00/0.38	48.00/1.05	70.00/0.66	67.00/0.56	48.00/1.03
Bulgarian	95.80/0.07	88.70/0.21	91.70/0.14	77.80/0.38	79.60/0.31	89.00/0.18	75.60/0.82	95.30/0.08	63.70/1.31	46.90/1.83	59.70/0.80	51.40/1.89
Catalan	98.00/0.04	95.90/0.12	95.00/0.12	89.40/0.14	87.60/0.21	95.60/0.10	92.10/0.14	96.30/0.09	91.60/0.15	76.90/0.43	87.90/0.20	56.00/0.96
Classical-syriac	**99.00/0.01**‡	**100.00/0.00**‡	**99.00/0.01**‡	87.00/0.18	**100.00/0.00**‡	**97.00/0.03**‡	**99.00/0.01**‡	88.00/0.16	76.00/0.30	65.00/0.40	80.00/0.23	94.00/0.06
Crimean-tatar	94.00/0.14	**98.00/0.04**‡	**99.00/0.03**‡	94.00/0.09	**98.00/0.04**‡	**95.00/0.08**‡	**98.00/0.04**‡	**98.00/0.04**‡	**97.00/0.06**‡	92.00/0.12	**96.00/0.07**‡	**95.00/0.09**‡
Czech	92.40/0.15	89.20/0.23	85.90/0.26	90.20/0.20	82.40/0.35	90.50/0.20	83.00/0.69	79.90/0.50	67.40/1.50	55.00/1.55	31.90/2.07	43.60/2.18
Danish	90.40/0.15	92.70/0.13	79.50/0.32	91.80/0.13	76.00/0.36	86.70/0.25	90.40/0.14	66.40/1.04	85.00/0.27	73.30/0.45	64.50/0.81	66.60/0.73
Dutch	94.20/0.11	85.10/0.34	87.20/0.24	82.20/0.13	82.30/0.26	87.70/0.22	88.60/0.22	86.70/0.24	77.00/0.50	59.40/0.90	—	53.20/1.20
English	**96.40/0.06**	95.80/0.07	85.30/0.22	93.80/0.11	94.70/0.08	**95.90/0.06**	**96.50/0.06**	91.60/0.12	88.50/0.27	88.00/0.26	—	70.90/0.70
Estonian	93.30/0.14	87.70/0.33	88.60/0.21	93.80/0.12	67.20/0.65	78.40/0.38	64.10/1.24	81.20/0.84	45.80/2.64	33.30/2.82	42.40/1.35	37.00/3.21
Faroese	79.20/0.42	79.60/0.44	72.90/0.54	76.30/0.52	56.30/0.84	75.90/0.49	76.80/0.39	40.10/1.90	56.60/0.87	56.80/0.91	27.60/1.50	48.40/1.18
Finnish	92.40/0.14	77.00/0.65	73.70/0.43	87.20/0.24	43.80/0.88	78.60/0.34	52.00/2.18	83.30/0.44	23.20/4.90	19.30/5.04	1.40/5.87	14.10/5.66
French	87.90/0.22	85.30/0.27	78.00/0.36	84.30/0.26	72.50/0.48	82.80/0.29	79.60/0.40	51.50/1.60	61.80/0.84	62.20/0.87	—	60.20/0.91
Friulian	**97.00/0.05**‡	**97.00/0.08**‡	**97.00/0.07**‡	78.00/0.24	85.00/0.17	**96.00/0.09**‡	**99.00/0.03**‡	88.00/0.26	81.00/0.31	89.00/0.15	**95.00/0.09**‡	83.00/0.27
Galician	97.60/0.04	96.70/0.08	94.90/0.09	89.90/0.12	93.90/0.10	95.10/0.09	95.00/0.08	97.50/0.04	86.60/0.23	74.30/0.45	91.10/0.13	62.40/0.78
Georgian	97.90/0.03	95.10/0.13	93.50/0.12	97.80/0.04	95.10/0.06	94.10/0.12	95.40/0.15	96.10/0.06	79.00/0.46	77.60/0.53	80.60/0.41	82.30/0.46
German	87.40/0.24	82.30/0.44	78.90/0.46	81.10/0.36	77.10/0.49	81.00/0.58	68.20/0.69	60.50/1.06	52.70/1.64			46.50/1.77
Greek	88.10/0.22	78.20/0.82	81.00/0.45	81.10/0.36	58.90/0.95	78.40/0.40	54.80/1.58	81.40/0.48	40.50/2.64	27.30/3.44	20.70/2.39	31.20/3.22
Haida	**96.00/0.05**‡	93.00/0.17	**95.00/0.09**‡	**96.00/0.06**‡	15.00/1.95	66.00/0.73	**100.00/0.00**‡	**95.00/0.12**‡	90.00/0.22	77.00/0.69	21.00/3.72	60.00/1.60
Hebrew	98.20/0.02	84.30/0.30	86.10/0.20	85.70/0.15	83.70/0.22	53.70/0.57	54.50/0.70	61.20/0.50	23.10/1.57	28.80/1.45	77.80/0.30	30.40/1.32
Hindi	**99.70/0.01**‡	**100.00/0.00**‡	**99.80/0.00**‡	89.40/0.14	98.70/0.02	93.00/0.08	80.00/0.43	98.80/0.03	65.60/1.43	73.40/1.16	83.50/0.83	2.50/3.01
Hungarian	82.10/0.40	76.90/0.54	78.60/0.47	79.50/0.46	59.20/0.79	69.50/0.68	80.80/0.36	50.90/1.16	64.80/0.84	50.20/1.25	16.20/2.93	38.40/1.99
Icelandic	81.10/0.36	80.90/0.41	72.80/0.54	80.60/0.37	55.20/0.78	77.10/0.46	79.30/0.36	63.60/0.69	43.60/1.26	37.00/1.44		46.80/1.24
Irish	89.10/0.33	67.20/1.16	71.20/0.79	81.80/0.48	56.30/1.17	53.00/1.13	34.10/2.88	59.00/1.50	16.90/4.39	14.70/5.28	14.10/3.00	8.50/6.09
Italian	97.30/0.05	94.20/0.16	94.20/0.12	90.00/0.15	88.80/0.17	77.50/0.69	63.70/1.30	96.00/0.07	63.10/0.91	52.30/1.63	32.60/1.73	58.80/1.50
Kabardian	94.00/0.06	**99.00/0.01**‡	**98.00/0.02**‡	92.00/0.12	**100.00/0.00**‡	86.00/0.14	**99.00/0.01**‡	89.00/0.13	82.00/0.26	82.00/0.28	**96.00/0.05**‡	94.00/0.11
Kannada	**96.00/0.08**‡	90.00/0.36	74.00/0.92	**99.00/0.01**‡	91.00/0.20	66.00/0.75	**97.00/0.03**‡	52.00/1.85	38.00/2.21	36.00/1.77	—	50.00/2.02
Khaling	93.00/0.11	72.00/0.89	73.50/0.36	44.70/0.82	77.30/0.37	53.70/0.87	17.10/1.80	51.70/1.16	8.50/3.46	15.60/2.53	87.50/0.20	18.40/2.57
Kurmanji	**94.50/0.06**	92.60/0.12	**94.60/0.07**	90.40/0.17	94.00/0.08	93.00/0.08	87.80/0.36	**93.90/0.07**	70.00/0.98	69.40/1.10	66.40/0.99	59.30/1.47
Ladin	**96.00/0.08**‡	93.00/0.17	94.00/0.12	86.00/0.23	79.00/0.29	92.00/0.18	87.00/0.18	90.00/0.17	88.00/0.29	84.00/0.28	**93.00/0.16**	74.00/0.53
Latin	69.80/0.46	46.20/1.28	56.70/0.67	16.20/1.97	18.10/2.05	48.00/0.81	37.20/1.43	51.30/1.06	55.20/0.95	32.20/1.52	9.10/3.15	36.10/1.57
Latvian	96.10/0.06	93.20/0.21	90.70/0.15	92.90/0.11	91.10/0.15	92.80/0.17	90.20/0.29	93.40/0.11	71.50/0.74	66.10/0.85	50.20/1.30	56.50/1.26
Lithuanian	84.80/0.21	70.60/0.68	80.90/0.28	65.20/0.41	41.70/1.11	64.10/0.48	52.00/0.85	79.00/0.41	68.90/0.59	48.10/1.17	36.20/1.68	41.20/1.41
Livonian	92.00/0.16	82.00/0.40	77.00/0.59	87.00/0.31	68.00/0.62	67.00/0.75	76.00/0.60	74.00/0.66	60.00/1.43	50.00/1.56	56.00/0.95	40.00/2.16
Lower-sorbian	94.00/0.11	94.20/0.13	91.30/0.17	93.70/0.13	83.50/0.30	88.30/0.22	95.50/0.09	72.60/0.59	72.70/0.48	70.60/0.50	74.20/0.40	61.20/0.71
Macedonian	95.60/0.07	92.70/0.12	89.10/0.17	91.90/0.10	88.90/0.16	91.20/0.15	94.20/0.10	85.80/0.22	75.80/0.56	65.30/0.70	50.50/1.07	60.50/1.07
Maltese	85.00/0.26	63.00/0.72	66.00/0.61	4.00/3.00	89.00/0.20	16.00/1.85	28.00/1.43	48.00/0.92	21.00/2.13	12.00/2.33	41.00/1.32	8.00/2.62
Middle-french	**98.90/0.02**	97.00/0.07	96.50/0.07	96.70/0.05	93.50/0.09	95.10/0.10	95.40/0.16	98.00/0.02	90.30/0.26	80.90/0.42		79.60/0.49
Navajo	86.50/0.29	43.60/2.19	49.30/1.78	79.00/0.54	25.80/2.25	38.60/2.06	6.80/3.25	37.10/1.93	12.40/3.11	10.70/3.31	27.20/1.80	9.20/3.75
Neapolitan	**96.00/0.06**‡	**94.00/0.24**‡	**95.00/0.14**‡	—	100.00/0.66	**95.00/0.13**‡	**95.00/0.09**‡	72.00/0.72	79.00/0.33	77.00/0.44	54.00/1.72	76.00/0.63
North-frisian	90.00/0.21	80.00/0.41	59.00/1.44	15.00/4.44	83.00/0.40	36.00/2.70	33.00/2.23	45.00/3.17	17.00/3.91	16.00/3.64	—	7.00/4.53
Northern-sami	96.30/0.08	61.70/1.17	74.30/0.44	94.70/0.17	47.50/1.16	62.70/0.70	75.50/0.35	69.50/1.05	67.10/0.60	51.70/1.00	47.20/1.29	46.40/1.27
Norwegian-bokmaal	85.90/0.20	**90.80/0.15**	79.20/0.31	88.90/0.19	81.70/0.28	**90.50/0.17**	87.20/0.20	77.80/0.34	72.20/0.57	70.90/0.53	49.80/1.13	66.50/0.68
Norwegian-nynorsk	82.40/0.28	82.80/0.30	70.40/0.55	79.40/0.34	56.60/0.71	74.70/0.42	88.00/0.20	57.00/0.81	76.60/0.43	50.00/1.03	39.00/1.35	45.10/0.97
Occitan	**97.00/0.05**‡	**94.00/0.15**‡	**95.00/0.07**‡	86.00/0.23	83.00/0.17	**96.00/0.06**‡	92.00/0.09	**94.00/0.17**‡	86.00/0.21	85.00/0.25	**96.00/0.06**‡	75.00/0.63
Old-armenian	88.00/0.22	84.90/0.33	82.80/0.35	80.40/0.36	68.00/0.62	78.90/0.46	82.20/0.36	58.40/1.10	57.80/0.91	64.70/0.79	62.60/0.68	58.90/0.98
Old-church-slavonic	82.00/0.35	**92.00/0.15**	**93.00/0.15**	9.00/2.10	**93.00/0.10**	81.00/0.45	88.00/0.16	52.00/1.20	67.00/0.58	66.00/0.59	33.00/0.97	71.00/0.47
Old-english	84.20/0.27	69.30/0.59	65.40/0.55	28.20/1.18	50.90/0.84	40.60/0.92	34.30/1.30	63.90/0.77	58.30/0.86	56.60/0.94	—	43.80/1.23
Old-french	89.80/0.18	80.80/0.48	82.40/0.37	—	61.80/0.78	80.80/0.40	82.00/0.39	55.10/1.26	75.90/0.51	62.90/0.81	54.10/0.88	57.00/0.87
Old-saxon	94.50/0.10	87.30/0.28	77.70/0.39	54.50/0.66	72.30/0.46	59.90/0.67	54.00/0.67	64.30/0.94	72.80/0.49	68.70/0.53	76.70/0.33	42.90/1.24
Pashto	89.00/0.19	92.00/0.11	82.00/0.47	84.00/0.25	87.00/0.16	71.00/0.63	78.00/0.42	56.00/1.41	31.00/1.63	37.00/1.46	82.00/0.29	30.00/1.81
Persian	98.20/0.03	63.70/1.50	90.80/0.20	95.60/0.08	90.80/0.17	80.70/0.53	62.60/1.38	98.20/0.03	56.60/2.63	50.50/2.48	29.30/3.33	3.70/4.30
Polish	88.60/0.23	87.60/0.33	82.40/0.37	87.80/0.26	76.40/0.45	87.00/0.26	82.90/0.56	80.40/0.62	61.60/1.33	44.60/1.82	—	49.00/1.78
Portuguese	96.90/0.05	97.30/0.06	95.10/0.08	84.00/0.23	87.80/0.14	96.60/0.06	94.60/0.08	**98.50/0.02**	88.30/0.19	77.40/0.41	76.40/0.42	55.50/0.96
Quechua	99.00/0.02	**99.80/0.00**‡	99.00/0.02	96.80/0.05	81.00/0.32	95.10/0.10	98.80/0.04	99.30/0.02	91.30/0.20	9.70/3.79	43.60/12.02	78.40/0.56
Romanian	81.20/0.49	82.60/0.53	77.70/0.58	82.00/0.49	69.20/0.75	79.70/0.54	62.40/1.33	56.40/1.87	44.90/2.34	41.40/2.65	40.40/1.83	33.80/2.76
Russian	91.90/0.20	88.00/0.33	82.20/0.45	86.80/0.40	85.20/0.35	86.50/0.44	76.10/0.70	86.70/0.62	63.80/1.38	53.20/1.64	—	46.00/2.20
Sanskrit	89.70/0.16	92.80/0.12	87.50/0.22	76.60/0.38	79.20/0.36	80.40/0.35	93.70/0.09	50.40/1.43	70.70/0.65	71.70/0.51	53.80/1.31	74.40/0.48
Serbo-croatian	87.60/0.24	87.40/0.29	84.50/0.32	88.00/0.27	75.20/0.46	83.10/0.36	69.10/1.13	61.90/1.50	35.50/2.94	44.70/2.54	26.20/2.35	33.20/2.84
Slovak	92.70/0.12	91.50/0.13	82.90/0.29	88.80/0.17	73.90/0.44	83.30/0.28	91.10/0.14	51.40/1.25	67.60/0.54	66.00/0.55	61.60/0.67	59.20/0.68
Slovene	33.00/0.79	7.00/1.61	17.80/1.18	93.40/0.10	84.80/0.24	84.90/0.24	90.90/0.16	40.80/0.74	88.30/0.21	72.20/0.49	0.70/8.23	33.90/1.66
Sorani	87.90/0.15	76.00/0.53	80.90/0.27	86.80/0.18	59.30/0.60	63.60/0.68	27.60/2.22	53.20/1.49	12.60/3.06	16.40/2.83	28.50/1.81	12.70/2.95
Spanish	96.80/0.05	94.40/0.17	93.10/0.13	72.70/0.34	93.60/0.11	92.40/0.20	81.30/0.64	95.60/0.07	72.80/0.93	64.90/1.27	59.30/0.85	46.80/1.44
Swahili	**98.00/0.02**‡	**98.00/0.06**‡	**99.00/0.01**‡	**98.00/0.02**‡	**98.00/0.02**‡	71.00/0.44	1.00/3.15	94.00/0.09	5.00/3.22	5.00/2.74	88.00/0.19	4.00/2.73
Swedish	89.50/0.18	88.00/0.22	59.90/0.80	85.20/0.27	75.60/0.42	85.00/0.27	88.50/0.23	84.50/0.27	72.70/0.61	60.70/0.94	33.10/2.01	49.50/1.34
Tatar	**97.00/0.03**‡	**99.00/0.01**‡	**99.00/0.01**‡	**95.00/0.06**‡	**97.00/0.03**‡	**96.00/0.04**‡	**97.00/0.03**‡	**99.00/0.01**‡	**97.00/0.03**‡	86.00/0.17	45.00/1.73	93.00/0.08
Turkish	97.00/0.04	87.90/0.26	93.90/0.09	79.30/0.44	75.40/0.53	73.20/0.70	95.90/0.08	97.30/0.04	77.20/0.54	59.50/1.14	23.30/2.88	51.50/1.62
Ukrainian	91.60/0.15	93.10/0.15	83.70/0.30	90.50/0.20	76.10/0.41	86.20/0.29	87.20/0.25	82.50/0.48	76.70/0.44	62.80/0.75	36.10/1.36	65.30/0.71
Urdu	98.40/0.03	99.30/0.01	99.10/0.02	43.50/0.78	99.00/0.01	95.90/0.05	83.70/0.38	95.10/0.21	74.40/1.11	72.70/1.10	97.00/0.04	5.90/3.60
Uzbek	**96.00/0.10**‡	**100.00/0.00**‡	**100.00/0.00**‡	—	**100.00/0.00**‡	**96.00/0.04**‡	**99.00/0.01**‡	44.00/2.20	61.00/0.66	61.00/0.81	8.00/2.87	76.00/0.51
Venetian	97.90/0.03	98.50/0.03	97.60/0.05	98.50/0.03	98.20/0.03	93.10/0.11	97.60/0.04	98.40/0.03	89.20/0.18	87.10/0.20	87.60/0.46	77.80/0.43
Votic	77.00/0.37	37.00/1.37	52.00/0.85	—	41.00/0.83	37.00/1.35	66.00/0.47	12.00/2.46	48.00/0.88	49.00/0.90	23.00/1.53	34.00/1.58
Welsh	**92.00/0.16**	82.00/0.47	79.00/0.43	**92.00/0.13**	72.00/0.47	72.00/0.54	88.00/0.16	82.00/0.44	75.00/0.41	85.00/0.29	**90.00/0.15**	52.00/0.96
West-frisian	84.00/0.27	82.00/0.51	72.00/0.70	—	92.00/0.10	67.00/0.78	67.00/0.56	47.00/1.17	54.00/1.02	45.00/1.07	17.00/1.73	33.00/1.52
Yiddish	**95.00/0.05**‡	**97.00/0.10**‡	**98.00/0.07**‡	92.00/0.19	**96.00/0.07**‡	94.00/0.14	**99.00/0.01**‡	94.00/0.13	94.00/0.06	84.00/0.31	80.00/0.29	86.00/0.29
Zulu	96.90/0.06	93.80/0.16	95.60/0.11	73.30/0.40	98.50/0.02	68.30/0.64	2.50/3.03	87.60/0.28	2.70/2.88	2.50/3.63	72.30/0.62	2.40/3.55

Table 14: Task 1 High Condition Part 2.

	oracle-fc	oracle-e	uzh-01	uzh-02	iitbhu-iiith-02	iitbhu-iiith-01	waseda-01	msu-04	msu-03	hamburg-01	iit-varanasi-01	msu-02
Adyghe	100.00/*	97.20/*	94.40/0.06	94.20/0.06	93.40/0.07	93.40/0.07	87.80/0.16	80.60/0.46	93.50/0.07	92.10/0.08	92.90/0.08	94.00/0.06
Albanian	100.00/*	95.00/*	88.10/0.30	87.20/0.33	88.80/0.24	87.30/0.27	72.70/1.29	78.80/0.54	77.20/0.58	79.00/0.59	39.20/1.63	72.80/1.01
Arabic	98.40/*	86.90/*	79.40/0.65	78.60/0.68	78.30/0.71	74.40/0.81	66.70/1.02	0.00/10.73	0.00/9.77	63.80/1.03	38.80/1.90	0.00/4.70
Armenian	97.00/*	97.10/*	92.80/0.13	92.40/0.13	90.80/0.16	88.70/0.19	85.30/0.26	86.80/0.23	86.80/0.24	88.20/0.19	67.40/0.80	80.50/0.47
Asturian	97.10/*	96.20/*	91.60/0.17	92.00/0.17	92.40/0.17	91.80/0.18	91.80/0.18	90.30/0.19	89.40/0.22	91.70/0.19	90.00/0.20	88.40/0.27
Azeri	99.00/*	99.00/*	95.00/0.11‡	94.00/0.15‡	96.00/0.08‡	92.00/0.14	84.00/0.34	96.00/0.11‡	92.00/0.16	89.00/0.19	94.00/0.14†	80.00/0.37
Bashkir	100.00/*	99.30/*	96.70/0.08	97.30/0.06	96.50/0.08	95.00/0.11	87.20/0.24	92.00/0.22	92.40/0.24	94.10/0.13	95.40/0.09	88.30/0.25
Basque	43.90/*	95.50/*	88.00/0.23†	86.00/0.27†	88.10/0.25†	86.50/0.28†	80.50/0.45†	59.50/0.91†	51.60/1.11†	33.10/1.66	69.20/0.58†	2.70/6.01
Belarusian	100.00/*	84.50/*	70.40/0.97	69.50/0.97	64.30/1.23	63.20/1.23	53.60/1.44	61.30/1.47	56.40/1.50	54.00/1.45	45.80/1.71	59.50/1.41
Bengali	100.00/*	99.00/*	99.00/0.05‡	99.00/0.05‡	97.00/0.11‡	96.00/0.12‡	96.00/0.14‡	88.00/0.29	95.00/0.15‡	92.00/0.22	97.00/0.10‡	84.00/0.31
Breton	93.00/*	97.00/*	95.00/0.11‡	96.00/0.10‡	92.00/0.25‡	90.00/0.29	93.00/0.17‡	93.00/0.18‡	91.00/0.14	88.00/0.22	94.00/0.20†	77.00/0.80
Bulgarian	100.00/*	92.70/*	83.30/0.26	83.80/0.25	81.00/0.29	78.00/0.33	80.80/0.31	76.90/0.37	77.80/0.33	78.80/0.35	35.00/1.36	72.20/0.48
Catalan	100.00/*	96.80/*	92.10/0.15	92.20/0.15	92.10/0.16	91.80/0.17	92.80/0.17	90.00/0.21	90.50/0.19	84.40/0.27	83.80/0.28	85.40/0.34
Classical-syriac	100.00/*	100.00/*	100.00/0.00‡	100.00/0.00‡	99.00/0.01‡	99.00/0.01‡	100.00/0.00‡	99.00/0.01‡	96.00/0.04‡	97.00/0.03‡	99.00/0.01‡	97.00/0.04‡
Cornish	92.00/*	88.00/*	70.00/0.74	66.00/0.76	70.00/0.76	70.00/0.74	46.00/2.44	58.00/0.86	36.00/1.62	52.00/1.00	66.00/0.70	10.00/2.78
Crimean-tatar	100.00/*	99.00/*	98.00/0.04‡	98.00/0.04‡	97.00/0.06‡	97.00/0.06‡	92.00/0.11	91.00/0.21	93.00/0.12	96.00/0.06‡	98.00/0.04‡	95.00/0.07‡
Czech	97.20/*	93.80/*	87.20/0.26	86.60/0.28	80.40/0.37	79.00/0.39	82.30/0.46	79.40/0.42	78.60/0.47	82.00/0.38	61.10/0.94	76.30/0.53
Danish	100.00/*	93.60/*	80.40/0.30	80.00/0.31	79.20/0.33	78.60/0.34	79.60/0.32	78.80/0.34	76.10/0.37	79.00/0.32	75.70/0.36	68.80/0.50
Dutch	100.00/*	96.20/*	85.70/0.22	85.60/0.21	82.00/0.28	81.90/0.28	77.10/0.37	80.40/0.31	84.00/0.25	77.80/0.38	71.00/0.49	65.90/0.52
English	100.00/*	97.20/*	94.50/0.10	94.20/0.10	94.20/0.10	93.50/0.11	91.50/0.14	91.50/0.14	94.40/0.09	90.20/0.14	90.90/0.15	86.40/0.25
Estonian	100.00/*	90.80/*	81.60/0.30	81.50/0.31	78.20/0.34	76.20/0.37	72.20/0.50	71.30/0.51	65.60/0.63	63.10/0.77	46.50/1.20	67.50/0.54
Faroese	100.00/*	86.60/*	72.60/0.59	71.70/0.60	69.10/0.61	68.00/0.62	68.20/0.72	68.00/0.68	66.20/0.71	56.10/0.84	48.90/1.02	60.10/0.78
Finnish	97.10/*	91.50/*	82.80/0.27	82.30/0.29	73.80/0.43	71.10/0.47	65.10/0.64	58.10/0.83	57.00/0.84	35.90/1.22	22.00/2.55	41.90/1.98
French	100.00/*	89.40/*	80.20/0.33	80.90/0.32	78.60/0.35	78.20/0.35	73.10/0.47	75.70/0.42	76.50/0.41	71.80/0.50	69.30/0.60	73.90/0.46
Friulian	100.00/*	99.00/*	96.00/0.06‡	96.00/0.06‡	97.00/0.05‡	97.00/0.05‡	96.00/0.06‡	95.00/0.07‡	93.00/0.09	81.00/0.24	92.00/0.14	92.00/0.12
Galician	99.90/*	95.70/*	90.80/0.16	90.40/0.17	88.90/0.18	88.40/0.18	88.90/0.18	85.80/0.27	82.90/0.29	86.00/0.23	82.50/0.29	82.80/0.33
Georgian	96.20/*	96.00/*	93.90/0.14	94.00/0.14	93.50/0.17	93.40/0.17	93.20/0.17	91.20/0.21	92.30/0.20	92.60/0.17	91.20/0.22	84.40/0.29
German	100.00/*	89.20/*	80.10/0.48	79.50/0.48	76.80/0.56	76.70/0.56	74.00/0.64	74.10/0.60	74.40/0.56	70.90/0.65	65.50/0.71	68.00/0.72
Greek	97.40/*	84.40/*	75.30/0.53	75.50/0.55	71.50/0.56	69.10/0.61	60.50/1.73	67.00/0.71	62.00/0.83	58.40/0.98	29.90/1.99	62.00/1.65
Greenlandic	100.00/*	100.00/*	98.00/0.02‡	98.00/0.02‡	88.00/0.20	86.00/0.22	74.00/2.40	68.00/0.38	80.00/0.22	68.00/0.40	84.00/0.22	70.00/0.38
Haida	100.00/*	96.00/*	94.00/0.12‡	94.00/0.12‡	87.00/0.32	85.00/0.36	62.00/1.98	91.00/0.19‡	92.00/0.20‡	16.00/2.15	90.00/0.19	81.00/0.38
Hebrew	100.00/*	96.10/*	85.40/0.19	84.50/0.20	84.50/0.21	83.10/0.23	76.90/0.32	81.70/0.25	80.10/0.26	77.90/0.30	64.70/0.52	64.40/0.47
Hindi	99.70/*	98.90/*	97.50/0.03	97.60/0.03	96.20/0.07	96.00/0.08	95.60/0.05	94.80/0.07	95.00/0.07	94.20/0.07	87.70/0.32	90.90/0.16
Hungarian	100.00/*	86.50/*	73.70/0.53	73.40/0.55	74.50/0.51	72.00/0.56	53.80/0.96	65.90/0.68	68.80/0.65	51.60/0.91	57.10/0.85	64.50/0.65
Icelandic	100.00/*	96.00/*	73.80/0.52	73.60/0.52	65.90/0.67	63.50/0.70	62.40/0.78	64.60/0.69	59.20/0.78	54.60/0.79	45.70/1.03	55.70/0.87
Ingrian	100.00/*	96.00/*	92.00/0.14‡	92.00/0.12‡	90.00/0.24‡	90.00/0.18‡	68.00/1.56	88.00/0.20‡	86.00/0.22‡	58.00/0.66	88.00/0.18‡	56.00/0.68
Irish	99.10/*	87.30/*	77.10/0.67	75.60/0.70	68.80/0.89	64.70/0.97	54.30/1.22	60.80/1.12	57.10/1.19	59.60/1.13	18.80/3.40	52.20/1.43
Italian	100.00/*	97.60/*	94.90/0.09	95.10/0.09	93.20/0.13	91.70/0.15	91.90/0.16	88.90/0.19	92.50/0.16	85.90/0.25	68.90/0.78	85.80/0.32
Kabardian	100.00/*	100.00/*	97.00/0.03‡	98.00/0.02‡	98.00/0.02‡	92.00/0.11	92.00/0.11	86.00/0.27	92.00/0.10	95.00/0.06‡	97.00/0.03‡	97.00/0.03‡
Kannada	100.00/*	99.00/*	94.00/0.12‡	94.00/0.12‡	92.00/0.14	91.00/0.15	93.00/0.11	87.00/0.26	87.00/0.23	86.00/0.24	85.00/0.26	64.00/1.19
Karelian	100.00/*	100.00/*	100.00/0.00‡	100.00/0.00‡	96.00/0.08‡	94.00/0.08‡	78.00/1.92	92.00/0.08‡	92.00/0.12‡	82.00/0.28	96.00/0.06‡	76.00/0.28
Kashubian	100.00/*	96.00/*	88.00/0.20‡	88.00/0.26‡	86.00/0.22‡	82.00/0.26	66.00/1.96	84.00/0.26	78.00/0.38	82.00/0.34	84.00/0.24	72.00/0.48
Kazakh	100.00/*	96.00/*	84.00/0.16	82.00/0.18	88.00/0.12‡	84.00/0.16	70.00/1.76	76.00/0.26	74.00/0.28	86.00/0.16‡	50.00/0.50	82.00/0.20
Khakas	100.00/*	98.00/*	98.00/0.04‡	98.00/0.04‡	98.00/0.04‡	98.00/0.04‡	64.00/1.54	98.00/0.04‡	98.00/0.02‡	96.00/0.06‡	98.00/0.04‡	98.00/0.04‡
Khaling	90.90/*	94.40/*	83.20/0.29	82.40/0.30	85.60/0.23	86.00/0.23	85.70/0.25	41.40/1.18	43.40/1.23	68.30/0.65	59.40/0.80	20.10/2.61
Kurmanji	97.20/*	97.30/*	93.20/0.10	92.30/0.11	91.10/0.18	90.60/0.19	88.30/0.32	74.20/0.55	87.20/0.21	90.00/0.13	86.10/0.34	91.00/0.22
Ladin	97.00/*	98.00/*	93.00/0.16‡	95.00/0.11‡	92.00/0.13	93.00/0.11‡	93.00/0.13‡	80.00/0.27	87.00/0.21	76.00/0.26	91.00/0.10	89.00/0.29
Latin	100.00/*	74.30/*	53.30/0.75	51.70/0.80	46.20/0.89	44.80/0.94	37.90/1.16	38.20/1.17	40.80/1.10	21.40/1.94	31.30/1.37	37.50/1.26
Latvian	99.60/*	94.90/*	90.60/0.15	89.80/0.19	88.00/0.24	86.50/0.27	88.20/0.26	85.30/0.31	84.40/0.31	86.30/0.26	73.70/0.55	86.50/0.25
Lithuanian	98.90/*	78.80/*	63.90/0.52	63.00/0.55	55.60/0.75	53.40/0.78	52.00/0.70	45.90/0.88	48.10/0.87	40.80/1.13	46.80/0.96	55.00/0.77
Livonian	99.00/*	94.00/*	82.00/0.35	79.00/0.42	75.00/0.45	77.00/0.40	74.00/0.50	67.00/0.61	63.00/0.68	70.00/0.59	62.00/0.75	54.00/1.14
Lower-sorbian	100.00/*	95.00/*	85.10/0.26	84.20/0.29	84.00/0.28	82.30/0.30	81.40/0.34	78.20/0.39	80.80/0.35	78.60/0.40	69.80/0.50	78.90/0.39
Macedonian	98.40/*	97.20/*	91.60/0.11	91.50/0.12	90.10/0.13	88.50/0.15	88.10/0.16	86.40/0.19	84.30/0.21	87.40/0.17	75.10/0.38	84.20/0.24
Maltese	99.00/*	98.00/*	95.00/0.10‡	94.00/0.11‡	91.00/0.20	90.00/0.19	89.00/0.22	77.00/0.35	84.00/0.25	82.00/0.38	85.00/0.24	59.00/0.73
Mapudungun	100.00/*	100.00/*	98.00/0.04‡	100.00/0.00‡	96.00/0.04‡	96.00/0.04‡	76.00/1.46	90.00/0.12‡	88.00/0.14	100.00/0.00‡	98.00/0.04‡	92.00/0.08‡
Middle-french	99.80/*	97.50/*	94.30/0.11	94.50/0.12	93.30/0.14	92.60/0.16	93.20/0.13	92.90/0.15	92.70/0.15	89.00/0.19	89.40/0.23	90.80/0.19
Middle-high-german	100.00/*	100.00/*	100.00/0.00‡	100.00/0.00‡	96.00/0.08‡	96.00/0.08‡	80.00/1.20	92.00/0.12‡	92.00/0.14‡	96.00/0.10‡	92.00/0.14‡	90.00/0.14‡
Middle-low-german	100.00/*	100.00/*	98.00/0.02‡	98.00/0.02‡	98.00/0.02‡	100.00/0.00‡	72.00/1.50	94.00/0.06‡	82.00/0.36	96.00/0.04‡	92.00/0.16‡	68.00/0.78
Murrinhpatha	100.00/*	100.00/*	96.00/0.04‡	96.00/0.04‡	90.00/0.20‡	86.00/0.22	70.00/1.34	76.00/0.52	78.00/0.50	88.00/0.22	96.00/0.10‡	44.00/1.26
Navajo	99.50/*	69.60/*	54.30/1.20	54.00/1.27	44.60/1.60	43.00/1.66	40.80/1.81	42.40/1.63	42.00/1.61	24.20/2.74	19.50/2.68	33.80/2.65
Neapolitan	99.00/*	99.00/*	99.00/0.03‡	99.00/0.03‡	98.00/0.05‡	98.00/0.05‡	95.00/0.08‡	96.00/0.06‡	93.00/0.11	49.00/0.71	98.00/0.06‡	94.00/0.20‡
Norman	100.00/*	94.00/*	84.00/0.38‡	86.00/0.34‡	88.00/0.24‡	88.00/0.24‡	66.00/2.08	38.00/1.10	34.00/1.28	58.00/0.94	26.00/1.62	46.00/2.04
North-frisian	100.00/*	94.00/*	91.00/0.24‡	89.00/0.27‡	88.00/0.29	89.00/0.27‡	87.00/0.30	78.00/0.67	70.00/0.74	75.00/0.61	85.00/0.39	49.00/1.98
Northern-sami	100.00/*	90.30/*	76.10/0.42	75.20/0.44	70.20/0.52	66.10/0.58	60.30/0.78	56.70/0.85	57.80/0.81	31.30/1.66	39.40/1.26	34.60/1.30
Norwegian-bokmaal	99.30/*	93.60/*	84.10/0.24	84.00/0.24	83.50/0.27	81.50/0.30	81.30/0.30	80.40/0.31	82.70/0.28	79.00/0.34	81.50/0.29	66.60/0.47
Norwegian-nynorsk	99.80/*	90.00/*	67.10/0.55	65.90/0.57	64.20/0.60	62.90/0.63	60.50/0.65	61.10/0.65	61.00/0.63	53.90/0.77	57.50/0.72	49.30/0.88
Occitan	100.00/*	97.00/*	94.00/0.10‡	95.00/0.11‡	94.00/0.10‡	94.00/0.10‡	96.00/0.10‡	92.00/0.12‡	89.00/0.22	81.00/0.22	93.00/0.12‡	89.00/0.23
Old-armenian	99.00/*	91.80/*	80.20/0.39	79.20/0.41	78.10/0.44	77.10/0.46	72.70/0.58	66.00/0.67	69.70/0.61	65.90/0.66	57.30/0.82	71.40/0.63
Old-church-slavonic	100.00/*	99.00/*	93.00/0.11	93.00/0.11	87.00/0.24	87.00/0.23	90.00/0.16	83.00/0.29	78.00/0.34	89.00/0.18	87.00/0.19	80.00/0.35
Old-english	100.00/*	83.90/*	65.60/0.58	65.00/0.58	62.70/0.64	60.30/0.69	56.30/0.72	52.90/0.77	58.30/0.70	45.70/0.93	42.40/1.13	33.50/1.20
Old-french	95.90/*	89.30/*	79.30/0.41	77.90/0.45	74.10/0.51	72.20/0.54	71.30/0.58	68.10/0.59	68.50/0.62	62.60/0.72	60.60/0.74	66.60/0.73
Old-irish	84.00/*	50.00/*	40.00/1.66‡	34.00/2.14	26.00/2.58	22.00/2.78	16.00/3.40	12.00/2.62	26.00/2.42	6.00/3.78	24.00/2.52	16.00/3.88
Old-saxon	97.60/*	92.40/*	80.70/0.34	80.90/0.33	74.90/0.39	74.10/0.41	70.30/0.49	70.90/0.49	71.10/0.47	67.40/0.55	64.70/0.60	47.60/1.04
Pashto	100.00/*	97.00/*	85.00/0.31	83.00/0.28	85.00/0.23	81.00/0.28	77.00/0.50	73.00/0.55	75.00/0.49	80.00/0.31	73.00/0.36	68.00/0.72
Persian	100.00/*	97.20/*	93.40/0.10	93.40/0.10	91.70/0.13	90.70/0.14	87.00/0.24	84.50/0.24	86.20/0.23	82.60/0.37	70.90/0.71	77.30/0.63
Polish	98.20/*	89.50/*	82.20/0.40	82.40/0.38	76.10/0.54	73.40/0.58	75.90/0.55	72.30/0.58	74.50/0.56	75.10/0.58	55.10/1.09	74.10/0.61
Portuguese	100.00/*	97.20/*	94.70/0.08	94.80/0.08	92.00/0.12	92.00/0.12	93.80/0.10	90.40/0.14	91.30/0.13	84.90/0.21	37.30/1.41	90.40/0.18
Quechua	85.90/*	99.60/*	98.90/0.02†	98.70/0.03†	98.60/0.03†	98.20/0.03†	70.90/1.49	96.70/0.06†	95.30/0.11†	78.40/0.40	77.30/0.55	73.30/1.45
Romanian	100.00/*	88.20/*	77.60/0.57	77.10/0.58	73.00/0.77	72.20/0.83	71.50/0.89	68.30/0.73	68.40/0.79	68.70/0.73	48.50/1.51	68.80/0.73
Russian	99.70/*	92.70/*	86.90/0.30	86.80/0.28	80.10/0.57	78.20/0.60	79.50/0.56	76.40/0.50	76.20/0.50	77.30/0.47	59.90/0.97	72.20/0.77
Sanskrit	99.30/*	93.20/*	85.90/0.23	85.90/0.23	85.50/0.25	84.70/0.26	79.10/0.36	78.50/0.36	77.70/0.39	79.80/0.33	68.80/0.54	79.60/0.36
Scottish-gaelic	100.00/*	96.00/*	92.00/0.10‡	92.00/0.14‡	94.00/0.12‡	94.00/0.08‡	72.00/1.66	84.00/0.28	72.00/0.50	88.00/0.18‡	86.00/0.18‡	88.00/0.24‡
Serbo-croatian	95.10/*	93.00/*	86.10/0.27	85.20/0.27	82.50/0.34	81.90/0.36	76.30/0.45	75.50/0.47	73.30/0.54	72.30/0.58	43.40/1.49	66.80/0.83
Slovak	100.00/*	92.40/*	78.60/0.37	77.90/0.39	73.90/0.45	72.30/0.47	73.90/0.47	71.00/0.46	68.90/0.50	70.30/0.51	58.70/0.67	68.40/0.54
Slovene	99.80/*	94.30/*	86.20/0.22	85.80/0.23	85.00/0.25	83.60/0.28	84.10/0.24	40.90/0.79	27.10/0.99	84.70/0.26	65.60/0.52	7.60/1.51
Sorani	97.40/*	93.00/*	79.60/0.32	79.20/0.33	80.20/0.30	77.80/0.34	72.00/0.49	64.20/0.61	64.40/0.61	49.30/0.81	55.90/0.90	56.40/1.19
Spanish	100.00/*	95.60/*	91.40/0.14	91.10/0.15	92.00/0.14	91.20/0.16	91.50/0.15	88.60/0.19	89.30/0.18	88.30/0.23	75.70/0.64	85.10/0.40
Swahili	100.00/*	99.00/*	99.00/0.01‡	99.00/0.01‡	97.00/0.05‡	95.00/0.07‡	92.00/0.14	85.00/0.22	84.00/0.28	95.00/0.09‡	87.00/0.29	92.00/0.13
Swedish	99.40/*	93.10/*	79.80/0.35	79.50/0.35	77.80/0.40	78.30/0.40	76.80/0.41	77.80/0.37	74.30/0.43	71.90/0.48	31.40/1.41	65.40/0.57
Tatar	100.00/*	99.00/*	97.00/0.03‡	98.00/0.02‡	95.00/0.05‡	95.00/0.05‡	92.00/0.11	94.00/0.06‡	95.00/0.07‡	93.00/0.09	96.00/0.04‡	94.00/0.07‡
Tibetan	100.00/*	72.00/*	52.00/0.78	56.00/0.64	50.00/0.90	40.00/1.00	38.00/1.36	44.00/0.86	44.00/0.94	46.00/0.74	22.00/1.36	52.00/0.80
Turkish	94.10/*	95.90/*	90.70/0.17	90.30/0.17	90.00/0.27	88.20/0.31	69.20/0.78	82.50/0.39	81.20/0.45	68.60/0.70	79.20/0.47	65.40/1.21
Turkmen	100.00/*	98.00/*	94.00/0.08‡	94.00/0.08‡	98.00/0.02‡	98.00/0.02‡	74.00/1.72	94.00/0.06‡	94.00/0.06‡	90.00/0.18‡	96.00/0.04‡	98.00/0.02‡
Ukrainian	99.30/*	93.50/*	81.40/0.35	80.40/0.38	77.60/0.42	76.00/0.43	74.00/0.49	73.00/0.46	71.70/0.47	77.50/0.41	46.60/0.85	69.80/0.50
Urdu	98.70/*	92.70/*	96.70/0.04	96.80/0.04	96.70/0.04	96.40/0.05	93.90/0.10	94.10/0.10	92.20/0.14	94.70/0.07	87.50/0.25	89.40/0.20
Uzbek	100.00/*	100.00/*	100.00/0.00‡	100.00/0.00‡	100.00/0.00‡	100.00/0.00‡	96.00/0.04‡	100.00/0.00‡	94.00/0.10	100.00/0.00‡	100.00/0.00‡	100.00/0.00‡
Venetian	99.30/*	98.10/*	94.40/0.08	95.10/0.08	92.80/0.10	92.30/0.11	93.10/0.10	91.60/0.11	91.90/0.12	91.90/0.12	91.90/0.11	88.50/0.17
Votic	100.00/*	90.00/*	86.00/0.16	88.00/0.14	86.00/0.18	83.00/0.22	74.00/0.43	67.00/0.53	71.00/0.44	42.00/0.82	78.00/0.32	49.00/0.90
Welsh	100.00/*	90.00/*	84.00/0.29	83.00/0.30	82.00/0.30	82.00/0.30	81.00/0.33	77.00/0.39	71.00/0.44	67.00/0.63	81.00/0.34	67.00/0.61
West-frisian	100.00/*	94.00/*	97.00/0.05‡	98.00/0.04‡	89.00/0.25	86.00/0.30	96.00/0.14‡	90.00/0.11	78.00/0.40	92.00/0.13	94.00/0.07	73.00/0.68
Yiddish	100.00/*	99.00/*	92.00/0.10	94.00/0.10‡	89.00/0.16	89.00/0.16	91.00/0.18	85.00/0.19	89.00/0.15	92.00/0.13	88.00/0.23	89.00/0.18
Zulu	96.90/*	94.60/*	87.20/0.28	87.30/0.27	85.20/0.35	82.80/0.40	82.80/0.38	70.40/0.68	68.40/0.70	81.80/0.39	52.60/1.14	71.60/0.70

Table 15: Task 1 Medium Condition Part 1.

	bme-01	bme-03	bme-02	msu-01	baseline	axsemantics-02	axsemantics-01	kucst-01	tuebingen-oslo-03	tuebingen-oslo-02	tuebingen-oslo-01
Adyghe	90.80/0.12	90.50/0.13	93.10/0.11	88.90/0.13	84.80/0.15	91.90/0.08	—	66.10/0.86	55.00/1.28	34.60/1.96	47.10/1.70
Albanian	46.20/1.41	46.20/1.41	46.30/1.38	65.50/1.01	60.70/1.44	26.50/3.21	—	10.50/3.78	3.30/6.25	3.40/6.60	2.00/7.59
Arabic	47.00/1.63	47.00/1.63	37.20/2.76	0.00/7.80	39.50/1.83	22.60/3.23	—	0.00/10.78	5.10/3.63	22.30/2.85	0.00/8.80
Armenian	58.70/1.00	58.70/1.00	58.00/1.13	77.40/0.53	71.00/0.55	63.40/1.06	—	12.30/3.18	9.80/3.67	8.30/4.11	8.00/4.29
Asturian	87.80/0.22	88.60/0.22	86.40/0.27	89.60/0.21	89.10/0.25	82.50/0.35	—	49.70/1.01	40.10/1.26	51.80/0.89	26.20/1.68
Azeri	56.00/0.89	56.00/0.89	65.00/0.83	81.00/0.40	50.00/1.91	89.00/0.20	—	11.00/2.36	54.00/1.10	46.00/1.34	34.00/1.74
Bashkir	92.40/0.14	91.50/0.17	93.20/0.21	93.70/0.13	72.30/0.66	93.90/0.12	—	65.40/0.84	59.40/1.03	51.40/1.17	45.20/1.53
Basque	37.70/1.38	37.70/1.38	34.20/1.60	10.40/3.73	1.80/5.63	0.70/3.17	—	49.40/1.17†	1.40/4.21	2.70/3.82	2.40/4.11
Belarusian	52.40/1.41	52.40/1.41	45.40/1.69	41.60/2.03	21.70/2.09	16.60/2.82	—	13.00/2.84	26.90/2.59	20.60/2.82	15.40/3.25
Bengali	87.00/0.32	87.00/0.32	85.00/0.39	83.00/0.37	76.00/0.33	72.00/0.37	—	66.00/0.82	43.00/1.04	45.00/1.09	46.00/1.04
Breton	88.00/0.33	90.00/0.26	**93.00/0.20‡**	70.00/0.69	67.00/1.09	81.00/0.33	—	66.00/0.67	42.00/1.21	55.00/0.71	30.00/1.59
Bulgarian	58.00/0.71	58.00/0.71	59.70/0.86	75.80/0.36	70.60/0.49	52.60/1.27	—	32.10/2.05	22.90/2.80	17.10/3.20	20.60/3.11
Catalan	84.50/0.29	84.20/0.33	88.10/0.21	86.10/0.27	85.70/0.31	79.50/0.37	—	23.30/1.99	37.30/1.47	43.40/1.28	14.10/2.36
Classical-syriac	**98.00/0.03‡**	**98.00/0.03‡**	**96.00/0.05‡**	91.00/0.09	**99.00/0.01‡**	**100.00/0.00‡**	—	81.00/0.26	67.00/0.45	71.00/0.30	90.00/0.11
Cornish	20.00/2.20	28.00/1.96	32.00/1.80	—	12.00/2.94	32.00/1.54	2.00/3.54	34.00/1.70	20.00/1.76	26.00/1.70	10.00/3.46
Crimean-tatar	**94.00/0.11‡**	**92.00/0.11**	**94.00/0.19‡**	90.00/0.19	78.00/0.31	**97.00/0.05‡**	—	61.00/0.93	50.00/1.31	52.00/1.17	58.00/1.11
Czech	35.50/1.47	35.70/1.73	32.90/1.69	69.00/0.70	79.70/0.48	61.10/1.09	—	7.20/4.19	10.50/3.61	17.40/3.13	8.60/4.20
Danish	72.10/0.46	71.90/0.45	71.50/0.56	70.90/0.47	77.60/0.37	72.00/0.41	—	31.30/1.97	24.00/2.65	30.80/2.39	27.90/2.21
Dutch	66.40/0.53	66.40/0.53	66.10/0.72	73.90/0.42	72.70/0.45	61.20/0.69	—	—	16.30/2.73	25.60/2.21	14.30/2.85
English	90.40/0.15	90.40/0.15	89.60/0.16	92.60/0.11	90.50/0.15	89.00/0.15	—	—	29.30/2.05	28.10/2.32	26.10/2.14
Estonian	31.70/1.57	31.70/1.57	27.00/1.98	59.90/0.81	62.70/0.77	36.10/1.82	—	8.30/3.48	14.60/3.86	3.40/4.84	3.70/5.09
Faroese	48.90/1.04	46.80/1.11	50.70/1.05	45.80/1.28	65.30/0.77	47.00/1.01	—	12.50/2.67	13.10/2.72	19.80/2.38	13.80/2.64
Finnish	31.70/1.88	31.70/1.88	26.20/2.34	51.20/1.04	44.20/1.53	21.40/3.01	—	0.00/8.23	0.20/7.52	1.20/7.45	1.10/8.10
French	73.40/0.47	73.40/0.47	74.60/0.45	74.60/0.46	73.10/0.47	66.90/0.66	—	—	14.50/2.58	29.80/2.04	22.30/2.39
Friulian	91.00/0.11	91.00/0.11	91.00/0.12	56.00/0.93	**92.00/0.11**	**94.00/0.11‡**	—	74.00/0.47	62.00/0.58	66.00/0.50	48.00/1.01
Galician	84.40/0.27	81.40/0.30	81.50/0.33	77.50/0.41	82.80/0.34	78.90/0.43	—	40.60/1.26	46.20/1.01	43.50/1.11	26.70/1.77
Georgian	90.20/0.31	90.20/0.31	91.50/0.33	91.10/0.22	92.10/0.21	91.40/0.30	—	35.40/1.72	30.50/2.09	43.90/1.53	28.10/2.33
German	67.50/0.79	67.50/0.79	66.00/0.95	73.50/0.57	71.60/0.71	67.60/0.80	—	—	12.10/3.72	14.10/3.58	11.90/3.64
Greek	14.90/2.65	15.10/2.34	16.40/3.21	52.90/1.16	59.30/1.03	34.40/2.27	—	4.20/4.51	5.90/4.82	4.50/5.21	4.90/5.45
Greenlandic	80.00/0.22	74.00/0.40	78.00/0.24	—	70.00/0.42	82.00/0.24	54.00/0.90	22.00/1.50	70.00/0.42	42.00/0.96	22.00/1.86
Haida	80.00/1.02	84.00/0.91	71.00/1.47	75.00/1.08	61.00/1.02	81.00/0.46	—	21.00/4.58	78.00/0.69	58.00/1.58	28.00/2.49
Hebrew	76.60/0.30	76.60/0.30	79.00/0.28	67.90/0.44	38.10/0.98	33.00/1.22	—	22.20/1.45	11.90/1.97	8.10/2.07	12.10/2.10
Hindi	87.40/0.30	87.40/0.30	86.40/0.47	94.80/0.08	87.20/0.18	74.40/0.53	—	71.80/1.02	47.30/1.68	52.20/1.54	0.80/3.28
Hungarian	58.60/0.83	58.60/0.83	51.10/1.35	65.30/0.77	44.40/1.42	56.80/0.82	—	1.50/4.83	5.90/4.34	7.80/3.95	2.40/4.92
Icelandic	51.70/0.94	51.70/0.94	49.90/1.06	44.20/1.15	58.80/0.83	44.90/1.04	—	10.80/2.79	11.60/3.04	16.30/2.64	9.70/2.99
Ingrian	78.00/0.36	**88.00/0.30‡**	**84.00/0.30**	—	46.00/0.86	80.00/0.30	44.00/1.28	68.00/0.54	46.00/0.88	36.00/1.00	24.00/1.40
Irish	45.40/1.75	45.40/1.75	43.30/1.92	47.90/1.68	44.10/1.57	19.50/3.79	—	3.00/5.48	1.70/6.88	3.70/6.84	4.20/7.16
Italian	77.50/0.44	78.30/0.43	79.10/0.45	87.30/0.23	72.50/0.81	50.60/1.56	—	10.90/3.02	13.20/3.08	1.50/5.54	11.40/3.74
Kabardian	**99.00/0.01‡**	**99.00/0.01‡**	**100.00/0.00‡**	42.00/1.31	83.00/0.17	**97.00/0.03‡**	—	46.00/0.74	81.00/0.27	79.00/0.29	75.00/0.41
Kannada	73.00/0.64	74.00/0.81	78.00/0.61	59.00/1.26	55.00/1.30	81.00/0.30	—	—	20.00/2.64	19.00/2.22	20.00/2.90
Karelian	**96.00/0.12‡**	**96.00/0.12‡**	**96.00/0.10‡**	—	42.00/1.00	**98.00/0.02‡**	62.00/0.90	60.00/1.24	58.00/0.80	50.00/0.82	26.00/1.42
Kashubian	**78.00/0.30**	**78.00/0.30**	**88.00/0.20‡**	—	68.00/0.58	60.00/0.64	**76.00/0.38**	6.00/2.12	74.00/0.38	56.00/0.70	32.00/1.36
Kazakh	24.00/1.42	24.00/1.42	4.00/5.68	—	48.00/1.14	**86.00/0.14‡**	44.00/1.08	16.00/1.74	0.00/4.34	44.00/0.66	38.00/0.88
Khakas	**98.00/0.02‡**	**98.00/0.02‡**	**98.00/0.04‡**	—	84.00/0.36	**96.00/0.06‡**	**96.00/0.06‡**	32.00/1.56	62.00/0.60	60.00/0.50	66.00/0.54
Khaling	62.20/0.97	53.80/1.33	56.20/1.28	15.30/2.59	18.00/2.01	5.30/2.56	—	27.20/2.09	5.50/3.65	6.80/3.42	5.40/3.86
Kurmanji	80.30/0.76	80.30/0.76	83.30/0.89	88.70/0.21	85.10/0.28	86.70/0.43	—	26.30/2.38	20.30/2.71	32.40/2.40	15.70/3.12
Ladin	**92.00/0.14**	**88.00/0.25**	**90.00/0.17**	79.00/0.33	86.00/0.35	77.00/0.37	—	62.00/0.57	67.00/0.53	63.00/0.63	24.00/1.77
Latin	22.60/2.05	22.60/2.05	22.60/2.32	27.90/1.63	37.90/1.16	11.20/2.31	—	2.60/3.91	2.90/4.00	5.20/3.40	3.20/4.18
Latvian	72.60/0.65	72.60/0.65	64.40/0.98	82.40/0.38	85.50/0.26	79.90/0.54	—	9.70/3.25	19.50/2.77	23.30/2.41	6.40/3.68
Lithuanian	26.70/1.77	26.50/1.64	23.60/2.13	39.50/1.17	52.00/0.70	25.20/1.59	—	3.60/3.36	18.20/2.29	12.20/2.56	3.40/3.54
Livonian	46.00/1.14	46.00/1.14	44.00/1.25	59.00/1.04	51.00/1.36	52.00/1.23	—	23.00/2.13	42.00/1.68	5.00/4.25	13.00/3.21
Lower-sorbian	69.30/0.54	69.30/0.54	65.70/0.64	57.90/0.88	68.90/0.60	68.60/0.52	—	15.50/2.06	27.30/1.61	29.70/1.38	20.30/1.85
Macedonian	71.50/0.47	71.50/0.47	71.50/0.50	73.80/0.37	82.60/0.32	79.50/0.32	—	14.20/2.38	18.00/2.38	20.40/2.43	21.20/2.37
Maltese	83.00/0.33	83.00/0.33	**90.00/0.15**	57.00/0.90	21.00/1.71	24.00/1.61	—	57.00/0.88	18.00/2.27	17.00/2.29	4.00/3.16
Mapudungun	**98.00/0.02‡**	**98.00/0.02‡**	**98.00/0.02‡**	—	82.00/0.20	**98.00/0.02‡**	**90.00/0.24‡**	**94.00/0.12‡**	52.00/0.86	54.00/0.78	32.00/1.38
Middle-french	85.40/0.32	85.40/0.32	90.20/0.22	93.10/0.14	90.20/0.18	86.00/0.32	—	54.70/1.09	61.30/0.97	19.90/2.51	31.40/1.74
Middle-high-german	66.00/0.72	66.00/0.72	**96.00/0.04‡**	—	54.00/0.66	52.00/0.88	84.00/0.26	78.00/0.34	40.00/1.00	48.00/0.84	30.00/1.40
Middle-low-german	86.00/0.30	86.00/0.30	**98.00/0.04‡**	—	38.00/1.44	30.00/1.38	76.00/0.64	—	58.00/1.10	60.00/1.06	36.00/1.92
Murrinhpatha	**84.00/0.38**	**90.00/0.26‡**	**90.00/0.26‡**	—	22.00/2.04	4.00/1.86	54.00/1.14	62.00/0.94	6.00/2.88	4.00/3.10	8.00/2.68
Navajo	30.30/2.13	30.30/2.13	33.60/2.26	29.60/2.10	30.40/2.49	4.30/5.01	—	9.10/3.40	3.00/4.36	3.10/4.41	0.80/5.44
Neapolitan	**98.00/0.06‡**	**98.00/0.06‡**	**98.00/0.06‡**	93.00/0.14	**94.00/0.17‡**	**96.00/0.09‡**	—	76.00/0.65	78.00/0.38	65.00/0.56	39.00/1.18
Norman	32.00/1.98	32.00/1.98	44.00/1.70	—	46.00/2.02	34.00/1.56	28.00/2.62	14.00/2.58	30.00/1.80	24.00/1.86	6.00/2.88
North-frisian	72.00/0.59	72.00/0.59	69.00/0.72	42.00/2.73	33.00/2.85	29.00/2.52	—	—	14.00/4.07	20.00/3.61	3.00/5.09
Northern-sami	44.60/1.22	44.60/1.22	47.50/1.42	33.00/2.02	34.90/1.38	23.10/1.72	—	8.30/3.43	13.10/2.61	8.20/2.70	2.60/3.85
Norwegian-bokmaal	77.00/0.38	77.00/0.38	77.30/0.43	81.40/0.29	80.50/0.31	77.30/0.34	—	26.70/2.13	28.50/2.33	28.30/2.36	29.40/1.84
Norwegian-nynorsk	56.90/0.70	56.90/0.70	58.60/0.70	57.20/0.71	60.50/0.65	54.40/0.77	—	15.20/2.40	18.00/2.54	19.80/2.64	20.60/2.08
Occitan	82.00/0.35	82.00/0.35	69.00/0.61	79.00/0.44	79.00/0.44	**92.00/0.16‡**	—	41.00/1.26	62.00/0.69	59.00/0.60	14.00/2.14
Old-armenian	42.10/1.32	42.20/1.23	43.30/1.27	41.00/1.41	67.30/0.71	55.00/0.93	—	13.00/2.34	14.00/2.31	24.40/1.95	17.20/2.40
Old-church-slavonic	**87.00/0.22**	**87.00/0.22**	**86.00/0.22**	63.00/0.85	77.00/0.53	83.00/0.22	—	39.00/0.94	54.00/0.67	49.00/0.67	47.00/0.82
Old-english	37.70/1.27	35.30/1.63	37.30/1.52	46.10/1.04	27.70/1.29	18.00/1.88	—	—	23.60/2.06	24.00/1.98	10.70/2.57
Old-french	60.50/0.83	58.60/0.77	62.60/0.78	56.00/0.98	63.00/0.74	55.80/0.89	—	20.20/2.02	27.40/1.79	27.10/1.80	18.40/2.17
Old-irish	6.00/3.26	6.00/3.26	6.00/3.46	—	10.00/3.80	3.00/2.94	8.00/2.82	6.00/3.26	8.00/3.22	6.00/3.50	4.00/3.96
Old-saxon	61.50/0.65	61.50/0.65	48.00/1.06	38.30/1.27	39.10/1.02	31.60/1.25	—	19.40/1.88	21.50/1.78	18.80/1.87	11.10/2.31
Pashto	65.00/0.67	65.00/0.67	70.00/0.59	46.00/1.51	68.00/0.71	57.00/0.77	—	43.00/1.02	18.00/1.82	7.00/3.29	18.00/2.46
Persian	72.60/0.73	72.60/0.73	76.30/0.52	80.40/0.35	66.50/1.01	49.90/1.80	—	48.80/1.63	37.50/2.83	29.40/3.38	1.30/5.04
Polish	49.70/1.21	49.70/1.21	49.40/1.20	62.60/0.90	73.50/0.64	60.80/0.99	—	—	9.50/3.61	7.50/3.92	9.60/3.73
Portuguese	89.30/0.17	88.60/0.20	80.80/0.31	89.10/0.18	92.40/0.13	84.30/0.24	—	26.30/1.78	35.60/1.50	11.90/2.76	22.90/1.98
Quechua	80.80/0.53	80.80/0.53	79.70/0.60	69.30/1.13	70.90/1.49	**95.90/0.09†**	—	21.00/3.08	48.60/1.33	1.90/6.31	21.70/2.92
Romanian	61.40/1.03	61.40/1.03	59.70/1.04	56.60/1.14	69.30/0.75	47.20/1.72	—	12.70/3.34	13.70/3.68	15.90/3.51	5.60/4.20
Russian	51.70/1.16	51.70/1.16	51.80/1.47	66.70/0.72	76.40/0.52	56.70/1.09	—	—	8.50/4.04	1.80/5.44	9.60/4.14
Sanskrit	64.80/0.70	64.80/0.70	65.30/0.71	36.50/2.33	60.10/0.76	76.30/0.37	—	14.10/2.48	21.70/2.05	21.50/1.76	26.50/1.98
Scottish-gaelic	**90.00/0.16‡**	**90.00/0.16‡**	**88.00/0.22‡**	—	50.00/0.74	50.00/1.30	70.00/0.74	56.00/0.74	48.00/0.96	52.00/0.88	36.00/1.66
Serbo-croatian	38.60/1.26	38.60/1.26	30.30/1.87	58.10/1.01	68.20/0.77	47.20/1.58	—	7.70/4.18	10.90/4.20	10.80/4.16	5.00/4.55
Slovak	56.60/0.73	56.60/0.73	58.00/0.85	53.50/0.95	71.30/0.53	62.30/0.64	—	10.50/2.12	21.80/1.72	26.90/1.46	17.60/1.79
Slovene	68.70/0.56	68.70/0.56	55.00/1.01	43.60/0.76	72.30/0.46	73.30/0.47	—	0.20/8.25	29.90/1.86	34.40/1.60	8.30/3.26
Sorani	40.30/1.35	40.10/1.44	46.10/1.19	28.40/2.35	52.10/1.05	15.50/2.66	—	30.70/1.80	6.40/3.58	6.60/3.70	1.60/4.42
Spanish	82.30/0.38	82.30/0.38	79.40/0.51	85.20/0.26	86.50/0.35	73.10/0.85	—	28.10/2.04	25.20/2.52	21.90/2.95	20.10/2.63
Swahili	84.00/0.34	86.00/0.27	85.00/0.35	77.00/0.42	73.00/0.37	1.00/3.21	—	72.00/0.59	1.00/3.35	3.00/3.30	10.00/4.16
Swedish	68.70/0.53	69.10/0.53	70.00/0.54	76.20/0.36	76.40/0.41	69.50/0.50	—	11.10/3.05	13.90/3.48	2.70/4.93	19.00/2.99
Tatar	92.00/0.10	92.00/0.10	90.00/0.17	**95.00/0.05‡**	90.00/0.14	90.00/0.08	—	53.00/1.30	62.00/1.00	57.00/1.11	**52.00/1.34**
Tibetan	26.00/1.30	26.00/1.30	30.00/1.40	—	36.00/1.00	42.00/1.00	44.00/0.88	24.00/1.32	26.00/1.24	38.00/1.04	**42.00/0.94**
Turkish	38.30/2.06	38.30/1.78	36.50/2.31	80.50/0.55	32.20/2.95	73.70/0.51	—	9.30/4.03	20.70/2.92	18.90/3.18	12.60/4.37
Turkmen	**96.00/0.04‡**	**94.00/0.06‡**	**96.00/0.06‡**	—	68.00/0.64	**94.00/0.06‡**	**96.00/0.04‡**	48.00/0.68	70.00/0.36	82.00/0.22	66.00/0.62
Ukrainian	66.80/0.62	66.80/0.62	61.10/0.72	69.20/0.61	74.00/0.49	62.70/0.66	—	14.50/2.20	19.10/2.10	25.20/1.94	20.40/2.23
Urdu	85.90/0.42	82.90/0.53	83.90/0.54	87.00/0.23	87.00/0.23	78.20/0.46	—	80.70/0.30	53.50/1.55	45.50/1.58	2.70/3.38
Uzbek	**100.00/0.00‡**	**100.00/0.00‡**	**100.00/0.00‡**	89.00/0.18	**96.00/0.04‡**	**100.00/0.00‡**	—	14.00/3.03	63.00/0.62	59.00/0.73	66.00/0.93
Venetian	86.40/0.18	86.10/0.31	82.00/0.26	77.00/0.42	88.90/0.16	89.80/0.17	—	45.40/1.27	56.00/0.74	58.40/0.69	20.10/1.81
Votic	78.00/0.37	79.00/0.38	79.00/0.37	19.00/2.05	37.00/1.39	64.00/0.48	—	59.00/0.78	45.00/0.94	39.00/1.03	21.00/1.62
Welsh	**81.00/0.38**	79.00/0.36	**85.00/0.29‡**	56.00/0.98	58.00/1.01	62.00/0.68	—	23.00/1.80	41.00/1.06	46.00/1.03	9.00/2.20
West-frisian	91.00/0.27	90.00/0.25	92.00/0.26	80.00/0.31	90.00/0.79	65.00/0.81	—	76.00/0.44	48.00/1.13	50.00/1.56	28.00/1.56
Yiddish	79.00/0.37	80.00/0.30	84.00/0.28	80.00/0.31	**87.00/0.22**	78.00/0.39	—	62.00/0.87	56.00/1.01	63.00/0.96	39.00/1.51
Zulu	60.00/0.93	60.00/0.93	54.00/1.05	67.40/0.78	53.60/0.98	1.70/3.34	—	15.80/2.42	1.20/3.73	1.50/4.41	0.80/5.04

Table 16: Task 1 Medium Condition Part 2.

	oracle-fc	oracle-e	axsemantics-01	uzh-02	uzh-01	ua-08	iitbhu-iiith-02	ua-05	iitbhu-iiith-01	ua-06	ua-03	waseda-01
Adyghe	98.30/*	98.40/*	—	90.30/0.10	90.00/0.10	90.60/0.14	89.10/0.17	82.10/0.22	85.50/0.21	88.90/0.17	81.00/0.23	73.10/0.51
Albanian	54.80/*	54.90/*	—	35.70/1.89	36.40/1.87	20.50/4.00	29.70/2.00	21.80/4.35	26.40/2.20	20.30/4.02	18.90/3.03	24.40/4.82
Arabic	54.20/*	57.40/*	—	44.30/1.80	45.20/1.77	35.80/2.24	35.20/2.04	19.80/5.28	31.90/2.19	35.50/2.23	0.10/6.27	27.60/3.33
Armenian	55.30/*	76.20/*	—	64.60/0.82†	64.90/0.77†	49.10/1.73	54.40/0.92	50.50/1.51	51.60/1.02	43.30/1.91	49.90/1.53	37.00/2.18
Asturian	65.20/*	82.80/*	—	74.60/0.47†	72.50/0.52†	58.00/0.95	70.30/0.55†	67.90/0.83	66.30/0.62	56.80/1.00	57.00/1.05	58.60/1.06
Azeri	71.00/*	79.00/*	—	62.00/0.82	62.00/0.86	46.00/1.31	65.00/0.76	48.00/1.17	63.00/0.81	24.00/2.62	36.00/1.63	39.00/1.35
Bashkir	98.00/*	94.90/*	—	70.10/0.51	67.20/0.53	77.50/0.48	77.20/0.44	42.90/1.10	77.80/0.44	61.90/1.42	42.10/1.11	39.40/1.84
Basque	5.60/*	31.20/*	—	12.70/3.05†	13.30/2.98†	11.40/3.29†	11.80/3.02†	6.70/3.88	9.60/3.13†	10.50/3.34†	3.30/3.96	6.50/3.70
Belarusian	86.30/*	54.80/*	—	30.20/2.18	30.00/2.16	33.40/1.97	22.90/2.35	16.20/2.52	21.20/2.45	31.30/2.04	16.20/2.52	10.30/2.72
Bengali	83.00/*	91.00/*	—	72.00/0.49	71.00/0.53	68.00/1.00	58.00/0.83	62.00/0.63	55.00/0.88	64.00/1.16	59.00/0.90	52.00/0.76
Breton	74.00/*	86.00/*	—	71.00/0.76	72.00/0.78	69.00/0.92	61.00/0.95	69.00/0.85	61.00/0.93	67.00/0.99	66.00/0.90	61.00/0.99
Bulgarian	66.10/*	80.90/*	—	58.50/0.70	58.20/0.70	62.90/1.02	54.00/0.81	50.40/0.97	51.50/0.89	62.40/1.02	49.30/0.98	50.00/0.90
Catalan	86.90/*	87.40/*	—	69.90/0.57	68.50/0.60	72.50/0.65	64.40/0.65	62.80/0.79	61.80/0.70	71.60/0.68	60.50/0.82	60.80/0.86
Classical-syriac	95.00/*	98.00/*	—	96.00/0.04‡	96.00/0.04‡	94.00/0.06‡	92.00/0.09	95.00/0.06‡	91.00/0.10	93.00/0.07‡	94.00/0.06‡	94.00/0.06†
Cornish	68.00/*	58.00/*	—	24.00/1.82	28.00/1.56	38.00/1.40	30.00/1.68	40.00/1.56	22.00/1.82	6.00/2.80	14.00/2.90	12.00/3.62
Crimean-tatar	98.00/*	98.00/*	—	89.00/0.15	89.00/0.15	89.00/0.17	91.00/0.14	81.00/0.25	89.00/0.17	85.00/0.21	71.00/0.39	67.00/0.43
Czech	56.70/*	58.30/*	—	46.50/1.97	46.50/1.80	40.00/2.09	37.00/1.51	42.30/1.80	33.80/1.68	40.00/2.09	39.80/1.83	39.30/2.14
Danish	96.20/*	91.10/*	—	69.90/0.51	70.00/0.50	87.20/0.24	65.20/0.58	68.20/0.49	65.80/0.58	87.70/0.24	68.10/0.48	64.70/0.67
Dutch	95.20/*	80.80/*	—	55.20/0.71	56.00/0.70	68.90/0.60	58.60/0.62	56.00/0.70	57.60/0.65	69.30/0.62	55.30/0.74	53.70/0.86
English	100.00/*	92.90/*	—	90.30/0.14	90.30/0.14	91.80/0.16	86.50/0.20	89.80/0.15	81.30/0.28	91.80/0.16	89.90/0.15	80.80/0.26
Estonian	70.30/*	62.20/*	—	33.60/1.49	35.20/1.36	33.30/2.17	33.00/1.59	28.70/1.73	29.00/1.72	31.80/2.22	29.00/1.74	30.80/1.79
Faroese	85.70/*	68.90/*	—	43.40/1.18	45.90/1.12	49.80/1.20	33.00/1.37	43.10/1.14	27.60/1.51	49.30/1.22	39.20/1.25	39.70/1.50
Finnish	58.10/*	39.80/*	—	24.90/2.05	25.70/2.01	20.00/3.29	19.90/2.31	21.30/2.90	19.00/2.37	19.30/3.31	20.80/2.91	19.50/2.59
French	85.50/*	78.50/*	—	66.60/0.61	65.20/0.61	60.80/1.03	55.00/0.83	59.00/0.96	53.10/0.90	58.90/1.08	55.60/0.76	58.90/0.97
Friulian	89.00/*	85.00/*	—	79.00/0.39	79.00/0.36	70.00/0.41	72.00/0.64	75.00/0.59	70.00/0.63	69.00/0.52	68.00/0.64	70.00/0.52
Galician	73.00/*	72.40/*	—	61.10/0.72	60.80/0.70	47.60/1.17	48.40/0.94	53.70/1.21	43.50/1.09	41.80/1.39	50.30/1.24	53.00/1.22
Georgian	93.80/*	92.40/*	—	84.50/0.35	84.00/0.34	88.20/0.30	80.40/0.41	83.00/0.38	77.70/0.46	87.50/0.33	83.40/0.38	70.60/0.58
German	79.60/*	85.60/*	—	62.00/0.78	62.40/0.76	55.00/1.14	57.00/0.93	59.30/0.83	53.50/1.00	55.00/1.14	67.10/0.69	52.00/1.04
Greek	57.70/*	49.00/*	—	32.20/1.93	32.30/1.83	23.90/2.89	27.10/1.96	28.90/2.32	26.10/2.01	23.40/2.90	26.90/2.36	25.10/2.71
Greenlandic	100.00/*	96.00/*	—	74.00/0.48	74.00/0.42	68.00/0.48	72.00/0.36	68.00/0.42	80.00/0.30	66.00/0.42	64.00/0.50	52.00/2.74
Haida	45.00/*	77.00/*	—	63.00/1.42†	60.00/1.77†	20.00/4.47	57.00/1.45	49.00/2.07	48.00/1.86	20.00/4.47	10.00/4.94	29.00/5.64
Hebrew	82.40/*	71.80/*	—	39.90/1.02	39.10/1.02	56.70/0.91	34.30/1.12	35.40/1.04	32.40/1.19	56.40/0.92	37.20/1.03	26.00/1.46
Hindi	38.80/*	85.80/*	—	78.00/0.79†	78.00/0.68†	45.80/1.57†	75.90/0.89†	70.80/1.17†	75.10/0.90†	39.60/1.66	49.40/1.22†	59.60/1.19†
Hungarian	78.90/*	65.40/*	—	41.30/1.19	40.30/1.18	48.20/1.41	39.20/1.35	33.10/1.37	33.50/1.54	47.90/1.42	28.00/1.58	25.90/1.83
Icelandic	92.20/*	71.80/*	—	48.90/1.04	48.20/1.01	56.20/0.94	31.70/1.39	42.60/1.16	29.30/1.49	55.50/0.95	40.60/1.19	38.90/1.49
Ingrian	100.00/*	66.00/*	—	36.00/1.58	36.00/1.34	20.00/1.78	46.00/1.10	32.00/1.14	34.00/1.32	38.00/0.92	26.00/1.36	4.00/2.88
Irish	82.70/*	50.40/*	—	37.60/2.18	37.70/2.09	35.30/2.40	26.00/2.58	34.80/2.11	22.30/2.74	35.50/2.38	35.10/2.13	34.10/3.03
Italian	82.80/*	73.80/*	—	57.40/1.02	57.00/1.17	47.80/1.64	47.30/1.07	42.20/2.06	45.40/1.09	46.50/1.71	38.40/1.97	42.20/2.05
Kabardian	99.00/*	100.00/*	—	90.00/0.10	92.00/0.08	88.00/0.21	87.00/0.13	86.00/0.18	84.00/0.16	86.00/0.25	84.00/0.20	75.00/0.32
Kannada	74.00/*	78.00/*	—	60.00/0.80	61.00/0.79	38.00/2.14	57.00/0.89	57.00/1.10	55.00/0.92	37.00/2.14	31.00/2.40	36.00/2.10
Karelian	88.00/*	98.00/*	—	88.00/0.20‡	88.00/0.16‡	70.00/0.60	92.00/0.14‡	94.00/0.10‡	90.00/0.18‡	56.00/0.78	64.00/0.70	46.00/2.54
Kashubian	100.00/*	82.00/*	—	64.00/0.72	66.00/0.72	44.00/1.16	58.00/0.88	68.00/0.70	52.00/1.14	58.00/0.76	54.00/1.08	56.00/0.90
Kazakh	100.00/*	92.00/*	—	86.00/0.14‡	80.00/0.20	62.00/0.50	78.00/0.22	76.00/0.30	84.00/0.16‡	34.00/1.48	42.00/0.94	38.00/2.18
Khakas	100.00/*	92.00/*	—	78.00/0.26	78.00/0.28	70.00/0.64	86.00/0.16‡	56.00/0.54	80.00/0.24	42.00/0.92	54.00/0.56	36.00/1.96
Khaling	22.00/*	53.20/*	—	22.30/2.13	23.00/2.04	33.80/2.32†	24.50/1.83	15.50/2.14	19.20/2.01	30.50/2.44†	15.50/2.14	12.10/2.89
Kurmanji	90.20/*	89.20/*	—	87.40/0.64	87.10/0.34	84.00/0.44	80.80/0.55	87.20/0.35	75.20/0.64	84.00/0.44	86.70/0.35	86.20/0.43
Ladin	77.00/*	83.00/*	—	71.00/0.55	72.00/0.52	59.00/0.80	68.00/0.62	67.00/1.03	64.00/0.68	58.00/0.80	55.00/0.89	58.00/0.96
Latin	52.30/*	42.00/*	—	17.10/2.42	17.70/2.32	33.00/1.84	15.30/2.48	16.90/2.46	14.00/2.52	33.10/1.84	17.40/2.44	16.10/2.84
Latvian	80.10/*	70.90/*	—	54.50/1.00	54.50/1.16	55.90/0.97	35.90/1.43	56.00/1.41	36.40/1.43	57.30/0.96	52.00/1.04	52.80/0.87
Lithuanian	65.40/*	44.30/*	—	20.70/1.84	20.40/1.78	32.40/1.97	16.90/1.91	23.20/1.87	14.50/2.03	32.60/1.97	19.20/2.15	23.00/1.89
Livonian	73.00/*	53.00/*	—	33.00/1.69	32.00/1.69	35.00/1.60	33.00/1.86	30.00/1.67	32.00/1.88	34.00/1.73	29.00/1.68	29.00/2.21
Lower-sorbian	75.90/*	77.00/*	—	45.60/1.04	46.20/1.02	54.20/1.08	40.90/1.15	48.70/0.98	37.50/1.23	54.30/1.10	50.50/0.97	36.30/1.38
Macedonian	79.20/*	85.90/*	—	59.80/0.61	60.20/0.60	67.60/0.63	57.40/0.60	56.50/0.68	53.70/0.65	68.80/0.62	54.20/0.76	49.80/0.89
Maltese	99.00/*	69.00/*	—	40.00/1.16	39.00/1.12	48.00/1.02	32.00/1.31	18.00/1.64	24.00/1.43	49.00/0.96	18.00/1.64	20.00/1.96
Mapudungun	88.00/*	100.00/*	—	78.00/0.34	80.00/0.36	84.00/0.38	84.00/0.28	86.00/0.24	84.00/0.28	70.00/0.60	76.00/0.46	68.00/1.64
Middle-french	86.70/*	93.40/*	—	84.50/0.32	83.10/0.34	74.50/0.66	83.10/0.34	81.40/0.36	82.60/0.39	68.80/0.67	74.20/0.55	76.90/0.49
Middle-high-german	94.00/*	90.00/*	—	84.00/0.30‡	82.00/0.34‡	58.00/0.80	70.00/0.62	36.00/2.46	70.00/0.62	32.00/0.98	34.00/1.32	18.00/2.84
Middle-low-german	92.00/*	64.00/*	—	50.00/1.34	54.00/1.28‡	24.00/2.26	42.00/1.44	34.00/1.32	36.00/1.50	30.00/1.54	34.00/1.32	18.00/2.84
Murrinhpatha	98.00/*	64.00/*	—	36.00/1.48	36.00/1.36	38.00/1.68	34.00/1.66	38.00/1.58	36.00/1.66	26.00/1.72	38.00/1.58	34.00/2.24
Navajo	88.90/*	30.00/*	—	19.80/3.42	20.80/2.96	12.10/3.75	10.30/3.46	8.00/6.97	8.80/3.53	12.00/3.75	13.70/3.99	16.10/3.75
Neapolitan	90.00/*	90.00/*	—	89.00/0.28†	86.00/0.31†	80.00/0.59	80.00/0.41	83.00/0.32	76.00/0.50	80.00/0.66	81.00/0.59	79.00/0.59
Norman	88.00/*	84.00/*	—	52.00/0.92	54.00/0.88	58.00/1.16	64.00/0.70	66.00/0.66	64.00/1.00	32.00/1.62	40.00/1.72	44.00/2.34
North-frisian	85.00/*	61.00/*	—	42.00/2.23	40.00/2.29	31.00/2.39	45.00/2.11	31.00/2.69	38.00/2.12	20.00/4.53	27.00/2.80	36.00/2.25
Northern-sami	69.10/*	50.70/*	—	20.70/2.02	21.10/1.90	35.80/2.29	15.40/2.33	16.80/2.35	12.30/2.48	34.00/2.34	14.80/2.54	16.40/2.35
Norwegian-bokmaal	99.30/*	94.10/*	—	79.10/0.32	78.70/0.33	83.60/0.39	69.60/0.47	78.30/0.35	68.40/0.51	90.10/0.20	76.80/0.37	73.30/0.40
Norwegian-nynorsk	98.30/*	89.30/*	—	56.70/0.73	56.80/0.74	83.60/0.39	54.80/0.79	57.30/0.70	52.30/0.85	82.90/0.42	56.50/0.72	54.60/0.81
Occitan	91.00/*	82.00/*	—	77.00/0.49‡	76.00/0.52	68.00/0.72	72.00/0.55	71.00/1.24	69.00/0.61	66.00/0.84	68.00/0.76	72.00/0.82
Old-armenian	47.40/*	59.70/*	—	42.00/1.32	41.80/1.30	32.90/1.50	29.70/1.58	36.10/1.70	24.30/1.77	31.10/1.53	31.20/1.46	30.50/1.79
Old-church-slavonic	97.00/*	76.00/*	—	48.00/1.06	46.00/1.08	50.00/0.88	53.00/0.78	42.00/1.11	50.00/0.87	50.00/0.92	34.00/1.20	40.00/1.14
Old-english	81.00/*	64.80/*	—	24.10/1.58	24.70/1.54	46.50/1.11	23.10/1.62	29.00/1.34	20.70/1.75	46.40/1.11	17.60/1.72	16.90/1.72
Old-french	65.80/*	68.70/*	—	46.20/1.10	46.10/1.05	36.30/1.48	39.50/1.23	34.90/1.67	36.70/1.32	34.80/1.53	32.90/1.78	36.00/1.31
Old-irish	46.00/*	16.00/*	—	8.00/3.62†	8.00/3.84‡	0.00/6.94	4.00/3.80	6.00/4.28†	4.00/3.84	4.00/3.90	4.00/4.54	8.00/4.34†
Old-saxon	68.30/*	64.50/*	—	30.00/1.32	31.40/1.29	46.50/1.06	25.10/1.52	29.30/1.38	22.20/1.61	46.60/1.06	28.70/1.41	22.80/1.84
Pashto	59.00/*	65.00/*	—	48.00/1.25	48.00/1.29	36.00/1.59	35.00/1.30	37.00/1.70	33.00/1.34	36.00/1.57	33.00/1.75	31.00/2.26
Persian	54.70/*	81.00/*	—	67.60/0.59†	67.50/0.55†	35.30/2.25	61.60/0.81†	34.80/2.98	56.20/0.94	25.20/2.87	28.70/2.77	36.60/1.78
Polish	75.90/*	66.20/*	—	45.30/1.43	44.60/1.47	49.10/1.87	32.50/1.72	44.60/1.49	29.00/1.83	49.40/1.86	43.60/1.50	42.00/1.72
Portuguese	73.70/*	87.00/*	—	75.80/0.40	73.80/0.43	62.50/0.72	59.20/0.69	63.90/0.80	57.80/0.69	61.70/0.74	56.50/1.01	62.60/0.83
Quechua	21.40/*	88.70/*	—	70.20/0.90†	69.00/0.93†	62.00/1.21†	61.60/1.02†	50.80/1.42†	56.50/1.10†	36.20/2.98†	26.40/2.79†	33.50/2.35†
Romanian	79.40/*	65.10/*	—	46.00/1.34	46.20/1.34	45.00/1.94	35.50/1.83	45.80/1.48	32.80/1.94	45.40/1.94	40.40/1.58	44.70/1.52
Russian	80.20/*	71.50/*	—	53.20/1.09	53.50/1.07	49.90/1.33	49.20/1.36	47.40/1.14	39.20/1.42	50.20/1.34	46.00/1.18	47.00/1.27
Sanskrit	68.90/*	74.20/*	—	56.80/0.90	58.00/0.93	43.50/1.53	52.20/1.07	46.20/1.23	51.40/1.08	39.20/1.73	46.00/1.33	42.40/1.24
Scottish-gaelic	100.00/*	84.00/*	—	68.00/0.62	70.00/0.58	58.00/0.98	74.00/0.50‡	50.00/0.82	60.00/0.78	62.00/0.94	46.00/0.82	38.00/2.50
Serbo-croatian	34.50/*	62.80/*	—	43.00/1.50†	43.50/1.53†	29.50/2.38	35.10/1.56	43.80/1.69†	34.20/1.68	28.70/2.40	44.80/1.70†	29.30/1.88
Slovak	90.00/*	71.00/*	—	51.80/0.96	51.10/0.97	48.00/1.06	42.30/1.11	51.30/1.00	39.30/1.18	48.00/1.06	49.00/1.02	48.40/1.09
Slovene	70.80/*	79.70/*	—	58.00/0.73	57.50/0.74	54.10/0.82	48.60/0.88	46.00/0.96	42.90/0.96	53.10/0.84	30.80/1.19	34.10/1.27
Sorani	38.20/*	55.00/*	—	38.90/1.55	40.10/1.32	28.60/2.16	26.40/1.70	24.80/2.38	22.90/1.83	27.50/2.20	24.20/2.39	19.90/3.35
Spanish	82.70/*	79.10/*	—	68.90/0.80	67.80/0.66	73.20/0.80	57.20/0.79	68.60/0.76	53.50/0.87	72.50/0.81	64.90/0.81	61.80/1.08
Swahili	39.00/*	80.00/*	—	58.00/0.70†	58.00/0.73†	36.00/1.49	72.00/0.51†	33.00/1.57	69.00/0.56†	33.00/1.59	33.00/1.57	70.00/0.51†
Swedish	95.00/*	86.90/*	—	68.40/0.51	67.90/0.52	79.00/0.40	61.40/0.70	62.00/0.67	58.50/0.75	77.70/0.42	60.30/0.72	61.70/0.62
Tatar	98.00/*	96.00/*	—	86.00/0.16	88.00/0.14	90.00/0.14	85.00/0.26	72.00/0.35	79.00/0.32	89.00/0.15	66.00/0.44	67.00/0.44
Telugu	86.00/*	98.00/*	72.00/0.96	96.00/0.12‡	92.00/0.24‡	96.00/0.12‡	96.00/0.16‡	96.00/0.06‡	94.00/0.22‡	82.00/0.74	82.00/0.42	54.00/2.90
Tibetan	100.00/*	82.00/*	—	52.00/0.78	52.00/0.76	36.00/1.10	48.00/0.80	34.00/0.98	58.00/0.62	54.00/0.66	38.00/0.84	34.00/1.02
Turkish	39.60/*	55.10/*	—	38.10/2.04	39.00/1.89	22.60/2.99	39.50/2.09	27.50/2.53	37.50/2.13	11.80/5.16	12.20/3.67	26.70/2.79
Turkmen	100.00/*	96.00/*	—	90.00/0.14‡	86.00/0.20‡	60.00/1.00	80.00/0.28	86.00/0.20‡	78.00/0.34	68.00/0.46	72.00/0.44	50.00/2.06
Ukrainian	85.40/*	71.40/*	—	48.90/0.92	49.40/0.92	56.50/0.92	38.10/1.05	47.70/0.98	30.70/1.22	57.10/0.92	47.50/1.01	46.60/0.99
Urdu	41.30/*	82.80/*	—	72.50/0.48†	71.90/0.48†	50.70/1.56†	69.60/0.60†	66.50/0.74†	65.90/0.66†	33.90/1.67	44.90/1.07†	58.90/0.84†
Uzbek	75.00/*	98.00/*	—	90.00/0.12†	92.00/0.10†	85.00/0.29†	91.00/0.14†	77.00/0.31	90.00/0.14†	43.00/2.01	46.00/1.13	63.00/0.78
Venetian	88.50/*	88.80/*	—	78.80/0.35	78.40/0.37	76.80/0.42	75.90/0.38	73.80/0.35	74.10/0.40	76.40/0.43	71.50/0.56	71.80/0.55
Votic	94.00/*	55.00/*	—	26.00/1.56	26.00/1.56	32.00/1.47	26.00/1.60	21.00/1.55	23.00/1.69	29.00/1.54	19.00/1.57	17.00/1.88
Welsh	88.00/*	75.00/*	—	55.00/1.08	55.00/1.01	50.00/1.40	50.00/1.12	48.00/1.11	45.00/1.27	51.00/1.35	43.00/1.17	42.00/1.25
West-frisian	100.00/*	72.00/*	—	53.00/1.04	56.00/1.01	46.00/1.13	51.00/1.05	51.00/1.17	48.00/1.08	47.00/1.12	40.00/1.26	50.00/1.23
Yiddish	100.00/*	96.00/*	—	82.00/0.31	83.00/0.30	87.00/0.23	71.00/0.39	82.00/0.30	68.00/0.44	82.00/0.29	78.00/0.35	78.00/0.38
Zulu	43.50/*	54.10/*	—	32.10/1.52	33.00/1.49	29.30/1.62	29.80/1.60	20.10/1.91	27.70/1.73	29.30/1.62	20.10/1.91	31.00/1.53

Table 17: Task 1 Low Condition Part 1.

	msu-02	ua-02	hamburg-01	ua-07	baseline	ua-01	msu-04	msu-03	iit-varanasi-01	ua-04	axsemantics-02	tuebingen-oslo-02
Adyghe	82.50/0.23	—	82.00/0.22	83.20/0.26	59.00/0.46	59.00/0.46	52.00/0.94	3.70/3.21	57.80/0.66	40.00/1.61	13.40/1.47	0.90/5.25
Albanian	25.40/4.57	12.60/7.09	16.10/2.69	13.50/7.10	22.00/4.37	22.00/4.37	5.50/4.88	4.40/5.10	0.80/6.08	2.90/6.88	0.00/12.09	0.00/8.87
Arabic	1.20/4.39	25.50/4.04	23.50/2.52	20.40/2.99	25.60/2.98	25.60/2.98	0.10/25.85	0.00/22.93	0.80/5.30	0.40/6.74	0.00/10.78	0.30/6.16
Armenian	37.70/2.27	47.70/2.28	39.80/1.44	37.80/2.09	37.00/2.18	37.00/2.18	16.60/2.33	18.20/2.48	5.80/3.80	4.10/4.28	10.70/2.87	0.10/6.56
Asturian	58.00/1.08	58.90/0.96	64.50/0.64	45.80/1.03	58.60/1.06	58.60/1.06	51.10/1.02	43.00/1.18	23.90/1.62	22.30/2.39	9.80/1.96	1.80/4.14
Azeri	43.00/1.96	48.00/1.19	37.00/1.40	47.00/1.27	24.00/2.84	24.00/2.84	26.00/2.11	34.00/1.55	28.00/2.10	12.00/2.98	24.00/1.74	1.00/4.77
Bashkir	45.50/1.07	—	58.20/0.76	75.40/0.50	39.40/1.84	39.40/1.84	27.20/2.08	14.50/3.16	35.80/1.35	24.50/2.08	22.30/1.26	0.20/4.96
Basque	0.10/6.56	0.50/5.48	1.70/4.06	6.20/3.53	0.10/6.52	0.10/6.52	0.90/4.72	0.10/5.43	0.50/4.71	6.70/3.88	0.00/10.18	0.20/5.45
Belarusian	20.60/2.38	6.50/3.47	17.10/2.44	17.80/3.07	6.80/2.44	6.80/2.44	17.20/2.50	12.30/2.61	2.90/3.68	3.40/3.90	0.00/8.99	0.30/5.72
Bengali	51.00/1.22	59.00/0.71	48.00/1.13	45.00/1.27	50.00/1.24	50.00/1.24	26.00/1.76	23.00/1.85	26.00/2.25	27.00/2.47	4.00/2.44	1.00/3.40
Breton	21.00/2.73	62.00/1.02	34.00/1.31	52.00/0.96	20.00/2.58	20.00/2.58	29.00/1.60	27.00/2.04	30.00/1.52	50.00/1.13	1.00/3.27	10.00/2.82
Bulgarian	31.00/1.92	27.50/2.59	38.50/1.24	33.80/1.98	30.90/1.69	30.90/1.69	21.90/1.96	13.30/2.08	9.70/2.85	13.80/2.95	4.70/2.98	0.00/6.02
Catalan	59.20/1.01	55.20/0.83	54.60/0.84	58.10/0.83	60.80/0.86	60.80/0.86	51.00/1.15	29.60/1.33	25.70/1.62	17.10/2.28	0.00/9.15	0.80/5.16
Classical-syriac	**93.00/0.08‡**	**93.00/0.08‡**	92.00/0.09	55.00/0.70	**94.00/0.06‡**	**94.00/0.06‡**	86.00/0.17	73.00/0.34	62.00/0.47	55.00/0.75	71.00/0.39	19.00/1.52
Cornish	12.00/4.02	8.00/3.94	22.00/2.40	38.00/1.40	10.00/4.10	10.00/4.10	4.00/3.12	8.00/2.74	**32.00/1.56**	40.00/1.56	0.00/7.76	4.00/3.58
Crimean-tatar	78.00/0.30	78.00/0.28	80.00/0.25	77.00/0.34	57.00/0.73	57.00/0.73	70.00/0.61	64.00/0.61	51.00/0.75	31.00/1.64	59.00/0.52	0.00/4.88
Czech	38.70/2.13	33.80/2.88	31.80/1.86	—	38.50/2.08	38.50/2.08	24.60/2.35	20.10/2.40	8.10/3.28	0.00/9.74	8.80/2.81	0.00/7.13
Danish	61.70/0.61	66.70/0.54	65.10/0.55	63.20/0.56	58.30/0.76	58.30/0.76	58.40/0.74	58.60/0.68	40.90/0.99	26.40/2.17	33.10/1.04	0.10/6.28
Dutch	47.50/0.84	49.80/0.88	43.00/1.01	44.20/1.05	50.80/0.73	50.80/0.73	40.70/1.17	34.60/1.22	8.90/2.54	12.10/2.73	19.80/1.51	0.10/5.72
English	81.60/0.32	87.60/0.18	90.40/0.14	42.70/1.21	77.60/0.39	77.60/0.39	75.30/0.49	74.10/0.40	61.80/0.60	42.70/1.21	45.50/0.69	0.20/5.39
Estonian	22.30/2.61	16.80/5.18	13.40/2.47	17.50/3.60	21.50/2.60	21.50/2.60	7.20/3.49	8.80/3.91	2.60/4.12	0.60/10.40	0.00/10.34	0.00/8.92
Faroese	40.90/1.23	38.90/1.33	23.80/1.56	25.70/1.56	34.40/1.45	34.40/1.45	19.60/1.82	18.00/1.75	9.60/2.49	4.50/3.51	9.20/2.13	0.00/5.82
Finnish	16.30/4.29	14.70/8.11	12.40/2.87	7.40/5.36	17.20/3.98	17.20/3.98	4.50/5.56	4.20/5.83	0.60/6.86	0.00/14.30	2.90/5.65	0.00/11.02
French	54.90/1.14	56.60/0.92	51.80/0.98	50.70/0.98	58.90/0.97	58.90/0.97	43.60/1.30	41.30/1.27	13.40/2.33	9.00/3.17	16.30/1.97	0.00/7.53
Friulian	**73.00/0.70**	**73.00/0.60**	55.00/0.68	59.00/0.81	70.00/0.52	70.00/0.52	69.00/0.55	46.00/0.97	39.00/1.13	26.00/1.71	36.00/1.16	8.00/2.67
Galician	53.00/1.32	48.30/1.15	47.50/1.09	42.90/1.16	53.00/1.22	53.00/1.22	42.10/1.21	32.70/1.45	15.30/2.06	5.40/3.78	5.80/2.26	0.40/4.50
Georgian	63.90/0.67	75.30/1.02	70.70/0.58	75.20/0.54	76.60/0.58	76.60/0.58	75.00/0.86	59.50/0.80	23.80/1.69	22.80/1.86	47.50/0.83	0.10/5.23
German	50.40/1.09	53.20/0.93	44.70/1.04	41.50/1.25	49.20/1.18	49.20/1.18	39.40/1.20	37.90/1.24	19.90/1.81	11.40/3.03	18.70/1.99	0.00/6.72
Greek	23.80/3.12	22.40/4.31	23.60/2.30	12.70/4.48	25.10/2.71	25.10/2.71	17.90/2.61	16.90/2.81	2.40/4.61	0.00/10.32	9.70/3.49	0.00/8.82
Greenlandic	48.00/0.92	48.00/0.88	42.00/0.78	68.00/0.48	50.00/0.78	50.00/0.78	48.00/0.88	34.00/1.14	60.00/0.58	68.00/0.58	30.00/1.16	24.00/1.30
Haida	27.00/5.89	44.00/2.25	0.00/5.01	35.00/3.03	29.00/5.64	29.00/5.64	8.00/4.74	2.00/7.43	12.00/3.69	47.00/2.30	0.00/17.05	3.00/5.14
Hebrew	27.80/1.30	20.10/2.01	24.20/1.42	20.50/1.53	24.40/1.31	24.40/1.31	16.20/1.71	14.70/1.82	5.20/2.44	5.20/2.66	4.20/2.15	0.10/3.85
Hindi	31.50/3.92	70.10/1.26†	68.70/0.88†	34.20/2.94	31.80/3.87	31.80/3.87	41.10/1.98	33.40/2.89	23.20/2.55	18.50/3.33	8.20/2.82	4.20/4.78
Hungarian	28.20/1.74	32.30/1.42	21.60/1.82	24.40/1.70	17.50/2.28	17.50/2.28	10.00/2.64	10.90/2.69	4.70/2.87	1.70/4.66	2.20/2.72	0.00/8.30
Icelandic	36.60/1.45	36.60/1.25	31.00/1.38	29.20/1.48	35.10/1.54	35.10/1.54	23.20/1.73	21.90/1.74	8.50/2.53	4.90/3.66	12.80/2.27	0.00/5.83
Ingrian	26.00/1.80	**28.00/1.72**	14.00/1.90	20.00/1.78	20.00/1.78	20.00/1.78	20.00/1.82	20.00/1.82	24.00/1.54	26.00/1.46	6.00/2.94	2.00/3.64
Irish	32.70/2.46	18.20/6.13	30.40/2.43	11.40/4.79	30.30/2.80	30.30/2.80	20.00/2.99	26.70/2.65	1.30/6.82	5.00/5.08	14.70/4.68	0.00/9.73
Italian	43.90/1.87	40.40/2.53	43.10/1.44	29.90/2.31	40.50/2.16	40.50/2.16	28.50/1.82	22.60/1.79	11.00/3.49	9.90/3.91	0.00/11.23	0.10/6.90
Kabardian	**89.00/0.13**	—	83.00/0.19	86.00/0.18	72.00/0.30	72.00/0.30	62.00/0.65	52.00/1.29	56.00/0.64	47.00/1.25	42.00/0.83	12.00/2.85
Kannada	37.00/1.95	56.00/1.08	37.00/1.41	34.00/2.04	33.00/2.09	33.00/2.09	14.00/2.38	24.00/1.98	29.00/2.55	27.00/3.21	0.00/6.95	0.00/5.73
Karelian	44.00/1.14	66.00/0.62	48.00/0.90	70.00/0.60	24.00/2.14	24.00/2.14	56.00/0.96	26.00/3.64	80.00/0.30	**88.00/0.24‡**	42.00/1.00	18.00/1.66
Kashubian	**58.00/0.72**	**60.00/0.96**	52.00/1.04	44.00/1.16	**60.00/0.70**	**60.00/0.70**	56.00/0.88	52.00/1.00	46.00/0.86	52.00/0.98	8.00/1.82	6.00/2.00
Kazakh	64.00/0.40	78.00/0.30	60.00/0.58	62.00/0.50	26.00/1.72	26.00/1.72	48.00/1.22	22.00/2.66	68.00/0.34	44.00/0.44	42.00/0.74	20.00/1.04
Khakas	62.00/0.42	—	60.00/0.52	70.00/0.64	26.00/2.42	26.00/2.42	68.00/0.58	50.00/0.88	62.00/0.54	36.00/1.70	42.00/0.44	16.00/2.40
Khaling	2.30/4.71	0.10/5.36	13.60/2.67	22.10/2.38	3.20/4.37	3.20/4.37	0.90/5.03	2.20/3.51	8.80/3.03	0.00/7.90	0.00/5.86	0.00/5.86
Kurmanji	82.90/0.46	86.00/1.11	80.30/0.40	14.50/2.95	82.70/0.45	82.70/0.45	71.40/0.66	49.30/1.01	25.40/1.76	14.50/2.95	63.10/0.81	0.20/5.57
Ladin	53.00/1.03	62.00/1.17	53.00/0.75	51.00/1.01	58.00/0.96	58.00/0.96	30.00/1.32	41.00/1.15	33.00/1.41	28.00/1.88	24.00/1.51	6.00/3.85
Latin	14.40/3.09	12.10/2.65	9.30/2.77	1.10/4.82	16.10/2.84	16.10/2.84	8.10/2.91	8.10/2.91	1.00/4.35	1.10/4.82	0.00/10.23	0.00/7.37
Latvian	48.30/1.01	51.50/1.63	40.50/1.16	26.80/1.86	52.80/0.87	52.80/0.87	35.60/1.25	31.00/1.41	9.00/2.68	5.40/3.68	5.40/2.14	0.00/6.39
Lithuanian	19.10/2.10	14.00/2.90	10.80/2.29	9.20/2.56	23.00/1.89	23.00/1.89	6.60/2.52	8.40/2.31	2.80/3.29	1.60/4.09	0.00/9.02	0.10/5.98
Livonian	**29.00/2.10**	24.00/3.00	24.00/2.01	16.00/2.35	**28.00/2.14**	**28.00/2.14**	14.00/2.67	11.00/2.72	6.00/3.40	8.00/4.01	10.00/3.10	0.00/5.68
Lower-sorbian	35.70/1.24	35.90/1.25	31.60/1.35	28.60/1.66	32.60/1.29	32.60/1.29	13.90/1.92	8.00/2.10	9.90/2.38	5.00/3.33	4.90/2.17	1.00/4.33
Macedonian	45.50/1.03	49.10/0.79	44.40/0.86	44.70/0.88	49.80/0.89	49.80/0.89	16.70/1.85	25.10/1.42	16.70/1.69	15.20/2.52	10.30/1.75	0.10/5.45
Maltese	18.00/1.97	7.00/8.76	14.00/2.03	17.00/2.22	10.00/2.37	10.00/2.37	16.00/1.90	14.00/1.85	8.00/2.78	7.00/3.81	3.00/3.73	0.00/3.60
Mapudungun	**68.00/0.80**	76.00/0.42	60.00/0.66	**84.00/0.38**	64.00/0.68	64.00/0.68	64.00/0.54	42.00/0.90	**74.00/0.36**	**86.00/0.24**	44.00/1.00	0.00/4.56
Middle-french	77.30/0.55	76.70/0.59	76.30/0.50	66.50/0.89	76.90/0.49	76.90/0.49	71.90/0.66	61.90/0.82	32.80/1.47	30.00/1.98	5.20/2.14	1.40/4.62
Middle-high-german	56.00/0.62	60.00/0.60	66.00/0.52	58.00/0.80	38.00/0.84	38.00/0.84	66.00/0.58	44.00/0.86	56.00/0.70	0.00/6.20	20.00/1.66	24.00/1.52
Middle-low-german	16.00/1.86	14.00/2.70	36.00/1.52	24.00/2.26	18.00/1.76	18.00/1.76	26.00/1.52	20.00/1.96	14.00/2.76	0.00/7.16	6.00/2.72	10.00/3.16
Murrinhpatha	14.00/2.40	0.00/8.04	20.00/2.00	**38.00/1.68**	6.00/2.72	2.00/4.22	20.00/2.00	10.00/2.12	**28.00/1.72**	36.00/1.80	2.00/2.94	0.00/3.98
Navajo	17.10/3.72	8.50/5.96	8.70/3.69	3.40/4.51	17.80/3.39	0.00/7.76	9.40/3.65	6.20/3.63	0.90/5.37	1.80/5.12	0.00/8.96	0.00/7.20
Neapolitan	79.00/0.94	**84.00/0.29**	36.00/0.94	59.00/0.96	79.00/0.59	79.00/0.59	61.00/0.76	45.00/0.98	45.00/1.02	59.00/0.79	24.00/1.47	6.00/3.04
Norman	30.00/2.48	48.00/0.96	40.00/1.42	**58.00/1.16**	30.00/2.22	30.00/2.22	34.00/1.50	8.00/2.32	52.00/1.10	**66.00/0.74**	22.00/2.16	20.00/2.60
North-frisian	29.00/3.24	15.00/32.10	34.00/2.36	29.00/2.39	29.00/3.34	29.00/3.34	17.00/3.86	13.00/4.05	18.00/3.01	27.00/2.82	12.00/5.22	1.00/6.29
Northern-sami	11.70/2.80	8.40/2.90	6.20/3.10	18.30/2.27	16.40/2.35	16.40/2.35	5.30/3.20	2.00/3.38	1.50/3.99	5.40/3.65	0.00/9.29	0.20/5.89
Norwegian-bokmaal	72.30/0.40	71.40/0.46	71.60/0.45	70.40/0.46	68.70/0.49	68.70/0.49	7.60/1.78	9.30/1.68	40.80/0.96	28.60/1.95	45.90/0.79	0.20/5.26
Norwegian-nynorsk	37.40/1.17	50.20/0.95	42.00/1.02	46.80/0.96	50.20/0.89	50.20/0.89	29.60/1.38	29.00/1.35	22.00/1.63	14.60/2.68	10.70/1.46	0.00/6.06
Occitan	68.00/0.99	68.00/1.31	60.00/0.77	62.00/0.85	**72.00/0.82**	**72.00/0.82**	56.00/0.92	49.00/1.19	31.00/1.44	21.00/2.11	1.00/2.76	5.00/3.59
Old-armenian	31.00/1.75	29.50/2.01	23.30/1.73	17.90/1.96	30.70/1.74	30.70/1.74	16.50/2.01	16.00/2.07	1.90/3.40	0.90/5.64	0.00/7.40	0.10/5.09
Old-church-slavonic	35.00/1.22	32.00/1.26	31.00/1.28	25.00/1.55	40.00/1.14	40.00/1.14	35.00/1.18	18.00/1.61	21.00/1.72	11.00/2.61	9.00/2.17	10.00/2.91
Old-english	12.10/2.15	12.60/2.17	13.70/1.94	15.30/2.10	17.60/1.72	17.60/1.72	12.60/2.04	10.70/2.15	8.60/2.75	6.70/4.17	3.60/2.74	0.60/4.63
Old-french	28.00/1.97	27.20/1.58	23.50/1.79	26.90/2.03	32.50/1.65	32.50/1.65	20.30/1.94	15.70/2.05	7.00/2.86	7.30/2.97	1.10/3.12	0.10/5.12
Old-irish	**8.00/4.30‡**	**6.00/6.08‡**	**6.00/3.86‡**	—	**8.00/4.06‡**	**8.00/4.06‡**	**4.00/3.74**	**2.00/4.06**	**2.00/4.04**	**0.00/6.94**	**2.00/4.68**	**0.00/5.68**
Old-saxon	17.10/2.16	20.90/1.90	12.90/1.97	15.70/1.99	22.80/1.84	22.80/1.84	10.90/2.29	9.50/2.23	5.60/2.79	5.90/3.27	4.60/2.51	0.60/4.41
Pashto	34.00/2.09	27.00/2.80	34.00/1.47	19.00/2.27	35.00/1.91	35.00/1.91	27.00/1.87	17.00/2.29	11.00/2.64	8.00/3.56	15.00/2.34	0.00/4.52
Persian	29.50/3.15	33.10/3.07	39.60/1.57	31.60/2.35	26.50/3.17	26.50/3.17	17.20/3.29	15.40/4.55	6.30/3.91	13.10/3.99	0.00/11.63	1.00/6.19
Polish	40.20/1.70	32.90/2.46	23.10/1.92	16.90/3.04	40.40/1.60	40.40/1.60	19.50/2.07	11.30/2.21	4.70/3.29	2.40/6.75	0.00/9.64	0.00/7.83
Portuguese	62.60/0.96	66.90/0.66	57.30/0.72	35.00/1.36	62.60/0.83	62.60/0.83	44.90/1.08	41.10/1.08	19.90/1.72	14.90/2.22	5.70/2.59	0.20/5.25
Quechua	15.60/6.47	50.70/1.42†	14.20/3.09	58.50/1.27†	15.90/6.46	15.90/6.46	10.50/4.34	6.10/4.69	15.00/3.19	22.20/3.49	0.00/13.64	0.00/10.05
Romanian	**44.30/1.60**	29.50/3.01	27.80/1.97	19.50/2.77	**44.70/1.52**	**44.70/1.52**	26.10/2.08	18.90/2.53	4.60/3.83	3.80/4.67	6.30/3.27	0.00/6.49
Russian	45.20/1.27	37.00/2.46	25.10/1.65	16.50/2.23	43.40/1.13	43.40/1.13	17.50/1.77	8.90/1.95	7.50/3.02	0.00/10.26	—	0.00/7.56
Sanskrit	41.80/1.52	43.80/1.27	23.60/1.87	32.80/1.66	33.70/1.50	33.70/1.50	12.60/2.80	17.30/2.37	6.70/3.04	6.00/3.92	6.60/2.90	0.00/6.36
Scottish-gaelic	58.00/0.70	42.00/1.68	**62.00/0.70**	54.00/1.34	46.00/0.96	46.00/0.96	54.00/0.92	46.00/1.08	48.00/1.40	46.00/1.38	32.00/1.70	40.00/2.14
Serbo-croatian	20.70/2.70	24.70/2.67	28.50/1.85	19.10/3.56	22.10/2.66	22.10/2.66	11.40/2.93	10.90/2.99	4.10/4.05	0.00/7.99	0.00/10.54	0.00/7.13
Slovak	44.80/1.10	42.20/1.15	39.20/1.09	—	37.70/1.15	37.70/1.15	25.70/1.48	16.60/1.62	9.60/2.23	0.00/6.89	11.60/1.71	0.10/4.69
Slovene	6.10/1.79	44.80/1.28	32.10/1.12	34.20/1.16	32.30/1.17	32.30/1.17	12.50/1.80	11.30/1.85	14.00/2.04	13.20/2.75	7.90/1.77	2.30/4.62
Sorani	19.50/3.58	7.00/4.32	16.00/2.07	13.20/2.52	19.90/3.35	19.90/3.35	1.90/4.46	1.30/4.63	1.30/4.08	2.20/4.17	0.80/4.55	0.10/5.54
Spanish	59.70/1.28	55.80/1.50	60.40/0.85	55.30/1.11	61.80/1.08	61.80/1.08	45.30/1.31	41.70/1.28	13.00/2.67	14.80/2.95	5.80/2.48	0.10/6.00
Swahili	35.00/2.48	0.00/4.73	41.00/1.09	20.00/2.08	32.00/2.51	0.00/6.10	9.00/2.74	2.00/3.27	4.00/2.79	32.00/1.82	0.00/4.48	2.00/4.55
Swedish	49.40/0.84	56.90/0.69	58.90/0.70	52.90/0.83	51.10/0.89	51.10/0.89	54.90/0.83	50.40/0.86	32.80/1.19	16.90/2.61	13.90/1.83	0.00/6.67
Tatar	72.00/0.35	79.00/0.28	66.00/0.44	74.00/0.39	50.00/0.85	50.00/0.85	37.00/1.34	52.00/0.95	44.00/0.95	20.00/2.22	53.00/0.73	0.00/5.42
Telugu	70.00/1.18	—	**86.00/0.24**	**96.00/0.12‡**	70.00/1.14	70.00/1.14	82.00/0.82	78.00/0.62	**94.00/0.18‡**	**96.00/0.06‡**	46.00/1.56	60.00/0.88
Tibetan	**46.00/0.84**	40.00/1.10	**48.00/0.82**	36.00/1.10	34.00/1.02	34.00/1.02	**46.00/0.98**	**44.00/0.94**	36.00/1.12	**46.00/0.92**	38.00/1.24	26.00/1.38
Turkish	17.50/4.42	27.50/2.53	13.90/3.14	22.50/3.00	13.30/4.56	13.30/4.56	9.70/3.79	4.40/4.49	10.70/3.66	2.70/5.85	3.80/3.81	0.00/8.73
Turkmen	**86.00/0.20‡**	78.00/0.28	64.00/0.54	60.00/1.00	34.00/1.98	34.00/1.98	62.00/0.86	44.00/1.44	64.00/0.52	64.00/0.78	64.00/0.42	28.00/1.60
Ukrainian	43.30/0.99	36.50/1.41	30.00/1.27	30.40/1.23	38.70/0.99	38.70/0.99	26.00/1.36	22.00/1.40	9.00/2.28	9.30/3.62	13.40/1.54	0.00/5.79
Urdu	32.00/4.13	61.90/0.95†	62.50/0.80†	47.70/1.66†	32.70/4.08	32.70/4.08	49.10/1.45†	44.40/1.40	32.60/1.87	37.80/2.21	0.00/10.84	4.70/3.64
Uzbek	54.00/1.75	—	69.00/0.66	83.00/0.33	52.00/1.77	52.00/1.77	67.00/0.78	19.00/3.09	82.00/0.29	**90.00/0.23†**	41.00/0.88	26.00/1.74
Venetian	70.90/0.58	71.50/0.38	67.50/0.45	59.90/0.69	71.80/0.55	71.80/0.55	66.00/0.51	59.00/0.77	31.10/1.32	26.30/1.77	23.20/1.43	4.10/3.43
Votic	18.00/2.03	13.00/1.89	14.00/2.04	**34.00/1.51**	17.00/1.88	17.00/1.88	11.00/2.43	12.00/2.32	20.00/1.91	22.00/1.86	6.00/2.66	3.00/3.52
Welsh	27.00/1.78	**51.00/1.22**	32.00/1.83	28.00/1.79	30.00/1.45	30.00/1.45	17.00/2.14	20.00/2.04	11.00/2.66	14.00/2.75	0.00/8.39	0.00/4.76
West-frisian	47.00/1.41	43.00/1.39	33.00/1.32	31.00/1.62	**50.00/1.23**	**50.00/1.23**	29.00/1.58	39.00/1.44	26.00/1.67	27.00/1.86	22.00/1.83	18.00/2.40
Yiddish	**80.00/0.36**	72.00/0.44	**79.00/0.29**	55.00/0.87	78.00/0.38	78.00/0.38	55.00/0.84	67.00/0.63	33.00/1.65	26.00/3.12	41.00/1.03	0.00/5.65
Zulu	17.90/2.49	1.30/7.43	15.50/2.00	—	15.70/2.35	15.70/2.35	2.40/3.59	1.00/4.17	1.10/4.96	0.00/8.77	0.20/4.79	0.00/6.39

Table 18: Task 1 Low Condition Part 2.

	bme-01	bme-03	kucst-01	bme-02	tuebingen-oslo-03	tuebingen-oslo-01
Adyghe	0.00/69.64	0.00/69.64	0.70/5.96	0.00/8.29	0.00/5.89	0.00/9.97
Albanian	0.00/8.93	0.00/8.93	0.00/9.40	0.00/9.88	0.00/9.93	0.00/10.98
Arabic	0.00/8.96	0.00/8.96	0.00/10.78	0.00/8.72	0.10/6.19	0.00/10.67
Armenian	0.00/8.20	0.00/8.20	0.10/7.32	0.00/10.20	0.00/7.07	0.00/9.34
Asturian	2.40/3.32	2.40/3.32	0.60/4.89	0.00/7.15	0.10/5.03	0.00/7.83
Azeri	0.00/5.65	0.00/6.11	0.00/5.07	0.00/6.75	0.00/5.72	0.00/8.63
Bashkir	0.00/7.63	0.00/7.63	0.50/5.17	0.00/7.81	0.00/5.58	0.00/7.52
Basque	0.10/6.66	0.10/6.66	0.50/5.01	0.10/6.03	0.00/6.05	0.00/8.44
Belarusian	0.10/5.66	0.10/5.66	0.20/5.96	0.10/7.43	0.00/6.88	0.00/7.71
Bengali	0.00/5.10	0.00/5.14	2.00/4.22	0.00/5.65	0.00/4.58	0.00/7.63
Breton	13.00/2.27	13.00/2.27	1.00/2.98	5.00/3.16	9.00/2.68	0.00/5.89
Bulgarian	0.00/8.20	0.00/8.20	0.00/6.47	0.00/8.23	0.00/7.86	0.00/8.24
Catalan	0.00/7.66	0.00/7.66	0.10/6.10	0.00/7.56	0.00/6.16	0.00/7.98
Classical-syriac	24.00/1.07	24.00/1.07	4.00/2.73	10.00/3.33	11.00/2.18	0.00/5.83
Cornish	12.00/3.16	6.00/3.12	14.00/3.04	6.00/3.42	0.00/2.82	0.00/6.96
Crimean-tatar	0.00/5.41	0.00/5.41	0.00/5.09	0.00/7.06	0.00/5.30	0.00/6.91
Czech	0.00/7.87	0.00/7.87	0.10/7.30	0.00/9.27	0.00/7.71	0.00/8.87
Danish	0.00/7.12	0.00/7.12	0.80/5.97	0.00/7.80	0.00/6.56	0.00/7.12
Dutch	0.00/7.24	0.00/7.24	—	0.00/7.17	0.00/6.60	0.00/7.28
English	0.00/7.63	0.00/7.63	—	0.00/7.56	0.00/6.03	0.00/7.64
Estonian	0.00/9.58	0.00/9.58	0.10/7.39	0.00/9.13	0.00/7.86	0.00/8.99
Faroese	0.00/6.87	0.00/6.87	0.30/5.50	0.00/6.95	0.00/6.18	0.00/7.18
Finnish	0.00/13.42	0.00/13.42	0.00/13.84	0.00/18.49	0.00/10.61	0.00/12.50
French	0.00/8.91	0.00/8.91	—	0.00/8.24	0.00/7.19	0.00/8.50
Friulian	12.00/2.60	16.00/1.87	3.00/3.59	11.00/4.41	1.00/4.19	0.00/6.64
Galician	1.10/3.62	1.10/3.62	0.20/5.16	0.00/7.08	0.00/5.92	0.00/7.51
Georgian	0.00/7.52	0.00/7.52	0.00/5.97	0.00/7.62	0.00/5.76	0.00/8.95
German	0.00/8.25	0.00/8.25	—	0.00/8.30	0.00/7.13	0.00/7.83
Greek	0.00/10.67	0.00/10.67	0.10/8.17	0.00/9.58	0.00/9.33	0.00/10.33
Greenlandic	14.00/1.80	14.00/1.80	6.00/2.52	24.00/1.54	0.00/3.40	0.00/8.06
Haida	3.00/8.06	1.00/8.57	0.00/7.63	3.00/7.95	0.00/8.49	0.00/13.62
Hebrew	0.40/3.50	0.40/3.50	0.40/3.56	0.00/4.76	0.00/4.07	0.00/5.57
Hindi	0.00/9.66	0.00/9.66	2.20/6.46	0.00/9.28	0.00/6.07	0.00/11.32
Hungarian	0.00/11.30	0.00/11.30	0.00/8.40	0.00/16.28	0.00/8.83	0.00/9.92
Icelandic	0.00/6.51	0.00/6.51	0.10/5.74	0.00/7.16	0.00/6.33	0.00/7.28
Ingrian	4.00/2.56	10.00/2.24	0.00/2.76	6.00/2.52	0.00/4.04	0.00/5.96
Irish	0.00/10.39	0.00/10.39	0.00/9.54	0.00/10.24	0.00/9.31	0.00/10.81
Italian	0.00/18.32	0.00/18.32	0.00/6.99	0.00/10.11	0.00/8.17	0.00/9.76
Kabardian	9.00/2.83	9.00/2.83	3.00/3.94	6.00/4.68	1.00/4.40	0.00/8.04
Kannada	6.00/5.82	6.00/5.82	—	0.00/5.95	0.00/5.55	0.00/7.34
Karelian	4.00/2.44	4.00/2.44	4.00/2.82	6.00/2.24	2.00/2.66	0.00/7.90
Kashubian	14.00/2.34	14.00/2.34	8.00/2.52	16.00/2.32	2.00/3.34	0.00/7.22
Kazakh	28.00/1.20	28.00/1.20	2.00/2.14	0.00/7.74	26.00/1.02	0.00/7.68
Khakas	14.00/2.16	14.00/2.16	0.00/3.04	10.00/2.60	2.00/3.54	0.00/6.88
Khaling	0.10/5.48	0.00/5.56	0.80/4.86	0.10/5.76	0.00/5.62	0.00/7.18
Kurmanji	0.00/7.80	0.00/7.80	0.00/6.41	0.00/14.05	0.00/6.30	0.00/7.04
Ladin	1.00/2.89	3.00/3.42	5.00/3.72	0.00/6.33	0.00/4.61	0.00/6.90
Latin	0.00/9.16	0.00/9.16	0.00/7.40	0.00/9.10	0.00/7.79	0.00/9.07
Latvian	0.00/7.99	0.00/7.99	0.30/6.80	0.00/8.04	0.00/7.79	0.00/8.61
Lithuanian	0.00/8.84	0.00/8.84	0.20/6.50	0.00/7.70	0.00/7.20	0.00/8.19
Livonian	0.00/6.91	0.00/6.91	0.00/5.42	0.00/7.16	0.00/6.16	0.00/7.68
Lower-sorbian	0.20/4.80	0.20/4.80	1.40/4.68	0.00/5.99	0.00/5.46	0.00/6.37
Macedonian	0.00/7.62	0.00/7.62	0.20/5.84	0.00/7.58	0.00/6.02	0.00/7.78
Maltese	4.00/3.24	4.00/3.24	2.00/3.70	0.00/5.17	0.00/4.20	0.00/6.13
Mapudungun	40.00/1.36	40.00/1.36	14.00/2.10	34.00/1.74	0.00/3.10	0.00/6.52
Middle-french	1.20/4.68	1.20/4.68	0.40/5.26	0.20/7.37	0.00/5.87	0.00/8.03
Middle-high-german	16.00/2.12	16.00/2.12	24.00/1.42	10.00/2.68	8.00/2.06	0.00/5.38
Middle-low-german	10.00/3.28	6.00/4.00	—	12.00/3.86	8.00/3.08	0.00/5.68
Murrinhpatha	16.00/2.48	16.00/2.48	20.00/2.42	12.00/2.88	4.00/2.80	0.00/4.76
Navajo	0.00/6.31	0.00/6.31	0.50/6.16	0.00/7.33	0.00/6.83	0.00/8.49
Neapolitan	17.00/3.25	13.00/2.70	2.00/3.52	16.00/2.53	0.00/4.79	0.00/8.88
Norman	20.00/2.38	20.00/2.38	8.00/3.44	12.00/3.18	4.00/2.54	0.00/7.22
North-frisian	4.00/4.42	4.00/4.30	—	4.00/4.60	1.00/5.46	0.00/6.96
Northern-sami	0.30/5.45	0.30/5.45	0.20/6.38	0.00/8.17	0.00/7.74	0.00/8.21
Norwegian-bokmaal	0.00/7.08	0.00/7.08	0.80/5.04	0.00/7.15	0.00/6.81	0.00/6.77
Norwegian-nynorsk	0.00/7.22	0.00/7.22	0.50/5.62	0.00/7.64	0.00/6.30	0.00/7.02
Occitan	7.00/2.54	7.00/2.54	2.00/4.38	1.00/6.01	0.00/4.68	0.00/7.36
Old-armenian	0.00/5.85	0.00/5.85	0.40/5.33	0.00/6.38	0.00/6.30	0.00/6.44
Old-church-slavonic	11.00/2.43	11.00/2.43	9.00/2.93	3.00/5.19	1.00/4.00	0.00/6.23
Old-english	0.00/6.59	0.00/6.59	—	0.00/6.55	0.00/5.55	0.00/6.40
Old-french	0.00/7.57	0.00/7.57	0.30/5.66	0.00/7.89	0.00/6.19	0.00/7.63
Old-irish	**0.00/4.68**	**0.00/4.68**	**0.00/4.72**	**0.00/5.24**	**0.00/5.16**	**0.00/6.80**
Old-saxon	0.00/6.03	0.00/6.03	0.90/4.70	0.00/6.34	0.10/5.34	0.00/6.92
Pashto	0.00/5.17	0.00/5.17	3.00/3.77	0.00/5.31	0.00/4.49	0.00/6.16
Persian	0.00/11.69	0.00/11.69	0.00/10.08	0.00/9.85	0.00/6.76	0.00/11.34
Polish	0.00/8.63	0.00/8.63	—	0.00/8.67	0.00/7.77	0.00/8.57
Portuguese	0.00/8.19	0.00/8.19	0.20/5.58	0.00/8.13	0.00/6.12	0.00/8.31
Quechua	0.00/6.95	0.00/8.16	0.10/7.54	0.00/10.77	0.00/7.99	0.00/12.01
Romanian	0.00/11.83	0.00/11.83	0.00/6.83	0.00/8.81	0.00/8.03	0.00/8.12
Russian	0.00/9.24	0.00/9.24	—	0.00/9.10	0.00/8.33	0.00/9.46
Sanskrit	0.20/5.93	0.20/5.93	0.80/5.64	0.10/6.84	0.00/6.43	0.00/8.11
Scottish-gaelic	18.00/3.38	18.00/3.38	28.00/2.34	2.00/6.28	10.00/3.78	0.00/8.34
Serbo-croatian	0.00/9.44	0.00/9.44	0.00/8.19	0.00/9.49	0.00/8.64	0.00/9.18
Slovak	0.00/6.29	0.00/6.29	0.80/4.68	0.00/6.23	0.00/5.12	0.00/6.33
Slovene	0.00/7.00	0.00/7.00	0.00/8.28	0.00/7.23	1.50/4.95	0.00/7.51
Sorani	0.00/7.01	0.00/7.01	0.20/5.72	0.00/6.87	0.00/5.46	0.00/7.88
Spanish	0.00/8.48	0.00/8.48	0.20/6.65	0.00/8.51	0.00/6.90	0.00/8.84
Swahili	3.00/3.88	3.00/3.88	4.00/3.68	2.00/5.54	0.00/5.07	0.00/7.38
Swedish	0.00/8.47	0.00/8.47	0.20/6.89	0.00/8.86	0.00/7.50	0.00/8.32
Tatar	0.00/7.30	0.00/7.30	1.00/5.37	0.00/7.42	0.00/6.09	0.00/7.29
Telugu	28.00/1.58	28.00/1.58	24.00/2.40	26.00/1.74	6.00/2.82	0.00/10.74
Tibetan	0.00/3.66	0.00/3.66	32.00/1.18	0.00/3.68	22.00/1.64	0.00/4.06
Turkish	0.00/8.69	0.00/8.69	0.10/8.64	0.00/16.38	0.00/9.48	0.00/10.71
Turkmen	2.00/2.38	2.00/2.38	2.00/2.68	2.00/4.38	0.00/4.66	0.00/7.00
Ukrainian	0.00/6.24	0.00/6.24	1.40/5.14	0.00/6.74	0.00/6.29	0.00/7.05
Urdu	8.40/3.76	8.40/3.76	3.90/4.82	1.60/9.69	0.20/5.54	0.00/10.49
Uzbek	7.00/2.75	7.00/2.75	0.00/3.96	5.00/2.95	20.00/1.59	0.00/9.48
Venetian	0.00/5.58	0.00/5.58	2.10/4.07	0.00/5.99	0.00/4.73	0.00/6.78
Votic	2.00/2.96	2.00/3.10	1.00/3.21	1.00/3.51	0.00/4.50	0.00/6.16
Welsh	0.00/5.76	0.00/5.76	1.00/4.91	0.00/7.30	0.00/5.65	0.00/7.92
West-frisian	8.00/3.09	1.00/3.47	6.00/2.71	3.00/3.74	3.00/2.95	0.00/4.99
Yiddish	0.00/11.50	0.00/11.50	0.00/4.50	0.00/6.76	0.00/5.59	0.00/8.03
Zulu	0.00/7.44	0.00/7.44	0.30/5.57	0.00/7.68	0.00/6.91	0.00/7.88

Table 19: Task 1 Low Condition Part 3.

KU-CST at CoNLL–SIGMORPHON 2018 Shared Task: a *Tridirectional* Model

Manex Agirrezabal

Centre for Language Technology (CST)
Department of Nordic Studies and Linguistics (NorS)
University of Copenhagen (KU)
`manex.aguirrezabal@hum.ku.dk`

Abstract

In this paper we describe our sequence-to-sequence model for morphological inflection. We have constructed a common Encoder-Decoder network that encodes the input lemma into a dense vector to translate it to an inflected form, based on input morphological tags. The main novelty of the model is that the input lemma is encoded in three different directions: left-to-right, right to left and boundaries-to-center. In this paper we report the accuracies of the model compared to the same bidirectional approach.

1 Introduction

In this work we present the neural network architecture prepared for the task of morphological inflection in the CoNLL–SIGMORPHON 2018 Shared Task (Cotterell et al., 2018). Both morphological analysis and morphological inflection are crucial in end-to-end Natural Language Processing pipelines, as they are one of the initial steps performed before solving more high-level problems such as Named-Entity Recognition, Sentiment Analysis, or others.

2 Task

In the CoNLL–SIGMORPHON 2018 Shared Task there were two tasks to solve. In this work we present a possible solution for the first task, in which word-forms have to be built without considering the context. The input in the task is a lemma and a list morphological tags. The system should be then able to produce the corresponding word form. The following is an example from the Spanish dataset

$$jaquear$$
$$V; COND; 1; PL$$
$$\downarrow$$
$$jaquearamos$$

in which the input lemma is *jaquear* and its morphological tags state that the word form should be a verb (*V*) in conditional tense (*COND*), first person (*1*) in plural (*PL*). The output word form is *jaquearamos*.

The models can be trained and tested in over 100 languages and in three different settings, low-, medium- and high-resource scenarios (100, 1,000 or 10,000 training instances, respectively).

2.1 Dataset

As mentioned above we trained and tested our models in the provided dataset, which contains morphological inflections for over 100 languages. The information is encoded using Unicode and morphological tags follow the UniMorph tagging schema (Kirov et al., 2018).

3 Method

Following previous successful attempts to morphological inflection (Kann and Schütze, 2016), we built a model based on Neural Networks, specifically an Encoder-Decoder network (Cho et al., 2014) with an attention mechanism (Bahdanau et al., 2014). Furthermore, instead of constructing a linguistically inspired model, we have shortly explored an engineering approach. The main novelty of our model is in the way the input is encoded.

In Lample et al. (2016) it is stated that recurrent architectures such as Recurrent Neural Networks are capable of encoding very long sequences, but the representation is biased towards the last explored items. Because of that, a bidirectional RNN could be expected to represent well the structure of a word, as it models both the ending (suffix) and the beginning (prefix) by the use of a forward encoder and a backward encoder, respectively.

Our model explores whether this architecture can be improved adding another encoder that en-

Proceedings of the CoNLL–SIGMORPHON 2018 Shared Task: Universal Morphological Reinflection, pages 28–32,
Brussels, Belgium, October 31, 2018. ©2018 Association for Computational Linguistics

codes the word starting at the boundaries and ending in the center, capturing in that way the central structure of the word. The architecture is shown in Figure 1.

Each input is encoded with three different encoders, left-to-right, right-to-left and boundaries-to-center, and those encoded representations are concatenated. Then, a many-hot encoding representation of the morphological tags is concatenated at the end. In this way, we generate the representation of our source lemma with its morphological information. This representation goes to the decoder so that the output word is generated character by character.

4 Model configuration

The implementation is based on a Machine Translation model created using the Pytorch framework. It encodes sentences using three Recurrent Neural Networks with 128 GRU cells in each encoder. In order to train the decoder, we use a teacher forcing ratio of 0.5. We started training all the models for 10 epochs, but we could observe that the models from the low-resource scenario did not converge and the ones in the high-resource scenario did not improve results after the fifth epoch. Because of that, we train our models for 20, 15 and 5 epochs in the low-, medium- and high-resource scenarios, respectively.

5 Results

We tested a bidirectional and a *tridirectional* model and our expectations were that the tridirectional one would show a better performance in the development set. As you can see in Table 1, the mean accuracy is slightly better than in the bidirectional model with the same exact configuration,[1] although these differences are not significant according to a bootstrap test.

In Table 2 you can see the accuracies for each language in each setting with the tridirectional approach[2]. In Figure 2 we plotted these accuracies together with the accuracies of the bidirectional model. In some cases, our tridirectional approach is sufficiently more accurate than the bidirectional

---

[1]Same number of epochs, same cell types, and same size of hidden memory size. We are aware, although, that the tridirectional approach has more parameters because it has three encoders instead of two.

[2]In order to make it more interpretable, we marked in bold results that are better than the current baseline presented for the shared task.

Mean accuracies			
	low	medium	high
Bidirectional model	2.3	28.4	54.8
Tridirectional model	**2.8**	**32.4**	**55.6**
Mean Levenshtein distances			
	low	medium	high
Bidirectional model	5.25	2.30	**1.28**
Tridirectional model	**5.21**	**2.11**	1.41

Table 1: Average results for the bidirectional and tridirectional approaches in three different settings.

one, such as in *Crimean-Tatar*, *Galician*, *Quechua* and *welsh* in the high setting, or *Bashkir*, *Crimean-Tatar*, *Ingrian*, *Napolitan*, *Tatar* and *Urdu* in the medium setting. There are other cases, although, that the bidirectional approach shows a higher accuracy. Check, for instance, *Persian* and *Tatar* in the high setting or *Kabardian* in the medium setting.

	low	medium	high
Adyghe	0.3	65.2	**99.0**
Albanian	0.2	11.9	13.4
Arabic	0.0	**7.1**	**41.9**
Armenian	0.0	13.0	48.0
Asturian	1.0	48.3	87.1
Azeri	1.0	11.0	44.0
Bashkir	1.0	68.3	62.9
Basque	0.3	**44.6**	**69.9**
Belarusian	0.5	13.0	**65.5**
Bengali	1.0	75.0	78.0
Breton	5.0	**68.0**	**60.0**
Bulgarian	0.0	33.2	58.1
Catalan	0.2	24.1	85.8
Classical-Syriac	0.0	67.0	76.0
Cornish	**18.0**	**46.0**	-
Crimean-Tatar	0.0	54.0	**99.0**
Czech	0.2	7.8	34.1
Danish	0.2	32.7	64.8
Estonian	0.1	7.1	43.3
Faroese	0.5	9.0	25.7
Finnish	0.0	0.0	1.5
Friulian	1.0	73.0	**98.0**
Galician	0.6	40.4	92.0
Georgian	0.2	36.2	82.2
Greek	0.2	4.2	21.2

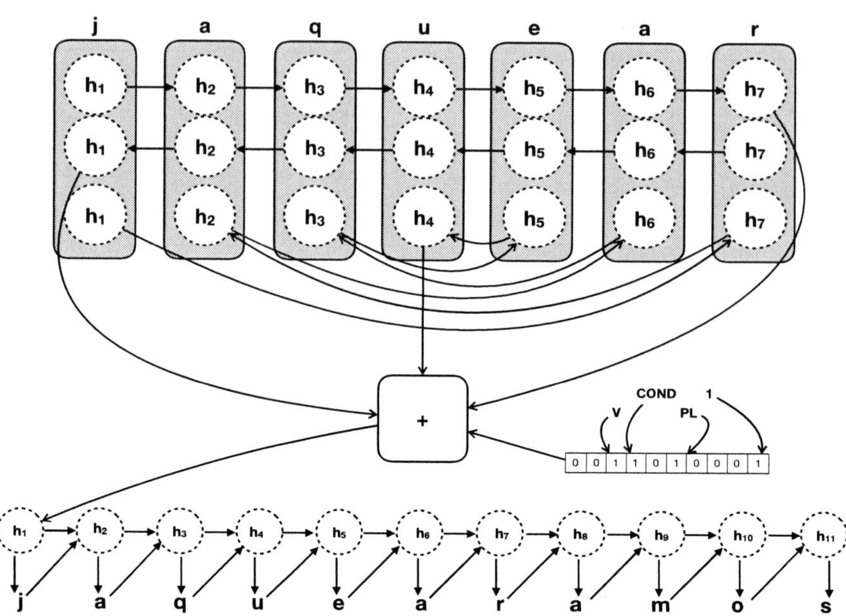

Figure 1: Architecture of our Tridirectional Encoder-Decoder model.

	low	medium	high		low	medium	high
Greenlandic	4.0	22.0	-	Middle-High-German	12.0	**90.0**	-
Haida	0.0	14.0	18.0	Murrinhpatha	**14.0**	**76.0**	-
Hebrew	0.4	24.3	**77.9**	Navajo	0.4	**9.7**	28.1
Hindi	1.1	73.2	84.6	Neapolitan	7.0	70.0	56.0
Hungarian	0.1	1.0	12.9	Norman	6.0	12.0	-
Icelandic	0.4	11.1	41.4	Northern-Sami	0.1	9.4	46.0
Ingrian	4.0	**58.0**	-	Norwegian-Bokmaal	0.8	26.2	47.8
Irish	0.2	3.6	13.8	Norwegian-Bynorsk	0.4	17.6	37.7
Italian	0.0	12.8	34.9	Occitan	1.0	40.0	**99.0**
Kabardian	6.0	58.0	**96.0**	Old-Armenian	0.0	11.8	60.7
Karelian	2.0	40.0	-	Old-Church-Slavonic	7.0	33.0	29.0
Kashubian	8.0	20.0	-	Old-French	0.0	18.2	53.9
Kazakh	0.0	22.0	-	Old-Irish	2.0	6.0	-
Khakas	2.0	22.0	-	Old-Saxon	0.6	15.1	**77.1**
Khaling	1.0	**28.8**	88.7	Pashto	2.0	48.0	**85.0**
Kurmanji	0.0	30.6	68.1	Persian	0.2	47.3	29.3
Ladin	5.0	60.0	93.0	Portuguese	0.2	25.9	72.6
Latin	0.0	3.5	9.6	Quechua	0.2	18.0	43.0
Latvian	0.2	8.3	50.9	Romanian	0.2	13.2	41.1
Lithuanian	0.2	3.9	37.3	Sanskrit	0.9	14.4	52.7
Livonian	1.0	25.0	57.0	Scottish-Gaelic	16.0	**54.0**	-
Lower-Sorbian	0.8	13.7	72.6	Serbo-Croatian	0.1	5.4	26.3
Macedonian	0.0	14.8	52.8	Slovak	0.7	10.6	59.3
Maltese	4.0	**57.0**	**47.0**	Slovene	1.2	**21.2**	**59.3**
Mapudungun	30.0	**96.0**	-	Sorani	0.3	28.0	29.3
Middle-French	1.1	52.8	83.1	Spanish	0.2	26.8	58.5

	low	medium	high
Swahili	**4.0**	**70.0**	90.0
Swedish	0.3	11.2	31.8
Tatar	1.0	53.0	44.0
Telugu	38.0	-	-
Tibetan	24.0	24.0	-
Turkish	0.0	7.9	23.4
Turkmen	6.0	36.0	-
Ukrainian	0.7	12.3	32.6
Urdu	4.4	79.8	95.9
Uzbek	2.0	16.0	8.0
Venetian	2.3	46.9	88.9
Votic	1.0	**55.0**	23.0
Welsh	0.0	23.0	**91.0**
West-Frisian	3.0	**88.0**	13.0
Yiddish	0.0	60.0	82.0
Zulu	0.3	**16.2**	**72.7**
Mean	2.8	32.4	55.6

Table 2: Accuracies for all languages in the low-, medium- and high-resource scenario using the *tridirectioal* Encoder-Decoder model. The last row shows the average accuracy for each resource scenario.

6 Conclusion and Future work

In this experiment we tried to approach morphological inflection using a slightly more complex Encoder-Decoder architecture, by encoding the lemmas in three different directions (left-to-right, right-to-left and boundaries-to-center).

Although the model works quite well in some cases, there is plenty room for improvement. The main improvement that must be done is to continue experimenting with more parameters to check whether the addition of parameters improves results. Both in the medium- and high-resource settings, there are some languages that show very bad performance, especially *Finnish*, *Hungarian* and *Latin*. We feel that there is a need of carefully analyzing their outputs so that to better understand the motivation for these low results.

Data augmentation techniques were successfully used in the last CoNLL–SIGMORPHON 2018 Shared Task (Bergmanis et al., 2017; Kann and Schütze, 2017; Nicolai et al., 2017; Silfverberg et al., 2017) and thus, we think that our model could see its results improved in the low- and the medium-resource setting by adding artificially generated data.

We expect that using external resources, such as Wikipedia, would have a positive effect. We could even analyze how much effect does a specific amount of text have in this task pretraining character embeddings with, for instance, 10,000, 50,000 or 100,000 characters.

Acknowledgments

I acknowledge the anonymous reviewers for their informative comments and possible extra future directions, and also the organizers of the CoNLL–SIGMORPHON 2018 Shared Task for giving us the opportunity of participating in such an exciting task.

References

Dzmitry Bahdanau, Kyunghyun Cho, and Yoshua Bengio. 2014. Neural machine translation by jointly learning to align and translate. *arXiv preprint arXiv:1409.0473*.

Toms Bergmanis, Katharina Kann, Hinrich Schütze, and Sharon Goldwater. 2017. Training data augmentation for low-resource morphological inflection. *Proceedings of the CoNLL SIGMORPHON 2017 Shared Task: Universal Morphological Reinflection*, pages 31–39.

Kyunghyun Cho, Bart Van Merriënboer, Caglar Gulcehre, Dzmitry Bahdanau, Fethi Bougares, Holger Schwenk, and Yoshua Bengio. 2014. Learning phrase representations using rnn encoder-decoder for statistical machine translation. *arXiv preprint arXiv:1406.1078*.

Ryan Cotterell, Christo Kirov, John Sylak-Glassman, Géraldine Walther, Ekaterina Vylomova, Arya D. McCarthy, Katharina Kann, Sebastian Mielke, Garrett Nicolai, Miikka Silfverberg, David Yarowsky, Jason Eisner, and Mans Hulden. 2018. The CoNLL–SIGMORPHON 2018 shared task: Universal morphological reinflection. In *Proceedings of the CoNLL–SIGMORPHON 2018 Shared Task: Universal Morphological Reinflection*, Brussels, Belgium. Association for Computational Linguistics.

Katharina Kann and Hinrich Schütze. 2016. Med: The lmu system for the sigmorphon 2016 shared task on morphological reinflection. In *Proceedings of the 14th SIGMORPHON Workshop on Computational Research in Phonetics, Phonology, and Morphology*, pages 62–70.

Katharina Kann and Hinrich Schütze. 2017. The lmu system for the conll-sigmorphon 2017 shared task on universal morphological reinflection. *Proceedings of the CoNLL SIGMORPHON 2017 Shared Task: Universal Morphological Reinflection*, pages 40–48.

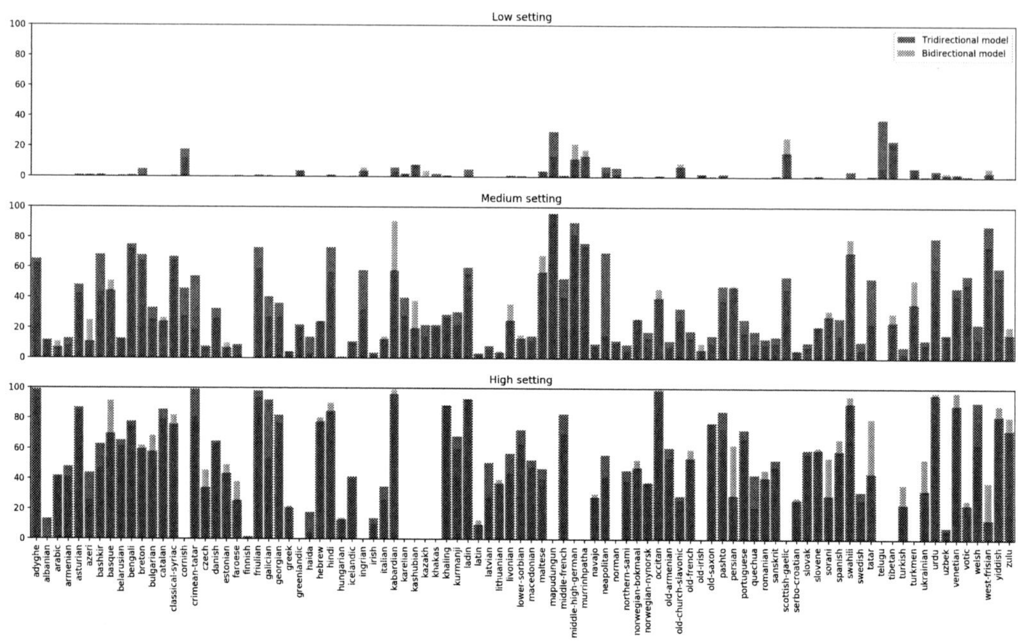

Figure 2: Accuracies of both the bidirectional and tridirectional models. As it can be seen in the figure, results from the two models are not very different as it was initially expected.

Christo Kirov, Ryan Cotterell, John Sylak-Glassman, Graldine Walther, Ekaterina Vylomova, Patrick Xia, Manaal Faruqui, Sebastian Mielke, Arya D. McCarthy, Sandra Kbler, David Yarowsky, Jason Eisner, and Mans Hulden. 2018. UniMorph 2.0: Universal Morphology. In *Proceedings of the Eleventh International Conference on Language Resources and Evaluation (LREC 2018)*, Miyazaki, Japan. European Language Resources Association (ELRA).

Guillaume Lample, Miguel Ballesteros, Sandeep Subramanian, Kazuya Kawakami, and Chris Dyer. 2016. Neural architectures for named entity recognition. *arXiv preprint arXiv:1603.01360*.

Garrett Nicolai, Bradley Hauer, Mohammad Motallebi, Saeed Najafi, and Grzegorz Kondrak. 2017. If you can't beat them, join them: the university of alberta system description. *Proceedings of the CoNLL SIGMORPHON 2017 Shared Task: Universal Morphological Reinflection*, pages 79–84.

Miikka Silfverberg, Adam Wiemerslage, Ling Liu, and Lingshuang Jack Mao. 2017. Data augmentation for morphological reinflection. *Proceedings of the CoNLL SIGMORPHON 2017 Shared Task: Universal Morphological Reinflection*, pages 90–99.

IPS-WASEDA system at CoNLL–SIGMORPHON 2018 Shared Task on morphological inflection

Rashel Fam   **Yves Lepage**
Graduate School of Information, Production, and Systems
Waseda University
2-7 Hibikino, Wakamatsu-ku, Kitakyushu-shi, 808-0135 Fukuoka-ken, Japan
`{fam.rashel@fuji., yves.lepage@}waseda.jp`

Abstract

This paper presents the system submitted by IPS-WASEDA University for CoNLL–SIGMORPHON 2018 Shared Task 1: Type level inflection. We develop a system based on a holistic approach which considers whole-word form as a unit, instead of breaking them into smaller pieces (e.g. morphemes) like the baseline systems does. We also implement an encoder-decoder model which has recently become the new standard in many natural language processing (NLP) tasks. The results show that the neural approach outperforms the baseline and our holistic approach on bigger resources settings. The use of data augmentation helps to improve the performance of the model in lower resources settings, although it still cannot beat the other systems. In the end, for the low resources setting, our holistic approach performs best in comparison to the baseline and the neural approach (even with data augmentation).

1   Introduction

Lemma:	*illustrate*
Target MSDs:	*V;V.PTCP;PRS*
Target form:	*illustrating*

Figure 1:   An example of inflection task in English: given the lemma *illustrate*, we are asked to generate the present participle form *illustrating*.

We address the problem of inflection task: given a **lemma** (e.g. the dictionary form of a word) and the target form's **morphosyntactic descriptions (MSD)**, generate a target inflected form. Figure 1 shows an example of inflection task in English.

Many NLP tasks, like machine translation, require analysis and generation of morphological word forms, even previously unseen ones. Different languages exhibit different richness of morphology. This makes the task an interesting prob-

lem. Dreyer and Eisner (2011) show that data sparsity is a common issue for language with rich morphology which usually leads to poor generalisations in machine learning.

There are three main approaches at the problem:

- **The hand-engineered rule-based approach** offers a high accuracy but costs time during construction. It usually faces the world coverage problem and is language-dependent.

- **The supervised approach** automatically induces the rules from a given training data and applies the best rules to generate the target forms by using some classification techniques (Ahlberg et al., 2015). It is practically language independent and relatively easier to build. However, the data sparsity is an issue.

- **The neural approach** is the model which triumphed in the task recently, especially the RNN encoder-decoder model (Kann and Schütze, 2016; Makarov et al., 2017). Some drawbacks of this approach are very long training times and the need for a large amount of training data.

This paper describes the systems we developed for the CoNLL–SIGMORPHON 2018 Shared Task 1 (Cotterell et al., 2018). The recent success of neural approach encouraged us to implement a sequence-to-sequence (seq2seq) model to solve the task. Knowing that the neural approach tends to need a large amount of training data, we also consider another approach as a back-off, which is a holistic approach. We treat the task of generating target forms as the task of solving analogical equations between words.

2   Languages and data

Task 1 consists of 93 different languages. 10 additional surprise languages are given in the middle of

33

Proceedings of the CoNLL–SIGMORPHON 2018 Shared Task: Universal Morphological Reinflection, pages 33–42,
Brussels, Belgium, October 31, 2018. ©2018 Association for Computational Linguistics

Feature	low			medium			high		
	Avg	Min	Max	Avg	Min	Max	Avg	Min	Max
# of characters (train)	29	14	51	33	14	63	40	19	86
# of unseen characters (dev)	4	0	21	1	0	8	0	0	4
# of lemmata (train)	77	5	100	487	5	989	2,308	15	8,643
# of unseen lemmata (dev)	414	0	984	295	0	960	98	0	743
# of MSDs (train)	22	5	43	23	5	48	25	7	48
# of unseen MSDs (dev)	1	0	8	0	0	2	0	0	1
# of MSD patterns (train)	45	4	95	94	4	726	126	5	1,649
# of unseen MSD patterns (dev)	44	0	695	8	0	414	0	0	6
# of rules (train)	98	26	100	838	147	1,000	5,642	815	9,842
# of unseen rules (dev)	561	12	997	504	30	995	398	22	971

Table 1: Statistics on the dataset given. Number of rules and unseen rules are based on rule extraction method explained in Section 5.3.1.

the development phase. The languages vary from Germanic, Celtic and Slavic languages, which are mainly used in Europe, to Indo-Aryan, Iranian, etc. The dataset consists of lines of triplet. A triplet consists of a lemma, a target form, and a target MSD pattern separated by tabulation characters. The MSDs are morphological tags presented in Unimorph Schema (Kirov et al., 2018).

The provided resources are categorized into:

- **train**: this dataset is the dataset which can be manipulated by the participant to solve the task. It consists of three different sizes:

    low   :   100 word forms
    medium :   1,000 word forms
    high   : 10,000 word forms

  Telugu has only the *low* training dataset. Some languages have only *low* and *medium* training datasets: Cornish, Greenlandic, Inggrian, Karelian, Kashubian, Kazakh, Khakas, Mapudungun, Middle-Low-German, Middle-High-German, Murrinh-patha, Norman, Old-Irish, Scottish-Gaelic, Tibetan, Turkmen.

- **dev**: this dataset is given to evaluate the performance of our system during the development phase. It consists of 1,000 word forms.

- **test**: this dataset is given at the test phase. This dataset does not contain the target forms. It consists of 1,000 word forms, similar to *dev* dataset.

For some languages, the size of the dataset is smaller than the one mentioned above.

Let us now look at some statistics on the given dataset shown in Table 1. Overall, we can observe a non-decreasing phenomenon from *low* to *high* for all of the number of pieces of information (features) found in the training dataset. On the opposite, we found a non-increasing pattern for the unseen information contained in the dev dataset relatively to training dataset. This shows that bigger resources gradually cover the unseen data encountered in the smaller ones.

Norman, Telugu, Cornish, and Uzbek are languages with a smaller number of lemmata in the training dataset. However, these languages tend to have less, even zero for some languages, unseen lemmata relatively to the dev dataset. They also have a smaller number of unseen characters. On the other hand, languages like Finnish, Russian, English, French, and German have the biggest number of unseen lemmata despite having the biggest number of lemmata in the training dataset compared to other languages.

Let us now turn to the number of MSDs and MSD patterns. These numbers can be interpreted as how large or complex the paradigm for that particular language is. Basque, Quechua, Turkish, Zulu are languages with a higher variety of unique MSD patterns. Basque, in particular, has astonishingly more than 1,600 patterns in comparison to the average of around 126 patterns per language in *high* datasets. The same thing can be seen for *low* and *medium* data. Almost all of the lines are associated with different MSD patterns in the *low* training dataset. Furthermore, Basque also topped as the language with the highest number of unseen MSD patterns for all dataset sizes.

(*substring*,	*replacement*,	*#_of_occurrences*)
'-ε'	'-ing'	1,121
'-e'	'-ing'	832
'-ize'	'-izing'	162
$\vdots$	$\vdots$	$\vdots$
'show'	'showing'	1
$\vdots$	$\vdots$	$\vdots$

Figure 2: Excerpt of affixes remembered by the baseline system from the training data. It memorizes all changes from lemma into target form in various character length.

We also count the number of rules found in the dataset (see the last two rows in Table 1). These rules are not the morphological rules defined by linguists but the one extracted from the method explained in Section 5.3.1. For all languages and all datasets, we count how many unique rules can be extracted and relatively unseen to the respective dev dataset. Telugu, Tatar, and Swahili are the languages with the lowest number of unseen rules. We expect to have good performance in these languages because it means that most of the transformations from lemma into the target form are present in the training data.

3 Baseline system: morpheme-based

The CoNLL–SIGMORPHON 2018 organizers provide a baseline system which is a morpheme-based approach. For each language, it determines whether the language is biased towards prefixing or suffixing. The string will be reversed if the language is biased to prefixing.

For each instance in the training data, it aligns the lemma and target form using Levenshtein distance to cut the word into three categories of candidate: prefix, stem, and suffix. Prefixing and suffixing rules are then extracted and grouped according to the given MSD pattern. The rules are stored as a knowledge in a list of triplets: substring to replace, string replacement, and the number of occurrences. Figure 2 illustrates how the baseline system stores the suffixing rules for English present participle.

In the generation step, it filters the candidate rules by the given target MSD pattern. First, the longest common suffixing rule with the highest number of occurrences is applied. Then the most frequent prefixing rule is applied in the succession to generate the predicted target form.

4 Holistic approach

Another view on the problem is to see that word forms are connected with other word forms systematically. Based on this observation, we can treat the inflection task as the task of solving analogical equation on words[1]:

$$\text{lemma}_t : \text{form}_t :: \text{lemma}_q : x \quad \Rightarrow \quad x = \text{form}_q$$

4.1 Proportional analogy

Analogy is a relationship between four objects: A, B, C, and D usually noted as $A : B :: C : D$. It states that A is to B as C is to D where the ratio between A and B is the same as the ratio between C and D. Here, we consider analogy as a possible way to explain derivation between words as it is already used from the ancient Greek and Latin grammatical tradition up to recent works on computational linguistics, like (Hathout, 2008, 2009).

Various formalisations of analogy have been proposed in (Yvon, 2003; Lepage, 2004; Stroppa and Yvon, 2005). In this work, we select the following definition[2].

$$A : B :: C : D \Rightarrow \begin{cases} d(A, B) = d(C, D) \\ d(A, C) = d(B, D) \\ |A|_a + |D|_a = |B|_a + |C|_a, \\ \forall_a \end{cases} \tag{1}$$

We can construct analogical grids (Fam and Lepage, 2017b, 2018) to give a compact view of different analogies that emerge from a set of words contained in a corpus. An analogical grid is a MxN matrix of words. The special property of this matrix is that any four words from two rows and two columns is an analogy (see Formula 2).

$$\begin{matrix} P_1^1 : P_1^2 : \cdots : P_1^m \\ P_2^1 : P_2^2 : \cdots : P_2^m \\ \vdots \ \ \vdots \qquad \ \ \vdots \\ P_n^1 : P_n^2 : \cdots : P_n^m \end{matrix} \stackrel{\Delta}{\Longleftrightarrow} \begin{matrix} \forall (i, k) \in \{1, \ldots, n\}^2, \\ \forall (j, l) \in \{1, \ldots, m\}^2, \\ P_i^j : P_i^l :: P_k^j : P_k^l \end{matrix} \tag{2}$$

4.2 Solving analogical equation to generate word form

In contrast to the baseline system which uses a morpheme-based approach, our holistic approach

---

[1] Both lemma_t and form_t are a pair of lemma and target form found in the training data; lemma_q is the lemma given in the question; and form_q is the predicted target form.

[2] $d(A, B)$ stands for the value of the LCS edit distance between two strings A and B that uses only insertions and deletions with cost of 1. $|A|_c$ is the number of occurrences of character c in string A.

Training data

lemma	inflected	morph. features
show	*showed*	*V;PST*
show	*showing*	*V;V.PTCP;PRS*
release	*released*	*V;PST*
release	*releasing*	*V;V.PTCP;PRS*
schmear	*schmeared*	*V;PST*
⋮	⋮	⋮

Question

Lemma: *illustrate*
Target MSDs: *V;V.PTCP;PRS*

LEMMA	:	*V;V.PTCP;PRS*	:	*V;PST*
release	:	*releasing*	:	*released*
revise	:	*revising*	:	*revised*
age	:	*aging*	:	*aged*
bake	:	*baking*	:	
show	:	*showing*	:	*showed*
enter	:		:	*entered*
reason	:	*reasoning*	:	*reasoned*
schmear	:		:	*schmeared*

release : releasing :: illustrate : x
$$\Rightarrow$$
$x = $ ***illustrating***

show : showing :: illustrate : x
$$\Rightarrow$$
$x = $ ~~***illustrateing***~~

Figure 3: How to generate target form (present participle) of the given lemma *illustrate* as solving analogical equation. Different analogical grids may generate different target forms.

does not break words in pieces (Singh, 2000; Singh and Ford, 2000; Neuvel and Singh, 2001). We generate the target form by solving analogical equation based on the evidence observed in the given training data.

First, the relevant analogical grid is selected according to the given target MSD pattern. If several candidates of analogical equation exist, we use some heuristic features to select the analogical equation. These heuristics are edit distance, longest common subsequence, longest common suffix, and longest common prefix, between the given lemma and lemmata existed in the training dataset. If there are still several candidates after using heuristic features, we solve all of the possible analogical equations to generate all the possible predicted target form. The most frequent answer is chosen as the predicted target form.

For example, Figure 3 illustrates how to generate the target form for the example given in Figure 1. Let us say that we are able to get two analogical grids according to the given MSD pattern. We construct the analogical equation as follows:

$$\text{lemma}_t : \text{form}_t :: illustrate : \text{form}_q$$

taken from the first and second column of the analogical grids according to the given MSD pattern. Based on longest common suffix, we choose to use the one in the *top* which produces the word form *illustrating* instead of the *bottom* one which produces *illustrateing*.

5 Neural approach

Following the recent success of neural approach in previous evaluation campaign, we implement a common architecture of seq2seq model. We treat the inflection task as the problem of translating the given target MSDs and lemma into target form. Thus, the input string for the example given in Figure 1 will be as follows.

V V.PTCP PRS i l l u s t r a t e

5.1 Seq2seq model

Our model is a standard seq2seq model with attention mechanism inspired from the one which is used for machine translation (Luong et al., 2015). The difference is that we consider a character or MSD as one token, instead of a word. Each token (character) is represented by a continuous vector representation learned in the embedding layer.

We use a bi-directional Gated Recurrent Unit (GRU) cell (Cho et al., 2014) which is a variation of Long Short-Term Memory (LSTM) cell (Hochreiter and Schmidhuber, 1997) that tries to solve the vanishing gradient problem. Our decoder is two layers of uni-directional GRU cell with attention mechanism. There are various implementations of attention mechanism like (Bahdanau et al., 2015; Luong et al., 2015). In this work, we use the one that has the weight normalization (Salimans and Kingma, 2016) to help the model converges faster.

To handle the unseen tokens, we remember them in a First-In-First-Out (FIFO) list and replace them with a special token *<UNK>* before feeding them into our model. These special tokens are reverted back to the character contained in the list after the decoding phase.

5.2 Hyperparameters

We fixed our hyperparameters for all languages and amounts of resources after doing some preliminary experiments. The number of hidden units is fixed to 100 for each layer in the encoder and decoder. The size of the embedding is 300. We optimize the model using ADAM (Kingma and Ba, 2015) with learning rate of 5×10^4 during training. To make the training process faster, we use mini-batch size of 20.

We trained the model using early-stop mechanism of 30 epochs without improvement on validation data which is a set of lines randomly selected from the original training data.

5.3 Simple data augmentation

Preliminary results show that the neural approach suffers from the lack of data. To tackle this problem, we perform a simple data augmentation which artificially creates additional training data from evidences seen in the original training data. Additional training data is expected to bring improvement to the performance of our model, especially on *low* data situation (Kann and Schütze, 2017; Bergmanis et al., 2017; Silfverberg et al., 2017; Zhou and Neubig, 2017; Nicolai et al., 2017).

5.3.1 Rule extraction

We find the longest common substring between lemma and target form. The left part is assumed as prefix candidate, while the right part is assumed as suffix candidate. Figure 4 shows several examples of rules extracted from the training data in three different languages.

To capture situational affixing where the next or previous character influences the changes, we added the first character from the longest common substring to the extracted prefix candidate and the last character for the suffix candidate. This, for

- Insertion

	Language:	Irish
	Lemma:	*fótaidhé-óid*
	Target MSDs:	*N;NOM;PL;DEF*
	Target form:	*na fótaidhé-óidí*

	prefix	root	suffix
lemma		*fótaidhé-óid*	
target form	*na*	*fótaidhé-óid*	*í*

- Substitution

	Language:	French
	Lemma:	*amoindrir*
	Target MSDs:	*V;SBJV;PST;3;SG*
	Target form:	*amoindrît*

	prefix	root	suffix
lemma		*amoindr*	*ir*
target form		*amoindr*	*ît*

- Insertion and substitution at the same time

	Language:	German
	Lemma:	*einschließen*
	Target MSDs:	*V;SBJV;PST;2;SG*
	Target form:	*schlössest ein*

	prefix	root	suffix
lemma	*ein*	*schl*	*ießen*
target form		*schl*	*össest ein*

Figure 4: Illustrations of rules extraction for data augmentation: simple insertion (Irish); substitution (French); insertion and substitution at the same time (German).

example, happens for regular past form in English where you add only *-d* as suffix for lemmata ended with *e*, instead of adding *-ed*

At a glance, it looks similar to how the baseline system extracts the affix rules. However, we only memorize the left (prefix candidate) and right part (suffix candidate), not all of the possible affix combinations with the stem as the baseline system does. It simplifies the rules extraction, and thus, gives us a smaller number of extracted rules in comparison to the baseline system.

5.3.2 Creating additional training data

For each rule which appears less than 10 times in the training data, we artificially create 5 instances of additional training data. The additional training

Method	Accuracy		
	low	medium	high
Baseline	39.3	63.4	77.1
Holistic	**39.6**	64.5	77.3
Seq2seq	13.1	71.3	**90.9**
Seq2seq+Aug	36.9	**78.5**	89.1

Table 2: Average accuracy scores on *dev* dataset.

data is constructed by using a random string with the length of random integer between 1 to 4. Here, we do not employ any language model to asses the probability of the character sequence like the one described in (Silfverberg et al., 2017). For example, we can create the following additional training instance for the examples given in Figure 4. Characters written in boldface are patterns from the extracted rules.

> Irish: *fbsód $\implies$ na fbsódí*
> French: *aifrir $\implies$ aifrît*
> German: *einsraftließen $\implies$ sraftlössest ein*

6 Experiment Protocol

We evaluate the performance of the systems using average on accuracy. Accuracy is the ratio of correctly predicted target forms by the total number of questions. Please refer to Formula 3 for the exact definition[3].

$$\text{Accuracy} = \frac{\sum_{i=1}^{N} \delta(\text{predicted}_i = \text{correct}_i)}{N} \times 100 \tag{3}$$

We carry experiments using training dataset and measure the accuracies on dev dataset for all the languages for all training dataset sizes. The system which has the highest score will be picked as our representative system in the test phase for that particular language and dataset size.

7 Results

Table 2 shows the average accuracy in all languages for each of the systems. Our holistic approach is able to perform as good as the baseline system, even slightly better under all of the three dataset sizes. This is the same observation found in (Fam and Lepage, 2017a) on previous year dataset.

The results show that the neural approach using seq2seq model left behind both the baseline

---

[3] N is the total number of questions. $\delta(A = B)$ equals to 1 if the two strings A and B are same, or else it is 0.

system and the holistic approach on *medium* and *high* data situation. The gap is around 15 accuracy points. However, the lack of training data exhibits the drawback of the neural approach as it performs poorly under *low* data situation. Furthermore, the use of data augmentation improves the performance in most cases. We can see an improvement of around 3 times better accuracy on *low* dataset although it still cannot overcome the performance of either the baseline nor the holistic approach.

The baseline system and the holistic approach shine over the neural approach particularly for languages like Albanian, Czech, Haida, Neapolitan, Norwegian-Bokmaal, and Uzbek. Our seq2seq model seems to struggle even on *high* data situation for some of these languages. On the other hand, our seq2seq model gets better accuracy than the baseline system or holistic approach even on *low* data situation in some languages like Azeri, Basque, Breton, Cornish, Greenlandic, Hindi, Karelian, Khaling, Maltese, Middle-Low-German, Middle-High-German, Murrinhpatha, Norman, North-Frisian, Persian, Swahili, Turkish, Turkmen, Welsh, Zulu.

The same trend can be seen on the results for similar languages, like Romance (Catalan, Galician, Portuguese, and Spanish), Semitic (Arabic and Hebrew), and Baltic (Latvian and Lithuanian) languages. The baseline system leads the score on *low* dataset size before started to be outperformed by our seq2seq model on the dataset with bigger sizes. For other language families like Indo-Aryan (Bengali, Hindi, Urdu), Finnic (Estonian and Finnish), and Turkic (Turkish and Turkmen) languages, our seq2seq model steadily leads the score for all dataset sizes. Please refer to Table 3 for detail results per language.

8 Discussion

The results for the baseline system and our holistic approach show the absence of necessity to break down the words into morpheme. The derivation between lemma and target form can also be acquired through analogy. However, selecting the candidates for constructing the analogical equation is a crucial thing. Thus, we need to improve our selection method or use better heuristic features. To handle the problem of unseen MSD patterns, the use of formal concept analysis (Ganter and Wille, 1999) is worth to consider.

Language	Accuracy											
	low				medium				high			
	B	H	S	S+Aug	B	H	S	S+Aug	B	H	S	S+Aug
adyghe	59.8	71.6	35.5	**73.8**	85.5	88.1	88.0	**89.5**	94.8	93.6	**95.6**	95.2
albanian	22.7	**24.5**	0.6	11.6	60.2	**71.5**	44.8	65.2	77.2	**86.4**	81.1	80.5
arabic	22.9	**24.7**	0.1	21.0	37.0	46.2	61.1	**67.9**	42.8	59.1	**93.0**	91.7
armenian	**37.9**	35.7	1.2	34.2	72.4	76.9	76.5	**83.7**	88.6	89.6	**94.1**	90.9
asturian	**59.8**	58.6	19.7	53.1	87.9	88.0	87.4	**89.7**	95.5	95.4	**97.8**	97.2
azeri	21.0	28.0	13.0	**37.0**	48.0	57.0	**69.0**	67.0	69.0	72.0	81.0	**82.0**
bashkir	**38.8**	38.6	11.5	35.9	73.8	71.8	**87.0**	81.0	89.1	86.7	**94.1**	92.6
basque	0.1	0.2	1.9	**8.6**	1.9	2.5	67.0	**79.2**	8.4	9.8	**97.4**	96.9
belarusian	7.2	**10.7**	4.6	5.7	22.5	25.3	44.6	**55.4**	41.4	42.3	**85.3**	80.9
bengali	44.0	43.0	14.0	**49.0**	75.0	74.0	94.0	**96.0**	84.0	84.0	98.0	**99.0**
breton	20.0	17.0	18.0	**61.0**	51.0	59.0	83.0	**88.0**	55.0	61.0	91.0	**92.0**
bulgarian	32.7	33.0	4.3	**49.8**	74.4	76.9	70.6	**82.1**	90.6	89.5	**95.4**	94.3
catalan	**54.3**	51.2	4.6	32.6	82.2	81.2	85.0	**92.3**	94.3	94.2	**98.1**	95.9
classical-syriac	**89.0**	87.0	41.0	72.0	**98.0**	**98.0**	94.0	**98.0**	98.0	97.0	98.0	**100.0**
cornish	2.0	0.0	7.5	**22.5**	4.0	2.0	47.5	**57.5**				
crimean-tatar	53.0	**66.0**	16.0	63.0	74.0	76.0	**95.0**	89.0	93.0	92.0	**99.0**	98.0
czech	38.1	**38.4**	1.6	26.1	78.8	**79.4**	51.1	76.6	89.0	**89.5**	85.5	86.3
danish	57.4	**65.2**	30.2	53.0	78.1	**79.7**	74.3	69.8	88.9	88.8	**91.3**	85.8
estonian	22.6	21.7	0.7	**28.4**	62.4	60.6	60.0	**70.3**	76.2	77.0	**90.6**	88.0
faroese	35.6	**38.3**	3.3	16.6	61.0	**63.0**	51.0	60.6	74.2	74.5	**79.8**	74.5
finnish	15.4	15.4	0.7	**18.7**	43.5	43.3	42.6	**69.9**	79.3	77.2	**84.1**	82.0
friulian	**51.0**	48.0	25.0	49.0	86.0	85.0	89.0	**94.0**	94.0	93.0	98.0	**99.0**
galician	**52.5**	51.9	9.1	30.7	82.3	81.2	77.9	**88.9**	93.7	93.2	**98.4**	97.4
georgian	**71.8**	70.5	17.2	58.9	89.7	90.0	82.9	**92.5**	93.8	94.0	**98.5**	98.4
greek	**27.7**	27.0	2.0	12.0	61.0	**63.0**	44.3	56.6	77.4	77.6	81.7	**83.3**
greenlandic	36.0	42.0	27.5	**57.5**	74.0	60.0	75.0	**85.0**				
haida	**43.0**	28.0	5.0	23.0	**59.0**	**59.0**	50.0	52.0	**71.0**	68.0	53.0	52.0
hebrew	27.9	**29.8**	4.1	13.8	40.0	49.0	**76.3**	**76.3**	55.9	60.7	**98.1**	97.2
hindi	34.9	31.8	23.9	**65.6**	86.1	83.9	94.3	**95.1**	93.6	93.5	**98.6**	97.5
hungarian	14.9	**22.0**	0.9	12.1	39.9	46.7	47.3	**53.1**	68.7	69.7	**77.5**	63.5
icelandic	35.8	**38.1**	6.5	14.9	60.4	**63.6**	52.3	61.3	77.2	77.1	**84.3**	78.7
ingrian	20.0	12.0	**27.5**	20.0	46.0	42.0	**80.0**	75.0				
irish	31.8	**35.7**	3.7	20.9	44.7	49.2	42.6	**57.7**	54.3	58.1	**83.0**	77.2
italian	43.3	**44.4**	3.3	41.3	70.5	83.1	81.3	**91.1**	77.2	93.1	**97.9**	95.4
kabardian	78.0	74.0	51.0	**83.0**	90.0	87.0	**95.0**	**95.0**	90.0	86.0	**96.0**	**96.0**
karelian	40.0	34.0	20.0	**67.5**	48.0	48.0	95.0	**97.5**				
kashubian	56.0	64.0	12.5	**57.5**	74.0	68.0	85.0	**92.5**				
kazakh	44.0	50.0	**52.5**	47.5	64.0	62.0	72.5	**77.5**				
khakas	36.0	48.0	27.5	**65.0**	92.0	92.0	85.0	**92.5**				
khaling	3.9	1.6	4.6	**11.2**	18.4	17.8	77.3	**86.4**	53.8	48.0	**99.6**	98.4
kurmanji	82.1	**85.8**	0.0	58.4	84.7	**88.9**	83.7	88.2	91.9	91.4	**92.8**	91.4
ladin	**59.0**	53.0	30.0	52.0	85.0	86.0	88.0	**95.0**	92.0	91.0	**98.0**	**98.0**
latin	**16.0**	12.6	0.8	5.4	**36.8**	28.5	25.2	36.2	45.6	37.1	**70.1**	55.5
latvian	**53.4**	50.9	4.1	18.3	85.8	**86.6**	60.5	82.4	92.0	91.2	**94.8**	**94.8**
lithuanian	**23.5**	19.4	0.8	5.6	**53.0**	50.3	33.7	51.6	64.7	63.6	**86.2**	84.1
livonian	25.0	**27.0**	1.0	**27.0**	47.0	47.0	69.0	**77.0**	58.0	59.0	**92.0**	**92.0**
lower-sorbian	30.7	**35.8**	2.9	19.3	70.4	79.3	64.1	**81.4**	88.1	87.9	**95.2**	94.8
macedonian	**51.4**	47.4	5.1	37.7	83.8	88.2	75.7	**89.8**	93.2	93.5	**96.4**	95.3
maltese	11.0	19.0	0.0	**23.0**	21.0	29.0	87.0	**93.0**	25.0	29.0	97.0	**98.0**
mapudungun	62.0	60.0	57.5	**95.0**	80.0	88.0	**97.5**	**97.5**				
middle-french	**78.7**	76.1	10.1	67.2	90.8	91.3	89.2	**93.0**	95.8	95.1	**98.8**	96.3
middle-high-german	44.0	48.0	35.0	**67.5**	54.0	60.0	**97.5**	**97.5**				
murrinhpatha	2.0	4.0	25.0	**35.0**	14.0	10.0	**95.0**	90.0				
navajo	14.3	**14.6**	2.0	13.8	31.8	31.2	35.8	**41.5**	40.0	40.5	**82.5**	76.0
neapolitan	**83.0**	81.0	25.0	65.0	94.0	93.0	91.0	**95.0**	**99.0**	98.0	95.0	95.0
norman	38.0	34.0	45.0	**60.0**	60.0	52.0	77.5	**80.0**				
northern-sami	**17.8**	13.1	2.1	11.6	38.8	35.0	43.2	**60.7**	64.5	62.4	**93.4**	88.0
norwegian-bokmaal	69.0	**73.2**	13.8	54.8	79.8	**81.0**	78.0	76.5	**90.6**	90.3	88.9	77.0
norwegian-nynorsk	51.4	**53.7**	11.9	37.6	**61.6**	61.1	52.5	57.0	74.7	75.1	**84.0**	75.8
occitan	**79.0**	77.0	15.0	55.0	87.0	87.0	94.0	**98.0**	94.0	92.0	**100.0**	**100.0**
old-armenian	27.6	**28.8**	1.5	14.8	64.9	68.0	48.9	**69.3**	76.7	79.3	**86.0**	85.1
old-church-slavonic	**34.0**	32.0	11.0	29.0	65.0	65.0	74.0	**78.0**	64.0	57.0	92.0	**96.0**
old-french	30.4	27.6	4.9	**35.4**	61.3	65.2	65.0	**68.9**	79.7	79.5	**87.5**	84.8
old-irish	**12.0**	**12.0**	5.0	5.0	20.0	18.0	20.0	**32.5**				
old-saxon	**25.3**	19.0	2.7	5.2	41.7	35.6	63.0	**68.0**	60.5	56.0	**95.3**	94.6

Language	Accuracy											
	low				medium				high			
	B	H	S	S+Aug	B	H	S	S+Aug	B	H	S	S+Aug
pashto	**41.0**	**41.0**	8.0	21.0	71.0	73.0	69.0	**75.0**	77.0	77.0	**100.0**	98.0
persian	27.1	29.3	2.8	**35.7**	67.3	71.7	82.1	**85.7**	81.0	83.7	**96.0**	95.4
portuguese	**65.7**	64.3	6.9	31.0	92.2	91.8	78.2	**92.5**	97.1	97.2	**97.6**	97.5
quechua	17.1	11.7	3.2	**31.2**	**71.5**	52.1	52.0	55.9	**95.2**	89.6	56.3	56.0
romanian	**44.1**	42.8	3.2	30.3	70.2	**73.0**	59.7	72.3	80.4	78.5	**84.6**	83.1
sanskrit	30.0	37.5	4.8	**42.7**	57.9	77.8	67.9	**80.7**	78.7	83.4	88.0	**88.3**
scottish-gaelic	42.0	38.0	25.0	**50.0**	46.0	44.0	80.0	**90.0**				
serbo-croatian	22.8	20.9	1.3	**25.4**	67.3	65.4	52.9	**74.1**	84.0	85.0	85.2	**86.9**
slovak	37.7	**46.3**	3.3	23.8	71.0	**72.9**	61.3	70.6	82.5	82.8	**90.0**	89.9
slovene	35.2	**37.4**	13.7	25.9	73.5	75.2	63.4	**86.0**	87.3	85.7	**95.2**	93.8
sorani	**20.5**	18.8	1.2	15.6	52.8	52.1	60.3	**71.4**	64.3	60.1	**88.0**	87.7
spanish	**62.4**	57.7	4.9	46.7	85.9	84.9	84.3	**90.3**	91.5	93.6	**97.1**	95.8
swahili	29.0	29.0	27.0	**66.0**	71.0	76.0	**94.0**	93.0	72.0	82.0	**100.0**	**100.0**
swedish	55.6	**62.8**	7.8	39.9	75.2	**76.8**	62.2	68.0	85.8	85.6	**86.1**	76.2
tatar	57.0	**68.0**	17.0	53.0	85.0	88.0	**94.0**	87.0	91.0	91.0	**100.0**	99.0
telugu	80.0	80.0	40.0	**82.5**								
tibetan	**54.0**	42.0	32.5	42.5	48.0	50.0	37.5	**52.5**				
turkish	11.8	12.3	1.1	**28.5**	32.1	40.1	**71.4**	68.3	72.3	74.4	**91.8**	87.0
turkmen	30.0	54.0	37.5	**60.0**	70.0	76.0	87.5	**92.5**				
ukrainian	39.4	**44.6**	6.7	23.3	**72.7**	71.8	55.3	71.3	84.8	84.3	**89.9**	87.1
urdu	29.9	27.4	24.9	**57.8**	86.8	85.7	91.5	**95.0**	96.0	95.7	97.4	**97.6**
uzbek	53.0	35.0	47.0	**74.0**	**93.0**	92.0	78.0	78.0	93.0	**94.0**	78.0	78.0
venetian	**69.0**	68.3	16.6	42.3	89.5	89.0	91.6	**93.1**	93.7	92.1	**99.6**	99.0
votic	**15.0**	12.0	11.0	13.0	38.0	39.0	68.0	**76.0**	41.0	39.0	**78.0**	**78.0**
welsh	26.0	23.0	11.0	**30.0**	55.0	56.0	83.0	**88.0**	71.0	70.0	**95.0**	**95.0**
west-frisian	**47.0**	44.0	8.0	40.0	66.0	64.0	86.0	**93.0**	66.0	62.0	91.0	**95.0**
yiddish	**70.0**	68.0	6.0	60.0	80.0	79.0	83.0	**92.0**	88.0	83.0	98.0	**99.0**
zulu	19.2	18.4	11.0	**33.3**	56.5	65.8	81.6	**86.7**	71.0	81.1	**99.2**	97.7
dutch	53.2	**54.2**	7.8	24.1	72.0	72.8	73.5	**79.4**	88.9	87.3	**96.2**	95.1
english	77.2	**81.7**	28.5	56.4	90.8	**91.4**	85.7	88.0	94.9	94.7	**95.6**	93.6
french	**56.8**	54.5	3.9	37.7	**74.1**	73.7	71.9	71.6	81.9	81.0	**83.7**	73.5
german	51.4	**54.2**	10.7	11.5	74.2	**77.8**	66.0	71.1	83.1	85.8	**88.4**	82.0
kannada	31.0	**36.0**	9.0	27.0	58.0	64.0	83.0	**90.0**	66.0	62.0	**95.0**	**95.0**
middle-low-german	20.0	18.0	22.5	**25.0**	34.0	30.0	90.0	**92.5**				
north-frisian	23.0	23.0	11.0	**27.0**	33.0	32.0	**85.0**	82.0	31.0	32.0	94.0	**95.0**
old-english	**16.7**	11.8	4.3	12.7	28.2	22.1	38.3	**53.3**	44.2	35.8	**83.8**	79.5
polish	40.7	**42.8**	1.8	13.9	73.6	**76.9**	60.0	76.1	88.4	88.6	88.1	**89.5**
russian	41.4	**41.6**	1.8	11.5	75.7	**77.8**	54.4	76.5	85.2	85.7	**89.2**	87.7
Average	39.3	**39.6**	13.1	36.9	63.4	64.5	71.3	**78.5**	77.1	77.3	**90.9**	89.1

Table 3: Accuracy scores on development set (*dev*) in each language for baseline system (**B**), holistic approach(**H**), our seq2seq model without data augmentation (**S**) and with data augmentation (**S+Aug**).

The improvement shown by using data augmentation seems promising. One may think to increase the amount of the artificially created additional training data. However, there is a trade-off between performance and training time. Another thing to consider is how many more additional training data should be created. We can see that the data augmentation seems not to improve the performance on *high* data situation anymore. In addition, the current method to extract the affix rules is very simple. Although it may capture circumfixes, it is still strongly biased to prefixing and suffixing only. A better method is expected to also capture other phenomena, such as parallel infixing (Arabic), repetition (Greek), and reduplication (Malay, Indonesian).

9 Conclusion

We developed several systems for morphological inflection task. The first one is based on a holistic approach. We generate the target forms by solving analogical equations on words. The second one is a seq2seq neural network model. A simple data augmentation is also implemented to help on low data situation. We evaluated their performance on the development dataset and choose the best system on each language and dataset size as our representative system for the submission.

Experimental results show that the neural approach using seq2seq model has the best performance in most cases on *medium* and *high* data situation. However, both baseline and our holistic approach are toe-to-toe on *low* data situation.

References

Malin Ahlberg, Markus Forsberg, and Mans Hulden. 2015. Paradigm classification in supervised learning of morphology. In *Proceedings of the 2015 Conference of the North American Chapter of the Association for Computational Linguistics: Human Language Technologies*, pages 1024–1029, Denver, Colorado. Association for Computational Linguistics.

Dzmitry Bahdanau, Kyunghyun Cho, and Yoshua Bengio. 2015. Neural machine translation by jointly learning to align and translate. In *Proceedings of the 3rd International Conference for Learning Representations (ICLR-15)*, San Diego.

Toms Bergmanis, Katharina Kann, Hinrich Schütze, and Sharon Goldwater. 2017. Training data augmentation for low-resource morphological inflection. In *Proceedings of the CoNLL SIGMORPHON 2017 Shared Task: Universal Morphological Reinflection*, pages 31–39, Vancouver. Association for Computational Linguistics.

Kyunghyun Cho, Bart van Merrienboer, Caglar Gulcehre, Dzmitry Bahdanau, Fethi Bougares, Holger Schwenk, and Yoshua Bengio. 2014. Learning phrase representations using rnn encoder–decoder for statistical machine translation. In *Proceedings of the 2014 Conference on Empirical Methods in Natural Language Processing (EMNLP)*, pages 1724–1734, Doha, Qatar. Association for Computational Linguistics.

Ryan Cotterell, Christo Kirov, John Sylak-Glassman, Géraldine Walther, Ekaterina Vylomova, Arya D. McCarthy, Katharina Kann, Sebastian Mielke, Garrett Nicolai, Miikka Silfverberg, David Yarowsky, Jason Eisner, and Mans Hulden. 2018. The CoNLL–SIGMORPHON 2018 shared task: Universal morphological reinflection. In *Proceedings of the CoNLL–SIGMORPHON 2018 Shared Task: Universal Morphological Reinflection*, Brussels, Belgium. Association for Computational Linguistics.

Markus Dreyer and Jason Eisner. 2011. Discovering morphological paradigms from plain text using a dirichlet process mixture model. In *Proceedings of the 2011 Conference on Empirical Methods in Natural Language Processing (EMNLP'2011)*, pages 616–627, Edinburgh, Scotland, UK. Association for Computational Linguistics.

Rashel Fam and Yves Lepage. 2017a. A holistic approach at a morphological inflection task. In *Proceedings of the 8th Language and Technology Conference (LTC-17)*, pages 88–92, Poznań, Poland. Fundacja uniwersytetu im. Adama Mickiewicza.

Rashel Fam and Yves Lepage. 2017b. A study of the saturation of analogical grids agnostically extracted from texts. In *Proceedings of the Computational Analogy Workshop at the 25th International Conference on Case-Based Reasoning (ICCBR-CA-17)*, pages 11–20, Trondheim, Norway.

Rashel Fam and Yves Lepage. 2018. Tools for the production of analogical grids and a resource of n-gram analogical grids in 11 languages. In *Proceedings of the 11th edition of the Language Resources and Evaluation Conference (LREC-18)*, pages 1060–1066, Miyazaki, Japan. ELRA.

Bernhard Ganter and Rudolf Wille. 1999. *Formal Concept Analysis: Mathematical Foundations.* Springer-Verlag Berlin Heidelberg.

Nabil Hathout. 2008. Acquistion of the morphological structure of the lexicon based on lexical similarity and formal analogy. In *Proceedings of the 3rd Textgraphs workshop on Graph-based Algorithms for Natural Language Processing*, pages 1–8, Manchester, UK. Coling 2008 Organizing Committee.

Nabil Hathout. 2009. Acquisition of morphological families and derivational series from a machine readable dictionary. *CoRR*, abs/0905.1609.

Sepp Hochreiter and Jürgen Schmidhuber. 1997. Long short-term memory. *Neural Computation*, 9(8):1735–1780.

Katharina Kann and Hinrich Schütze. 2016. Med: The LMU system for the SIGMORPHON 2016 Shared Task on morphological reinflection. In *Proceedings of the 2016 Meeting of SIGMORPHON*, Berlin, Germany. Association for Computational Linguistics.

Katharina Kann and Hinrich Schütze. 2017. The LMU system for the CoNLL-SIGMORPHON 2017 Shared Task on universal morphological reinflection. In *Proceedings of the CoNLL SIGMORPHON 2017 Shared Task: Universal Morphological Reinflection*, pages 40–48, Vancouver. Association for Computational Linguistics.

Diederik P. Kingma and Jimmy Ba. 2015. Adam: A method for stochastic optimization. In *Proceedings of the 3rd International Conference for Learning Representations (ICLR-15)*, San Diego.

Christo Kirov, Ryan Cotterell, John Sylak-Glassman, Géraldine Walther, Ekaterina Vylomova, Patrick Xia, Manaal Faruqui, Sebastian Mielke, Arya D. McCarthy, Sandra Kübler, David Yarowsky, Jason Eisner, and Mans Hulden. 2018. UniMorph 2.0: Universal Morphology. In *Proceedings of the Eleventh International Conference on Language Resources and Evaluation (LREC 2018)*, Miyazaki, Japan. European Language Resources Association (ELRA).

Yves Lepage. 2004. Analogy and formal languages. *Electronic notes in theoretical computer science*, 53:180–191.

Thang Luong, Hieu Pham, and Christopher D. Manning. 2015. Effective approaches to attention-based neural machine translation. In *Proceedings of the*

2015 Conference on Empirical Methods in Natural Language Processing, pages 1412–1421, Lisbon, Portugal. Association for Computational Linguistics.

Peter Makarov, Tatiana Ruzsics, and Simon Clematide. 2017. Align and copy: UZH at SIGMORPHON 2017 Shared Task for morphological reinflection. In *Proceedings of the CoNLL SIGMORPHON 2017 Shared Task: Universal Morphological Reinflection*, pages 49–57, Vancouver. Association for Computational Linguistics.

Sylvain Neuvel and Rajendra Singh. 2001. Vive la différence ! what morphology is about. *Folia Linguistica*, 35(3-4):313–320.

Garrett Nicolai, Bradley Hauer, Mohammad Motallebi, Saeed Najafi, and Grzegorz Kondrak. 2017. If you can't beat them, join them: the University of Alberta system description. In *Proceedings of the CoNLL SIGMORPHON 2017 Shared Task: Universal Morphological Reinflection*, pages 79–84, Vancouver. Association for Computational Linguistics.

Tim Salimans and Diederik P Kingma. 2016. Weight normalization: A simple reparameterization to accelerate training of deep neural networks. In D. D. Lee, M. Sugiyama, U. V. Luxburg, I. Guyon, and R. Garnett, editors, *Advances in Neural Information Processing Systems 29*, pages 901–909. Curran Associates, Inc.

Miikka Silfverberg, Adam Wiemerslage, Ling Liu, and Lingshuang Jack Mao. 2017. Data augmentation for morphological reinflection. In *Proceedings of the CoNLL SIGMORPHON 2017 Shared Task: Universal Morphological Reinflection*, pages 90–99, Vancouver. Association for Computational Linguistics.

Rajendra Singh, editor. 2000. *The Yearbook of South Asian Languages and Linguistics-200*. Sage, Thousand Oaks.

Rajendra Singh and Alan Ford. 2000. In praise of Sakatayana: some remarks on whole word morphology. In Rajendra Singh, editor, *The Yearbook of South Asian Languages and Linguistics-200*. Sage, Thousand Oaks.

Nicolas Stroppa and François Yvon. 2005. An analogical learner for morphological analysis. In *Proceedings of the Ninth Conference on Computational Natural Language Learning (CoNLL-2005)*, pages 120–127, Ann Arbor, Michigan. Association for Computational Linguistics.

François Yvon. 2003. Finite-state machines solving analogies on words. Technical report, ENST.

Chunting Zhou and Graham Neubig. 2017. Morphological inflection generation with multi-space variational encoder-decoders. In *Proceedings of the CoNLL SIGMORPHON 2017 Shared Task: Universal Morphological Reinflection*, pages 58–65, Vancouver. Association for Computational Linguistics.

AX Semantics' Submission to the CoNLL-SIGMORPHON 2018 Shared Task

Andreas Madsack, Alessia Cavallo, Johanna Heininger and **Robert Weißgraeber**

AX Semantics, Stuttgart, Germany

`{firstname.lastname}@ax-semantics.com`

Abstract

This paper describes the AX Semantics submission to the SIGMORPHON 2018 shared task on morphological reinflection.

We implemented two systems, both solving the task for all languages in one codebase, without any underlying language specific features. The first one is a classifier, that chooses the best paradigms to inflect the lemma; the second system is a neural sequence model trained to generate a sequence of copy, insert and delete actions. Both provide reasonably strong scores on solving the task in nearly all 103 languages.

1 Introduction

This paper describes our implementation and results for Task 1 of the CoNLL-SIGMORPHON 2018 Shared Task: Universal Morphological Reinflection (Cotterell et al., 2018). The task is to generate inflected word forms given the lemma and a feature specification (Kirov et al., 2018). See Figure 1 for an example in German.

sehen (V;IND;PST;3;PL) → sahen

Figure 1: Task 1 Example, German: putting the verb "sehen" into 3rd person past tense.

Including the surprise languages the task consists of 103 languages. Three differently-sized training sets were made available, namely a low dataset containing only 100 samples, a medium set with 1000, and a high set with 10000 samples. Most of the languages had all three sizes (89 languages), some only low and medium (13 languages), and one language only low.

We tackled the problem with two very different approaches. System 1 is training a classifier to predict an abstract paradigm according to which the inflected form is created and the system 2 is a character-based recurrent neural network.

2 System 1 - Paradigm classification

Our first approach to solve the task is based on the system proposed by Sorokin (2016), which participated in the SIGMORPHON-2016 Shared Task (Cotterell et al., 2016). It realizes the automatic inflection of word forms via the classification of abstract paradigms created through the method of longest common subsequence (LCS).

The idea of abstract paradigms was introduced in Ahlberg et al. (2014) and implies the representation of a lemma and an inflected form as a list of patterns, where common parts of both words are replaced by variables. Given e.g. the lemma *write* and the target form *writing* the abstract paradigm is **1+e#1+ing**. In order to create such a paradigm the LCS of both words has to be determined, which later will be replaced by variables. Such a representation suggests that the LCS is the stem of both words and the symbols not in the LCS characterize the inflection.

Unlike Sorokin (2016) and Ahlberg et al. (2014), who applied a finite state machine to extract the LCS and Ahlberg et al. (2015) who used an SVM classifier, we made use of a sequence alignment function provided by Biopython[1]. With the input parameters *write* and *writing* the method returns the alignment shown in Figure 2, based on which the LCS and later the paradigm can be constructed. Another system searching for best edit pairs is Morfette (Grzegorz Chrupala and van Genabith, 2008), which in contrast to our approach first reverses the strings to find the shortest sequence of insert and delete commands instead of the LCS.

If multiple alignments and hence LCS exist, we rate the options based on a set of rules and thereafter choose the alignment with the minimum score. More specifically, 0.5 points are given for a

---

[1] https://github.com/biopython/biopython

43

Proceedings of the CoNLL–SIGMORPHON 2018 Shared Task: Universal Morphological Reinflection, pages 43–47,
Brussels, Belgium, October 31, 2018. ©2018 Association for Computational Linguistics

```
write__
||||...
writing
```

Figure 2: Formatted output of the pairwise2 function in Biopython for the strings *write* and *writing*

gap (specified by _) in one of both words, 1 point is given for each unequal character in the alignment (specified by .), and an additional amount of 100 is added to the score if the alignment creates following variables in the part of the abstract paradigm representing the lemma. The latter part is especially important as the value of subsequent variables, the common part in both words they stand for, can't be determined unambiguously. This poses a problem when the target form has to be constructed based on the variables in the lemma paradigm. We will discuss this issue in more detail in the last part of this section.

Following the procedure described above we created an abstract paradigm for each lemma and inflected form provided in the maximum available training set (if no high set was available we used the medium or low one respectively) for each language and predicted the corresponding proper test data. Thereupon we could train a classifier to predict the correct abstract paradigm given a lemma and the morphosyntactic description (e.g. N;NOM;PL) of its inflected form. Apart from the morphosyntactic description (MSD), we used 3 prefixes, as well as 5 suffixes of the lemma as input features for the classification. We applied one-hot-encoding on the features, creating a sparse matrix consisting of only 0s and 1s (Table 1) and eliminated all pre- and suffixes that occurred less than three times in the lemmas of the training set. This type of feature selection is the main difference between our system and the one described in Sorokin (2016), which apart from excluding the features seen less than 3 times only kept 10% of all features according to an ambiguity measure.

en	sch	rite	ite	e	..	PST	NOM
1	0	0	0	1	..	1	0
0	0	1	1	0	..	0	1
..	..	..	..	..	..	..	..

Table 1: Abstract illustration of a feature matrix used for the classification

In order to find the best performing classifier we inspected several algorithms available in the sklearn library for Python and conducted a randomized search for the best hyperparameters of each classifier. For 90 out of 103 languages a neural network yielded the best results on the development-set followed by the Decision Tree (8 languages), Support Vector Machines (3 languages), Random Forest (1 language), and Logistic Regression (1 language) algorithm.

After the classification of an abstract paradigm for a lemma and a MSD, the only task left is constructing the inflected form based on the abstract paradigm and the lemma. The basic procedure for the generation is to first identify the value of the variables in the abstract paradigm and then to insert these letter sequences into the abstract pardigm representing the inflected target form. However, as previously indicated, this procedure does not always deliver an unambiguous result. For example for the German lemma *sehen* (*to see*) and the MSD V;IND;PST;3;PL, which would be the target form *sahen* (*they saw*), the classifier should correctly predict the abstract paradigm **1+e+2#1+a+2**. Now there are two fitting value combinations, which would reconstruct the lemma, namely 1=s, 2=hen and 1=seh, 2=n, and hence two possible target forms exist (*sahen* and *sehan*), only one of which is the right target. The depicted example is fairly simple, but more complex samples, especially when the lemma paradigm consists of subsequent variables, could produce an even larger number of possible targets. The fraction of samples that yields more than one combination and the number of combinations if this is the case depends heavily on the language of interest. English e.g. has only one possible target form for 995 out of 1000 test samples and two possibilities for the remaining five, whereas Arabic produces a much more complicated result (1 combination = 5698 times, 2 combinations = 2677 times, 3 combinations = 1205 times, 4 combinations = 267 times, 5 combinations = 43 times, 6 combinations = 1 times).

To address the problem of multiple possible combinations we constructed a set of decision hierarchy based on which one combination is chosen. For each sample in the training set we recorded the value combination that led to the inflected form. A combination was coded as the index of the fitting value of a variable in the list of all possible values sorted by length. Then we could identify the combination that most frequently led

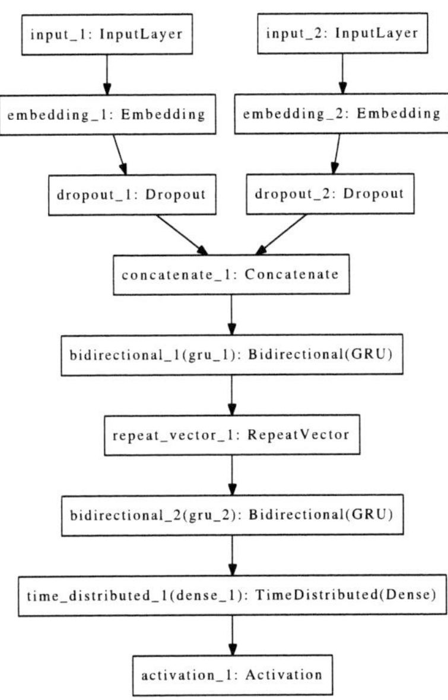

Figure 3: Sequence model for System 2

to the correct target for a specific set of variables with a specific number of possible values for each variable. In the example above we have two variables, $1 = [s, she]$ and $2 = [hen, n]$, with two possible values each. For this specific case we can now look up the index of the values that most often led to a correct target during training and choose the combination which consists of these values for the generation of the inflected form.

3   System 2 - Sequence Neural Model

Our second system is based on the paper by (Makarov et al., 2017) which participated in the SIGMORPHON2017 Shared Task (Cotterell et al., 2017).

We used hamming distance (similar to the baseline code given by the organizers) to align the lemma and the expected result. On this alignment we generated `Copy`, `Delete` and `Insert` operations to transfer the lemma to the inflected form (analogous to Makarov et al. (2017, chaper 4.1)). For each language we trained a different model with a different charmap only consisting of the characters in the given language. This charmap is used for Insert operations. The sequence model is implemented using keras and Tensorflow. See model overview in Figure 3. The character based lemma input and the feature matrix are both en-

coded in their own embeddings. The feature matrix is a list of all possible features in all languages. This list is the same as the one for System 1.

The hyperparameters of the model are a dropout of 0.2, the number of features is 370, lemma input and output lengths are 100, and length of feature sequence is set to 20. The 2 bidirectional GRUs (Chung et al., 2015) have 256 hidden units. The activation function used is softmax as the output is a sequence of `Stop`, `Copy`, `Delete` and `Insert` of a character from the charmap. Every time the full sequence accuracy improved the model is saved. The full sequence accuracy is defined by the fact that all characters in a sequence are correct. The optimizer used is adam (Kingma and Ba, 2014).

4   Results

The performance of the presented systems on the test data is shown in Table 2 and Table 3 (on page 4). It can be seen that the first system yields slightly better results compared to the second system. The paradigm model outperforms the baseline in 77 cases whereas the sequence model beats the baseline in 53 out of 103 languages. Overall, both systems do fairly well compared to the baseline in nearly all languages, whereas when the baseline comes close the difference is only a minor fractions of the accuracy percentages. Regarding the paradigm model it has to be stated that the displayed values are probably lower than the classification accuracy, meaning that in some cases the correct paradigm may have been predicted, but the right target could not be constructed. We can't verify this assumption for the test data, but on the development data we observed that for some languages the classification performance was a lot better than the final accuracy. Irish e.g. had a classification accuracy of nearly 78% for the abstract paradigms, but the final performance amounted only to ca. 68% due to the mistakes made during the target creation. Improving the method of handling multiple possible targets could therefore further enhance the performance of the paradigm model.

Unsurprisingly, languages that provided lower numbers of data size don't perform very well overall.

For comparison of the error intensity of the two systems we calculated the Levenshtein distance between the system results and the expected in-

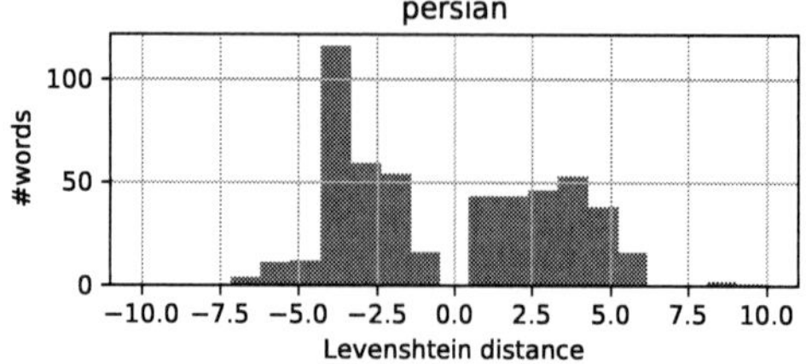

Figure 4: Levenshtein distance histogram for Persian. Errors left for system 1; right for system 2. Distances without error are removed.

language	data size	system 1	system 2	baseline
cornish	medium	2	**32**	12
greenlandic	medium	54	**82**	72
karelian	medium	62	**98**	42
kashubian	medium	**76**	60	68
kazakh	medium	44	**86**	50
khakas	medium	**96**	**96**	84
mapudungun	medium	90	**98**	82
middle-high-german	medium	**84**	52	54
middle-low-german	medium	**76**	30	38
murrinhpatha	medium	**54**	4	0
norman	medium	28	34	**46**
old-irish	medium	8	8	**16**
scottish-gaelic	medium	**70**	50	50
telugu	low	**72**	46	70
tibetan	medium	**44**	42	36
turkmen	medium	**96**	94	68

Table 2: Results for test data compared to baseline (medium and low)

flected forms. Of course if the system has a better accuracy on the task, it makes fewer errors than the other system. This calculation is not very conclusive, but allows for some basic predicates, see Figure 4 for a histogram of error distributions. When both systems are equally strong the sums of the distances are not that divergent. For example for *Persian* the sum of Levenshtein distances for system 1 is 919 and for system 2 it is 804 but for *Georgian* the distance for system 1 is 40 and for system 2 it is 55.

5 Conclusion

Our goal is to improve our morphology system component in our Natural Language Generation SaaS (Weißgraeber and Madsack, 2017). The two systems described herewithin compete against a handcrafted morphology and a reasonable lexicon. The handcrafted morphology and the lexicon is always better on very regular POS types (i.e. German adjectives). So all three systems (the two described in this paper and the handcrafted one) are evaluated for every language and POS type, and can be combined into a best-of-breed selection scheme by preferring the most appropriate system for each POS type and language combination.

language	data size	system 1	system 2	baseline
adyghe	high	99.0	**99.6**	91.6
albanian	high	**88.9**	40.9	79.5
arabic	high	**58.2**	34.0	4.1
armenian	high	**90.3**	73.4	86.6
asturian	high	**95.3**	91.1	95.2
azeri	high	94.0	**100.0**	70.0
bashkir	high	**99.8**	**99.8**	90.7
basque	high	**8.2**	5.4	7.3
belarusian	high	47.3	**52.8**	41.0
bengali	high	**96.0**	78.0	81.0
breton	high	80.0	**85.0**	73.0
bulgarian	high	88.7	75.6	**89.0**
catalan	high	**95.9**	92.1	95.7
classical-syriac	high	**100.0**	99.0	97.0
crimean-tatar	high	**98.0**	**98.0**	95.0
czech	high	89.2	83.0	**90.6**
danish	high	**92.7**	90.4	87.0
dutch	high	85.1	**88.6**	87.7
english	high	95.8	**96.5**	95.9
estonian	high	**87.7**	64.1	78.0
faroese	high	**79.6**	76.8	76.1
finnish	high	77.0	52.0	**78.0**
french	high	**85.3**	79.6	83.0
friulian	high	97.0	**99.0**	96.0
galician	high	**96.7**	95.0	95.1
georgian	high	95.1	**95.4**	93.9
german	high	**82.3**	**82.3**	81.1
greek	high	78.2	54.8	**78.3**
haida	high	93.0	**100.0**	66.0
hebrew	high	**84.3**	54.5	53.7
hindi	high	**100.0**	80.0	93.0
hungarian	high	76.9	**80.9**	68.8
icelandic	high	**80.9**	79.3	76.9
ingrian	high	44.0	**80.0**	46.0
irish	high	**67.2**	34.1	53.0
italian	high	**94.2**	63.7	77.5
kabardian	high	**99.0**	**99.0**	86.0
kannada	high	90.0	**97.0**	66.0
khaling	high	**72.0**	17.1	53.7
kurmanji	high	92.6	87.8	**92.9**
ladin	high	**93.0**	87.0	92.0
latin	high	46.2	37.2	**47.6**
latvian	high	**93.2**	90.2	92.8
lithuanian	high	**70.6**	52.0	64.2
livonian	high	**82.0**	76.0	67.0
lower-sorbian	high	94.2	**95.5**	88.1
macedonian	high	92.7	**94.2**	91.2
maltese	high	**63.0**	28.0	16.0
middle-french	high	**97.0**	95.4	95.1
navajo	high	**43.6**	6.8	0.0
neapolitan	high	94.0	**95.0**	**95.0**
northern-sami	high	61.7	**75.5**	62.3
north-frisian	high	**80.0**	33.0	37.0
norwegian-bokmaal	high	90.8	87.2	**91.0**
norwegian-nynorsk	high	82.8	**88.0**	74.8
occitan	high	94.0	92.0	**96.0**
old-armenian	high	**84.9**	82.2	79.2
old-church-slavonic	high	**92.0**	88.0	80.0
old-english	high	**69.3**	34.3	40.9
old-french	high	80.8	**82.0**	80.7
old-saxon	high	**87.3**	54.0	60.1
pashto	high	**92.0**	78.0	72.0
persian	high	63.7	62.6	**80.7**
polish	high	**87.6**	82.9	87.1
portuguese	high	**97.3**	94.6	96.7
quechua	high	**99.8**	98.8	95.1
romanian	high	**82.6**	62.4	79.8
russian	high	**88.0**	76.1	86.5
sanskrit	high	92.8	**93.7**	80.6
serbo-croatian	high	**87.4**	69.1	83.0
slovak	high	**91.5**	91.1	83.1
slovene	high	7.0	**90.9**	79.7
sorani	high	**76.0**	27.6	63.6
spanish	high	**94.4**	81.3	92.4
swahili	high	**98.0**	1.0	0.0
swedish	high	88.0	**88.5**	84.7
tatar	high	**99.0**	97.0	95.0
turkish	high	87.9	**95.9**	73.2
ukrainian	high	**93.1**	87.2	86.3
urdu	high	**99.3**	83.7	95.9
uzbek	high	**100.0**	99.0	96.0
venetian	high	**98.5**	97.6	93.0
votic	high	37.0	**66.0**	34.0
welsh	high	82.0	**88.0**	72.0
west-frisian	high	**82.0**	67.0	67.0
yiddish	high	97.0	**99.0**	94.0
zulu	high	**93.8**	2.5	0.2

Table 3: Results for test data compared to baseline (high)

Of course, all three systems have pros and cons. The handcrafted one fails on completely new words (or even rare words), that are not regularly inflected. The paradigm system is in some languages better compared to the sequence model and the errors of the paradigm system are not that disturbing, since they are usually more plausible, whereas the sequence model tends to make more arbitrary errors.

On error the sequence model may return for example something like this: *gerksent* for *murksen* `V.PTCP;PST` (German, correct form: *gemurkst*). An examplary major error for the paradigm system would be *kiefen* for *kaufen* `V;PST;3;PL` (correct form: *kauften*), where a native speaker can see the relation to the inflection of *laufen*, where the past form is *liefen*. This kind of errors are greatly reduced by training with *a lot* more data.

In the future we will try to improve especially the sequence model for the languages we use on our platform.

References

Malin Ahlberg, Markus Forsberg, and Mans Hulden. 2014. Semi-supervised learning of morphological paradigms and lexicons. In *Proceedings of the 14th Conference of the European Chapter of the Association for Computational Linguistics*, pages 569–578. Association for Computational Linguistics.

Malin Ahlberg, Markus Forsberg, and Mans Hulden. 2015. Paradigm classification in supervised learning of morphology. In *Proceedings of the 2015 Conference of the North American Chapter of the Association for Computational Linguistics: Human Language Technologies*, pages 1024–1029, Denver, Colorado. Association for Computational Linguistics.

Junyoung Chung, Çaglar Gülçehre, KyungHyun Cho, and Yoshua Bengio. 2015. Gated feedback recurrent neural networks. *CoRR*, abs/1502.02367.

Ryan Cotterell, Christo Kirov, John Sylak-Glassman, Géraldine Walther, Ekaterina Vylomova, Arya D. McCarthy, Katharina Kann, Sebastian Mielke, Garrett Nicolai, Miikka Silfverberg, David Yarowsky, Jason Eisner, and Mans Hulden. 2018. The CoNLL–SIGMORPHON 2018 shared task: Universal morphological reinflection. In *Proceedings of the CoNLL–SIGMORPHON 2018 Shared Task: Universal Morphological Reinflection*, Brussels, Belgium. Association for Computational Linguistics.

Ryan Cotterell, Christo Kirov, John Sylak-Glassman, Géraldine Walther, Ekaterina Vylomova, Patrick Xia, Manaal Faruqui, Sandra Kübler, David Yarowsky, Jason Eisner, and Mans Hulden. 2017. The CoNLL-SIGMORPHON 2017 shared task: Universal morphological reinflection in 52 languages. In *Proceedings of the CoNLL-SIGMORPHON 2017 Shared Task: Universal Morphological Reinflection*, Vancouver, Canada. Association for Computational Linguistics.

Ryan Cotterell, Christo Kirov, John Sylak-Glassman, David Yarowsky, Jason Eisner, and Mans Hulden. 2016. The SIGMORPHON 2016 shared task—morphological reinflection. In *Proceedings of the 2016 Meeting of SIGMORPHON*, Berlin, Germany. Association for Computational Linguistics.

GD Grzegorz Chrupala and J van Genabith. 2008. Learning morphology with morfette. In *Proceedings of LREC*, volume 8.

Diederik P. Kingma and Jimmy Ba. 2014. Adam: A method for stochastic optimization. *CoRR*, abs/1412.6980.

Christo Kirov, Ryan Cotterell, John Sylak-Glassman, Graldine Walther, Ekaterina Vylomova, Patrick Xia, Manaal Faruqui, Sebastian Mielke, Arya D. McCarthy, Sandra Kbler, David Yarowsky, Jason Eisner, and Mans Hulden. 2018. UniMorph 2.0: Universal Morphology. In *Proceedings of the Eleventh International Conference on Language Resources and Evaluation (LREC 2018)*, Miyazaki, Japan. European Language Resources Association (ELRA).

Peter Makarov, Tatiana Ruzsics, and Simon Clematide. 2017. Align and copy: Uzh at sigmorphon 2017 shared task for morphological reinflection. In *Proceedings of the CoNLL SIGMORPHON 2017 Shared Task: Universal Morphological Reinflection*, pages 49–57. Association for Computational Linguistics.

Alexey Sorokin. 2016. Using longest common subsequence and character models to predict word forms. In *Proceedings of the 14th SIGMORPHON Workshop on Computational Research in Phonetics, Phonology, and Morphology*, pages 54–61. Association for Computational Linguistics.

Robert Weißgraeber and Andreas Madsack. 2017. A working, non-trivial, topically indifferent nlg system for 17 languages. In *Proceedings of the 10th International Conference on Natural Language Generation*, pages 156–157. Association for Computational Linguistics.

Experiments on Morphological Reinflection: CoNLL 2018 Shared Task

Rishabh Jain
IIT (BHU), Varanasi, India
rishabh.j.017@gmail.com

Anil Kumar Singh
IIT (BHU), Varanasi, India
nlprnd@gmail.com

Abstract

We present a system for the task of morphological inflection, i.e., finding a target morphological form, given a lemma and a set of target tags. System is trained on datasets of three sizes: low, medium and high. The system uses a simple Long Short-Term Memory (LSTM) based encoder-decoder based model. The performance for low size dataset is poor in general while it improves significantly for medium and high sized training dataset. The average performance over all languages is poor as compared to baseline for low dataset, it is comparable for medium dataset, and significantly more for high dataset.

1 Introduction

The CoNLL-SIGMOPRHON 2018 shared task consists of two subtasks out of which we participate only in the first subtask, which involves generating a target inflected form from a given lemma with its morphosyntactic descriptions (MSDs) provided as a set of features. For instance, the word thinking is the present continuous inflected form of the lemma think. The models were trained on three differently-sized datasets. The low-sized datasets had around 100 training samples, the medium-sized datasets had around 1000 training samples and the high-sized datasets had around 10000 samples for most languages. Datasets were provided for a total of 103 languages including surprise data.

2 Background

Prior to neural network based approaches to morphological reinflection, most systems used a 3-step approach to solve the problem:
1) String alignment between the lemma and the target (morphologically transformed form),
2) Rule extraction from spans of the aligned strings and
3) Rule application to previously unseen lemmas to transform them.
(Durrett and DeNero, 2013) and (Ahlberg et al., 2014, 2015) used the above approaches, with each of them using different string alignment algorithms and different models to extract rules from these alignment tables. However, in these kinds of systems, the types of rules to be generated must be specified, which should also be engineered to take into account language-specific transformational behaviour.

(Faruqui et al., 2016) proposed a neural network based system which abstracts away the above steps by modeling the problem as one of generating a character sequence, character-by-character. (Kann and Schütze, 2016) proposed a highly competetive implementation in previous year tasks (Cotterell et al., 2016, 2017).

Akin to machine translation systems, this system uses an encoder-decoder LSTM model as proposed by (Hochreiter and Schmidhuber, 1997). The encoder is a bidirectional LSTM, while the decoder LSTM feeds into a softmax layer for every character position in the target string. Decoder predicts the output sequence character by character using feedback until stop is predicted. This model takes into account the fact that the target and the root word are similar, except for the parts that have been changed due to inflection, by feeding the root word directly to the decoder as well. A separate neural net is trained for every language.

3 System Description

We have modelled our system based on the system proposed by (Faruqui et al., 2016), as described in the previous section. However we have made some modifications to the above system, to account for the three different sizes of datasets and to

Proceedings of the CoNLL–SIGMORPHON 2018 Shared Task: Universal Morphological Reinflection, pages 48–57,
Brussels, Belgium, October 31, 2018. ©2018 Association for Computational Linguistics

account for the behaviour of morphological transformations of independent languages.

In the model, some structural and hyperparameter features remain the same. The characters in the root word and morphological features of the tatrget word are represented using one hot vectors. The major change in our model is the size of LSTM layers which is kept variable (depending on vocabulary size) as opposed to fixed as in system proposed by (Faruqui et al., 2016) based on assumption that bigger vocabulary would require bigger layers to extract features and system is trained for more epochs.

The embedding size for each language is different depending upon the alphabet set of that language available in the given dataset and similarly for morphological tags which are split into individual components. We use a bidirectional encoder to which we feed the input word embeddings. The output of the encoder, concatenated with the root word embedding and morphological features, feeds into the decoder. All recurrent units have variable hidden layer dimensions depending upon the embedding size of root word and morphological features. Over the decoder layer is a softmax layer that is used to predict the character that must occur at each character position of the target word. In order to maintain a constant word length, we use paddings of 0 characters. All models use categorical cross-entropy as the loss function and the RMSProp optimizer for optimization.

The model was trained for 100 epochs for each size. Keras API (Chollet et al., 2015) was used for writing neural networks. For low dataset, batch size of 10 was used, for medium 100, and for high 250/500 depending of hardware limitations.

Submission

Following are tables showing top 5 accuracies obtained by our system on test data as opposed to baseline model.

3.1 Low-sized Dataset

Language	Baseline	Enc-Dec
Telugu	70	94
Uzbek	52	82
Karelian	24	80
Mapudungun	64	74
Kazakh	26	68

Table 1: Top 5 Accuracies for languages for low data

3.2 Medium-sized Dataset

Language	Baseline	Enc-Dec
Uzbek	96	100
Classical-syriac	99	99
Crimean-tatar	78	98
Khakas	84	98
Mapudungun	82	98

Table 2: Top 5 Accuracies for languages for medium data

3.3 High-sized Dataset

Language	Baseline	Enc-Dec
Classical-syriac	97	100
Crimean-tatar	95	100
Haida	66	100
Swahili	N/A	100
Kannada	66	100

Table 3: Top 5 Accuracies for languages for high data

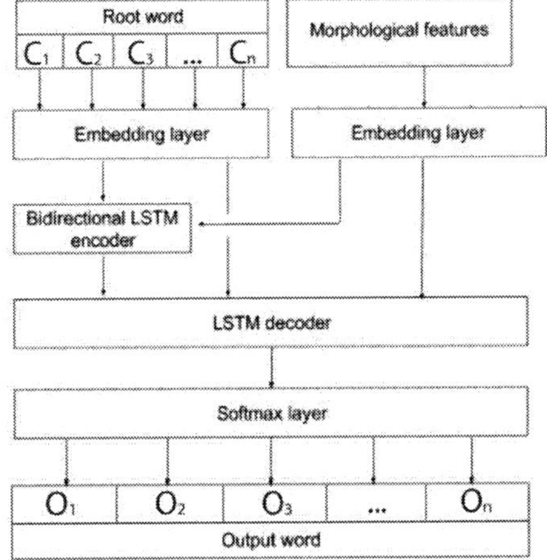

Figure 1: C1, .., Cn represent characters of the root word while O1, ..,On represent characters of the output word.

4 Evaluation

4.1 Results on Test Set

The evaluation results were obtained using the evaluation script and the test set provided by the shared task organizers.

The best five baseline accuracies, accuracies for the first submission and accuracies for the second submission can be found in Table 1, Table 2 and Table 3 for each of the three dataset sizes: low, medium and high respectively.

The complete set of accuracies and Levenshtein distances for all languages have been included in Appendix (tables 4 to 6).

4.2 Observations

We performed some experiments, where the choice of hyperparameters was guided by intuitions developed from analysis of the dataset and results obtained on smaller subsets of the data. We have presented some key observations from our analysis in the ensuing sub-sections.

4.2.1 Number of layers

We observed that increasing number of layers does not result in significant increase in performance, even reduced performance in some cases whereas increased computation time significantly. So instead of adding more layers, adding more complexity and features in current layer is bound to improve performance.

4.2.2 Embedding of Morphological features

Multiple types of embedding to represent morphological features was tried some of which were: binary vectors, one hot vectors, integer vectors. One hot vectors resulted in best performance for our model.

4.2.3 Size of encoder layer

Increasing size of encoder after certain multiple of total embedding size ($\sim$5) results in saturation of performance.

4.2.4 Hyperparameter Optimization

Various hyperparameters need to be optimized such as batch-size, dropout rate, number of epochs etc. which may be different for each language, to obtain optimal performance.

5 Conclusions

There are two main conclusions. One is that different configurations of deep neural networks work well for different languages. The second is that deep learning may not be the right approach for low-sized data or some other pre-processing and post-processing may need to be done to increase performance. Data augmentation is one alternative to deal with low resource languages.

Results for low-size were poor for almost all languages. So, deep learning cannot extract features adequately from low resources without data augmentation. It is to be noted that we used purely deep learning. If deep learning is augmented with other transduction, rule-based or knowledge-based methods, the results for low-size could perhaps be improved.

Very high accuracies ($>$95%) are observed for some languages in high sized datasets, neural networks is probably the best choice for processing such languages.

References

Malin Ahlberg, Markus Forsberg, and Mans Hulden. 2014. Semi-supervised learning of morphological paradigms and lexicons. In *Proceedings of the 14th Conference of the European Chapter of the Association for Computational Linguistics: Language Technology (Computational Linguistics)*, pages 569–578.

Malin Ahlberg, Markus Forsberg, and Mans Hulden. 2015. Paradigm classification in supervised learning of morphology. In *Proceedings of the 2015 Conference of the North American Chapter of the Association for Computational Linguistics: Human Language Technologies*, pages 1024–1029.

François Chollet et al. 2015. Keras. `https://keras.io`.

Ryan Cotterell, Christo Kirov, John Walther, Sylak-Glassman Géraldine, Ekaterina Vylomova, Patrick Xia, Manaal Faruqui, Sandra Kübler, David Yarowsky, Jason Eisner, and Mans Hulden. 2017. The conllsigmorphon 2017 shared task: Universal morphological reinflection in 52 languages. In *Proceedings of the CoNLL-SIGMORPHON 2017 Shared Task: Universal Morphological Reinflection*.

Ryan Cotterell, Christo Kirov, John Walther, Sylak-Glassman Géraldine, Ekaterina Vylomova, Patrick Xia, Manaal Faruqui, David Yarowsky, Jason Eisner, and Mans Hulden. 2016. The sigmorphon 2016 shared taskmorphological reinflection. In *Proceedings of the 14th SIGMORPHON Workshop on Computational Research in Phonetics, Phonology, and Morphology*. ACL.

Greg Durrett and John DeNero. 2013. Supervised learning of complete morphological paradigms. In *Proceedings of the 2013 Conference of the North American Chapter of the Association for Computational Linguistics: Human Language Technologies*, pages 1185–1195.

Manaal Faruqui, Yulia Tsvetkov, Graham Neubig, and Chris Dyer. 2016. Morphological inflection generation using character sequence to sequence learning. In *Proceedings of NAACL*.

Sepp Hochreiter and Jürgen Schmidhuber. 1997. Long short-term memory. *Neural Comput.*, 9(8):1735–1780.

Katharina Kann and Hinrich Schütze. 2016. Med: The lmu system for the sigmorphon 2016 shared task on morphological reinflection. In *Proceedings of the 14th SIGMORPHON Workshop on Computational Research in Phonetics, Phonology, and Morphology*, pages 62–70.

A Appendix

In Tables 4 to 6 (on this page and the next), BA stands for baseline accuracy, L.D. for Levenshtein Distance, Acc for Accuracy, dev for development data.

Table 4: Results for all languages for low data.

languages	BA	Acc - dev	Avg. L.D. -dev	Acc -test
adyghe	59	56.9	0.908	57.8
albanian	22.3	0.9	6.736	0.8
arabic	25.6	0.5	5.489	0
armenian	37	5	4.575	5.8
asturian	58.6	24	1.882	23.9
azeri	24	22	2.3	28
bashkir	39.4	37.5	1.468	35.8
basque	0.1	1	4.949	0.5
belarusian	6.8	4.9	4.062	2.9
bengali	50	22	2.43	26
breton	20	36	1.49	30
bulgarian	30.7	9.3	3.162	9.7
catalan	60.8	20.7	1.867	25.7
classical-syriac	94	63	0.54	62
cornish	10	28	1.9	32
crimean-tatar	56	48	0.81	51
czech	38.5	7.3	3.294	8.1
danish	58.3	42.1	1.159	40.9
estonian	21.5	2.3	4.851	2.6
faroese	34.4	10.5	2.915	9.6
finnish	17.3	0.4	7.573	0.6
friulian	70	38	1.37	39
galician	53	17.3	2.349	15.3
georgian	70.6	23.1	2.087	23.8
greek	25.3	2.8	4.75	2.4
greenlandic	50	54	0.72	60
haida	29	20	4.66	12
hebrew	24.4	4.8	2.556	5.2
hindi	31.8	23.5	2.603	23.2
hungarian	17.4	4.3	3.166	4.7
icelandic	35.6	8	2.647	8.5
ingrian	20	18	2.14	24
irish	30.3	1.6	7.413	1.3
italian	40.5	10.7	3.916	11
kabardian	72	54	1.13	56
karelian	24	60	0.58	80
kashubian	60	46	0.9	46
kazakh	26	78	0.3	68
khakas	26	72	0.44	62
khaling	3.1	2.7	3.872	2.2
kurmanji	82.7	25.6	1.927	25.4
ladin	58	32	1.41	33
latin	16	0.5	4.697	1
latvian	52.2	8.1	2.757	9
lithuanian	23.3	2.5	3.789	2.8

livonian	28	6	3.51	6
lower-sorbian	32.1	7.1	2.705	9.9
macedonian	49.8	16.1	1.884	16.7
maltese	9	4	2.73	8
mapudungun	64	82	0.3	74
middle-french	76.9	33.3	1.728	32.8
middle-high-german	38	60	0.86	56
murrinhpatha	2	26	1.98	28
navajo	0	0.6	5.847	0.9
neapolitan	79	46	1.27	45
norman	30	62	0.9	52
northern-sami	16.4	2.2	4.433	1.5
norwegian-bokmaal	67.8	43.7	1.012	40.8
norwegian-nynorsk	48.9	22.4	1.749	22
occitan	72	43	1.5	31
old-armenian	31	2	3.7	1.9
old-church-slavonic	39	24	1.95	21
old-french	32.5	6	3.315	7
old-irish	8	4	3.68	2
old-saxon	22.8	3.7	3.016	5.6
pashto	35	7	2.64	11
persian	26.3	6.4	4.253	6.3
portuguese	62.6	20	1.981	19.9
quechua	15.9	15.9	3.963	15
romanian	44.8	4.3	4.352	4.6
sanskrit	33.7	6	3.339	6.7
scottish-gaelic	46	38	2.02	48
serbo-croatian	21.7	3.9	4.542	4.1
slovak	37.7	9.8	2.241	9.6
slovene	32.3	12.2	2.064	0.4
sorani	19.3	2.5	4.466	1.3
spanish	61.8	12.2	3.076	13
swahili	0	6	3.06	4
swedish	51.1	33.2	1.383	32.8
tatar	52	40	1.07	44
telugu	70	100	0	94
tibetan	34	36	1.2	36
turkish	13.2	9.4	4.398	10.7
turkmen	34	62	0.68	64
ukrainian	38.7	8.6	2.485	9
urdu	32.7	30.9	2.203	32.6
uzbek	52	83	0.36	82
venetian	71.8	29	1.457	31.1
votic	17	20	1.92	20
welsh	30	9	3.04	11
west-frisian	50	22	2.14	26
yiddish	78	29	2.15	33
zulu	0.1	1.3	5.114	1.1
dutch	50.8	9	2.665	8.9
english	77.6	58.9	0.78	61.8
french	59	11.6	2.772	13.4

german	49.2	19.6	1.991	19.9
kannada	33	17	3.65	29
middle-low-german	18	24	2.5	14
north-frisian	31	14	3.65	18
old-english	17.6	7.1	2.879	8.6
polish	40.4	4.5	3.403	4.7
russian	43.4	6.5	3.398	7.5

Table 5: Results for all languages for medium data.

languages	BA	Acc - dev	Avg. L.D. -dev	Acc -test
adyghe	84.8	94.2	0.11	92.9
albanian	61.8	39.2	1.901	39.2
arabic	39.5	39.4	2.108	1.6
armenian	70.4	62.8	1.085	67.4
asturian	89.1	87.9	0.26	90
azeri	50	89	0.35	94
bashkir	72.6	94.3	0.118	95.4
basque	1.9	66.7	0.83	69.2
belarusian	21.5	45.9	1.997	45.8
bengali	76	94	0.17	97
breton	67	86	0.37	94
bulgarian	70.8	36.6	1.524	35
catalan	85.6	83.2	0.391	83.8
classical-syriac	99	97	0.03	99
cornish	12	64	0.58	66
crimean-tatar	78	94	0.06	98
czech	79.9	61	1.07	61.1
danish	77.8	76.3	0.478	75.7
estonian	62.9	49.8	1.442	46.5
faroese	65.2	47.1	1.159	48.9
finnish	44.1	19.8	3.105	22
friulian	92	92	0.15	92
galician	82.8	81.3	0.385	82.5
georgian	92.1	87.8	0.348	91.2
greek	59.3	33.8	2.15	29.9
greenlandic	72	66	0.54	84
haida	61	93	0.16	90
hebrew	38.1	61.9	0.714	64.7
hindi	86.5	88.2	0.315	87.7
hungarian	44.4	56.7	0.89	57.1
icelandic	58.9	47	1.101	45.7
ingrian	46	84	0.4	88
irish	44	20.7	3.73	18.8
italian	72.5	67.1	0.948	68.9
kabardian	83	99	0.01	97
karelian	42	96	0.08	96
kashubian	68	80	0.22	84
kazakh	50	62	0.46	50

khakas	84	94	0.1	98
khaling	17.9	60.6	0.956	59.4
kurmanji	85.2	85.4	0.401	86.1
ladin	86	91	0.15	91
latin	37.6	28.3	1.56	31.3
latvian	85.5	73.7	0.591	73.7
lithuanian	52.2	44.9	1.216	46.8
livonian	51	60	0.84	62
lower-sorbian	68.9	65.7	0.644	69.8
macedonian	82.6	77.6	0.408	75.1
maltese	20	90	0.17	85
mapudungun	82	100	0	98
middle-french	90.3	91.2	0.242	89.4
middle-high-german	54	98	0.08	92
murrinhpatha	0	96	0.08	96
navajo	0	16.4	3.227	19.5
neapolitan	94	98	0.02	98
norman	46	20	2.18	26
northern-sami	34.8	41.6	1.554	39.4
norwegian-bokmaal	80.7	80.5	0.321	81.5
norwegian nynorsk	61.1	56	0.746	57.5
occitan	92	94	0.15	93
old-armenian	67.3	53.7	1.168	57.3
old-church-slavonic	76	83	0.32	87
old-french	63.1	61.5	0.989	60.6
old-irish	16	30	1.7	24
old-saxon	39	63.2	0.715	64.7
pashto	69	70	0.68	73
persian	65.7	70.1	0.899	70.9
portuguese	92.4	33.5	1.858	37.3
quechua	70.9	76.7	0.693	77.3
romanian	69.4	48	1.752	48.5
sanskrit	59.7	65.9	0.645	68.8
scottish-gaelic	50	80	0.5	86
serbo-croatian	68.2	39.1	1.866	43.4
slovak	71.1	58	0.76	58.7
slovene	72.3	68	0.575	9.9
sorani	51.7	52.4	1.22	55.9
spanish	86.3	76.6	0.744	75.7
swahili	0	87	0.36	87
swedish	76.5	32	1.572	31.4
tatar	89	93	0.07	96
tibetan	36	30	1.42	22
turkish	32.8	78.9	0.661	79.2
turkmen	68	92	0.16	96
ukrainian	74.1	44.6	1.041	46.6
urdu	87.6	88.7	0.306	87.5
uzbek	96	100	0	100
venetian	89.1	92.3	0.116	91.9
votic	34	81	0.32	78
welsh	58	85	0.32	81

west-frisian	65	95	0.12	94
yiddish	87	83	0.47	88
zulu	0.1	57	1.387	52.6
dutch	72.4	69.4	0.644	71
english	90.5	90.1	0.205	90.9
french	73.2	68.2	0.881	69.3
german	71.7	69.7	0.827	65.5
kannada	55	92	0.21	85
middle-low-german	38	94	0.06	92
north-frisian	33	85	0.36	85
old-english	27.8	41.4	1.3	42.4
polish	73.5	56.9	1.151	55.1
russian	76.4	60.7	1.212	59.9

Table 6: Results for all languages for high data.

languages	BA	Acc - dev	Avg. L.D. -dev	Acc -test
adyghe	91.6	99.6	0.008	99.8
albanian	79.5	97.5	0.044	96.5
arabic	47.1	84.5	0.538	2.9
armenian	86.6	94.4	0.133	93.7
asturian	95.2	98.3	0.037	98.5
azeri	70	99	0.01	99
bashkir	90.7	99.8	0.003	99.7
basque	7.3	98.4	0.033	98
belarusian	41	88.4	0.235	88.4
bengali	81	98	0.05	99
breton	73	89	0.24	93
bulgarian	89	93.9	0.115	94.5
catalan	95.7	97.6	0.062	98
classical-syriac	97	100	0	100
crimean-tatar	95	100	0	100
czech	90.6	88.4	0.26	88
danish	87	91.2	0.158	91.3
estonian	78	97.2	0.075	95.9
faroese	76.1	80	0.437	81.1
finnish	78	76	0.603	76.4
friulian	96	100	0	99
galician	95.1	98.7	0.02	98.7
georgian	93.9	97.7	0.058	97.3
greek	78.3	82.6	0.407	80.8
haida	66	100	0	100
hebrew	53.7	97	0.063	97.3
hindi	93	99.6	0.006	99.4
hungarian	68.8	82.7	0.392	82.3
icelandic	76.9	86.5	0.297	83.9
irish	53	68.9	1.062	67.2
italian	77.5	95.5	0.106	95.7
kabardian	86	100	0	99

khaling	53.7	99.3	0.016	98.4
kurmanji	92.9	92.1	0.127	93.5
ladin	92	98	0.07	98
latin	47.6	59.6	0.652	61.5
latvian	92.8	92.8	0.162	92.8
lithuanian	64.2	86.7	0.234	88.1
livonian	67	92	0.2	97
lower-sorbian	88.1	95.9	0.078	94.3
macedonian	91.2	96.1	0.111	94.6
maltese	16	80	0.37	69
middle-french	95.1	98.6	0.038	96.7
navajo	0	79.9	0.603	75.3
neapolitan	95	98	0.02	97
northern-sami	62.3	94	0.145	92.6
norwegian-bokmaal	91	90.1	0.159	89
norwegian-nynorsk	74.8	83.6	0.295	82.6
occitan	96	100	0	99
old-armenian	79.2	84.1	0.381	87.3
old-church-slavonic	80	94	0.11	97
old-french	80.7	83.8	0.431	86.5
old-saxon	60.1	97.1	0.055	96.3
pashto	72	100	0	100
persian	80.7	98.5	0.028	98.9
portuguese	96.7	97.7	0.06	98.5
quechua	95.1	99.4	0.009	99.4
romanian	79.8	80.8	0.742	79
sanskrit	80.6	92.4	0.151	92.1
serbo-croatian	83	83.4	0.439	84.1
slovak	83.1	91.3	0.164	92.8
slovene	84.9	94.5	0.113	34.6
sorani	63.6	88.4	0.206	89
spanish	92.4	93.2	0.166	93.4
swahili	0	87	0.36	100
swedish	84.7	85.2	0.325	87.2
tatar	95	100	0	99
turkish	73.2	97.4	0.088	97.3
ukrainian	86.3	91.1	0.151	92.5
urdu	95.9	99.7	0.004	99.7
uzbek	96	99.3	0.012	98
venetian	93	95	0.14	99.1
votic	34	68	0.58	66
welsh	72	96	0.08	94
west-frisian	67	80	0.43	74
yiddish	94	98	0.08	99
zulu	0.2	97.8	0.055	97.2
dutch	87.7	94.8	0.102	93.1
english	95.9	94.7	0.133	95.8
french	83	80	0.514	81.1
german	81.1	85.8	0.395	83.7
kannada	66	99	0.01	100
north-frisian	37	93	0.15	96

old-english	40.9	84.9	0.307	83.4
polish	87.1	85.5	0.379	82.8
russian	86.5	84.4	0.509	85.4

The NYU System for the CoNLL–SIGMORPHON 2018 Shared Task on Universal Morphological Reinflection

Katharina Kann[1]
kann@nyu.edu

Stanislas Lauly[1]
stanislas.lauly@nyu.edu

Kyunghyun Cho[1,2]
kyunghyun.cho@nyu.edu

[1]Center for Data Science
New York University
New York, USA

[2]Dept. of Computer Science
New York University
New York, USA

Abstract

This paper describes the NYU submission to the CoNLL–SIGMORPHON 2018 shared task on universal morphological reinflection. Our system participates in the low-resource setting of Task 2, track 2, i.e., it predicts morphologically inflected forms in context: given a lemma and a context sentence, it produces a form of the lemma which might be used at an indicated position in the sentence. It is based on the standard attention-based LSTM encoder-decoder model, but makes use of multiple encoders to process all parts of the context as well as the lemma. In the official shared task evaluation, our system obtains the second best results out of 5 submissions for the competition it entered and strongly outperforms the official baseline.

1 Introduction

The extreme type sparsity in text in a morphologically rich language, i.e., a language which relies strongly on changes in the surface form of words to express properties like gender, tense or number, requires natural language processing (NLP) systems which are able to handle inflected words in a systematic way. The SIGMOR-PHON and CoNLL–SIGMORPHON shared tasks on morphological reinflection, which have been held since 2016 (Cotterell et al., 2016, 2017a), encourage the development of computational models for inflection in a large number of languages.

This year's edition (Cotterell et al., 2018) features two different tasks. The datasets for Task 1 consist of triplets of lemma, morphological tag (also called the "target tag") and the corresponding inflected form, which is given for training and should be produced at test time. This is the standard inflection setup which has also been subject of the shared tasks in the last years. Task 2, in contrast, is again split into two different subtasks (called "tracks"). Both are focused on inflection in

context. Here, a sentence is given, in the context of which the inflected form of which only the lemma is known should be used. The setup of the first subtask assumes that the lemmas and tags of all surrounding words are available and can be used for predicting. These might be used as desired, e.g., the tags of the previous and next words are often strong indicators for the tag of the form to be produced, which is unknown. Track 2, on the other hand, requires systems to produce inflected forms only from their lemma and the inflected context words; no tags or lemmas are given for the context. Thus, track 2 is both a more realistic and a harder version of track 1. All tasks and tracks feature 3 different settings: a low-resource setting (LOW), a medium-resource setting (MEDIUM) and a high-resource setting (HIGH).

In this paper, we describe the New York University (NYU) submission to the CoNLL–SIGMORPHON 2018 shared task on universal morphological reinflection. The system we submitted was exclusively designed for Task 2, track 2, LOW. Thus, we only focus on this particular competition and do not report numbers for other setups (though, in theory, every system which works for track 2 of Task 2 can also produce output for track 1; the same holds true for LOW/MEDIUM/HIGH). Overall, our system obtains the second highest test accuracy out of 5 submitted systems and outperforms the official shared task baseline by a wide margin.

2 Morphological Inflection in Context

The system presented in this paper is designed for morphological inflection in context, i.e., predicting an inflected form which fits an indicated position in a sentence, given its lemma. Here, we will describe the task in a more formal way.

Let $\mathcal{T}$ be the set of morphological tags being

Proceedings of the CoNLL–SIGMORPHON 2018 Shared Task: Universal Morphological Reinflection, pages 58–63,
Brussels, Belgium, October 31, 2018. ©2018 Association for Computational Linguistics

expressed in a language and w a lemma in the same language. We then define the morphological paradigm π of w as follows:

$$\pi(w) = \left\{ \left(f_k[w], t_k \right) \right\}_{k \in \mathcal{T}(w)} \qquad (1)$$

Here, $f_k[w]$ denotes the inflected form which corresponds to tag t_k, and both w and $f_k[w]$ are strings consisting of letters from an alphabet Σ. Note that, even though we follow the convention to describe word forms as functions of the lemma, in the huge majority of the cases, each inflected form is uniquely defined given any other word form of the same paradigm together with its morphological tag.

The task of *morphological inflection* consists of predicting a target form $f_i[w]$ from a paradigm, given the lemma w, as well as the tag t_i of the target form.

Building on this, the task of *morphological inflection in context* consists of predicting a target form $f_i[w]$ from the lemma w, as well as the context c, i.e., the sentence surrounding the target form. For the track of the shared task we are interested in, the context consists of inflected forms. Further, this task is ambiguous: for many languages, usually several morphological tags and, thus, inflected forms are acceptable for any given context.

3 Model Description

Our model is based on the standard LSTM encoder-decoder model with an attention mechanism (Bahdanau et al., 2015). Following several previous approaches (cf. Section 5), we apply it at the character level, i.e., the input to the system is the character sequence of the input lemma, represented by embeddings. The output is the (predicted) character sequence of the inflected form.

Additionally, we include the sentence context as follows: Given a sentence $s = [w_1, w_2, \ldots, w_{i-1}, l, w_{i+1}, \ldots, w_n]$, where l is the lemma of the inflected form of interest, and $w_1, \ldots, w_n$ with $n \neq i$ are the surrounding context words, we split the past context $c_{prev} = [w_1, w_2, \ldots, w_{i-1}]$ and the future context $c_{fut} = [w_{i+1}, \ldots, w_n]$ into subword units using byte pair encoding (BPE, Sennrich et al. (2016)). We then use two additional encoders to encode the sequences of subword units of both contexts.

Using bidirectional encoders, the final hidden states produced by each encoder are concatena-

tions of the respective forward and backward hidden states:

$$h_i = [\overrightarrow{h_i}, \overleftarrow{h_i}] \qquad (2)$$

with

$$\overrightarrow{h_i} = \text{LSTM}(emb_1, \ldots, emb_i), \text{and} \qquad (3)$$
$$\overleftarrow{h_i} = \text{LSTM}(emb_z, \ldots, emb_i) \qquad (4)$$

$emb = emb_1, \ldots, emb_z$ represents the respective sequence of embeddings, i.e., either the embeddings of the lemma's characters or the embeddings of the subword units of either context.

Our model then uses 3 attention mechanisms— one for each encoder—to produce a context vector for each output position: H_t for the lemma, H_t^p for the past context and H_t^f for the future context.

The input to the decoder LSTM at each timestep is the concatenation of all contexts and the embedding of the last output character. Embeddings are shared between the character encoder and the decoder, BPE embeddings are shared between the two context encoders.

An overview of our model architecture is shown in Figure 1. Our final system in an ensemble of 5 random restarts of the model, combined via majority voting.

3.1 Training and Hyperparameters

Using the shared task development sets, we decide on the following hyperparameters: We employ 100-dimensional BPE and character embeddings, and the encoder and decoder hidden states are 300-dimensional. Dropout (Srivastava et al., 2014) is used with a probability of 0.5 for all hidden states when used as input to the next layer, as well as for the embedding layer. For training, we employ ADAM (Kingma and Ba, 2014). Whenever performance does not improve for 20 steps, we halve the learning rate and restart from the best performing model. Training stops when the learning rate gets below 0.0001; the best performing model is used for the final predictions. We do not use batching, since it hurts performance in our experiments on the development sets.

For decoding, we apply beam search with a beam of width 5.

4 Official System Evaluation

4.1 Datasets

The data for Task 2, track 2, LOW consists of sentences taken from the Universal Dependencies

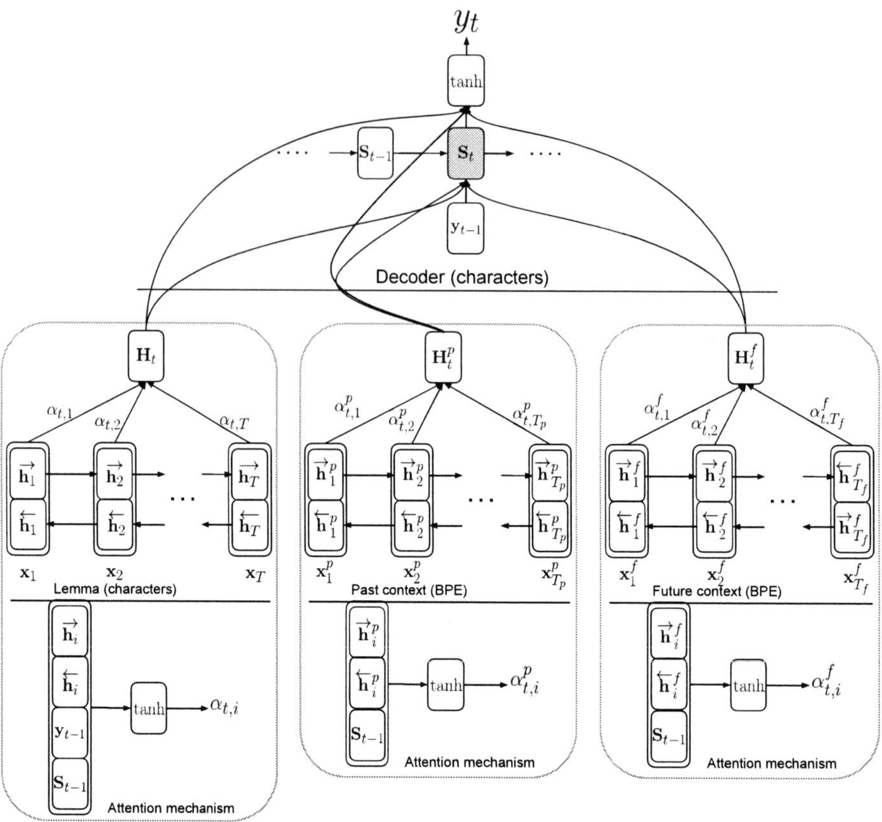

Figure 1: Overview of our employed model architecture.

(UD) treebanks (Nivre et al., 2017). All context forms, as well as the lemma of the target inflected form are given for each sentence. Training and development sets feature exactly one correct target form, while, for the test set, additional plausible target forms have been manually given by the shared task organizers (Cotterell et al., 2018).

The languages we experiment on are German, English, Spanish, Finnish, French, Russian and Swedish.

4.2 Baseline System

The official baseline system of the shared task is a character-level LSTM encoder-decoder model with attention (Bahdanau et al., 2015). The main input to the system is the lemma of the inflected form which is to be generated. Further, the context is taken into account: each character of the lemma is concatenated with 7 additional embeddings representing (i) the lemma of the word at the previous position in the sentence, (ii) the previous word itself, (iii) the tag of the previous word, (iv)

the lemma of the word at the next position in the sentence, (v) the next word itself, (vi) the tag of the next word, (vii) the lemma of the inflected form to generate and given to the encoder. Note that, since no tags or lemmas are available for track 2 of Task 2, but the architecture is identical to that used for track 1 of the same task, all embeddings but those for the previous and the next word, as well as the lemma are set to default vectors.

Given the character embedding-context representations produced by the encoder, the LSTM decoder generates the character sequence of the output inflected form, using an attention mechanism.

More details on the shared task baseline system can be found in Cotterell et al. (2018).

4.3 Official Test Results

Two official results are reported. First, system performance is calculated by just taking the gold solution into account, i.e., all generated inflected forms that do not match the UD gold standard are counted as wrong. Second, performance is com-

	BL	BME-HAS	CPH	CUB	*NYU*	UZH
de	0.10	27.81	18.91	11.02	*44.08*	**59.15**
en	2.22	56.90	59.42	58.91	*66.57*	**68.08**
es	8.98	27.77	31.84	27.91	*27.49*	**32.68**
fi	0.38	8.89	12.33	7.88	*15.37*	**24.40**
fr	0.00	9.57	**29.53**	23.01	*26.48*	25.05
ru	2.71	19.68	22.69	21.08	*22.09*	**28.11**
sv	0.96	22.34	30.96	16.49	*31.60*	**32.77**
av.	2.19	24.71	29.38	23.76	*33.38*	**38.60**

Table 1: Test accuracies when considering only the gold solution; BL = BASELINE; CPH = COPENHAGEN; CUB = CUBoulder. Best results per language in bold; our results in italic.

	BL	BME-HAS	CPH	CUB	*NYU*	UZH
de	0.10	31.14	21.54	11.53	*48.43*	**61.38**
en	2.92	62.64	66.87	66.36	*72.21*	**74.02**
es	11.08	33.52	**37.31**	31.42	*31.98*	37.17
fi	0.89	11.18	16.14	10.04	*18.68*	**28.21**
ru	2.71	21.29	24.40	22.59	*23.29*	**30.42**
sv	0.96	27.34	36.38	19.04	*37.13*	**39.36**
av.	3.11	31.18	33.77	26.83	*38.62*	**45.09**

Table 2: Test accuracies when counting all plausible forms as correct; BL = BASELINE; CPH = COPENHAGEN; CUB = CUBoulder. Best results per language in bold; our results in italic.

puted by taking all plausible target inflected forms into account, i.e., all forms that *could be correct* in any way of reading the sentence are accepted as correct. The final results for all systems are shown in Tables 1 and 2, respectively.

As can be seen, the baseline performs poorly in the low-resource setting we consider here. In particular, its accuracy is far worse than that of any participating system.

Looking at our system's performance, we can see that it is the second best one for German, English, Finnish, French, and Slovene, as well as on average, when only considering the gold solution. Taking all plausible forms into account, our systems obtains the second highest accuracy for German, English, Finnish, and Slovene, as well as on average.[1]

The best performing system on average is UZH, and CPH outperforms our model for Spanish, French and Russian for gold solutions, and Spanish and Russian for all plausible forms. BME-HAS and CUB perform worse than our system for all languages.

A final observation is that the accuracy differ-

---

[1]No results with all plausible forms are available for French.

ence between the evaluation with the gold solution and the evaluation with all plausible forms is $0.92 - 6.49$, depending on the system.

5 Related Work

Most recent work on morphological reinflection was done in the context of the SIGMORPHON 2016 and the CoNLL–SIGMORPHON 2017 shared tasks.

The first edition of the shared task in 2016 (Cotterell et al., 2016) resulted in 3 different types of systems: "pipeline approaches" (unsupervised alignment algorithms applied to the source-target pairs, followed by a model which predicts edit operations), "neural approaches", and "linguistically inspired systems". The winning system was a neural network, namely a character-based RNN encoder-decoder model with attention, similar to the one we use here (Kann and Schütze, 2016). Hence, neural models gained popularity in the 2017 edition of the shared task (Cotterell et al., 2017a). In 2017, explicit low-resource settings were first introduced to the shared task. These settings demonstrated the effectiveness of hard attention in neural sequence-to-sequence models if training data are limited (Makarov et al., 2017).

Research not immediately done for the shared tasks included papers on multi-source reinflection (Cotterell et al., 2017b; Kann et al., 2017a), cross-lingual transfer for reinflection (Kann et al., 2017b), or first intents of neural inflection systems which make use of context for lemmatization (Bergmanis and Goldwater, 2018).

Older work on morphological inflection includes Ahlberg et al. (2014); Durrett and DeNero (2013); Nicolai et al. (2015); Faruqui et al. (2016), inter alia.

6 Conclusion

We presented the NYU system for Task 2, track 2, LOW of the CoNLL–SIGMORPHON 2018 shared task on universal morphological reinflection. The system was designed for the task of morphological inflection in context: it predicts an inflected form for an indicated position in a sentence, given the sentence context and the lemma. In the official evaluation, which consisted of experiments in German, English, Spanish, Finnish, French, Russian and Slovene, our system was the second best performing one out of 5 submissions.

References

Malin Ahlberg, Markus Forsberg, and Mans Hulden. 2014. Semi-supervised learning of morphological paradigms and lexicons. In *EACL*.

Dzmitry Bahdanau, Kyunghyun Cho, and Yoshua Bengio. 2015. Neural machine translation by jointly learning to align and translate. In *ICLR*.

Toms Bergmanis and Sharon Goldwater. 2018. Context sensitive neural lemmatization with lematus. In *NAACL*.

Ryan Cotterell, Christo Kirov, John Sylak-Glassman, Géraldine Walther, Ekaterina Vylomova, Arya D. McCarthy, Katharina Kann, Sebastian Mielke, Garrett Nicolai, Miikka Silfverberg, David Yarowsky, Jason Eisner, and Mans Hulden. 2018. The CoNLL–SIGMORPHON 2018 shared task: Universal morphological reinflection. In *CoNLL–SIGMORPHON*.

Ryan Cotterell, Christo Kirov, John Sylak-Glassman, Géraldine Walther, Ekaterina Vylomova, Patrick Xia, Manaal Faruqui, Sandra Kübler, David Yarowsky, Jason Eisner, and Mans Hulden. 2017a. The CoNLL-SIGMORPHON 2017 shared task: Universal morphological reinflection in 52 languages. In *CoNLL-SIGMORPHON*.

Ryan Cotterell, Christo Kirov, John Sylak-Glassman, David Yarowsky, Jason Eisner, and Mans Hulden. 2016. The SIGMORPHON 2016 shared task— morphological reinflection. In *SIGMORPHON*.

Ryan Cotterell, John Sylak-Glassman, and Christo Kirov. 2017b. Neural graphical models over strings for principal parts morphological paradigm completion. In *EACL*.

Greg Durrett and John DeNero. 2013. Supervised learning of complete morphological paradigms. In *NAACL-HLT*.

Manaal Faruqui, Yulia Tsvetkov, Graham Neubig, and Chris Dyer. 2016. Morphological inflection generation using character sequence to sequence learning. In *NAACL-HLT*.

Katharina Kann, Ryan Cotterell, and Hinrich Schütze. 2017a. Neural multi-source morphological reinflection. In *EACL*.

Katharina Kann, Ryan Cotterell, and Hinrich Schütze. 2017b. One-shot neural cross-lingual transfer for paradigm completion. In *ACL*.

Katharina Kann and Hinrich Schütze. 2016. MED: The lmu system for the SIGMORPHON 2016 shared task on morphological reinflection. In *SIGMOR-PHON*.

Diederik P Kingma and Jimmy Ba. 2014. Adam: A method for stochastic optimization. *arXiv preprint arXiv:1412.6980*.

Peter Makarov, Tatiana Ruzsics, and Simon Clematide. 2017. Align and copy: UZH at SIGMORPHON 2017 shared task for morphological reinflection. In *CoNLL-SIGMORPHON*.

Garrett Nicolai, Colin Cherry, and Grzegorz Kondrak. 2015. Inflection generation as discriminative string transduction. In *NAACL-HLT*.

Joakim Nivre, Željko Agić, Lars Ahrenberg, Maria Jesus Aranzabe, Masayuki Asahara, Aitziber Atutxa, Miguel Ballesteros, John Bauer, Kepa Bengoetxea, Riyaz Ahmad Bhat, Eckhard Bick, Cristina Bosco, Gosse Bouma, Sam Bowman, Marie Candito, Gülşen Cebirolu Eryiit, Giuseppe G. A. Celano, Fabricio Chalub, Jinho Choi, Çar Çöltekin, Miriam Connor, Elizabeth Davidson, Marie-Catherine de Marneffe, Valeria de Paiva, Arantza Diaz de Ilarraza, Kaja Dobrovoljc, Timothy Dozat, Kira Droganova, Puneet Dwivedi, Marhaba Eli, Tomaž Erjavec, Richárd Farkas, Jennifer Foster, Cláudia Freitas, Katarína Gajdošová, Daniel Galbraith, Marcos Garcia, Filip Ginter, Iakes Goenaga, Koldo Gojenola, Memduh Gökrmak, Yoav Goldberg, Xavier Gómez Guinovart, Berta Gonzáles Saavedra, Matias Grioni, Normunds Grūzitis, Bruno Guillaume, Nizar Habash, Jan Hajič, Linh Hà M, Dag Haug, Barbora Hladká, Petter Hohle, Radu Ion, Elena Irimia, Anders Johannsen, Fredrik Jørgensen, Hüner Kaşkara, Hiroshi Kanayama, Jenna Kanerva, Natalia Kotsyba, Simon Krek, Veronika Laippala, Phng Lê Hng, Alessandro Lenci, Nikola Ljubešić, Olga Lyashevskaya, Teresa Lynn, Aibek Makazhanov, Christopher Manning, Cătălina Mărănduc, David Mareček, Héctor Martínez Alonso, André Martins, Jan Mašek, Yuji Matsumoto, Ryan McDonald, Anna Missilä, Verginica Mititelu, Yusuke Miyao, Simonetta Montemagni, Amir More, Shunsuke Mori, Bohdan Moskalevskyi, Kadri Muischnek, Nina Mustafina, Kaili Müürisep, Lng Nguyn Th, Huyn Nguyn Th Minh, Vitaly Nikolaev, Hanna Nurmi, Stina Ojala, Petya Osenova, Lilja Øvrelid, Elena Pascual, Marco Passarotti, Cenel-Augusto Perez, Guy Perrier, Slav Petrov, Jussi Piitulainen, Barbara Plank, Martin Popel, Lauma Pretkalnia, Prokopis Prokopidis, Tiina Puolakainen, Sampo Pyysalo, Alexandre Rademaker, Loganathan Ramasamy, Livy Real, Laura Rituma, Rudolf Rosa, Shadi Saleh, Manuela Sanguinetti, Baiba Saulite, Sebastian Schuster, Djamé Seddah, Wolfgang Seeker, Mojgan Seraji, Lena Shakurova, Mo Shen, Dmitry Sichinava, Natalia Silveira, Maria Simi, Radu Simionescu, Katalin Simkó, Mária Šimková, Kiril Simov, Aaron Smith, Alane Suhr, Umut Sulubacak, Zsolt Szántó, Dima Taji, Takaaki Tanaka, Reut Tsarfaty, Francis Tyers, Sumire Uematsu, Larraitz Uria, Gertjan van Noord, Viktor Varga, Veronika Vincze, Jonathan North Washington, Zdeněk Žabokrtský, Amir Zeldes, Daniel Zeman, and Hanzhi Zhu. 2017. Universal dependencies 2.0. LINDAT/CLARIN digital library at the Institute of Formal and Applied Linguistics, Charles University.

Rico Sennrich, Barry Haddow, and Alexandra Birch. 2016. Neural machine translation of rare words with subword units. In *ACL*.

Nitish Srivastava, Geoffrey Hinton, Alex Krizhevsky, Ilya Sutskever, and Ruslan Salakhutdinov. 2014. Dropout: A simple way to prevent neural networks from overfitting. *The Journal of Machine Learning Research*, 15(1):1929–1958.

Attention-free encoder decoder for morphological processing

Stefan Daniel Dumitrescu and Tiberiu Boros
Research Institute for Artificial Intelligence "Mihai Drăgănescu"
Romanian Academy
13 September, no. 13, Bucharest, Romania
`sdumitrescu@racai.ro, tibi@racai.ro`

Abstract

We present RACAI's Entry for the CoNLL-SIGMORPHON 2018 shared task on universal morphological reinflection. The system is based on an attention-free encoder-decoder neural architecture with a bidirectional LSTM for encoding the input sequence and a unidirectional LSTM for decoding and producing the output. Instead of directly applying a sequence-to-sequence model at character-level we use a dynamic algorithm to align the input and output sequences. Based on these alignments we produce a series of special symbols which are similar to those of a finite-state-transducer (FST).

1 Introduction

Languages with rich morphology convey morphological attributes such as gender, case, number, obliqueness through character/grapheme variations applied to the dictionary form of the word (lemma). It is often the case where these variations are obtained by suffixing the word rather than altering random characters, but this does not hold for all languages or irregular word forms. Sill, the variations inside the lemma are usually small, requiring the system just to replace an average of 2.3 letters for the irregular word forms.

In our approach we exploit this property and employ an encoder-decoder sequence-to-sequence model that doesn't require an attention mechanism. This mitigates attention issues such as repeating or skipping character sequences and reduces the need for models with high representational capacity.

We exploit the property that alignments between the input and output character sequences are *monotonic*: for example wordform *men* and lemma *man* share two letters (alignments) in the same order, without inversions. The standard attention mechanism is well-suited for machine learning tasks; however, when it comes to monotonic alignments it sometimes fails to achieve satisfactory results, in most cases due to the fact that repeated characters or character sequences in the input sequence confuse the attention mechanism making it generate loops or skip characters.

There are several proposed methods that try to solve this task with attention mechanisms such as guided attention (Tachibana et al., 2017), location-sensitive attention (Chorowski et al., 2015) and other variations. Still, given the particularities of morphological reinflection, we argue that there is no need for an explicit attention mechanism. Instead we train the decoder to focus on a single input symbol at each time-step and "self-attend" by shifting the input cursor with one position at a time. This method, though developed independently, closely resembles that of Makarov et al. (2017).

In our previous experiments we used this architecture to perform lemmatization (the opposite task of morphological reinflection) and we obtained state-of-the-art results.

In what follows, we will present the attention-free encoder-decoder architecture (Section 2), we show our experimental results (Section 3) and finally we draw conclusions (Section 4).

2 Attention-free encoder-decoder

The architecture of our neural network is fairly simple. We use an encoder that "sees" the sequence in both directions and a decoder which is conditioned to produce the output sequence using **focused encoder states** (see below for details) concatenated with trainable embeddings computed on morphological attributes.

As mentioned before, the classical attention mechanism is not well suited for tasks where the alignments between the input and output se-

Proceedings of the CoNLL–SIGMORPHON 2018 Shared Task: Universal Morphological Reinflection, pages 64–68,
Brussels, Belgium, October 31, 2018. ©2018 Association for Computational Linguistics

quences are monotonic. Instead, connectionist temporal classification (CTC) (Graves et al., 2006) provides better results in these cases. However, CTC requires that the number of input time-steps is much higher than the number of output labels. This renders CTC unsuitable for morphological reinflection as the number of output labels is almost always greater than the number of input characters.

Instead, we propose a simpler algorithm that reduces the model complexity and computational load. Our method requires preexisting alignments between the input and output sequences. These alignments are easy to obtain by exploiting a basic property of morphological reinflection, which also holds for lemmatization: **regardless of the language and irregularity of the word-form, the lemma and the inflected word form share many symbols**.

This implies a high likelihood of aligning identical input and output symbols and does not require Expectation Maximization (EM) for computing alignment probabilities. With this in mind, we propose the following algorithm that:

1. Computes an alignment matrix using dynamic programming;

2. Reads the two sequences in reverse and uses the previously computed matrix, favoring diagonal alignments over other alignments;

3. Generates alignment pairs, whenever the input and output symbols are identical.

Figure 1 describes our approach step-by-step.

The algorithm is a slightly modified dynamic algorithm in the sense that (a) it favors diagonal alignments (to cope with repeating consecutive letters) and (b) it only considers an alignment pair (i, j) if the characters from the source (s) and destination (d) at the two indexes are identical (i.e. $s_i = d_j$).

Next, we use the produced alignments to generate the training data for our attention-free encoder-decoder model. For our algorithm to work, we need the decoder to keep track of the focused-on character in the input sequence. This is achieved by simulating a FST using neural networks. Given the input sequence s, the decoder must produce an output sequence d' which is composed of three specialized labels and arbitrary characters in the vocabulary. The output symbols are:

```
s - input sequence of size n
d - output sequence of size m

a <- zeros(n+1, m+1)
#initialization
for i=(0,n): a[i,0]<-i
for i=(0,m): a[0,i]<-i

for i=(1,n):
        for j=(1,m):
        if s[i-1]==d[j-1]:
                cost<-0
        else:
                cost<-1
                a[i,j]<-cost+
                    min(a[i-1,j-1],
                        a[i-1,j],
                        a[i,j-1])

alignments={}; pi<-n; pj<-m
while i!=1 or j!=1:
        if i==1: j<-j-1
    else if j==1: i<-i-1
    else:
        if a[i-1,j-1]<=a[i-1,j] and
            a[i-1][j-1]<=a[i,j-1]:
                i<-i-1; j<-j-1
        else if a[i-1][j]<a[i][j-1]:
                i<-i-1
        else:
                j<-j-1
    if s[i]==d[j]:
        alignments<-
                alignments+(i-1,j-1)
return alignments
```

Figure 1: Alignment algorithm

- **Special symbol _INC_:** This means that the current focus-index of the input sequence must be incremented by 1;

- **Special Symbol _COPY_:** The character at the current focus-index must be "copied" in order to compose the final sequence;

- **Special Symbol _EOS_:** The output sequence is complete and the algorithm stops;

- **Any arbitrary character in the vocabulary:** This means that the final sequence must be obtained by adding this character.

At runtime we start by setting the focus-index at

0 and the final sequence to the void string ("") and we follow the instructions of the decoder output in order to construct the final sequence. During training, it is highly important to do sanity checks on the current focus-index to avoid index out-of-bounds exceptions during the first training epochs when the model has not yet converged. Once the loss is small enough, we found that the model rarely generates these exceptions. However, it is still recommended to keep these checks in place.

To obtain the output sequence d' on which we train our network we use a **fixed-oracle algorithm** that is summarized as:

1. Take every symbol in the output sequence and check if it aligns with a symbol in the input sequence (based on the *alignments* produced by the algorithm in Figure 1);

2. If the output symbol does not align with any character, instruct the decoder to generate it (the case of the arbitrary character in the vocabulary);

3. If the output symbol aligns, instruct the decoder to generate _INC_ symbols until the focus-index would reach the corresponding input character, and then generate an _COPY_ symbol;

4. When the sequence is completely generated, instruct the decoder to generate an _EOS_ symbol.

Because English reinflection is fairly simple, we chose an entry from the Romanian dataset for which we present a step-by-step example.

Assume the lemma is "face" (en. "to do") and is has to be reinflected for the morphological description **V;IND;PST;3;PL;IPFV**. The decoder has to generate word form "făceau" (en. "they were doing"). This means that the inflected form is obtained by replacing the character 'a' with the character 'ă' and by adding the suffix "au".

Figure 2 shows the alignments obtained via dynamic programming between the characters of the lemma (up) and the characters of the word form (down). The dashed lines correspond to alignments where the characters in the source and destination are not identical. The final alignments pairs are (according to the straight lines): (0,0), (2,2) and (3,3).

Based on these alignments, the FST symbols generated by the fixed-oracle algorithm are:

COPY, 'Ă', _INC_, _INC_, _COPY_, _INC_, _COPY_, 'A', 'U', _EOS_. Notice that after copying the first symbol ('F') to the output, the oracle immediately generates the vocabulary item 'Ă', because it is not aligned with any symbol in the source lemma. However, the next (3rd) symbol in the destination string is aligned with a character in the source string and the index is incremented with two _INC_ commands. The rest of the sequence is generated in a similar fashion.

Figure 2: Alignment example

Note 1: Fixed-oracle training is known to produce suboptimal results, when compared with dynamic-oracle training. However, we did not have time to experiment with the later mentioned training method and leave this for future work.

3 Training details and experimental results

For our implementation is based on DyNET (Neubig et al., 2017), which is a dynamic computation graph network framework. That means that we do not require any padding when we prepare mini-batches.

We evaluated our approach on the data provided during the SIGMORPHON 2018 Shared Task on morphological reinflection (Cotterell et al., 2018). During the evaluation campaign, each language was provided with 3 datasets of different sizes (high, medium and low). Because, neural approaches traditionally require more training data to generalize better, we only built models for the "high" datasets, which were composed of 10K training examples for each language.

Our model was trained using ADAM optimization (Kingma and Ba, 2014), with the default parameters $\alpha = 1e^{-3}$, $\beta_1 = 0.9$ and $\beta_2 = 0.999$. We used a mini-batch size of 1K words and we used trained each model until the accuracy on the development set stopped improving for 20 iterations. At the end, we used the best performing model for each languages.

Language	Acc.	Acc.*	Language	Acc.	Acc.*	Language	Acc.	Acc.*
adyghe	92.00	97.90	irish	81.80	86.90	sanskrit	76.60	94.10
albanian	95.60	97.10	italian	90.00	91.10	serbo-croatian	88.00	90.70
arabic	88.50	90.00	kabardian	92.00	94.00	slovak	88.80	92.60
armenian	0.00	93.90	khaling	44.70	45.40	slovene	93.40	94.10
asturian	95.40	97.00	kurmanji	90.40	92.10	sorani	86.80	89.00
azeri	90.00	99.00	ladin	86.00	90.00	spanish	72.70	75.00
bashkir	0.00	98.10	latin	16.20	16.20	swahili	98.00	99.00
basque	86.80	96.40	latvian	92.90	97.40	swedish	85.20	92.10
belarusian	3.80	5.10	lithuanian	65.20	66.20	tatar	95.00	97.00
bengali	99.00	99.00	livonian	87.00	97.00	turkish	79.30	80.20
breton	0.00	82.00	lower-sorbian	93.70	96.30	ukrainian	90.50	94.80
bulgarian	77.80	79.90	macedonian	91.90	94.60	urdu	43.50	44.30
catalan	89.40	89.70	maltese	4.00	91.00	uzbek	0.00	36.00
classical-syriac	87.00	98.00	middle-french	96.70	96.30	venetian	98.50	98.70
crimean-tatar	94.00	96.00	navajo	79.00	84.00	votic	0.00	73.00
czech	90.20	92.50	neapolitan	0.00	40.00	welsh	92.00	92.00
danish	91.80	94.90	northern-sami	90.70	93.10	west-frisian	0.00	93.00
estonian	93.80	97.00	nor-bokmaal	88.90	92.50	yiddish	92.00	99.00
faroese	76.30	88.80	nor-nynorsk	79.40	93.10	zulu	73.30	74.40
finnish	87.20	92.20	occitan	83.00	83.00	dutch	92.20	94.80
friulian	78.00	79.00	old-armenian	80.40	82.30	english	93.80	95.10
galician	89.90	91.10	old-church-slv.	9.00	74.00	french	84.30	89.80
georgian	97.80	98.40	old-french	0.00	00.00	german	37.40	42.50
greek	81.10	85.90	old-saxon	54.50	54.80	kannada	99.00	98.00
haida	96.00	93.00	pashto	84.00	89.00	north-frisian	15.00	69.00
hebrew	85.70	87.20	persian	95.60	97.70	old-english	28.20	30.00
hindi	89.40	90.60	portuguese	84.00	84.50	polish	87.80	90.40
hungarian	79.50	86.50	quechua	96.80	98.30	russian	86.80	91.40
icelandic	80.60	89.90	romanian	82.00	88.00	**Average**	**72.49**	**83.77**

Table 1: Accuracy figures for all languages in the SIGMORPHON Shared Task 2018

For all languages we used a two-layer encoder with 200 LSTM cells (in each direction - total 400 cells per layer) and a two-layer decoder of 200 unidirectional cells. Each character in the vocabulary is embedded as a 100-dimensional vector. We also use a 100-dimensional embedding size for each unique morphological descriptor.

Table 1 summarizes the testset results for all languages in the SIGMORPHON Challenge 2018. During the official evaluation campaign, our system was affected by a bug which caused all weights belonging to non-recurrent cells to be constant (not trainable during backprop). This issue had a strong negative impact on the results. After this, we retrained our models and we include the unofficial results in the same table, under the "Acc.*" column. For almost all languages, after correcting the bug, the accuracy strongly in-

creased; for Welsh we observed no increase, and only for 2 languages did we observe a less than 1 point decrease (probably due to weight initialization compounded by small models where the LSTMs overcame the fixed random weights of the dense layers). Overall, we observed a strong result increase, from an average of 72.49 to 83.77. For example, for West Frisian where initially the model would not converge (0.00), we now obtain 93.00; similarly, for Armenian, we have gone from 0.00 to 93.9.

4 Conclusions

We introduced a specially designed attention-free encoder-decoder model for morphological reinflection. Aside for mitigating standard attention issues, such as repeated or skipped character sequences, this approach allows training simpler models. This is mainly (a) because our model introduces the _COPY_ operation and reduces the representational load of the encoder-decoder model and (b) and because we keep track of the focus-index externally.

Also, we reduce the computational complexity of the model by completely removing calculation involved in the soft attention mechanism ($n * m$ matrix multiplications, where n is the size of the input sequence and m the size of the output sequence).

Moreover, the fact that the decoder does not require taking the previous output and embedding it as input for the next step, demonstrates that there is far less representational overhead involved in generating the output sequence.

As a side note, in our previous experiments with lemmatization, we observed that using this model yields a 2-5% absolute increase in accuracy over the standard soft-attention sequence-to-sequence model.

Acknowledgments

The research presented here is funded by the Romanian Government through the Executive Agency for Higher Education, Research, Development and Innovation Funding (UEFISCDI), programme "Experimental demonstration project (PED) PED-2016", project ID: PN-III-P2-2.1-PED-2016-1974, contract number 229PED.

References

Jan K Chorowski, Dzmitry Bahdanau, Dmitriy Serdyuk, Kyunghyun Cho, and Yoshua Bengio. 2015. Attention-based models for speech recognition. In *Advances in neural information processing systems*, pages 577–585.

Ryan Cotterell, Christo Kirov, John Sylak-Glassman, Géraldine Walther, Ekaterina Vylomova, Arya D. McCarthy, Katharina Kann, Sebastian Mielke, Garrett Nicolai, Miikka Silfverberg, David Yarowsky, Jason Eisner, and Mans Hulden. 2018. The CoNLL–SIGMORPHON 2018 shared task: Universal morphological reinflection. In *Proceedings of the CoNLL–SIGMORPHON 2018 Shared Task: Universal Morphological Reinflection*, Brussels, Belgium. Association for Computational Linguistics.

Alex Graves, Santiago Fernández, Faustino Gomez, and Jürgen Schmidhuber. 2006. Connectionist temporal classification: labelling unsegmented sequence data with recurrent neural networks. In *Proceedings of the 23rd international conference on Machine learning*, pages 369–376. ACM.

Diederik P Kingma and Jimmy Ba. 2014. Adam: A method for stochastic optimization. *arXiv preprint arXiv:1412.6980*.

Peter Makarov, Tatiana Ruzsics, and Simon Clematide. 2017. Align and copy: Uzh at sigmorphon 2017 shared task for morphological reinflection. In *Proceedings of the CoNLL SIGMORPHON 2017 Shared Task: Universal Morphological Reinflection*, pages 49–57, Vancouver. Association for Computational Linguistics.

Graham Neubig, Chris Dyer, Yoav Goldberg, Austin Matthews, Waleed Ammar, Antonios Anastasopoulos, Miguel Ballesteros, David Chiang, Daniel Clothiaux, Trevor Cohn, et al. 2017. Dynet: The dynamic neural network toolkit. *arXiv preprint arXiv:1701.03980*.

Hideyuki Tachibana, Katsuya Uenoyama, and Shunsuke Aihara. 2017. Efficiently trainable text-to-speech system based on deep convolutional networks with guided attention. *arXiv preprint arXiv:1710.08969*.

UZH at CoNLL–SIGMORPHON 2018 Shared Task on Universal Morphological Reinflection

Peter Makarov   **Simon Clematide**

Institute of Computational Linguistics
University of Zurich, Switzerland

makarov@cl.uzh.ch   simon.clematide@cl.uzh.ch

Abstract

This paper presents the submissions by the University of Zurich to the CoNLL–SIGMORPHON 2018 Shared Task on Universal Morphological Reinflection. Our system is based on the prior work on neural transition-based transduction (Makarov and Clematide, 2018b; Aharoni and Goldberg, 2017). Unlike the prior work, we train the model in a fully end-to-end fashion—without the need for an external character aligner—within the framework of imitation learning. In the type-level morphological inflection generation challenge (Task I), our five-strong ensemble outperforms all competitors in all three data-size settings. In the token-level inflection generation challenge (Task II), our single model achieves the best results on three out of four sub-tasks that we have participated in.

1 Introduction

The CoNLL–SIGMORPHON 2018 Shared Task on Universal Morphological Reinflection (Cotterell et al., 2018) focuses on inflection generation at the type level (Task I) and in context (Task II). Both tasks feature three settings depending on the maximum number of training examples: low, medium, and high. The team from the University of Zurich has taken part in both tasks with submissions featuring neural transition-based transducers (Aharoni and Goldberg, 2017; Makarov and Clematide, 2018b). The model transduces a string by a sequence of traditional character edit operations. The neuralized transducer, which conditions edits on the entire input string and captures unbounded dependencies in the output, has proven very effective in the past editions of the SIGMORPHON shared task (Aharoni et al., 2016; Makarov et al., 2017). Typically, this model is trained by maximizing the likelihood of gold action sequences that come from a separate character aligner. This year, we train with an imitation learning method (Makarov and Clematide, 2018a) that enforces optimal alignment in the loss and additionally supports action-space exploration and the optimization of a task-specific objective. Our method entirely eliminates the need for a character aligner and results in substantially stronger models, at the expense of slight increase in training time. The resulting models evaluate favorably on both CoNLL–SIGMORPHON 2018 tasks. On Task I, our five-strong ensemble `uzh-02` outperforms the nearest competitor by over 1% absolute accuracy in the high setting (24.4% error reduction) and over 2% absolute in the medium setting and 4% absolute in the low setting (13.9% and 8.6% error reduction, respectively). The larger ensemble `uzh-01` further improves the result slightly in the high and medium settings (1% and 2% error reduction, respectively). For Task II, we submit a single model to only the low and medium settings. The single model dominates the low setting, being also the only system that beats the predict-the-lemma baseline. The model comes second in the track 1 medium setting with almost 4% absolute accuracy behind the winner (8.5% error increase), and is the best in the track 2 medium setting with almost 4% absolute above the runner-up (6.7% error reduction).

2 Task description

The now classic Task I requires mapping a lemma form (e.g. "Schlüssel" meaning "key" in Swiss German) to an inflected form ("Schlüssle") given a morpho-syntactic description (N;DAT;PL). The new Task II requires mapping a lemma ("Schlüssel") to an inflected form ("Schlüssle") given sentential context ("Du muesch de ______ Sorg gäh." / "You need to take care of the keys.").

This year's edition of Task I features an unprecedented 102 languages. As in 2017, the low

69

Proceedings of the CoNLL–SIGMORPHON 2018 Shared Task: Universal Morphological Reinflection, pages 69–75,
Brussels, Belgium, October 31, 2018. ©2018 Association for Computational Linguistics

setting offers just 100 training samples per language, and it is at most 1,000 and 10,000 samples in the medium and high settings, respectively.

Task II features six Indo-European languages (German, English, Swedish; Spanish, French; Russian) and one Uralic language, Finnish. Track 1 of Task II additionally provides the morpho-syntactic specifications of all context words.

3 State of the Art

Over the past two years, type-level inflection generation in the high setting has been dominated by general sequence-to-sequence models (seq2seq) with soft attention (Kann and Schütze, 2016; Bergmanis et al., 2017). Neuralized counterparts of traditional transition-based transducers have proven highly competitive, being particularly effective in lower-resource settings (Aharoni et al., 2016; Makarov et al., 2017). Inflection generation in context is a novel SIGMORPHON challenge and, generally, a less studied problem. Recently, Wolf-Sonkin et al. (2018) propose a context-aware deep generative graphical model that generates sequences of inflected words.

4 Methods

Our model is a version of the transition-based transducer with a designated copy action (Makarov and Clematide, 2018b). The model edits the lemma into the inflected form by a sequence of single-character edit actions (DELETE, COPY, INSERT(c) for any output character c). Through the use of a recurrent neural network, the choice of edit is conditioned on the globally contextualized representation of an input character and the full history of edits. Concretely, at timestep t, the probability distribution over edits a_t is computed with a softmax classifier:

$$P(a_t \mid \mathbf{a}_{<t}, \mathbf{x}) = \mathrm{softmax}(\mathbf{W} \cdot \mathbf{s}_t + \mathbf{b}), \quad (1)$$

where $\mathbf{W}$ and $\mathbf{b}$ are classifier weights and $\mathbf{s}_t$ is the output of the long short-term memory cell (Hochreiter and Schmidhuber, 1997, LSTM):

$$\mathbf{s}_t = \mathrm{LSTM}(\mathbf{c}_{t-1}, [E(a_{t-1}); \mathbf{h}_i; \mathbf{f}]). \quad (2)$$

Vector $\mathbf{c}_{t-1}$ denotes the previous hidden state, $E(a_{t-1})$ is the embedding of the previous edit, $\mathbf{f}$ is the embedding of the morpho-syntactic description (MSD), and $\mathbf{h}_i$ is the encoding of an input character x_i with a bidirectional LSTM (Graves and Schmidhuber, 2005). Given the set $\{f_h\}_{h=1}^{H}$ of all morpho-syntactic features seen at training, we compute the embedding $\mathbf{f}$ of an MSD as a concatenation of individual feature embeddings $[F(f_1); \ldots ; F(f_H)]$ where we use a designated embedding $F(0)$ instead of $F(f_h)$ if f_h does not occur in the MSD. Also, we use the same embedding for input character c and action INSERT(c).

Our submission differs from the previous work in the way we train this model.

4.1 Task I: Type-level Inflection Generation

The transducer is typically trained to maximize the conditional likelihood of a gold edit action sequence given a lemma (Aharoni and Goldberg, 2017). Gold actions are generated by a character alignment algorithm, such as minimal edit distance (Levenshtein, 1966), applied to lemma-word pairs. The performance of the transducer, therefore, hinges on the quality of character alignments that, in turn, might depend on the amount of training data (e.g. if we employ a statistical alignment model such as a Bayesian nonparametric aligner). On the one hand, it is unsatisfactory to have to choose aligners for different settings. On the other, multiple edit sequences are often equally likely, and yet the choice of a single gold sequence does not depend on the MSD. This leads to the learning of a suboptimal transducer.

Our solution, therefore, is to remove the aligner entirely and instead optimize a sequence-level loss that enforces optimal alignment. Concretely, our loss is a weighted sum of (i) the minimal edit distance between the target word $\mathbf{y}$ and prediction $\hat{\mathbf{y}}$ and (ii) the cost of the sequence of edits from lemma $\mathbf{x}$ to prediction $\hat{\mathbf{y}}$:

$$\ell(\mathbf{a}, \mathbf{x}, \mathbf{y}) = \beta\, \mathrm{distance}(\mathbf{y}, \hat{\mathbf{y}}) + \mathrm{cost}(\mathbf{a}) \quad (3)$$

The first term is the task objective. The second term pushes the model to achieve the objective with the least number of edits. To compute the terms, we use unit costs for DELETE and INSERT(c) for any output character c and zero cost for COPY. $\beta \geq 1$ is a penalty for unit distance.

While there exist many techniques that minimize a non-differentiable loss, most of them require initialization with a pretrained model (Ranzato et al., 2016; Bahdanau et al., 2017; Shen et al., 2016). They assume that at each specific timestep, the gold transition is unknown. Training signal comes from the entire sequence of transitions, which is typically too sparse for a cold start (Leblond et al., 2018). This assumption is not valid for morphological string transduction, and it is easy to design an efficient procedure that returns edits that result in the lowest sequence-level loss (assuming that all future transitions are, too, selected optimally). Specifically, such a procedure should return an edit that leads to the completion of the suffix of target $\mathbf{y}$ using a transition sequence with the lowest edit cost. For example, if the partial prediction $\hat{\mathbf{y}}$ for the lemma-word pair ("Schlüssel", "Schlüssle") is "Schlüss" and the model attends to $x_6 = e$, the procedure returns DELETE. Using this technique, we collect per-timestep losses that reflect the impact of single edits on the sequence-level loss.

Our training method is thus an instance of imitation learning (Daumé III et al., 2009; Ross et al., 2011; Chang et al., 2015), also familiar from transition-based dependency parsing (Goldberg and Nivre, 2012). For the submission, we train the model by maximizing the marginal log-likelihood (Riezler et al., 2000; Goldberg, 2013; Ballesteros et al., 2016) with a variant of stochastic gradient ascent:

$$\mathcal{L}(\mathbf{x},\mathbf{y},\Theta) = \sum_{t=1}^{m} \log \sum_{a \in A_t} P(a \mid \mathbf{a}_{<t}, \mathbf{x}, \Theta) \quad (4)$$

Θ are the model parameters and A_t is the set of optimal edits at timestep t. To train with exploration, which addresses the exposure bias, we use a roll-in schedule and model roll-outs (Chang et al., 2015). In the *roll-in* phase, the next edit a_{t+1} is either sampled uniformly at random from the set A_t of optimal edits (expert roll-in) or from the current model's distribution over valid edits (model roll-in). This choice is controlled by a Bernoulli random variable that depends on the training epoch η. We use a roll-in schedule that gradually adds sampling from the model as training proceeds. In the *roll-out* phase, we estimate the future effect of some next action a_{t+1} on the sequence-level loss $l(\mathbf{a}, \mathbf{x}, \mathbf{y})$ by either using the optimal procedure outlined above (expert roll-out) or running the model for the rest of the input (model roll-out). Again, this choice is controlled by a Bernoulli random variable. The purpose of β from Eq. 3 is to cut down the number of expensive model roll-outs: In case a_{t+1} results in accuracy error (e.g. by inserting a letter that does not occur in the target $\mathbf{y}$),

Hyperparameter	Value
char. & action embedding (E)	100
feature embedding (F)	20
context char. embedding (Task II)	20
context feat. embedding (Task II)	10
batch size	1
epochs / patience (high)	30 / 5
epochs / patience (medium)	50 / 15
epochs / patience (low)	60 / 20
optimization	ADADELTA
β	5
roll-in	$\frac{k}{k+\exp(\eta/k)}, k = 12$
roll-out	0.5
beam width	4

Table 1: Model hyperparameters.

we set the sequence-level loss associated with this edit to β.

The model hyperparameters and optimization details are given in Table 1.

4.2 Task II: Inflection Generation in Context

Our submission involves a minor change to the model described above. Similar in spirit to the baseline of Task II, we compress the immediate context into context vector $\mathbf{g}$ and use it in place of the feature vector. For track 2 of Task II, the context vector is a concatenation of the character LSTM encodings of the words to the immediate right and left. For track 1 of Task II, the context vector also includes the embeddings of their MSDs, which we compute just as the feature vector $\mathbf{f}$ in the type-level model. We use smaller dimensions in the computation of context vectors (Table 1). We also considered larger context windows. For French and Swedish in the medium setting, our submission uses as context two words to the left and two words to the right since we observe substantial gains in accuracy over the two-word context window.

Following the baseline, we train on verbs, nouns, and adjectives for track 1 and all words paired with lemmas for track 2. We do not exploit any knowledge of the development and test sets[1] and assume that test sentences contain multiple gaps as in the development set. We do, however, use the fact that the official evaluation script ignores case distinctions. We lowercase all the

---

[1] At least for some languages (e.g. Russian and English), the development and test sets differ in the types of lexical categories to be predicted.

	uzh-01	uzh-02	#	avg	baseline	compet.
Task I						
development set						
H	96.18	**96.29**	10	94.98	78.12	–
M	87.60	**87.87**	12	85.66	63.05	–
L	57.52	**58.30**	15	54.73	38.81	–
test set						
H	**96.00**	95.97	–		77.42	94.66
M	**86.64**	86.38	–		63.53	84.19
L	57.18	**57.21**	–		38.89	53.22

Table 2: Overview of Task I results. H, M, L=high, medium, low settings; #=number of models that the average is taken over; compet.=nearest competitor.

	UZH--01--2	baseline	predict lemma	compet.
Task II				
development set				
M 1	53.05	41.44		–
M 2	49.53	33.55	35.09	–
L 1	41.75	1.61		–
L 2	38.40	1.58		–
test set				
M 1	53.02	44.09		**56.70**
M 2	**48.88**	38.56	36.62	45.18
L 1	**42.42**	1.85		29.86
L 2	**38.60**	2.19		33.38

Table 3: Overview of Task II results.

low-setting data, which results in an improvement.

4.3 `uzh-01` and `uzh-02`: Ensembling Strategies for Task I

Ensembling addresses the effects of random initialization when the objective function is not concave (Reimers and Gurevych, 2017). Both our Task I submissions are majority-vote ensembles. For each language, we compute 15 models for the low setting, 12 for the medium setting, and 10 for the high setting. For each language, run `uzh-02` is an ensemble over five models with the highest development set accuracies. Run `uzh-01` is an ensemble over all computed models. Ties are broken at random.

The Task II submission contains only a single model for each language.

All models are decoded with beam search.

5 Results and Discussion

5.1 Task I Results and Discussion

In Task I, our five-model majority-vote ensemble (`uzh-02`) outperforms the nearest competitor in the high setting (`mbe-02`) by 1.3% absolute accuracy (24.4% error reduction), and by 2.2% absolute in the medium setting (`iitbhu-iiith-02`) and 4.0% in the low setting (`ua-08`) (13.8% and 8.5% error reduction, respectively). The larger ensemble `uzh-01` is somewhat stronger in the medium and high settings than `uzh-02` and only marginally weaker in the low setting (Table 2). Ensembling adds consistent improvement over the single-model average, which suggests an uncomplicated way to improve our Task II results.

We also compare the performance of `uzh-02` to the highest accuracy achieved for each language and data setting by any of our competitors (Figure 1).[2] In the low setting, `uzh-02` is occasionally much behind the best achieved result (e.g. for Latin, Old English, Hebrew, Norwegian, and Danish) and behind the average 59.22% with a 4.9% relative error increase. For low-setting Lithuanian, `uzh-02` fails to improve over the baseline whereas `ua-08` and `ua-06` beat it by a large margin. In the medium and high settings, there are very few languages in which `uzh-02` is beaten by a competitor. `uzh-02` is more accurate on average (86.38% vs 84.79% in the medium setting and 95.97% vs 95.43% in the high setting) with error reductions of 10.4% and 12.0%, respectively.

Thus, with an appropriate training method, the neural transition-based model can be very strong in the high data setting. This is in line with the results for the SIGMORPHON 2016 dataset in Makarov and Clematide (2018a). On the other hand, we expect that gains can be made with the general soft-attention seq2seq model (or any latent-alignment model), by applying the same training method or other existing alternatives (Edunov et al., 2017).

Following a reviewer's request, we also compare the performance of the new model to that of the copy-enhanced variant of the hard attention model trained by maximizing the conditional likelihood of separately derived gold edits (Makarov and Clematide, 2018a, CA). (This model outperformed all competitors in last year's low setting.) Due to limited resources, we only compute low-setting CA models. The new model makes substantial gains: `uzh-01` and `uzh-02` achieve 8.5% and 7.8% error reduction over their CA ensemble counterparts (53.21% vs 57.18% and 53.62% vs 57.21%, respectively). This is con-

---

[2]Thus, this does not include the results from run `uzh-01`.

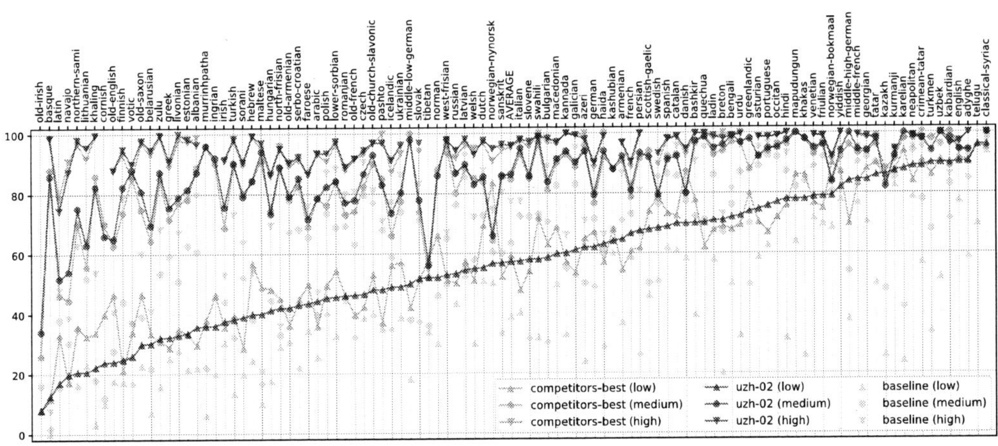

Figure 1: Test set accuracies for all languages and data-size settings of Task I: `uzh-02` (blue), the best result by any of the competitors (orange), and the official baseline (green).

sistent with the improvements that Makarov and Clematide demonstrate with the new model on the 2017 SIGMORPHON shared task data.

5.2 Task II Results and Discussion

We submit one model (`UZH--02--1`) to only the medium and low settings. The model comes second in the medium setting (track 1), behind `COPENHAGEN--01--2` with an absolute accuracy difference of 3.7% and an error increase of 8.5%. It outperforms by 3.7% absolute accuracy and an error reduction of 6.7% the nearest competitor (`COPENHAGEN--01--2`) in the medium setting (track 2) and by 12.6% (track 1, `CUBoulder--02--2`) and 5.2% absolute (track 2, `NYU--01--2`) in the low setting (17.9% and 7.8% error reduction, respectively) (Table 3).

Our model is the only system in the low setting that beats the baseline that makes prediction by copying over the lemma string ("predict lemma" in Table 3). Moreover, for individual languages, it is always as good as or better than this baseline, with the largest improvements for Spanish (8.8% and 6.7% absolute accuracy in tracks 1 and 2), French (11.2% in track 1), and Russian (18.6% and 5.9%).

We take a closer look at the Russian and French data to better understand the task that our system solves. About 98% of the gaps in the Russian development data correspond to nouns, and it is 100% verbs for French. We sample uniformly

at random 100 development set examples with MSDs (track 1) for each language and limit the context to two words to the left and two words to the right. A native speaker (with a linguistic background) attempts to predict the correct word form; additionally, they indicate whether their prediction is fully determined by the local context (and the MSD).

Human accuracy is 78% for Russian and 72% for French. Local context determines exactly 39% and 29% of examples. A good choice of the default prediction can be very effective: The upper bound formed by predicting based on local context and otherwise copying over the lemma is 57% for Russian (and 29% for French, which is unsurprising since the French infinitive is a relatively infrequent verb form). Except for long-range dependencies (e.g. conjunction, sequence of tenses), whose frequency is fairly low for nominal categories, bridging the gap to human performance primarily requires the knowledge of the word's lexical properties (e.g. being an uncountable noun) and usage, rather than morpho-syntactic information about other words in the sentence.

6 Conclusion

We use an imitation learning method to train a neural transition-based transduction model, which has previously been shown to be highly competitive on inflection generation and other morphological tasks and particularly strong in the limited-resource setting. The new training method eliminates the need for an external character aligner, integrating alignment into the training objective and thereby avoiding error propagation due to suboptimal alignments. Further improvement comes from optimizing the task metric and performing action-space exploration. Importantly, the new training method produces very strong models in the high data-size setting, which has previously been dominated by general soft-attention seq2seq models. In type-level inflection generation, our five-model majority-vote ensemble outperforms all competitors in all three data settings. Our single model submission comes out on top in three out of six challenges in inflection generation in context.

Acknowledgment

We would like to thank the organizers for the great effort. We thank Anne Göhring and Michi Amsler for their linguistic help and the reviewers for their interest and comments. Peter Makarov is supported by European Research Council Grant No. 338875. Simon Clematide is supported by the Swiss National Science Foundation under grant CRSII5_173719.

References

Roee Aharoni and Yoav Goldberg. 2017. Morphological inflection generation with hard monotonic attention. In *ACL*.

Roee Aharoni, Yoav Goldberg, and Yonatan Belinkov. 2016. Improving sequence to sequence learning for morphological inflection generation: The BIU-MIT systems for the SIGMORPHON 2016 shared task for morphological reinflection. In *14th Annual SIGMORPHON Workshop on Computational Research in Phonetics, Phonology, and Morphology at ACL 2016*.

Dzmitry Bahdanau, Philemon Brakel, Kelvin Xu, Anirudh Goyal, Ryan Lowe, Joelle Pineau, Aaron Courville, and Yoshua Bengio. 2017. An actor-critic algorithm for sequence prediction. In *ICLR*.

Miguel Ballesteros, Yoav Goldberg, Chris Dyer, and Noah A Smith. 2016. Training with exploration improves a greedy stack-LSTM parser. In *EMNLP*.

Toms Bergmanis, Katharina Kann, Hinrich Schütze, and Sharon Goldwater. 2017. Training data augmentation for low-resource morphological inflection. *Proceedings of the CoNLL SIGMORPHON 2017 Shared Task: Universal Morphological Reinflection*.

Kai-Wei Chang, Akshay Krishnamurthy, Alekh Agarwal, Hal Daume III, and John Langford. 2015.

Learning to search better than your teacher. In *ICML*.

Ryan Cotterell, Christo Kirov, John Sylak-Glassman, Géraldine Walther, Ekaterina Vylomova, Arya D. McCarthy, Katharina Kann, Sebastian Mielke, Garrett Nicolai, Miikka Silfverberg, David Yarowsky, Jason Eisner, and Mans Hulden. 2018. The CoNLL–SIGMORPHON 2018 shared task: Universal morphological reinflection. In *Proceedings of the CoNLL–SIGMORPHON 2018 Shared Task: Universal Morphological Reinflection*, Brussels, Belgium. Association for Computational Linguistics.

Hal Daumé III, John Langford, and Daniel Marcu. 2009. Search-based structured prediction. *Machine learning*, 75(3).

Sergey Edunov, Myle Ott, Michael Auli, David Grangier, and Marc'Aurelio Ranzato. 2017. Classical structured prediction losses for sequence to sequence learning. In *NAACL*.

Yoav Goldberg. 2013. Dynamic-oracle transition-based parsing with calibrated probabilistic output. In *Proc. of IWPT*.

Yoav Goldberg and Joakim Nivre. 2012. A dynamic oracle for arc-eager dependency parsing. In *COLING*.

Alex Graves and Jürgen Schmidhuber. 2005. Framewise phoneme classification with bidirectional LSTM and other neural network architectures. *Neural Networks*, 18(5).

Sepp Hochreiter and Jürgen Schmidhuber. 1997. Long short-term memory. *Neural computation*, 9(8).

Katharina Kann and Hinrich Schütze. 2016. MED: The LMU system for the SIGMORPHON 2016 shared task on morphological reinflection. In *14th Annual SIGMORPHON Workshop on Computational Research in Phonetics, Phonology, and Morphology at ACL 2016*.

Rémi Leblond, Jean-Baptiste Alayrac, Anton Osokin, and Simon Lacoste-Julien. 2018. SEARNN: Training RNNs with global-local losses. In *ICLR*.

Vladimir I Levenshtein. 1966. Binary codes capable of correcting deletions, insertions, and reversals. *Soviet physics doklady*, 10(8).

Peter Makarov and Simon Clematide. 2018a. Imitation learning for neural morphological string transduction. In *To appear in EMNLP*.

Peter Makarov and Simon Clematide. 2018b. Neural transition-based string transduction for limited-resource setting in morphology. In *COLING*.

Peter Makarov, Tatiana Ruzsics, and Simon Clematide. 2017. Align and copy: UZH at SIGMORPHON 2017 shared task for morphological reinflection. In *Proceedings of the CoNLL SIGMORPHON 2017 Shared Task: Universal Morphological Reinflection*.

Marc'Aurelio Ranzato, Sumit Chopra, Michael Auli, and Wojciech Zaremba. 2016. Sequence level training with recurrent neural networks. In *ICLR*.

Nils Reimers and Iryna Gurevych. 2017. Reporting score distributions makes a difference: Performance study of LSTM-networks for sequence tagging. In *EMNLP*.

Stefan Riezler, Jonas Kuhn, Detlef Prescher, and Mark Johnson. 2000. Lexicalized stochastic modeling of constraint-based grammars using log-linear measures and EM training. In *ACL*.

Stéphane Ross, Geoffrey Gordon, and Drew Bagnell. 2011. A reduction of imitation learning and structured prediction to no-regret online learning. In *Proceedings of the fourteenth international conference on artificial intelligence and statistics*.

Shiqi Shen, Yong Cheng, Zhongjun He, Wei He, Hua Wu, Maosong Sun, and Yang Liu. 2016. Minimum risk training for neural machine translation. In *ACL*.

Lawrence Wolf-Sonkin, Jason Naradowsky, Sebastian J Mielke, and Ryan Cotterell. 2018. A structured variational autoencoder for contextual morphological inflection. In *ACL*.

Finding the way from ä to a:
Sub-character morphological inflection for the SIGMORPHON 2018 Shared Task

Fynn Schröder[*]   **Marcel Kamlot**[*]   **Gregor Billing**[*]   **Arne Köhn**
Department of Computer Science
Universität Hamburg
Germany
`{7schroed,6kamlot,5billing,koehn}@informatik.uni-hamburg.de`

Abstract

In this paper we describe the system submitted by UHH to the *CoNLL–SIGMORPHON 2018 Shared Task*: Universal Morphological Reinflection. We propose a neural architecture based on the concepts of UZH (Makarov et al., 2017), adding new ideas and techniques to their key concept and evaluating different combinations of parameters. The resulting system is a language-agnostic network model that aims to reduce the number of learned edit operations by introducing equivalence classes over graphical features of individual characters. We try to pinpoint advantages and drawbacks of this approach by comparing different network configurations and evaluating our results over a wide range of languages.

1 Introduction

The system described in this paper[1] was submitted for the *CoNLL–SIGMORPHON 2018 Shared Task* (Cotterell et al., 2018), part 1 only. This assignment challenges the participants to design systems that generate inflected forms based on an input lemma and feature set as shown in Figure 1.

Training data is usually provided in three different volumes (see Table 1), all conforming to the *UniMorph* standard proposed by Kirov et al. (2018). The entire data set comprises 103 languages, although not every training volume is available for every language. In addition, some languages have significantly less training samples than the maximum depicted in Table 1.

With such a high count of diverse languages, our system is not tailored towards specific linguistic

---

[*]These authors contributed equally

[1]Source code available at `https://gitlab.com/nats/sigmorphon18`

bungas   N;INST;PL
⇓
bungām

Figure 1: An example for word inflection in *Latvian*, ”a drum/drums”

	# of Samples	
Volume	max	avg
low	100	99.6
medium	1.000	934.5
high	10.000	8553.6

Table 1: Maximum training data volumes

features of a language, but instead learns transition-based character actions to transform a lemma into its inflected form. We try to limit the number of output actions that our network has to learn by grouping certain characters into common groups based on graphical features like accents or symbol modifiers. Lastly, we propose a method to enhance the training data of the low setting without the use of external resources.

2 String Transducer

The inflection process itself is realized in our system through a finite set of edit actions, resulting in a standard transducer process. An input string is traversed left-to-right via an index pointer that indicates which symbol is currently being regarded. The following actions are available:

- EMIT s (for any symbol s): Appends s to the output string, irrespective of pointer symbol
- COPY: Append the pointer symbol to the output string
- PATCH x: Apply the graphical patch matrix x (cf. Section 3) to the pointer symbol and append the result to the output string
- MOVE: Increment the pointer to continue

Proceedings of the CoNLL–SIGMORPHON 2018 Shared Task: Universal Morphological Reinflection, pages 76–85,
Brussels, Belgium, October 31, 2018. ©2018 Association for Computational Linguistics

traversing the input word

- EOW (end <u>o</u>f <u>w</u>ord): Stop traversing the string and consider the current output string as the final inflection result

2.1 Alignment

We chose to implement our own mechanism to align input lemma and output strings, to accommodate for our patch concept.

The aligner itself is based on plain Levenshtein metrics (Levenshtein, 1966), with the additional constraint that two symbols a, b are considered equal (cost 0) if there is a patch that transforms a into b. We then pick the alignment with the lowest cost according to this customized Levenshtein metric to encourage our system to learn COPY and PATCH actions as much as possible.

2.2 Oracle Algorithm

The actions needed to transform an input lemma w into the inflected target form t are generated through a deterministic algorithm that acts as static oracle gold standard. This algorithm works with an aligned pair (w', t') as input, where the original w and t are filled with arbitrary characters not appearing in the original strings. The exact procedure can be seen in algorithm 1 with #-symbols being used as gap fill characters.

Algorithm 1 Deriving oracle actions gold standard from aligned input strings

---

for all (c_w, c_t) **in** alignment **do**
  if $c_w = \#$ **then**
    $actions$.append(EMIT c_t)
  else if $c_t = \#$ **then**
    $actions$.append(MOVE)
  else if $c_w = c_t$ **then**
    $actions$.append(COPY)
    $actions$.append(MOVE)
  else if $patchtable$.contains(c_w, c_t) **then**
    $actions$.append(PATCH c_w to c_t)
    $actions$.append(MOVE)
  else if $c_w \neq c_t$ **then**
    $actions$.append(EMIT c_t)
    $actions$.append(MOVE)
  end if
end for
$actions$.append(EOW)
return $actions$

Lemma	Inflection	Features
Baumhaus	Baumhäuser	N;ACC;PL
Kanarienvogel	Kanarienvögeln	N;DAT;PL
Milchkuh	Milchkühen	N;DAT;PL

Table 2: *German* noun declension examples: tree house, Canary bird, (milk-)cow

Lemma	Inflection	Features
chacer	chaçons	V;POS;IMP;1;PL
évincer	évinçant	V.PTCP;PRS
concevoir	conçusse	V;SBJV;PST;1;SG

Table 3: *French* verb conjugation examples: to hunt, to cut up, to conceive (of)

3 Patches

An essential part of our system concept is to introduce so-called *patches* that act as string transducer actions. A *patch* in this context is a shortcut operation between two graphically similar characters (see Figure 2), like the acute accent that transforms the letter a into the letter á. It acts as a partial function $p(x)$, so that the same patch can be applied to the letter e to yield $p(\text{e}) = \text{é}$ — however it does not produce a valid result character when applied to the letter b for example.

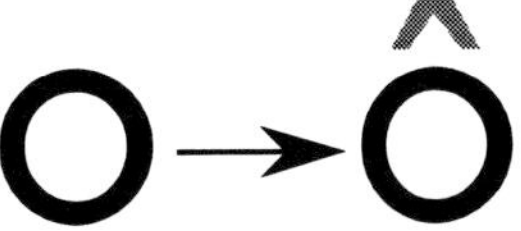

Figure 2: Example patch generated from o to ô (on the right)

3.1 Idea and Motivation

The basic idea for these patches comes from the tendency of some languages to slightly modify the root of the word during inflection. This can either be due to phonological requirements (Kendris, 2001) or historical linguistic influences (Wiese, 2009; Wunderlich, 1999). Two examples for inflection in *German* (note the added *Umlaut* symbols for the inflected forms) and *French* (with added *cedilla* marks) can be seen in Table 2 and 3, respectively. The underlying intention is to capture this modification to the word stem while retaining the idea that it still is based on the same letter or group of letters. A plain transducer would identify n and ñ as different symbols, and consequently generate EMIT actions the same way it would for f and g.

Another motivation was the previous work performed on machine translation systems by Liu et al. (2017). They achieved promising results by exploring visual features on the sub-character level for machine translation, and their ideas and implementations proved useful as a starting ground for the concept presented in this section.

3.2 Generation

To calculate meaningful patches, we render all unique and distinct symbols contained in a given training set into binary 2D pixel matrices that contain information whether a pixel is set/black or not. The resulting matrices are then compared with an element-wise XOR operation that yields all pixels different between the two images. We furthermore only consider patch matrices that are based on the same ASCII character and that don't surpass a certain heuristic threshold of set pixels. Through these checks, patches from i.e. x to m get discarded because although possible, it does not produce any advantage to use them in the transducing component. The resulting effect would be the exact same as a straight-forward EMIT action.

The only non-intuitive heuristic involves the letter i, which contains a dot on top of a vertical bar that "disappears" when applying typical patches like accents. To counter this effect, we introduced a hard-coded set of replacement rules where the letter i is effectively replaced by the Turkish dotless ı in graphical representations, in order to fool the system into correctly applying modifications. A similar principle might apply to other symbols in languages unknown to the authors, so the proposed architecture is capable of extending to more symbol exceptions if desired.

3.3 NFD Unicode Decomposition

The Unicode standard proposes normalization forms[2] that are capable of converting between composite symbols and their integral parts. In particular, the *NFD* normalization achieves an effect very similar to our patch concept.

However, when designing the system we consciously decided against the use of such a feature, mostly because we were not aware of the complex NFD standard and coding a similar system by hand was not a viable alternative at all.

3.4 Font Choice and Rendering

The font choice for our system has to focus on two main aspects:

1. It has to always render all characters in the exact same position
2. It should have high Unicode coverage to be able to render as many foreign alphabets' symbols as possible

Regarding point 1, we only considered mono-space fonts and examined 14 of them. Most of them were appropriate, only two of them still had issues with pixel-perfect alignment of the target symbols on several occasions. Regarding Point 2, we did not find a single font that covered all alphabets in use for this Shared Task, so we had to take some drawbacks and accept rendering of "unknown symbol" placeholders for some languages.

The symbol rendering is handled through the *pygame*[3] library. More sophisticated alternatives perform anti-aliasing that nullifies the desired effect of pixel-based comparison. An anti-aliased letter a looks slightly different than the same letter ä with German *Umlaut* added on top, and the resulting patch would contain this noise and therefore be different from the one between e.g. o and ö.

3.5 Equivalence Classes

After rendering, all resulting patch matrices are grouped by pixel similarity, resulting in a finite number of equivalence classes that can later be used as actions for the transducer. These actions are symmetrical, so that irrespective of lemma and inflection order we define $p(p(c)) = c$.

Once the patches are grouped, the original pixel representation is discarded so that our data can be arranged as a simple lookup table where patches are represented by numerical indices – as can be seen in Table 4.

We deal with unseen characters during prediction by populating the lookup table over a big portion of the entire Unicode plane, and then filtering the result based on a given input alphabet: We keep all rows of any patch p in the pre-populated table if at least one example of p was observed in the input alphabet. Although this computation is quite costly, we can still keep runtime demands at a minimum because the whole overview only has to be computed once. Individual languages can then be filtered out "on demand" while holding a complete

---

[2]see `http://www.unicode.org/reports/tr15/`

[3]see `https://www.pygame.org/docs/ref/font.html`

Symbol	Patch	Result
e	3	è
a	3	à
	. . .	
o	17	ø

Table 4: Symbol patch lookup table

copy of the Unicode-based lookup table in memory.

4 Enhancing Training Data

To improve our training on low data quantities, our system can enhance training data by generating artificial samples based only on the existing data. By detecting patterns in words with the same features and generating more data with the same patterns, we assumed that this would aid the network in detecting and applying patterns, such as common prefix and suffix changes.

Similar approaches were taken by submissions for previous CoNLL–SIGMORPHON Shared Tasks. The winning submission (Kann and Schütze, 2016) of the 2016 Shared Task employed data enhancement for the low resource setting. The team of the 2017 submission from Bergmanis et al. (2017) used two variants of a sequence autoencoder, with one using lemmas and target forms as inputs and the other using randomly generated strings. The additional training data proved to increase the average performance on development sets. Kann and Schütze (2017) used several augmentation methods, including a rule based system. Silfverberg et al. (2017) employ a data augmentation system splitting a word in three parts - inflectional prefix, word stem and inflectional suffix - and then generating new words using existing pre- and suffixes. Further works using data augmentation are provided by Zhou and Neubig (2017) and Nicolai et al. (2017).

4.1 Basic Enhancement Process

To generate artificial training samples for a data set, our system sorts the input data into groups of inflections that share the same features. Within each group, it aligns and compares each pair of lemma and inflected form with every other pair, only retaining the common characters at the aligned positions. The different characters are replaced semi-randomly using a language model based on n-grams with one gap each. Finally, these gaps are filled with letters from the dataset based on their

n-gram	Letter	Frequency	p
?ad	r	433	0.4446
	p	182	0.1869
	t	107	0.1099
	. . .	. . .	. . .
?ade	r	265	0.5311
	p	91	0.1824
	n	46	0.0922
	. . .	. . .	. . .

Table 5: Excerpt from the language model for *swedish* (low volume)

frequency (an example is discussed in Section 4.2), using the same letters for both the artificial lemma and inflected form. If there are still any gaps left, more characters are selected based on n-grams from the language model.

The system produces a specified number of words per alignment match. While creating the system we found that more than five enhanced words per match is not beneficial to the end result, with one word generated per match being the best option for most languages. We have also tried adding a constraint regarding the minimum number of occurrences of a pattern necessary to produce artificial words, but found no improvement overall by specifying this minimum support during development.

4.2 Language Model Example

In Table 6, after inserting `iomm`, one more gap (symbolized by #) is left to fill. To find an appropriate letter, the current word is compared to the language model's n-grams, starting with $n = 5$ and reducing n while shifting the beam from left to right until an n-gram with the corresponding gap is found in the language model. In this case, the longest n-gram found is the 4-gram `?ade` that can also be seen in Table 5. Through using each letter's probability (the frequency of the n-gram in the dataset where the letter replaced the ?-symbol) the letter to replace the ? gets chosen; in this example it is `p`.

Theoretically, this system improves with bigger data sets as there are potentially more patterns to be discovered. Unfortunately this also means that for low quantities of data, where enhancement would be most beneficial, the quality of the enhanced data is lower than for higher quantities of data, where it is not as needed.

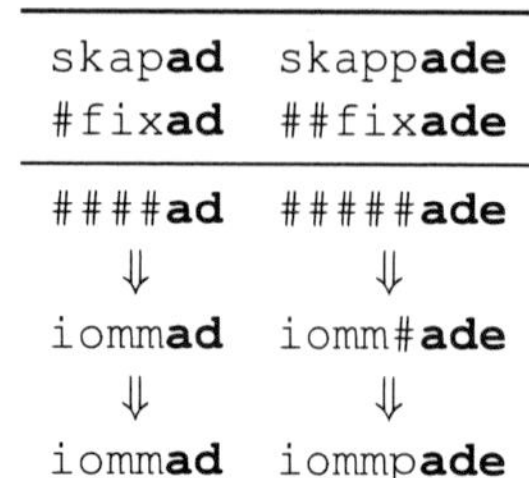

skap**ad**	skapp**ade**
#fix**ad**	##fix**ade**
####**ad**	#####**ade**
⇓	⇓
iomm**ad**	iomm#**ade**
⇓	⇓
iomm**ad**	iommp**ade**

Table 6: An example for creating artifical data for *skapad – skapade* (ADJ;DEF), "created"

5 System Architecture

The system proposed in this work is an encoder-decoder recurrent neural network combined with hard attention and the string-based transducer shown in Section 2. The architecture is displayed in Figure 3. After processing the inputs through both encoder and decoder the resulting action sequence is applied on the lemma string by the transducer to produce the inflected word.

5.1 Baseline

The baseline system that was distributed along with the details for this Shared Task by the organizers is based on pattern matching in strings. It is heavily inspired by the methods proposed in the research of Liu and Mao (2016).

For any given pair of aligned input lemma and output form, the baseline extracts prefix and suffix rules throughout the entire string, and then greedily applies them on a new input lemma that is to be inflected. The replacement rules are derived incrementally, so that if multiple rules would match a new sample, the longest one gets applied to produce the most accurate results possible.

Further details about the baseline system can be found in the proceedings of last year's Shared Task (Cotterell et al., 2017), as the architecture is virtually identical.

5.2 Neural Network Model

We use the same neural network architecture across all 103 languages and training set sizes (low, medium, high). The neural network acts as an oracle for the string transducer shown in Section 2. Its inputs are the lemma of a word and the features of the inflected target form. The outputs correspond to the defined transducer actions (COPY, PATCH p, MOVE, EMIT s and EOW).

We use an encoder-decoder architecture (Cho et al., 2014; Sutskever et al., 2014) to transform

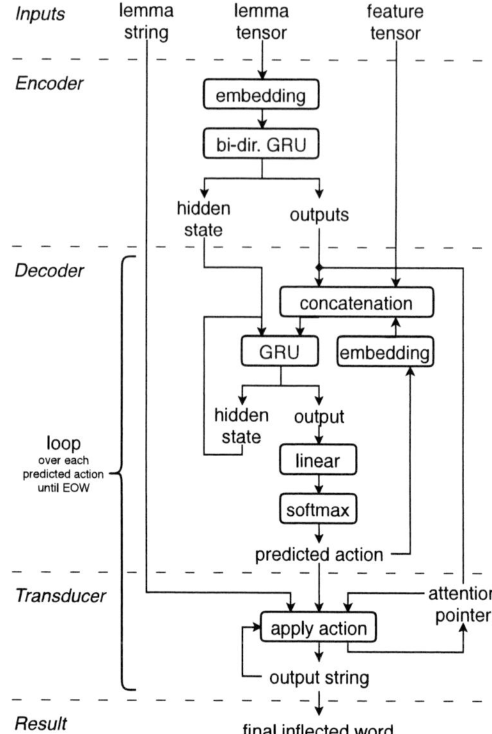

Figure 3: System architecture

a sequence of characters into a sequence of transducer actions. The decoder uses hard monotonic attention which has been found beneficial for the task of morphological inflection (Aharoni and Goldberg, 2016; Aharoni et al., 2016) and allows our system to meaningfully perform COPY and PATCH operations.

Both encoder and decoder contain a single gated recurrent unit (GRU) introduced by Cho et al. (2014) and character embeddings to obtain a dense numerical representation from each input symbol. The encoder is using a bi-directional GRU whose outputs are summed up from both directions. Since the encoder is uni-directional we only use the forward path of the hidden encoder state to start the decoder. The decoder concatenates the character embedding, attention context and feature tensor as a combined input to the GRU. The decoder GRU output is fed into a linear transform followed by a log softmax layer to obtain the log-likelihoods for each transducer action.

Biases and weights for the GRUs and linear layers are initialized randomly from a uniform distribution $\mathcal{U}(-\sqrt{1/s}, \sqrt{1/s})$ where s is the size of the hidden layer (GRU) or number of input features (linear layer). The embedding weights are initialized randomly from a normal distribution $\mathcal{N}(0, 1)$.

The input lemma is processed at once by the encoder, generating output representations for every input character and hidden state representations for the whole input sequence. By using an external loop the decoder produces one transducer action per step. In each step the previous hidden state and output action, inflection features, as well as the attended encoder output is put into the decoder. Which encoder output is being attended is controlled by the index pointer of the transducer. If the network outputs a MOVE action, the index pointer is increased so that the decoder will see the next encoder output in the following loop iteration. Actions moving the index pointer beyond the input lemma are discarded.

To improve the prediction performance we implemented a beam-search decoding process. This results in multiple paths out of which the path with the highest probability is selected to produce the final inflected word. An additional transducer state object stores the decoder hidden state, predicted action and its log-likelihood plus the resulting output string for each step and path in the beam.

5.3 Training

As the network outputs a sequence of transducer actions, the training targets are not the inflected words but an action sequence which produces the correct inflected form when applied on the lemma. This action sequence is generated by looping over the aligned lemma and inflection word in lockstep. For each character combination the corresponding actions are appended to the new output sequence. The detailed algorithm is described in Section 2.2.

Training updates are performed via backpropagation with the Adam optimizer (Kingma and Ba, 2014) using the following parameters: Learning rate $\alpha = 0.005$, momentum decays $\beta_1 = 0.9$, $\beta_2 = 0.999$, numerical stabilizer $\epsilon = 10^{-8}$ and a weight decay (L2 penalty) of 0.001.

The beam-decoding allows a global normalization of the model according to Andor et al. (2016). Unfortunately, training the model with global normalization in beam-search failed to converge. Andor et al. (2016) used pre-training with local normalization to overcome this difficulty, but since we could not find a robust way to switch local to global normalization during training for all 103 languages, we used local normalization only. Once the correct path falls out of the beam, the log-likelihoods of

the correct path build the basis of our custom loss function.

The loss function shown in eq. (1) is based on the locally normalized path probability presented in eq. (4) of Andor et al. (2016). It calculates the negated sum over the log-likelihood l of the correct action in each step of the path. Dividing by the natural logarithm of the sequence length s results in a consistent loss magnitude, thus helping the training process to converge more easily. We assume this is the case because we sum up the error across all steps, also punishing the correct predictions if the system was not 100% confident. The resulting loss L is used to perform the training update back through the entire network.

$$L = -\frac{\sum_i^s l_i}{\ln(1 + s)} \tag{1}$$

Although local normalization restored convergence of learning, we could not find a significant advantage in using multiple beams during training. One explanation why our model did not benefit from beam-search might be that it requires many training updates. Punishing the correct steps in the decoding process leads to many updates while with beam-search updates may be too infrequent.

Our final training and evaluation is done with a beam-size of 1. However, the architecture is prepared to utilize both beam-search and global normalization in the future. Training with a single beam and evaluating with multiple beams to find better predictions is also supported. Due to the complex implementation of beam search and combined batching the system works on single training samples by using a batch size of 1.

5.4 Comparison to previous architectures

Although our approach follows the "Align and Copy" idea of Makarov et al. (2017) the architectures differ. Makarov et al. proposed two different models: Hard attention model with copy mechanism (HACM) and hard attention model over edit actions (HAEM). Both contain an encoder-decoder with LSTMs. HACM uses a mixture of character generation and copying probability distribution to implement the copy mechanism.

Our architecture is more similar to HAEM. The latter uses additional LSTMs storing representations of the predicted inflected form, action history and deleted lemma characters. The decoder feeds a concatenation of the feature vector, currently attended encoder output and extra representations through a rectified linear unit followed by a soft-max to produce outputs like COPY, WRITE and DELETE.

6 Tuning and Evaluation

While we used the same architecture for all languages and training set sizes, we performed individual hyperparameter optimization for each language-size-pair. The parameters tested are the hidden size of encoder/decoder $(32, 64, 128)$, size of the character embeddings $(8, 16)$, whether to use patches or not and what amount of additional training data to hallucinate with the enhancer $(1\times, 5\times)$.

During the development we noticed that the results are strongly influenced by the random initialization of the network weights. We therefore tested every parameter combination with five different random seeds to mitigate this issue. Our final evaluation on the test set used the best parameters we found during the hyperparameter search on the development set for each language-size-pair.

Furthermore, we observed our model sometimes fails to output EOW and instead either tries to copy non-existent lemma characters or endlessly EMITs the same character. The string transducer includes fixes for these issues when the pointer has moved beyond the input lemma. In this case COPY and PATCH do not modify the output sequence at all and EMIT actions cannot append the previously written character again. However, this results in a few missing characters at the end of inflected forms in some corner cases.

7 Results and Discussion

Compared to the other *CoNLL–SIGMORPHON 2018 Shared Task* submissions, our system proved to be in the mid-range (top 59%-67%). By average accuracy, it improved the most over other submissions for the medium volume datasets. While the average accuracy increased from 40.3% on the low set by 33.7 points to 74.0% on the medium set, it improved by only 3.5 more points from the medium set to 77.5% on the high set.

An overview over the results on the medium data set is shown in Table 7. It shows that this system is working exceptionally well on some languages compared to the baseline, such as *Swahili* or *Murrinhpatha*. Likewise, this system performs remarkably worse on some languages, such as *Haida* and *Neapolitan*.

	Language	Ours	BL
Top languages	Uzbek	100.0	96.0
	Mapudungun	100.0	82.0
	Classical-Syriac	97.0	99.0
Worst languages	Old-Irish	6.0	16.0
	Haida	16.1	61.0
	Latin	21.4	37.6
max(Ours - BL)	Swahili	95	0.0
	Murrinhpatha	88.0	0.0
	Zulu	81.8	0.1
max(BL - Ours)	Neapolitan	49.0	94.0
	Haida	16.0	61.0
	Latin	21.4	37.6

Above baseline: 73   **avg. diff.:** 20.2
Below baseline: 29   **avg. diff.:** -7.7

Table 7: Results for our system compared to the baseline. Languages with the best and worst accuracies and languages that were the furthest above and below the baseline, trained on the medium set and evaluated on the test set.

7.1 Patches

Our system is generally able to deduce a meaningful set of patches (that is, a lookup table with more than one trivial entry) for about one third of all languages. While the precise numbers differ per training volume, the overall performance is justified given the font choice discussed in Section 3.4. We could possibly achieve a higher coverage by combining different fonts for different languages, but for us the manual tuning process did not outweigh the work efforts this selection would have required.

We can still observe that out of 42 languages with patches, our hyperparameter tuning algorithm opted to use patches in 17 cases on the low environment. While $\frac{17}{42} = 40,4\%$ clearly signifies little to no global improvement, the same fraction rises to $\frac{29}{42} = 69\%$ when evaluating on the medium environment.

In other words, the usefulness of patches rises (among languages that use patches at all) when training our system on larger quantities of data. However at the same time, the selection of which languages actually use patches to achieve maximum accuracy partially differs. Only slightly more than half of the 17 positively patching languages in the low environment also apply patches on medium, so it is imperative to consider the actual linguistical structures behind the data in order to maximise the benefit of this method.

Lastly, one could combine the NFD system explored in Section 3.3 with the already implemented font rendering to achieve hybrid patch generation in an effort to maximise its effectiveness. This idea was not pursued further by us and is left open as future work.

7.2 Data Enhancer

On low volume, the accuracy on the development set increased for 42 of the enhanced data sets (best of enhancement by 1 / by 5) when compared to the accuracy on the regular data set. For 53 sets they decreased, no matter the enhancement proportion. The probability of these being random observances is 0.3049 (Zar, 1998). However, by testing the accuracy of the enhanced and the regular training data for each language on the development set, we can select which languages will be enhanced and which will not. This is part of the hyperparameter search from Section 6. On the low development set, the enhancer is leading to a total improvement of 1.245% in accuracy and a negligible 0.044 characters in Levenshtein distance, with improvements for single languages of up to 10.8% (*french*). The average improvement is 3.6667%.

7.3 Network Hiccups

Our system's accuracy is poor on *Haida* and *Neapolitan* compared to other submissions and the baseline. The reason is that for both languages the post-processing used to combat a missing EOW is often triggered erroneously. The example below shows our system missing the last character in the output because the transducer discards the second identical action to EMIT an a in this case.

- ñíiyä → ñíiyä'wa (prediction)
- ñíiyä → ñíiyä'wa**a** (target)

As the inflected words are almost correct, the Levenshtein distance is much lower than the accuracy might indicate. For *Haida* the Levenshtein distance is even significantly lower than the baseline results. In hindsight, it would have been better to replace non-ending predictions with the lemma instead of trying to clean the output as the negative side-effects most likely outweigh any benefits. In the future, a better approach would be to improve the training process by using a dynamic oracle for the target sequence and correctly implementing global normalization with beam-search decoding. These changes are likely to eliminate the need for any post-processing.

Another weakness of our system is the inability to transform a prefix into a suffix or vice versa as shown in the following *German* language example:

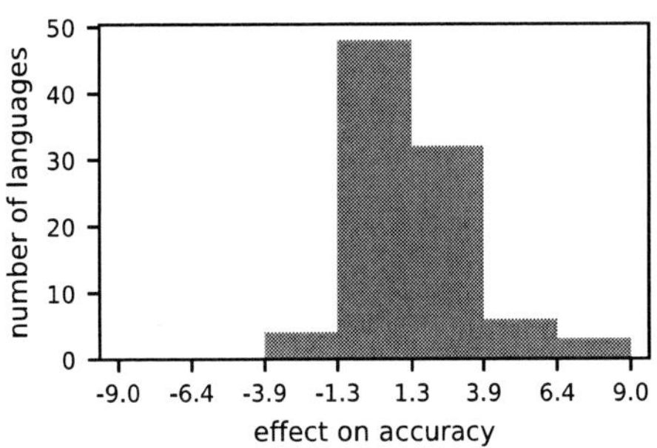

Figure 4: Histogram showing the effect of beam size 16 compared to size 1 on the test set (trained on low)

- abstellen → stellt __ (prediction)
- abstellen → stellt ab (target)

This behavior is expected as our neural network works with hard monotonic attention. It would need to store the information within the hidden-state over the whole sequence as it cannot attend the encoder outputs from the beginning again. A cure for this symptom would be to use a model with soft attention – which in turn cannot meaningfully use COPY or PATCH operations on the input lemma.

7.4 Beam-Decoding

While we did not use beam-decoding for the official results, we experimented with the evaluation performance after the submission. Figure 4 shows the number of languages for which beam-decoding with 16 beams makes a difference in comparison to greedy decoding. For half of the languages there are either no or only negligible differences in accuracy. About one third shows a small positive effect. Some languages show a larger accuracy increase while only few languages show a small accuracy decrease. A binomial test shows that the probability of the increase being random is as low as 2.4×10^{-10}. Beam-decoding therefore clearly leads to an increase in accuracy which matches the intuition of beam-decoding producing better or equal results compared to greedy decoding.

Acknowledgements

We would like to thank the two anonymous reviewers for their help, including making us aware of the Unicode NFD standard. We also appreciate the work of the organisers to realise the exciting Shared Task.

References

Roee Aharoni and Yoav Goldberg. 2016. Sequence to sequence transduction with hard monotonic attention. *CoRR* abs/1611.01487. http://arxiv.org/abs/1611.01487.

Roee Aharoni, Yoav Goldberg, and Yonatan Belinkov. 2016. Improving sequence to sequence learning for morphological inflection generation: The biu-mit systems for the sigmorphon 2016 shared task for morphological reinflection. In *Proceedings of the 14th SIGMORPHON Workshop on Computational Research in Phonetics, Phonology, and Morphology*. Association for Computational Linguistics, pages 41–48. https://doi.org/10.18653/v1/W16-2007.

Daniel Andor, Chris Alberti, David Weiss, Aliaksei Severyn, Alessandro Presta, Kuzman Ganchev, Slav Petrov, and Michael Collins. 2016. Globally normalized transition-based neural networks. *CoRR* abs/1603.06042. http://arxiv.org/abs/1603.06042.

Toms Bergmanis, Katharina Kann, Hinrich Schütze, and Sharon Goldwater. 2017. Training data augmentation for low-resource morphological inflection. In *The CoNLL-SIGMORPHON 2017 Shared Task*. https://doi.org/10.18653/v1/K17-2002.

Kyunghyun Cho, Bart van Merrienboer, Çaglar Gülçehre, Fethi Bougares, Holger Schwenk, and Yoshua Bengio. 2014. Learning phrase representations using RNN encoder-decoder for statistical machine translation. *CoRR* abs/1406.1078. http://arxiv.org/abs/1406.1078.

Ryan Cotterell, Christo Kirov, John Sylak-Glassman, Géraldine Walther, Ekaterina Vylomova, Arya D. McCarthy, Katharina Kann, Sebastian Mielke, Garrett Nicolai, Miikka Silfverberg, David Yarowsky, Jason Eisner, and Mans Hulden. 2018. The CoNLL–SIGMORPHON 2018 shared task: Universal morphological reinflection. In *Proceedings of the CoNLL–SIGMORPHON 2018 Shared Task: Universal Morphological Reinflection*. Association for Computational Linguistics, Brussels, Belgium.

Ryan Cotterell, Christo Kirov, John Sylak-Glassman, Géraldine Walther, Ekaterina Vylomova, Patrick Xia, Manaal Faruqui, Sandra Kübler, David Yarowsky, Jason Eisner, and Mans Hulden. 2017. Conll-sigmorphon 2017 shared task: Universal morphological reinflection in 52 languages. *CoRR* abs/1706.09031. http://arxiv.org/abs/1706.09031.

Katharina Kann and Hinrich Schütze. 2016. Med: The lmu system for the sigmorphon 2016 shared task on morphological reinflection. In *Proceedings of the 14th SIGMORPHON Workshop on Computational Research in Phonetics, Phonology, and Morphology*. Association for Computational Linguistics, Berlin, Germany, pages 62–70. http://anthology.aclweb.org/W16-2010.

Katharina Kann and Hinrich Schütze. 2017. The lmu system for the conll-sigmorphon 2017 shared task on universal morphological reinflection. In *Proceedings of the CoNLL SIGMORPHON 2017 Shared Task: Universal Morphological Reinflection*. Association for Computational Linguistics, Vancouver, pages 40–48. http://www.aclweb.org/anthology/K17-2003.

Christopher Kendris. 2001. *French Grammar*. Barron's Educational Series.

Diederik P. Kingma and Jimmy Ba. 2014. Adam: A method for stochastic optimization. *CoRR* abs/1412.6980. http://arxiv.org/abs/1412.6980.

Christo Kirov, Ryan Cotterell, John Sylak-Glassman, Géraldine Walther, Ekaterina Vylomova, Patrick Xia, Manaal Faruqui, Sebastian Mielke, Arya D. McCarthy, Sandra Kübler, David Yarowsky, Jason Eisner, and Mans Hulden. 2018. UniMorph 2.0: Universal Morphology. In Nicoletta Calzolari (Conference chair), Khalid Choukri, Christopher Cieri, Thierry Declerck, Sara Goggi, Koiti Hasida, Hitoshi Isahara, Bente Maegaard, Joseph Mariani, Hélène Mazo, Asuncion Moreno, Jan Odijk, Stelios Piperidis, and Takenobu Tokunaga, editors, *Proceedings of the Eleventh International Conference on Language Resources and Evaluation (LREC 2018)*. European Language Resources Association (ELRA), Miyazaki, Japan.

Vladimir I Levenshtein. 1966. Binary codes capable of correcting deletions, insertions, and reversals. In *Soviet physics doklady*. volume 10, pages 707–710.

Frederick Liu, Han Lu, Chieh Lo, and Graham Neubig. 2017. Learning character-level compositionality with visual features. *CoRR* abs/1704.04859. http://arxiv.org/abs/1704.04859.

Ling Liu and Lingshuang Jack Mao. 2016. Morphological reinflection with conditional random fields and unsupervised features. In *Proceedings of the 14th SIGMORPHON Workshop on Computational Research in Phonetics, Phonology, and Morphology*. Association for Computational Linguistics, pages 36–40. https://doi.org/10.18653/v1/W16-2006.

Peter Makarov, Tatiana Ruzsics, and Simon Clematide. 2017. Align and copy: UZH at SIGMORPHON 2017 shared task for morphological reinflection. *CoRR* abs/1707.01355. http://arxiv.org/abs/1707.01355.

Garrett Nicolai, Bradley Hauer, Mohammad Motallebi, Saeed Najafi, and Grzegorz Kondrak. 2017. If you can't beat them, join them: the university of alberta system description. In *Proceedings of the CoNLL SIGMORPHON 2017 Shared Task: Universal Morphological Reinflection*. Association for Computational Linguistics, Vancouver, pages 79–84. http://www.aclweb.org/anthology/K17-2008.

Miikka Silfverberg, Adam Wiemerslage, Ling Liu, and Lingshuang Jack Mao. 2017. Data augmentation for morphological reinflection. In *Proceedings of the CoNLL SIGMORPHON 2017 Shared Task: Universal Morphological Reinflection*. Association for Computational Linguistics, Vancouver, pages 90–99. http://www.aclweb.org/anthology/K17-2010.

Ilya Sutskever, Oriol Vinyals, and Quoc V. Le. 2014. Sequence to sequence learning with neural networks. *CoRR* abs/1409.3215. http://arxiv.org/abs/1409.3215.

Richard Wiese. 2009. The grammar and typology of plural noun inflection in varieties of german. *The Journal of Comparative Germanic Linguistics* 12(2):137–173.

Dieter Wunderlich. 1999. German noun plural reconsidered. *Behavioral and Brain Sciences* 22(6):1044–1045.

Jerrold H. Zar. 1998. *Biostatistical Analysis (4th Edition)*. Prentice Hall.

Chunting Zhou and Graham Neubig. 2017. Morphological inflection generation with multi-space variational encoder-decoders. In *Proceedings of the CoNLL SIGMORPHON 2017 Shared Task: Universal Morphological Reinflection*. Association for Computational Linguistics, Vancouver, pages 58–65. http://www.aclweb.org/anthology/K17-2005.

Morphological Reinflection in Context: CU Boulder's Submission to CoNLL-SIGMORPHON 2018 Shared Task

Ling Liu and **Ilamvazhuthy Subbiah** and **Adam Wiemerslage** and
Jonathan Lilley and **Sarah R. Moeller**
University of Colorado
`first.last@colorado.edu`

Abstract

This paper describes two systems for the second subtask of CoNLL-SIGMORPHON 2018 shared task on universal morphological reinflection submitted by the University of Colorado Boulder team. Both systems are implementations of RNN encoder-decoder models with soft attention. The first system is similar to the baseline system with minor differences in architecture and parameters, and is implemented using PyTorch. It works for both track 1 and track 2 of the subtask and generally outperforms the baseline at low data settings in both tracks. The second system predicts the morphosyntactic description (MSD) of the lemma to be inflected using an MSD prediction model. The data for subtask 2 is processed and reformatted to subtask 1 data format to train an inflection model. Then the inflection model predicts the inflected form for the target lemma given the predicted MSD. This system achieves higher accuracies than the first system when the training data is the most limited, though it does not perform better when the training data is abundant.

1 Introduction

Several natural language processing tasks can benefit from representational power in a computational model at the level of morphology. The task of morphological inflection has been explored recently in great depth (Cotterell et al., 2016, 2017), resulting in several effective models for that task. Of particular note is an architecture proposed by Kann and Schütze (2016), which is modeled after an encoder-decoder model that found success in machine translation (Cho et al., 2014).

A related, but relatively unexplored task is that of morphological inflection in context. This paper documents the University of Colorado Boulder's system for that task (subtask2) in the CoNLL-SIGMORPHON 2018 shared task. We experimented with a model very similar to the provided baseline, which computes the context for a given inflection as the concatenation of word and MSD embeddings to the left and right of the word that is to be inflected. During encoding of an input sequence, the context vector is concatenated with the character embedding at each time step.

We also experimented with an encoder comprising of three separate LSTMs whose output states are concatenated and used to predict the MSD for the lemma to be inflected. We then use a second encoder-decoder network to perform inflection over the given lemma according to that MSD, thus formulating the second portion into the problem in task1 where the training data are pairs of lemma, inflected word form, and the MSD for the inflection and the task is to predict the inflected word form given the lemma and MSD.

We find that the first system described here outperforms the second one when there is ample training data, whereas the latter performs better when the training data is scarce.

2 Task and data description

The shared task is broken into 2 subtasks. This paper presents systems that participated only in subtask2. There are seven languages for this task: German, English, Spanish, Finnish, French, Russian, and Swedish; and 3 data settings: low ($<$ 100 sentence examples), medium ($<$ 900 sentence examples), and high ($<$ 8000 sentence examples). Each data setting varies across languages with regard to the number of training sentence examples.

Within subtask 2 there are two tracks. Both tracks present each problem in context, that is, given some lemma and the word forms surrounding it in a sentence, the goal is to generate the correctly inflected form of that lemma. In track one, the MSD and lemma for each word in the sentence

Proceedings of the CoNLL–SIGMORPHON 2018 Shared Task: Universal Morphological Reinflection, pages 86–92,
Brussels, Belgium, October 31, 2018. ©2018 Association for Computational Linguistics

is available, whereas in track 2 only the inflected word form is available. For testing in both tracks, only the lemma of the form that should be inflected is provided. More details about the tasks and data can be found in Cotterell et al. (2018).

3 System description

3.1 System 1

Our first system is similar to the subtask 2 baseline system provided by the shared task organizers (Cotterell et al., 2018) but with a few changes in the architecture and parameters. It is an encoder-decoder model with soft attention (Bahdanau et al., 2015) implemented with PyTorch based on the PyTorch tutorial of translation with a sequence to sequence network and attention,[1] and it works for both track 1 and track 2.

Architecture The encoder is a single layer Gated Recurrent Unit (GRU) (Cho et al., 2014). It takes as input the concatenation of the context embedding and the embedded characters in the lemma, and outputs a sequence of state vectors, which are then translated into a sequence of embeddings by a one-layer GRU decoder using an attention mechanism. The embeddings are then transformed into output characters by a log softmax layer. For track 1, the context embedding is the concatenation of word embeddings for the previous inflected word form, previous lemma, previous MSD, current lemma, next inflected word form, next lemma, and next MSD. If a word is at the beginning of the sentence, we add a special symbol $\langle SOS \rangle$ as its history context, and if a word is at the end of the sentence, we add another special symbol $\langle EOS \rangle$ as its future context. The context embedding for track 1 is illustrated in the bottom part of Figure 1. For track 2, the context embedding is the concatenation of word embeddings for the previous inflected word form, current lemma, and next inflected word form as is shown in Figure 2. Special symbols indicating the beginning and end of sentences are also used. For the character embedding of lemmas, we also used $\langle SOS \rangle$ and $\langle EOS \rangle$ to indicate the beginning and end of the lemma.

The decoder starts decoding with input as $\langle SOS \rangle$ and hidden state as the last hidden state of the encoder. An attention mechanism is implemented to

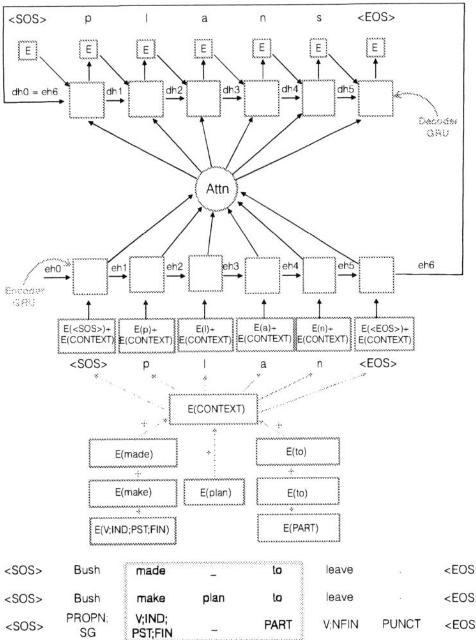

Figure 1: Architecture of system 1 with track 1 context embedding

allow the decoder network to focus on different parts of the encoder's outputs at each step of generation. It is implemented as another feed-forward layer which takes as its input the decoder's input and hidden states and calculates a set of attention weights. We multiply the attention weights with the encoder output vectors to create a weighted combination. This weighted combination will go through a non-linear ReLU layer before going to the GRU process. In addition, a dropout layer is added to the decoder input to deal with overfitting. The dropout rate is 0.1. The decoding process stops when the end symbol $\langle EOS \rangle$ is generated. It may also stop early when a maximum prediction length has been reached. The maximum prediction length is set at 50. The overall architecture of this system as to track 1 is shown in Figure 1. For track 2, only the context embedding is different, i.e. the context is the concatenation of the previous inflected word form, the target lemma and next inflected word form embeddings.

Data To train the model for track 1, the model is trained to make predictions for only entries whose part-of-speech (POS) are verbs, nouns, or adjectives. For track 2, the model is trained to make

---

[1] https://pytorch.org/tutorials/
intermediate/seq2seq_translation_
tutorial.html

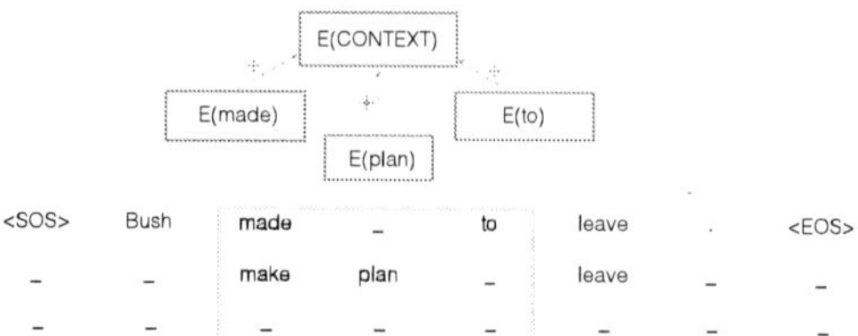

Figure 2: Context embedding for system 1 at track 2

predictions for entries where the lemma form is provided.

Settings and Hyper-parameters The model is trained to minimize the negative log likelihood loss (NLLLoss) on the training data. The optimization method is the Adam algorithm (Kingma and Ba, 2015) with a learning rate of 0.00005. As to other hyper-parameters, we use an embedding size of 100 for the character, lemma, word-form and MSD embeddings. The hidden size is 800 for track 1 and 400 for track 2.

3.2 System 2: MSD prediction and inflection

In our second approach we reformulate the task 2 problem as a task 1 problem. This approach involves predicting the morphosyntactic descriptions of the lemma in question, given the inflected word forms, the lemmas and the MSDs for the rest of the sentence. Once we have the predicted MSDs, we use a task 1 inflection model to get the inflected form. This section describes the architecture for the MSD prediction model followed by the inflection model. This system is only for track 1 as it relies on the morphosyntactic descriptions.

3.2.1 MSD prediction model

The MSD prediction model uses a many-to-one encoder-decoder neural network to predict the MSDs of the lemma to be inflected.

Architecture The encoder uses three separate single-layer bidirectional LSTMs ($LSTM_{left}$, $LSTM_{base}$ and $LSTM_{right}$) to encode the input into a fixed length vector c. It is based on Vylomova et al. (2017). $LSTM_{left}$ takes as input the sequence that is to the left of the current lemma in the sentence and computes the hidden states $h_l^{(t)} \in \mathbb{R}^H$.

$$h_l^{(t)} = f_l(x^{(t)}, h_l^{(t-1)})$$

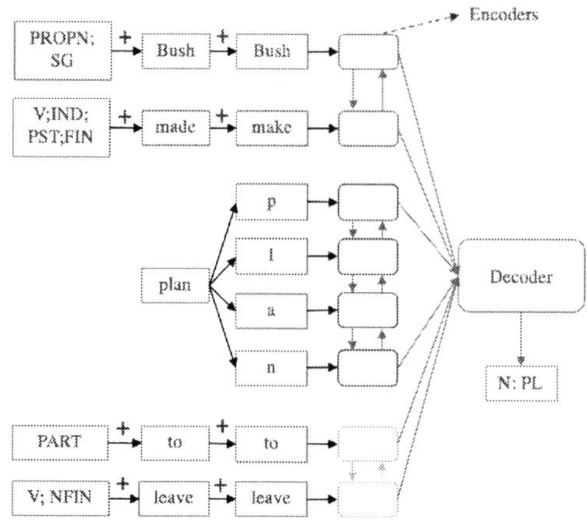

Figure 3: Architecture of the MSD prediction model

where $x^{(t)} \in \mathbb{R}^{3E}$ is a concatenation of the inflected word form embedding $e(w_t)$, the lemma embedding $e(l_t)$ and the MSD embedding $e(msd_t)$ for some word t in the sentence; $e(w_t), e(l_t), e(msd_t) \in \mathbb{R}^E$, where E is the dimension of the embedding layer.

In a similar fashion, $LSTM_{right}$ takes as input the sequence that is to the right of the current lemma in the sentence.

$$h_r^{(t)} = f_r(x^{(t)}, h_r^{(t-1)})$$

$LSTM_{base}$ takes as input the sequence of character embeddings, $e(c_t)$, concatenated with the lemma embedding, $e(l)$, for every character c in the lemma.

$$h_b^{(t)} = f_b(x_b^{(t)}, h_b^{(t-1)})$$

The input to the decoder is the vector $c \in \mathbb{R}^{3H}$ which is the concatenation of the final states from the three encoder LSTMs.

$$c = [h_l^{(T_l)}; h_r^{(T_r)}; h_b^{(T_b)}]$$

The decoder acts as a classifier that classifies the input into one of the possible MSD combinations.

$$h_d = f_d(c, h_d^{(0)})$$

$$P_{msd} = softmax(W.h_d + b)$$

The high level architecture of the model is shown in Figure 3.

Data To train the MSD prediction model,

we used only lemmas whose POS are verbs, nouns or adjectives.

Settings and Hyper-parameters We used a hidden size of 100 and an embedding size of 100 for the character, lemma, word and MSD embeddings. We used Adam as the optimizer with a learning rate of 0.0005.

3.2.2 Inflection model

The Inflection model outputs the inflected word-form given a lemma and its associated morphosyntactic features (for example, *touch + V;V.PTCP;PRS* ⇒ *touching*). It is an encoder-decoder soft-attention based neural network that takes as input the sequence of lemma characters and the morphosyntactic descriptions, and produces a sequence of characters as output. The Inflection model is based on University of Colorado Boulder's submission to CoNLL-SIGMORPHON 2017 Shared Task (Silfverberg et al., 2017).

Architecture The encoder is a single layer bi-directional GRU that takes as input the embeddings $e(.)$ of lemma characters and the morphosyntactic descriptions, and produces a sequence of state vectors. The decoder then uses this sequence of state vectors to generate the sequence of output embeddings. At each stage in the decoding process, the decoder uses the following to compute the current state vector:

- the previous decoder hidden state.

- the previous output embedding.

- A weighted sum of all the encoder states.

The decoding process starts with the embedding for the word boundary symbol $\langle EOS \rangle$ and a randomly initialized hidden state h_0. The weights for the encoder states is computed using an Attention mechanism which uses the previous decoder state as input. The weights are normalized using a softmax function. The overall architecture of the inflection model is shown in Figure 4.

Data The data to train the inflection model was generated from the task2 training data by taking out entries of verbs, nouns or adjectives and putting them into task 1 data format. The amount of training data we get in this way is comparable

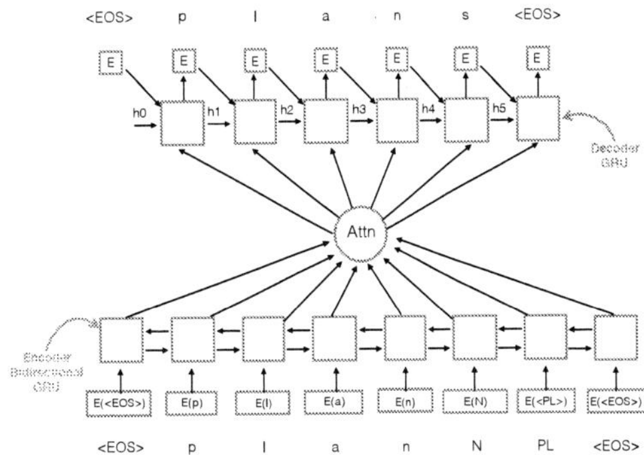

Figure 4: Architecture of the inflection model

to the data size of task 1 at different data settings for all the 7 languages; more than 10000 examples for the high data setting, more than 2000 examples for the medium data setting, and more than 250 examples for the low data setting.

Settings and Hyper-parameters The inflection model uses an embedding size of 100 and a hidden state of size 100 for the encoder and the decoder. The data is processed in batches of 20. Masking is used to mask part of the input sequences which are shorter than the maximum length in the batch. Stochastic Gradient Descent (SGD) with gradient clipping is used for optimization and the loss function is NLLLoss.

4 Experiments

4.1 Exploratory experiment: lemma copying

As the first exploration of the task and an evaluation of task complexity, we experimented by copying the lemma directly. In other words, we simply guess that the inflected form of a lemma in the context is the lemma itself. This experiment will be referred to as the copy system going further.

4.2 System 1

We tuned the architecture and the parameters for the first system on track 1 and finally settled on the architecture and parameters described in section 3.1 for track 1 and track 2. For both tracks, we train the model for 50 epochs at the low data setting and 40 epochs at medium and high data settings, and use the model at the epoch which gets the highest accuracy on the development set to make predictions on the test set.

LANGUAGE	HIGH				MEDIUM				LOW			
	COPY	SYS 1	SYS 2	BASELINE	COPY	SYS 1	SYS 2	BASELINE	COPY	SYS 1	SYS 2	BASELINE
DE	58.95	63.3	62.49	**64.51**	**58.95**	55.11	55.11	54.4	**58.95**	10.41	*32.15*	0.2
EN	62.64	**76.23**	68.58	72.91	62.64	65.16	**66.57**	60.02	**62.64**	57.6	*59.62*	1.81
ES	25.53	51.75	36.75	**53.44**	25.53	**41.8**	32.68	23.14	25.53	25.53	**27.77**	8.98
FI	22.36	43.07	30.24	**49.05**	22.36	23.38	23	**28.21**	**22.36**	7.12	*11.44*	0.76
FR	23.63	58.04	60.9	**63.54**	23.63	44.2	42.16	**45.01**	23.63	25.66	**26.88**	0
RU	18.37	65.16	55.52	**71.18**	18.37	44.58	40.46	**50.3**	18.37	15.06	**22.09**	0
SV	32.45	60.53	37.77	**62.23**	32.45	**49.68**	34.57	47.55	**32.45**	20.74	*29.04*	1.17
AVERAGE	34.85	59.73	50.32	**62.41**	34.85	**46.27**	42.08	44.09	**34.85**	23.16	*29.86*	1.85

Table 1: Track 1 accuracies for original form of the copy system, system 1, system2, and baseline

LANGUAGE	HIGH				MEDIUM				LOW			
	COPY	SYS 1	SYS 2	BASELINE	COPY	SYS 1	SYS 2	BASELINE	COPY	SYS 1	SYS 2	BASELINE
DE	58.95	59.96	-	**65.72**	**58.95**	49.54	-	56.93	**58.95**	11.02	-	0.1
EN	62.64	**70.8**	-	70.39	**62.64**	61.53	-	57.6	**62.64**	58.91	-	2.22
ES	25.53	45.86	-	**51.05**	25.53	35.34	-	**41.23**	25.53	**27.91**	-	8.98
FI	22.36	24.02	-	**34.82**	**22.36**	17.15	-	19.19	**22.36**	7.88	-	0.38
FR	23.63	48.27	-	**58.45**	23.63	**36.05**	-	21.38	**23.63**	23.01	-	0
RU	18.37	39.76	-	**46.89**	18.37	27.21	-	**30.52**	18.37	**21.08**	-	2.71
SV	32.45	**54.15**	-	54.04	32.45	41.17	-	**43.09**	32.45	16.49	-	0.96
AVERAGE	34.85	48.97	-	**54.48**	34.85	38.29	-	**38.56**	34.85	23.76	-	2.19

Table 2: Track 2 accuracies for original form of the copy system, system 1, system2, and baseline

4.3 System 2

In our experiments for System 2, we train the MSD prediction model for 10 epochs on all data settings. To train the inflection model we used 200 epochs for the low data setting and 100 epochs for the medium and high data settings. We also experimented with higher embedding and hidden sizes of 200 for the MSD prediction model and we found no significant improvements.

5 Results and discussion

The evaluation result as to original forms for track 1 is shown in Table 1. In general, our first system (SYS 1) outperforms the second system (SYS 2) in both high and medium data settings, though neither of them get a higher averaged accuracy than the baseline system when the training data size is high and the first system is only marginally better than the baseline when the training data is of medium size. For the four systems summarized in the table, our first system performs the best only with English at high data setting, and it achieves the highest accuracies with Spanish and Swedish at medium data setting. The second system outperforms the other three systems with English at medium data setting. However, when the training data is the most limited, i.e. at the low data setting, the second system outperforms both the first system and the baseline as to average accu-

racy over the seven languages, though it is still worse than the copy system. To be specific, direct lemma copy produces the best results for German, English, Finnish and Swedish among the four systems at the low data setting. The second system outperforms the other three systems with Spanish, French, and Russian.

Table 2 provides the evaluation results for the baseline system, our first system and the copy system, as to original forms for track 2. Our second system relies on the prediction of MSDs and does not work for track 2. For this track, we see the pattern of the system performance is similar to that of track 1. That is, the baseline system generally outperforms our first system and the copy system at the high data setting and gets very close to the first system in terms of averaged accuracies at the medium data setting, and our first system outperforms the baseline by a large margin at the low data setting though it is still worse than the copy system.

When the training data is the most limited, comparing the results of system 1 for track 1 and track 2, shows that track 1 results are not better than track 2 results, indicating that the MSD and lemma information does not really help with the performance of the first system when a limited amount of data is available. However, the second system outperforms the first system on track 1 for all languages, and the results of SYS 2 on track 1 are higher than the results of SYS 1 on track 2 on most languages (except Spanish, for which SYS 2 track 1 is a mere 0.14% lower). This suggests that, when training data is very limited, the MSDs introduce a lot of ambiguity if only used as contextual information. On the other hand, if we first predict the MSD as our second system does, the ambiguity is reduced and thus the system generates better predictions. German is the language where the second system is most significantly better than the first system on the track 1 low data setting. German is a language with much ambiguity in its inflected forms. For a German word form, there can be as many as 40 different readings (Müller and Schütze, 2015). This fact also supports the ambiguity explanation for the difference in the performance of our first and second systems.

In the low setting, Finnish, German and Russian have the lowest scores for our first model. Finnish and Russian are the two languages with the most complex inflection systems in the sense that they have the highest number of distinct MSDs. In the high data setting, counting only the parts-of-speech the model is supposed to predict, i.e. nouns, verbs and adjectives, there are 346 distinct MSDs in Finnish training data and 345 in Russian training data. The rich inflection requires more data for the model to learn. Though German has less distinct MSDs than Finnish and Russian, its inflection is also complex in the sense that it's less predictable: Unlike Russian and Finnish which use almost exclusively suffixes, German is not primarily suffixing but employs prefixing, circumfixing, and umlauting. Its inflectional rules are less regular than Finnish or Russian. A qualitative analysis of the predictions in the low data setting, finds that our first model tends to make changes in the stem for German though not for Finnish and Russian, and the wrong changes in the stem cause wrong predictions for German words while for Finnish and Russian the errors are mainly wrong suffixation. This agrees with the distinct features of their inflection systems.

The intuition behind just copying the lemma when the training data is limited, is the linguistic observation that the lemma form is usually the most frequently used form and thus any uninformative inflection tends to be less likely than the lemma.

6 Conclusion

For this task, we explored the performance of RNN encoder-decoder models with soft attention as to predicting the inflected forms of a lemma in context. We developed two systems by implementing the encoder-decoder model in different ways. We found that when the training data is very limited, morpho-syntactic descriptions contribute to better prediction results. Though both of our systems outperform the baseline at the low data setting, none of the systems are better than the blind guess of the inflected form being the lemma itself. However, when the training data is abundant, neural network systems outperform the lemma copying approach.

References

Dzmitry Bahdanau, Kyunghyun Cho, and Yoshua Bengio. 2015. Neural machine translation by jointly learning to align and translate. In *International Conference on Learning Representations*.

Kyunghyun Cho, Bart Van Merriënboer, Caglar Gulcehre, Dzmitry Bahdanau, Fethi Bougares, Holger Schwenk, and Yoshua Bengio. 2014. Learning phrase representations using RNN encoder-decoder for statistical machine translation. *arXiv preprint arXiv:1406.1078*.

Ryan Cotterell, Christo Kirov, John Sylak-Glassman, Géraldine Walther, Ekaterina Vylomova, Arya D. McCarthy, Katharina Kann, Sebastian Mielke, Garrett Nicolai, Miikka Silfverberg, David Yarowsky, Jason Eisner, and Mans Hulden. 2018. The CoNLL–SIGMORPHON 2018 shared task: Universal morphological reinflection. In *Proceedings of the CoNLL–SIGMORPHON 2018 Shared Task: Universal Morphological Reinflection*, Brussels, Belgium. Association for Computational Linguistics.

Ryan Cotterell, Christo Kirov, John Sylak-Glassman, Géraldine Walther, Ekaterina Vylomova, Patrick Xia, Manaal Faruqui, Sandra Kübler, David Yarowsky, Jason Eisner, and Mans Hulden. 2017. The CoNLL-SIGMORPHON 2017 shared task: Universal morphological reinflection in 52 languages. In *Proceedings of the CoNLL-SIGMORPHON 2017 Shared Task: Universal Morphological Reinflection*, Vancouver, Canada. Association for Computational Linguistics.

Ryan Cotterell, Christo Kirov, John Sylak-Glassman, David Yarowsky, Jason Eisner, and Mans Hulden. 2016. The SIGMORPHON 2016 shared task: Morphological reinflection. In *Proceedings of the 14th SIGMORPHON Workshop on Computational Research in Phonetics, Phonology, and Morphology*, Berlin, Germany. Association for Computational Linguistics.

Katharina Kann and Hinrich Schütze. 2016. MED: The LMU system for the SIGMORPHON 2016 shared task on morphological reinflection. In *Proceedings of the 14th SIGMORPHON Workshop on Computational Research in Phonetics, Phonology, and Morphology*, Berlin, Germany. Association for Computational Linguistics.

Diederik P. Kingma and Jimmy Lei Ba. 2015. Adam: a method for stochastic optimization. In *International Conference on Learning Representations*.

Thomas Müller and Hinrich Schütze. 2015. Robust morphological tagging with word representations. In *Proceedings of the 2015 Conference of the North American Chapter of the Association for Computational Linguistics: Human Language Technologies*, pages 526–536.

Miikka Silfverberg, Adam Wiemerslage, Ling Liu, and Lingshuang Jack Mao. 2017. Data augmentation for morphological reinflection. *Proceedings of the CoNLL SIGMORPHON 2017 Shared Task: Universal Morphological Reinflection*, pages 90–99.

Ekaterina Vylomova, Ryan Cotterell, Timothy Baldwin, and Trevor Cohn. 2017. Context-aware prediction of derivational word-forms. *CoRR*, abs/1702.06675.

Copenhagen at CoNLL–SIGMORPHON 2018: Multilingual Inflection in Context with Explicit Morphosyntactic Decoding

Yova Kementchedjhieva
University of Copenhagen
yova@di.ku.dk

Johannes Bjerva
University of Copenhagen
bjerva@di.ku.dk

Isabelle Augenstein
University of Copenhagen
augenstein@di.ku.dk

Abstract

This paper documents the Team Copenhagen system which placed first in the CoNLL–SIGMORPHON 2018 shared task on universal morphological reinflection, Task 2 with an overall accuracy of 49.87. Task 2 focuses on morphological inflection in context: generating an inflected word form, given the lemma of the word and the context it occurs in. Previous SIGMORPHON shared tasks have focused on context-agnostic inflection—the "inflection in context" task was introduced this year. We approach this with an encoder-decoder architecture over character sequences with three core innovations, all contributing to an improvement in performance: (1) a wide context window; (2) a multi-task learning approach with the auxiliary task of MSD prediction; (3) training models in a multilingual fashion.

1 Introduction

This paper describes our approach and results for Task 2 of the CoNLL–SIGMORPHON 2018 shared task on universal morphological reinflection (Cotterell et al., 2018). The task is to generate an inflected word form given its lemma and the context in which it occurs.

Morphological (re)inflection from context is of particular relevance to the field of computational linguistics: it is compelling to estimate how well a machine-learned system can capture the morphosyntactic properties of a word given its context, and map those properties to the correct surface form for a given lemma.

There are two tracks of Task 2 of CoNLL–SIGMORPHON 2018: in Track 1 the context is given in terms of word forms, lemmas and morphosyntactic descriptions (MSD); in Track 2 only word forms are available. See Table 1 for an example. Task 2 is additionally split in three settings based on data size: high, medium and low, with high-resource datasets consisting of up to 70K instances per language, and low-resource datasets consisting of only about 1K instances.

The baseline provided by the shared task organisers is a *seq2seq* model with attention (similar to the winning system for reinflection in CoNLL–SIGMORPHON 2016, Kann and Schütze (2016)), which receives information about context through an embedding of the two words immediately adjacent to the target form. We use this baseline implementation as a starting point and achieve the best overall accuracy of 49.87 on Task 2 by introducing three augmentations to the provided baseline system: (1) We use an LSTM to encode the entire available context; (2) We employ a multi-task learning approach with the auxiliary objective of MSD prediction; and (3) We train the auxiliary component in a multilingual fashion, over sets of two to three languages.

In analysing the performance of our system, we found that encoding the full context improves performance considerably for all languages: 11.15 percentage points on average, although it also highly increases the variance in results. Multi-task learning, paired with multilingual training and subsequent monolingual finetuning, scored highest for five out of seven languages, improving accuracy by another 9.86% on average.

2 System Description

Our system is a modification of the provided CoNLL–SIGMORPHON 2018 baseline system, so we begin this section with a reiteration of the baseline system architecture, followed by a description of the three augmentations we introduce.

Proceedings of the CoNLL–SIGMORPHON 2018 Shared Task: Universal Morphological Reinflection, pages 93–98,
Brussels, Belgium, October 31, 2018. ©2018 Association for Computational Linguistics

WORD FORMS	We	were	☐	to	feel	very	welcome	.
LEMMAS	we	be	make	to	feel	very	welcome	.
MSD TAGS	PRO;NOM;PL;1	AUX;IND;PST;FIN	☐	PART	V;NFIN	ADV	ADJ	PUNCT

Table 1: Example input sentence. Context MSD tags and lemmas, marked in gray, are only available in Track 1. The cyan square marks the main objective of predicting the word form *made*. The magenta square marks the auxiliary objective of predicting the MSD tag *V;PST;V.PTCP;PASS*.

2.1 Baseline

The CoNLL–SIGMORPHON 2018 baseline[1] is described as follows:

> The system is an encoder-decoder on character sequences. It takes a lemma as input and generates a word form. The process is conditioned on the context of the lemma [...] The baseline treats the lemma, word form and MSD of the previous and following word as context in track 1. In track 2, the baseline only considers the word forms of the previous and next word. [...] The baseline system concatenates embeddings for context word forms, lemmas and MSDs into a context vector. The baseline then computes character embeddings for each character in the input lemma. Each of these is concatenated with a copy of the context vector. The resulting sequence of vectors is encoded using an LSTM encoder. Subsequently, an LSTM decoder generates the characters in the output word form using encoder states and an attention mechanism.

To that we add a few details regarding model size and training schedule:

- the number of LSTM layers is one;

- embedding size, LSTM layer size and attention layer size is 100;

- models are trained for 20 epochs;

- on every epoch, training data is subsampled at a rate of 0.3;

- LSTM dropout is applied at a rate 0.3;

- context word forms are randomly dropped at a rate of 0.1;

- the Adam optimiser is used, with a default learning rate of 0.001; and

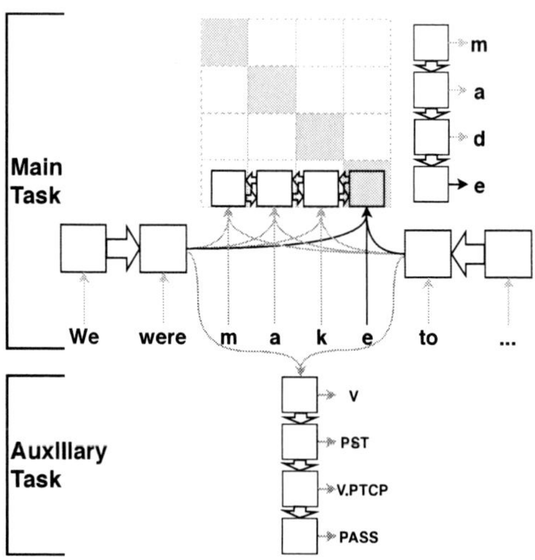

Figure 1: Schematic representation of our approach. The focus here is on the prediction of the final character, *e*, of the word form *made*. The attention matrix indicates that this character should be based on the final state of the encoder, which contains information about the final character of the input form, and the past and future context. The input and output of the auxiliary decoder are marked in magenta.

- trained models are evaluated on the development data (the data for the shared task comes already split in train and dev sets).

2.2 Our system

Here we compare and contrast our system[2] to the baseline system. A diagram of our system is shown in Figure 1.

2.2.1 Entire Context Encoded with LSTMs

The idea behind this modification is to provide the encoder with access to all morpho-syntactic cues present in the sentence. In contrast to the baseline, which only encodes the immediately adjacent context of a target word, we encode the *entire context*. All context word forms, lemmas, and MSD

---

[1] Code available at:
`https://github.com/sigmorphon/conll2018`

[2] Code available at: `https://github.com/YovaKem/inflection_in_context`

		Track 1		Track 2	
		base	our	base	our
high	DE	64.51	**72.40**	**65.72**	64.81
	EN	72.91	**77.84**	70.39	**71.90**
	ES	53.44	**56.24**	**51.05**	48.95
	FI	49.05	**55.27**	**34.82**	32.40
	FR	63.54	**70.67**	58.45	**61.51**
	RU	71.18	**77.91**	46.89	**49.00**
	SV	62.23	**69.26**	54.04	**55.96**
med.	DE	54.40	**62.18**	56.93	**57.33**
	EN	60.02	**66.67**	57.60	**66.67**
	ES	23.14	**51.33**	41.23	**42.50**
	FI	28.21	**35.71**	19.19	**22.24**
	FR	45.01	**60.29**	21.38	**45.62**
	RU	50.30	**63.05**	30.52	**35.94**
	SV	47.55	**57.66**	43.09	**45.96**
low	DE	0.20	**4.85**	0.10	**18.91**
	EN	1.81	**33.84**	2.22	**59.42**
	ES	8.98	**31.42**	8.98	**31.84**
	FI	0.76	**12.83**	0.38	**12.33**
	FR	0.00	**34.42**	0.00	**29.53**
	RU	0.00	**25.90**	2.71	**22.69**
	SV	1.17	**27.55**	0.96	**30.96**

Table 2: Official shared task test set results.

tags (in Track 1) are embedded in their respective high-dimensional spaces as before, and their embeddings are concatenated. However, we now reduce the entire past context to a fixed-size vector by encoding it with a forward LSTM, and we similarly represent the future context by encoding it with a backwards LSTM.

2.2.2 Auxiliary Task: MSD of the Target Form

We introduce an auxiliary objective that is meant to *increase the morpho-syntactic awareness of the encoder* and to regularise the learning process—the task is to predict the MSD tag of the target form. MSD tag predictions are conditioned on the context encoding, as described in 2.2.1. Tags are generated with an LSTM one component at a time, e.g. the tag *PRO;NOM;SG;1* is predicted as a sequence of four components, $\langle$PRO, NOM, SG, 1$\rangle$.

For every training instance, we backpropagate the sum of the main loss and the auxiliary loss without any weighting.

As MSD tags are only available in Track 1, this augmentation only applies to this track.

2.2.3 Multilinguality

The parameters of the entire MSD (auxiliary-task) decoder are shared across languages.

Since a grouping of the languages based on language family would have left several languages in single-member groups (e.g. Russian is the sole representative of the Slavic family), we experiment with random *groupings of two to three languages*. Multilingual training is performed by randomly alternating between languages for every new minibatch. We do not pass any information to the auxiliary decoder as to the source language of the signal it is receiving, as we assume abstract morpho-syntactic features are shared across languages.

Finetuning After 20 epochs of multilingual training, we perform 5 epochs of monolingual finetuning for each language. For this phase, we reduce the learning rate to a tenth of the original learning rate, i.e. 0.0001, to ensure that the models are indeed being finetuned rather than retrained.

2.2.4 Model Size and Training Schedule

We keep all hyperparameters the same as in the baseline. Training data is split 90:10 for training and validation. We train our models for 50 epochs, adding early stopping with a tolerance of five epochs of no improvement in the validation loss. We do not subsample from the training data.

2.2.5 Ensemble Prediction

We train models for 50 different random combinations of two to three languages in Track 1, and 50 monolingual models for each language in Track 2. Instead of picking the single model that performs best on the development set and thus risking to select a model that highly overfits that data, we use an ensemble of the five best models, and make the final prediction for a given target form with a majority vote over the five predictions.

3 Results and Discussion

Test results are listed in Table 2. Our system outperforms the baseline for all settings and languages in Track 1 and for almost all in Track 2—only in the high resource setting is our system not definitively superior to the baseline.

Interestingly, our results in the low resource setting are often higher for Track 2 than for Track 1, even though contextual information is less explicit in the Track 2 data and the multilingual multi-tasking approach does not apply to this track. We interpret this finding as an indicator that a simpler model with fewer parameters works better in a setting of limited training data. Nevertheless, we focus on the low resource setting in the analysis below due to time limitations. As our Track 1 results are still substantially higher than the baseline results, we consider this analysis valid and insightful.

3.1 Ablation Study

We analyse the incremental effect of the different features in our system, focusing on the low-resource setting in Track 1 and using development data.

Entire Context Encoded with LSTMs Encoding the entire context with an LSTM highly increases the variance of the observed results. So we trained fifty models for each language and each architecture. Figure 2 visualises the means and standard deviations over the trained models. In addition, we visualise the average accuracy for the five best models for each language and architecture, as these are the models we use in the final ensemble prediction. Below we refer to these numbers only.

The results indicate that encoding the full context with an LSTM highly enhances the performance of the model, by 11.15% on average. This observation explains the high results we obtain also for Track 2.

Auxiliary Task: MSD of the Target Form Adding the auxiliary objective of MSD prediction has a variable effect: for four languages (DE, EN, ES, and SV) the effect is positive, while for the rest it is negative. We consider this to be an issue of insufficient data for the training of the auxiliary component in the low resource setting we are working with.

Multilinguality We indeed see results improving drastically with the introduction of multilingual training, with multilingual results being 7.96% higher than monolingual ones on average.

We studied the five best models for each language as emerging from the multilingual training (listed in Table 3) and found no strong linguistic patterns. The EN–SV pairing seems to yield good models for these languages, which could be explained in terms of their common language family

DE	FI	SV	FI, SV	RU, FR	FR, FI
EN	RU, SV	RU, FI	RU,FR	SV, ES	SV, FR
ES	DE	FI	SV, DE	SV,EN	SV,FR
FI	DE	ES	FR, ES	EN,RU	RU,SV
FR	SV,EN	EN,ES	DE,FI	SV,EN	EN,SV
RU	SV	DE,FR	EN,SV	SV,FR	EN,FI
SV	EN,DE	FI,EN	FR,RU	ES,EN	RU, EN

Table 3: Five best multilingual models for each language.

and similar morphology. The other natural pairings, however, FR–ES, and DE–SV, are not so frequent among the best models for these pairs of languages.

Finally, monolingual finetuning improves accuracy across the board, as one would expect, by 2.72% on average.

Overall The final observation to be made based on this breakdown of results is that the multi-tasking approach paired with multilingual training and subsequent monolingual finetuning outperforms the other architectures for five out of seven languages: DE, EN, FR, RU and SV. For the other two languages in the dataset, ES and FI, the difference between this approach and the approach that emerged as best for them is less than 1%. The overall improvement of the multilingual multi-tasking approach over the baseline is 18.30%.

3.2 Error analysis

Here we study the errors produced by our system on the English test set to better understand the remaining shortcomings of the approach. A small portion of the wrong predictions point to an incorrect interpretation of the morpho-syntactic conditioning of the context, e.g. the system predicted *plan* instead of *plans* in the context *Our _ include raising private capital*. The majority of wrong predictions, however, are nonsensical, like *bomb* for *job*, *fify* for *fixing*, and *gnderrate* for *understand*. This observation suggests that generally the system did not learn to copy the characters of lemma into inflected form, which is all it needs to do in a large number of cases. This issue could be alleviated with simple data augmentation techniques that encourage autoencoding (see, e.g., Bergmanis et al., 2017).

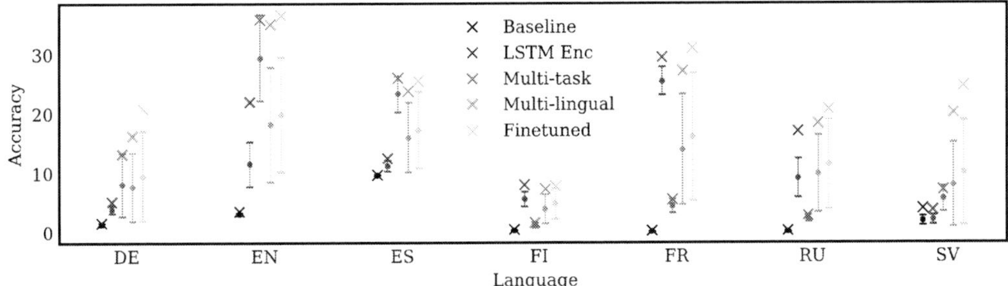

Figure 2: Mean (●) and standard deviation (error bars) over 100 models trained for each language and architecture, and average (×) over the 5 best models. *LSTM Enc* refers to a model that encodes the full context with an LSTM; *Multi-task* builds on *LSTM Enc* with an auxiliary objective of MSD prediction; *Multilingual* refers to a model with an auxiliary component trained in a multilingual fashion; *Finetuned* refers to a multilingual model topped with monolingual finetuning.

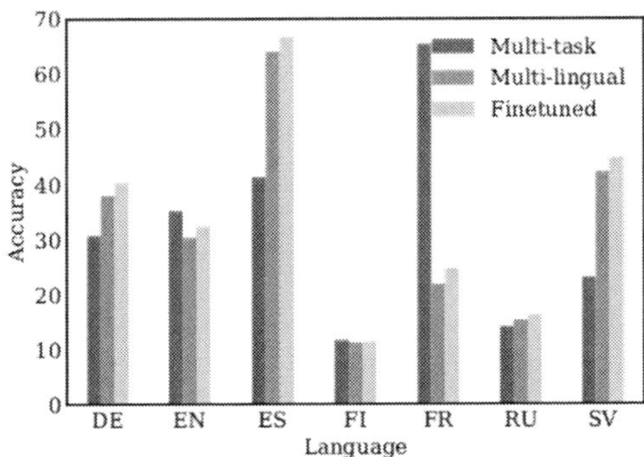

Figure 3: Accuracy on the auxiliary task of MSD prediction with different models. See the caption of Figure 2 for more details.

3.3 MSD prediction

Figure 3 summarises the average MSD-prediction accuracy for the multi-tasking experiments discussed above.[3] Accuracy here is generally higher than on the main task, with the multilingual finetuned setup for Spanish and the monolingual setup for French scoring best: 66.59% and 65.35%, respectively. This observation illustrates the added difficulty of generating the correct surface form even when the morphosyntactic description has been identified correctly.

We observe some correlation between these numbers and accuracy on the main task: for DE, EN, RU and SV, the brown, pink and blue bars here pattern in the same way as the corresponding ×'s in Figure 2. One notable exception to this

---

[3] As MSD tags are not available for target forms in the development data, the accuracy of MSD prediction is measured over all other nouns, adjectives and verbs in the dataset.

pattern is FR where inflection gains a lot from multilingual training, while MSD prediction suffers greatly. Notice that the magnitude of change is not always the same, however, even when the general direction matches: for RU, for example, multilingual training benefits inflection much more than in benefits MSD prediction, even though the MSD decoder is the only component that is actually shared between languages. This observation illustrates the two-fold effect of multi-task training: an auxiliary task can either inform the main task through the parameters the two tasks share, or it can help the main task learning through its regularising effect.

4 Related Work

Our system is inspired by previous work on multi-task learning and multi-lingual learning, mainly building on two intuitions: (1) jointly learning related tasks tends to be beneficial (Caruana, 1997; Søgaard and Goldberg, 2016; Plank et al., 2016; Bjerva et al., 2016; Bjerva, 2017b); and (2) jointly learning related languages in an MTL-inspired framework tends to be beneficial (Bjerva, 2017a; Johnson et al., 2017; de Lhoneux et al., 2018). In the context of computational morphology, multilingual approaches have previously been employed for morphological reinflection (Bergmanis et al., 2017) and for paradigm completion (Kann et al., 2017). In both of these cases, however, the available datasets covered more languages, 40 and 21, respectively, which allowed for linguistically-motivated language groupings and for parameter sharing directly on the level of characters. De Lhoneux et al. (2018) explore parameter sharing between related languages for dependency parsing, and find that sharing is more beneficial in the case of closely related languages.

5 Conclusions

In this paper we described our system for the CoNLL–SIGMORPHON 2018 shared task on Universal Morphological Reinflection, Task 2, which achieved the best performance out of all systems submitted, an overall accuracy of 49.87. We showed in an ablation study that this is due to three core innovations, which extend a character-based encoder-decoder model: (1) a wide context window, encoding the entire available context; (2) multi-task learning with the auxiliary task of MSD prediction, which acts as a regulariser; (3) a multilingual approach, exploiting information across languages. In future work we aim to gain better understanding of the increase in variance of the results introduced by each of our modifications and the reasons for the varying effect of multi-task learning for different languages.

Acknowledgements

We gratefully acknowledge the support of the NVIDIA Corporation with the donation of the Titan Xp GPU used for this research.

References

Toms Bergmanis, Katharina Kann, Hinrich Schütze, and Sharon Goldwater. 2017. Training data augmentation for low-resource morphological inflection. *Proceedings of the CoNLL SIGMORPHON 2017 Shared Task: Universal Morphological Reinflection*, pages 31–39.

Johannes Bjerva. 2017a. *One Model to Rule them all – Multitask and Multilingual Modelling for Lexical Analysis*. Ph.D. thesis, University of Groningen.

Johannes Bjerva. 2017b. Will my auxiliary tagging task help? Estimating Auxiliary Tasks Effectivity in Multi-Task Learning. In *NoDaLiDa*, pages 216–220.

Johannes Bjerva, Barbara Plank, and Johan Bos. 2016. Semantic tagging with deep residual networks. In *COLING*, pages 3531–3541.

Rich Caruana. 1997. Multitask learning. *Machine Learning*, 28 (1):41–75.

Ryan Cotterell, Christo Kirov, John Sylak-Glassman, Géraldine Walther, Ekaterina Vylomova, Arya D. McCarthy, Katharina Kann, Sebastian Mielke, Garrett Nicolai, Miikka Silfverberg, David Yarowsky, Jason Eisner, and Mans Hulden. 2018. The CoNLL–SIGMORPHON 2018 Shared Task: Universal Morphological Reinflection. In *Proceedings of the CoNLL–SIGMORPHON 2018 Shared Task: Universal Morphological Reinflection*, Brussels, Belgium. Association for Computational Linguistics.

Melvin Johnson, Mike Schuster, Quoc V. Le, Maxim Krikun, Yonghui Wu, Zhifeng Chen, Nikhil Thorat, Fernanda Viégas, Martin Wattenberg, Greg Corrado, Macduff Hughes, and Jeffrey Dean. 2017. Google's multilingual neural machine translation system: Enabling zero-shot translation. *Transactions of the Association for Computational Linguistics*, 5:339–351.

Katharina Kann, Ryan Cotterell, and Hinrich Schütze. 2017. One-shot neural cross-lingual transfer for paradigm completion. In *Proceedings of the 55th Annual Meeting of the Association for Computational Linguistics (Volume 1: Long Papers)*, pages 1993–2003. Association for Computational Linguistics.

Katharina Kann and Hinrich Schütze. 2016. MED: The LMU system for the SIGMORPHON 2016 shared task on morphological reinflection. In *Proceedings of the 14th SIGMORPHON Workshop on Computational Research in Phonetics, Phonology, and Morphology*, pages 62–70.

Miryam de Lhoneux, Johannes Bjerva, Isabelle Augenstein, and Anders Søgaard. 2018. Parameter sharing between dependency parsers for related languages. In *Proceedings of EMNLP*.

Barbara Plank, Anders Søgaard, and Yoav Goldberg. 2016. Multilingual Part-of-Speech Tagging with Bidirectional Long Short-Term Memory Models and Auxiliary Loss. In *Proceedings of ACL (Short Papers)*.

Anders Søgaard and Yoav Goldberg. 2016. Deep multi-task learning with low level tasks supervised at lower layers. In *Proceedings of ACL (Short Papers)*.

What can we gain from language models for morphological inflection?

Alexey Sorokin

Moscow Institute of Physics and Technology / Institutskij per., 9,
Faculty of Innovations and High Technologies, 141701, Dolgoprudny, Russia
Moscow State University / GSP-1, Leninskie Gory, 1
Faculty of Mathematics and Mechanics, 119991, Moscow, Russia
`alexey.sorokin@list.ru`

Abstract

This paper investigates the attempts to augment neural-based inflection models with character-based language models. We found that in most cases this slightly improves performance, however, the effect is marginal. We also propose another language-model based approach that can be used as a strong baseline in low-resource setting.

1 Introduction

Morphological inflection is a task of automatic reconstruction of surface word form given its source form, called lemma, and morphological characteristic of required form. For example, in Spanish the input word *contar* together with features v;fin;ind;imp;pst;3;pl should be transformed to *contaban*. The obvious way to solve such a task is to handcode transformations using finite-state rules. However, this approach requires an expert knowledge of the language under consideration and can be extremely time-consuming for the languages with complex morphology. Therefore a machine learning algorithm should be developed to efficiently solve this task for any language. Such an algorithm must be able to generalize from known lemma-features-word triples to previously unseen ones, mimicking human behaviour when inflecting a neologism in its native language or an unknown word in a foreign one. In this setting automatic inflection becomes an instance of string transduction problem, which makes conditional random fields a natural baseline model as suggested in (Nicolai et al., 2015). Another popular approach is to predict transformation pattern, either as a pair of prefix and suffix changes as used in the baseline model for Sigmorphon 2018 Shared Task (Cotterell et al., 2018). For example, consider a Czech adjective *krásný* and its superlative form *nejkrásnější*. The inflection pattern can

be encoded as a pair of prefix rule \$ $\rightarrow$ \$*nej* and a suffix rule *ý* $\rightarrow$ *ejší*. Such encoding is, however, too weak to deal with infixation and root vowel alterations, required, for example, for Spanish verb *volver* and its +Pres+Sg+1 form *vuelvo*. An *abstract paradigm* approach (Ahlberg et al., 2015; Sorokin, 2016) compresses this transformation to 1+o+2+er#1+ue+2+o, where digits stand for variables (the parts of verb stem), and constant fragments define the paradigm. In both cases in order to predict the inflected word form one suffices to guess the transformation pattern, thus solving a standard classification problem. Both mentioned models (CRFs and abstract paradigms) were quite successful in Sigmorphon 2016 Shared Task (Cotterell et al., 2016), however, they were clearly outperformed by neural network approaches.

Indeed, string transduction problems are successfully solved using neural methods, for example, in machine translation. The work of (Kann and Schütze, 2016) adopts the seq2seq model with soft attention of (Bahdanau et al., 2014). It defeated not only non-neural systems mentioned earlier, but also other neural approaches. It shows that attention mechanism is crucial for word inflection. However, in contrast to machine translation, a symbol of output word is less prone to depend from multiple input symbols, than a translated word from multiple source words. Consequently, the attention weight is usually concentrated on a single source symbol, being more a pointer than a distributed probability mass. Moreover, this pointer traverses the source word from left to right in order to generate the inflected form. All that motivated the hard attention model of (Aharoni and Goldberg, 2017), which outperformed the soft attention approaches. The key feature of this model is that it predicts not only the output word, but also the alignment between source and target using an additional step symbol which shifts the pointer to the

Proceedings of the CoNLL–SIGMORPHON 2018 Shared Task: Universal Morphological Reinflection, pages 99–104,
Brussels, Belgium, October 31, 2018. ©2018 Association for Computational Linguistics

next symbol. This model was further improved by (Makarov et al., 2017), whose system was the winner of Sigmorphon 2017 evaluation campaign (Cotterell et al., 2017). The approach of Makarov et al. was especially successful in low and medium resource setting, while in high resource setting it achieves an impressive accuracy of over 95%[1].

Does it mean that no further research is required and hard attention method equipped with copy mechanism is the final solution for automatic inflection problem? Actually, not, since the quality of the winning approach was much lower on medium (about 85%) and low (below 50%) datasets. This lower quality is easy to explain since in low resource setting the system might even see no examples of the required form[2] or observe just one or two inflection pairs which do not cover all possible paradigms for this particular form. For example, Russian verbs has several tens of variants to produce the +Pres+Sg+1 form. Consequently, to improve the inflection accuracy the system should extract more information from the whole language, not only the instances of the given form. This task is easier for agglutinative languages with regular inflection paradigm: to predict, say, the +Pres+Sg+1 form in Turkish, the system has just to observe several singular verb form (not necessarily of the first person) to extract the singular suffix and several first person form (of any number and tense). In presence of fusion, like in Russian and other Slavonic languages, the decomposition is not that easy or even impossible.

However, this decomposition is already realised in model of (Makarov et al., 2017) since the grammatical features are treated as a list of atomic elements, not as entire label. A new source of information about the whole language are the laws of its phonetics. For example, to detect the vowel in the suffix of the Turkish verb one do not need to observe any verbs at all, but to extract the vowel harmony patterns from the inflection of nouns. A natural way to capture the phonetic patterns are character language models. They were already applied to the problem of inflection in (Sorokin, 2016) and produced a strong boost over the baseline system. The work of Sorokin used simple ngram models, however, neural language models

(Tran et al., 2016) has shown their superiority over earlier approaches for various tasks.

Summarizing, our approach was to enrich the model of (Makarov et al., 2017) with the language model component. We followed the architecture of (Gulcehre et al., 2017), whose approach is simply to concatenate the state of the neural decoder with the state of the neural language model before passing it to the output projection layer. We expected to improve performance especially in low and medium resource setting, however, our approach does not have clear advantages: our joint system is only slightly ahead the baseline system of (Makarov et al., 2017) for most of the languages. We conclude that the language model job is already executed by the decoder. However, given the vitality of language model approach in other areas of modern NLP (Peters et al., 2018), we describe our attempts in detail to give other researchers the ideas for future work in this direction.

2 Model structure

2.1 Baseline model

As the state-of-the-art baseline we choose the model of Makarov et al. (Makarov et al., 2017), the winner of previous Sigmorphon Shared Task. This system is based on earlier work of Aharoni and Goldberg (Aharoni and Goldberg, 2017). We briefly describe the structure of baseline model (we call it AGM-model further) and refer the reader to these two papers for more information. AGM-model consists of encoder and decoder, where an encoder is just a bidirectional LSTM. Each element of the input sequence contains a 0-1 encoding of a current letter and two LSTMs traverse this sequence in opposite directions. After encoding, each element of obtained sequence contains information about current letter and its context.

The main feature of the encoder is that it operates on the level on alignments, not on the level of letter sequences. Assume a pair *volver-vuelvo* appears in the training set. The natural alignment is

$$
\begin{array}{cccccc}
v & u & e & l & v & o \\
| & | &   & | & | & | \\
v & o &   & l & v & e & r
\end{array}
$$

It is transformed to the source-target pair in Figure 1. Here the step symbol denotes pointer shift, for precise algorithm of transformation see (Aharoni and Goldberg, 2017):

The decoder is one-directional LSTM. It obtains

---

[1] Averaged over all languages of (Cotterell et al., 2017) dataset

[2] it was provided with 100 inflection pairs for entire language, which is often several times lower than the number of possible grammeme combinations

begin	v	step	u	e	step	l	step	v	step	o	step	step	end
begin	v	v	o	o	o	l	l	v	v	e	e	r	end

Figure 1: Transformation of alignment to source-target pair.

as input the lower string of Figure 1. Let i be the number of current timestep and j be current position in the input string. On i-th step the decoder takes a concatenation of 3 vectors: x_j — the j-th element in the output of the encoder, $\tilde{f} = W_{feat} f$ — the embedding of the grammatical feature vector and $g_i = W_{emb} y_{i-1}$ — the embedding of previous output symbol. The feature vector is obtained as $0/1$-encoding of the list of grammatical features. We actually take the concatenation of output vectors for $d \geq 1$ previous output symbols as y_{i-1}, in our experiments d was set to 4.

On each step the decoder produces a vector z_i as output and propagates updated hidden state vector h_i to the next timestep. z_i is then passed to a two-layer perceptron with ReLU activation on the intermediate layer and softmax activation on the output layer, which produces the output distribution p_i over output letters, formally:

$$
\begin{aligned}
\widehat{z}_i &= \max\left(W_p z_i + b_p, \overline{0}\right), \\
p_i &= \text{softmax}(W_o \widehat{z}_i + b_o), \\
y_i &= \text{argmax}_k\, p_{ik}
\end{aligned}
$$

If y_i is the index of step symbol, we move the pointer to the next input letter. We also use the copy gate from (Makarov et al., 2017): since the neural network copies the vast majority of its symbols, the output distribution $\widehat{p}_i$ is obtained as a weighted sum of singleton distribution which outputs current input symbol and the preliminary distribution p_i specified above. The weight σ_i is the output of another one-layer perceptron:

$$
\begin{aligned}
\sigma_i &= \text{sigmoid}(W_\sigma z_i + b_\sigma), \\
\widehat{p}_i &= \sigma_i I(k = c_j) + (1 - \sigma_i) p_i, \\
y_i &= \text{argmax}_k\, \widehat{p}_{ik}
\end{aligned}
$$

2.2 Character-based model

Our proposal is to explicitly equip the decoder with the information from the character-based language model. We suppose it will help the model to avoid outputting phonetically implausible sequences of letters. We choose the simplest possible architecture of the language model, namely, on each step it takes a concatenation of d previous symbol embeddings $u_i = [g_{i-d}, \ldots, g_{i-1}]$ and applies an LSTM

cell to obtain a vector v_i and update LSTM hidden state h_i. v_i is propagated through a two-layer perceptron to predict the next output symbol analogously to the output layer of the baseline model:

$$
\begin{aligned}
\widehat{u}_i &= \max\left(W_p^{LM} u_i + b_p^{LM}, \overline{0}\right), \\
p_i^{LM} &= \text{softmax}(W_o^{LM} \widehat{u}_i + b_o^{LM}), \\
y_i &= \text{argmax}_k\, p_{ik}^{LM}
\end{aligned}
$$

The model is trained to predict next output symbol separately from the basic model. In principle, one can use more complex neural architectures, for example, a multilayer LSTM or apply attention mechanism. However, our preliminary experiments have shown that attention over recent history as in (Tran et al., 2016) leads to slightly worse performance.

To join the baseline model and the language model we concatenate the decoder output z_i with the analogous vector from the language model z_i^{LM}. The language model is conditioned over previously output vectors (excluding step symbol). That is the fusion mechanism as used in (Gulcehre et al., 2017). We also experimented with concatenating the pre-output vectors $\widehat{z}_i, \widehat{z}_i^{LM}$, however, the former variant leads to slightly better performance. To avoid exposure bias we mask language model state with all zeros with the probability of 0.4 (it teaches the model to recover from language model errors).

3 Data and implementation

3.1 Implementation

The initial alignment was obtained using longest common subsequence (LCS) method. Then this alignment was optimized using Chinese Restaurant process as in (Cotterell et al., 2016). The optimization phase did 5 passes over training data. The aligner trained on the training set was also used to align the validation data.

We implemented our model using Keras library with Tensorflow backend[3]. For all the setting we used the encoder with 96 hidden units in each direction, the decoder contained 128 units and the

---

[3]`https://github.com/AlexeySorokin/Sigmorphon2018SharedTask`

pre-output projection layer was of dimension 96. Morphological features were embedded to 48 dimensions. We used batch size of 32 when training, the batches contained the words of approximately the same size to reduce the amount of padding. We trained the model for 100 epochs with Adam optimizer, training was stopped when the accuracy on the validation data did not improve for 15 epochs. During decoding, the beam search of width 10 was applied.

When learning the weights of a language model, we used the same training and validation sets as for inflection network. The language model used history of 5 symbols and contained 64 units in LSTM layers. The number of layers was set to 2. The rate of dropout was the same as for basic model. The model was trained for 20 epochs, training was stopped when perplexity on validation set did not improve for 5 epochs.

3.2 Dataset

We tested our model in Sigmorphon 2018 Shared Task (Cotterell et al., 2018). For an extended description we refer the reader to this papers. The dataset contained three subsets: high, medium and low. The size of the training dataset was 10000 words in the high subset[4], 1000 in medium and 100 in low. The dataset also contained a development set containing 1000 instances most of the time, for all languages we used this subset as validation data. Overall, there were 86 languages in the high setting, 102 in medium and 103 in low.

4 Results and discussion

We submitted three systems, one replicating the algorithm of (Makarov et al., 2017), the second equipped with language models. The third one used only the language models: we extracted all possible abstract inflection paradigms for a given set of grammatical features and created a set of possible candidate forms applying all paradigms to the lemma. For example, consider the word *делать* and paradigms 1+атъ#1+ет, 1+атъ#1+ит, 1+ь#1 and 1+чъ#1+жет; the first three produce the forms *делает, делит, делат*, while the fourth yields nothing since the given word does not end in *-чъ*. Then all these forms are ranked using sum of logarithmic probabilities from forward and backward language models.

Our results are mostly negative, since our language-model based architecture produced only marginal improvement over the model of Makarov et al. which it is based on. Moreover, for the low-resource setting the performance of both system was mediocre, even our third paradigm-based system was able to overperform them despite its obvious weakness. The results are presented in Table 1[5], M1 stands for the baseline model and M2 – for the LM-based one. The numbers in brackets count the number of large gaps (more than 2% for high dataset, 3% for medium and 5% for low).

We observe that the influence of language models is marginal, the strength of this effect grows with the size of training data, which contradicts our expectations. In low and medium setting we expected slightly higher performance, which probably implies that our choice of hyperparameters is suboptimal. We made several observations when comparing our two models: first, the LM-based one demonstrates the highest quality after reducing output history of the baseline model from 4 to 2 and setting LM state dropout to 0.4. It shows that memory containing last output symbols plays the role of a language model for local dependencies and the memory of LSTM encoder – for global and often there is no need to duplicate them. However, most of the time LM-based variant converges much faster which implies that language model learns to throw out incorrect sequences of letters, but seems to overfit in the same time. In any case, these questions require future investigation.

However, language models demonstrate its utility even when little training data is available. The results for low subtask (see 2) demonstrate that they are powerful enough to discriminate between correct and incorrect variants proposed by the abstract paradigm generator. This is especially impressive since this method simply returns the input form in case it has not seen the given set of grammatical features. So it cannot recover the value of missing paradigm cells generalizing other elements of the paradigm table, which clearly limits its performance. Moreover, even for an observed grammatical values a small training set does not cover all possible inflection patterns, either due to their irregularity and multiplicity, like in case of Arabic or Latin, or complex phonetic rules as in case of Navajo. Nevertheless, this approach clearly

---

[4]For several languages it was smaller, but exceeded 1000 instances

[5]We measured accuracy on the test subset of the dataset and averaged the scores over all languages.

Dataset	M1	M2	$M1 > M2$	$M2 > M1$
high	94.23	94.56	27(2)	45(6)
medium	79.37	79.51	40(8)	47(12)
low	39.13	39.18	49(7)	50(10)

Table 1: Comparison of baseline and LM-equipped models

beats our neural models since it requires less data when the number of possible inflection patterns is small.

So language models are actually good in ranking inflection variants even in case of little data available. What remains is to generate enough candidate forms to improve their recall. We tried to solve this problem by adding top 10 candidates proposed by the neural network model to the list of possible outputs. However, this approach fails: for most languages the results fall below the level of neural models themselves. Doing a quick error analysis, we found that in low setting neural networks often are not able to discriminate between different forms, predicting a correct variant for another tense or person. The language model also does not learn enough well to distinguish different inflectional affixes due to the same lack of data. Therefore it favors either a shorter form or the endings it has observed more frequently, even if these endings does not refer to the set of features under consideration. On the contrary, abstract paradigms simply do not produce these variants, making the choice more easy. A possible workaround may be to predict the set of grammatical features for the generated form, however, we have not implemented this method due to the lack of time.

This reranking approach appears to be less successful for medium and high datasets. In this case the number of proposed candidate paradigms becomes too high. Some of these paradigms generate phonetically plausible forms but are applicable only in particular conditions not satisfied by a given word. For example, consider the Russian input *делать*;v;prs;ind;3;sg; the paradigm 1+ать#1+ит produces the form *делит*, which is correct, but for another verb *делить*. Therefore the application of language models in case of more training data looks problematic: we tried to use them to filter out forms generated by neural models without reranking remaining candidates. That marginally improved performance for complex languages like Navajo and Latin but had a slight negative effect in most other cases.

Acknowledgements

I thank the organizers of Sigmorphon2018 Shared task, especially Ryan Cotterell, for preparing the data and organizing the Shared Task. I am grateful to all the members of Neural Networks and Deep Learning Lab at MIPT (http://ipavlov.ai) for helpful discussions during my investigations. The research was conducted under support of National Technological Initiative Foundation and Sberbank of Russia. Project identifier 0000000007417F630002.

5   Conclusion

We investigated the applications of character language models to automatic reinflection. Despite their usefulness for other task, they do not produce significant boost, though improve the quality for all the settings. However, reranking-based approach, which also uses language models, reaches slightly higher scores in case of low amount of training data. In case of larger training sets the phonetic plausibility is effectively checked by the neural decoder itself without applying additional mechanisms. The relative success of paradigm-based approach in low-resource setting implies that neural networks lack control mechanism provided by abstract paradigms. Therefore the combination of neural networks with finite state techniques seems a perspective direction of study. Another promising direction not touched in the current work are different methods of data augmentation, either by training on data from related languages, or by generating additional training instances. At least for the second approach character language models seem useful to check the quality of generated source-target pairs.

References

Roee Aharoni and Yoav Goldberg. 2017. Morphological inflection generation with hard monotonic attention. In *Proceedings of the 55th Annual Meeting of the Association for Computational Linguistics (Volume 1: Long Papers)*, volume 1, pages 2004–2015.

Dataset	M1	M2	$M1 > M2$	$M2 > M1$
low	39.13	41.61	49(37)	52(44)

Table 2: Comparison of baseline and LM-paradigm models

Malin Ahlberg, Markus Forsberg, and Mans Hulden. 2015. Paradigm classification in supervised learning of morphology. In *Proceedings of the Conference of the North American Chapter of the Association for Computational Linguistics Human Language Technologies (NAACL-HLT 2015), Denver, CO*, pages 1024–1029.

Dzmitry Bahdanau, Kyunghyun Cho, and Yoshua Bengio. 2014. Neural machine translation by jointly learning to align and translate. *arXiv preprint arXiv:1409.0473*.

Ryan Cotterell, Christo Kirov, John Sylak-Glassman, Géraldine Walther, Ekaterina Vylomova, Arya D. McCarthy, Katharina Kann, Sebastian Mielke, Garrett Nicolai, Miikka Silfverberg, David Yarowsky, Jason Eisner, and Mans Hulden. 2018. The CoNLL–SIGMORPHON 2018 shared task: Universal morphological reinflection. In *Proceedings of the CoNLL–SIGMORPHON 2018 Shared Task: Universal Morphological Reinflection*, Brussels, Belgium. Association for Computational Linguistics.

Ryan Cotterell, Christo Kirov, John Sylak-Glassman, Gèraldine Walther, Ekaterina Vylomova, Patrick Xia, Manaal Faruqui, Sandra Kübler, David Yarowsky, Jason Eisner, et al. 2017. CoNLL–SIGMORPHON 2017 shared task: Universal morphological reinflection in 52 languages. *Proceedings of the CoNLL SIGMORPHON 2017 Shared Task: Universal Morphological Reinflection*, pages 1–30.

Ryan Cotterell, Christo Kirov, John Sylak-Glassman, David Yarowsky, Jason Eisner, and Mans Hulden. 2016. The SIGMORPHON 2016 shared task—morphological reinflection. In *Proceedings of the 2016 Meeting of SIGMORPHON*, Berlin, Germany. Association for Computational Linguistics.

Caglar Gulcehre, Orhan Firat, Kelvin Xu, Kyunghyun Cho, and Yoshua Bengio. 2017. On integrating a language model into neural machine translation. *Computer Speech & Language*, 45:137–148.

Katharina Kann and Hinrich Schütze. 2016. Single-model encoder-decoder with explicit morphological representation for reinflection. *arXiv preprint arXiv:1606.00589*.

Peter Makarov, Tatiana Ruzsics, and Simon Clematide. 2017. Align and copy: Uzh at sigmorphon 2017 shared task for morphological reinflection. *Proceedings of the CoNLL SIGMORPHON 2017 Shared Task: Universal Morphological Reinflection*, pages 49–57.

Garrett Nicolai, Colin Cherry, and Grzegorz Kondrak. 2015. Inflection generation as discriminative string transduction. In *Proceedings of the Conference of the North American Chapter of the Association for Computational Linguistics Human Language Technologies (NAACL-HLT 2015), Denver, CO*, pages 923–931.

Matthew E Peters, Mark Neumann, Mohit Iyyer, Matt Gardner, Christopher Clark, Kenton Lee, and Luke Zettlemoyer. 2018. Deep contextualized word representations. *arXiv preprint arXiv:1802.05365*.

Alexey Sorokin. 2016. Using longest common subsequence and character models to predict word forms. In *Proceedings of the 14th SIGMORPHON Workshop on Computational Research in Phonetics, Phonology, and Morphology*, pages 54–61.

Ke Tran, Arianna Bisazza, and Christof Monz. 2016. Recurrent memory networks for language modeling. *arXiv preprint arXiv:1601.01272*.

IIT(BHU)–IIITH at CoNLL–SIGMORPHON 2018 Shared Task on Universal Morphological Reinflection

Abhishek Sharma *
IIT (BHU), Varanasi

Ganesh Katrapati
Language Technologies Research Center
IIIT Hyderabad

Dipti Misra Sharma
Language Technologies Research Center
IIIT Hyderabad

Abstract

This paper describes the systems submitted by IIT (BHU), Varanasi/IIIT Hyderabad (IITBHU–IIITH) for Task 1 of CoNLL–SIGMORPHON 2018 Shared Task on Universal Morphological Reinflection (Cotterell et al., 2018). The task is to generate the inflected form given a lemma and set of morphological features. The systems are evaluated on over 100 distinct languages and three different resource settings (low, medium and high). We formulate the task as a sequence to sequence learning problem. As most of the characters in inflected form are copied from the lemma, we use Pointer-Generator Network (See et al., 2017) which makes it easier for the system to copy characters from the lemma. Pointer-Generator Network also helps in dealing with out-of-vocabulary characters during inference. Our best performing system stood 4th among 28 systems, 3rd among 23 systems and 4th among 23 systems for the low, medium and high resource setting respectively.

1 Introduction

Morphological Inflection is the process of inflecting a lemma according to a set of morphological features so that the lemma becomes in accordance with other words in the sentence. It is useful for alleviating data sparsity, especially in morphologically rich languages during Natural Language Generation. For example, Minkov et al. (2007) translate words from the source language to lemmas in the target language and then use Morphological Inflection as a post-processing step to make the words of the output sentence in agreement with each other. Not only their approach reduces the data sparsity by decreasing the number of candidate words while translating, it also gives better results.

CoNLL–SIGMORPHON 2018 Shared Task on Universal Morphological Reinflection consisted of two tasks. Participants could compete in either or both of the tasks. We participated in Task 1 only. The task was to build a system which could inflect a lemma given a set of morphological tags. The systems were evaluated on over 100 distinct languages, out of which 10 were surprise languages. An example showing input and the expected output of the system is given below.

$$(\text{touch, V;V.PTCP;PRS}) \rightarrow \text{touching}$$

To assess the system's ability to generalize in different resource settings, three varying amounts of labeled training data (low, medium, high) were given. The systems were evaluated separately for each language and the three data quantity conditions. Accuracy (the fraction of correctly predicted forms) and the average Levenshtein distance between the prediction and the truth across all predictions were used as metrics. An aggregated performance measure separate for each of the resource setting was obtained by averaging the results for individual languages.

Morphological Inflection is accomplished by different morphological processes such as prefixation, infixation, suffixation (attaching bound morpheme in front, within and at the end of stem respectively) and ablaut depending on the language. As the systems were evaluated on over 100 distinct languages, we were motivated to use neural network based approaches because they do not require any manual feature engineering. But neural networks require a lot of training data to work. We try to address this challenge by designing neural network architectures which work well even on the low resource setting of the task.

Our system is based on attention based encoder-decoder models (Bahdanau et al., 2014). The

---

This research was conducted during the authors internship at IIIT Hyderabad.

Proceedings of the CoNLL–SIGMORPHON 2018 Shared Task: Universal Morphological Reinflection, pages 105–111,
Brussels, Belgium, October 31, 2018. ©2018 Association for Computational Linguistics

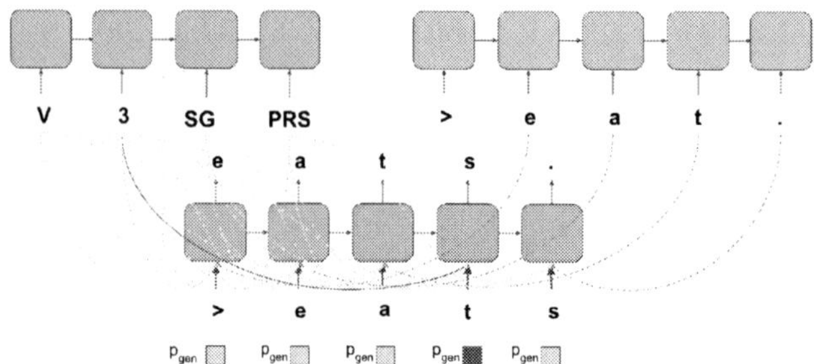

Figure 1: Neural network architecture for our system. The two encoders are shown at the top, while the decoder is shown at the bottom. At each time step, the decoder computes attention distribution over both the lemma and the tags separately. Attention mechanism is shown by the dotted lines (darker colour corresponds to more weight). A scalar - generation probability $p_{gen} \in [0, 1]$ (shown as the square, the lighter the colour the less the value) is also calculated at each time step, which corresponds to how likely a character will be generated from the vocabulary instead of a character being copied from the lemma.

lemma and the tags are encoded using two separate encoders. While decoding, the decoder reads relevant parts of the lemma and the tags using attention mechanism. As most of the characters in the inflected form are copied from the lemma, it is necessary to design a system with strong tendency to copy. We use Pointer-Generator Network (See et al., 2017) which facilitates copying of characters of lemma and tackles the problem of out-of-vocabulary tokens during prediction. Compared to other similar performing systems, our system is trained end-to-end, doesn't require data augmentation techniques and uses soft attention over hard monotonic attention which makes it more flexible.

Our best performing system outperforms the baseline by 14.21%, 22.41% and 19.13% for the low, medium and high resource settings respectively. It stood 4th among 28 systems, 3rd among 23 systems and 4th among 23 systems for the low, medium and high data conditions respectively.

The remainder of this paper is organized as follows. We present prior work on Morphological Inflection in Section 2. We describe our system in Section 3. The results of the shared task are presented in Section 4. In Section 5, we present ablation studies and discuss the contribution of the specific design decisions we made to the performance of our systems. We conclude the paper with Section 6.

2 Background

Traditional approaches for morphological inflection involve crafting hand-engineered rules. Although these rules offer high accuracy, they are very expensive to create.

Machine learning based approaches treat morphological inflection as a string transduction task (Durrett and DeNero, 2013; Hulden et al., 2014; Ahlberg et al., 2015; Nicolai et al., 2015). These approaches extract rules automatically from the data, but they still require language specific feature engineering.

Neural network based approaches successfully solve this problem. These approaches require no feature engineering and the same architecture works for different languages. Faruqui et al. (2016) were the first to formulate morphological inflection as neural sequence to sequence learning problem (Cho et al., 2014; Sutskever et al., 2014; Bahdanau et al., 2014). Kann and Schütze (2016) improved on their approach by using a single model instead of separate models for each morphological feature. They fed morphological tags into the encoder along with the sequence of characters of lemma. They also used attention mechanism (Bahdanau et al., 2014). Aharoni and Goldberg (2017) present an alternative to the soft attention in form of hard monotonic attention which models the almost monotonic alignment between characters in lemma and the inflected form.

The best performing system (Makarov et al., 2017) of the previous edition of this shared task extended the hard monotonic attention model of Aharoni and Goldberg (2017) with a copy mechanism (HACM model). To deal with low training data especially in the low and medium resource settings, some teams used data augmentation techniques (Kann and Schütze, 2017; Bergmanis et al.,

2017; Silfverberg et al., 2017; Zhou and Neubig, 2017; Nicolai et al., 2017).

3 System Description

In this section, we describe our system in detail. We report the neural network architecture, the training process, the hyperparameters and our submissions.

3.1 Neural network architecture

Our neural network architecture is based on Pointer-Generator Network (See et al., 2017) with some subtle differences.

Characters of the lemma c_i along with the additional start and stop characters are fed one by one into a bidirectional LSTM encoder producing a sequence of hidden states h_{l_i}. Similarly, using a separate bidirectional LSTM encoder, the tags tg_i are encoded and another sequence of hidden states h_{tg_i} is obtained.

We use a unidirectional LSTM as the decoder. The decoder's hidden state s_i is initialised by applying an affine transformation on the concatenation of the last hidden states of the lemma and the tag encoders. As the input and output sequences have different semantics, this affine transformation gives the model the ability to learn transformation of semantics from input to output (Faruqui et al., 2016).

$$s_0 = W_{initial}[h_{l_N}; h_{tg_N}] + b \qquad (1)$$

While decoding, at each time step t, the decoder computes an attention distribution over the lemma and the tag separately denoted as a_l^t and a_{tg}^t (Bahdanau et al., 2014).

$$e_{l_i}^t = v^T \tanh(W_{h_l} h_{l_i} + W_{s_l} s_{t-1} + b_l) \qquad (2)$$
$$e_{tg_i}^t = v^T \tanh(W_{h_{tg}} h_{tg_i} + W_{s_{tg}} s_{t-1} + b_{tg}) \qquad (3)$$
$$a_l^t = \text{softmax}(e_l^t) \qquad (4)$$
$$a_{tg}^t = \text{softmax}(e_{tg}^t) \qquad (5)$$

The context vectors h_l^* and h_{tg}^* are computed as the weighted sum over the encoder hidden states h_{l_i} and h_{tg_i} with the attention distribution mass a_l^t and a_{tg}^t as weights.

$$h_{l_t}^* = \sum_i a_{l_i}^t h_{l_i} \qquad (6)$$
$$h_{tg_t}^* = \sum_i a_{tg_i}^t h_{tg_i} \qquad (7)$$

The combined context vector is obtained by simply concatenating the lemma and the tag context vector.

$$h_t^* = [h_{l_t}^*; h_{tg_t}^*] \qquad (8)$$

The combined context vector h_t^* and the embedding of character predicted at the previous time step, y_{t-1} (while training to speed up convergence we use the ground truth label y_{t-1}^* instead) is given as input to the decoder. At the first time step, start character is given as input in place of y_{t-1}.

$$s_t = f(s_{t-1}, h_t^*, y_{t-1}) \qquad (9)$$

where f is a nonlinear function.

A probability distribution over the characters in the vocabulary is calculated which corresponds to how likely will a particular character be generated (if a character is generated at all).

$$P_{vocab} = \text{softmax}(V[s_t; h^*] + b) \qquad (10)$$

At each time step, a generation probability $p_{gen} \in [0, 1]$ is calculated. The generation probability determines if the decoder will generate a character from the vocabulary or copy a character from the lemma.

$$p_{gen} = \sigma(w_h h_t^* + w_s s_t + w_y y_{t-1} + b) \qquad (11)$$

Note that here p_{gen} is calculated using y_{t-1} (the embedding of output produced at the previous time step) instead of the decoder input x_t as in See et al. (2017).

The probability of predicting a character c is computed as the sum of probability of generating c weighted by the generation probability p_{gen} and the total attention distribution over c weighted by the probability of copying it $(1 - p_{gen})$.

$$P(c) = p_{gen}P_{vocab}(c) + (1 - p_{gen}) \sum_{i:c_i=c} a_{l_i}^t \qquad (12)$$

The decoder keeps predicting characters until the stop character is predicted or a fixed number of time steps are reached.

3.2 Training

We use negative log likelihood to compute the loss. The loss for time step t, where c_t^* is the target character is given by,

$$loss_t = -\log P(c_t^*) \qquad (13)$$

	low	medium	high
embedding size	100	100	300
hidden units	100	100	100
dropout probability (p)	0.5	0.5	0.3
initial epochs (e_1)	300	80	60
extended epochs (e_2)	100	20	10

Table 1: Hyperparameters for low, medium and high resource settings.

The loss for the overall sequence is,

$$loss = \frac{1}{T} \sum_{t=0}^{T} loss_t \qquad (14)$$

We use Adam Optimiser (Kingma and Ba, 2014) with initial learning rate 0.001 and batch size 32 to train the neural network. To deal with exploding gradient problem, we clip the norm computed over all the gradients together to 3. We apply dropout (Srivastava et al., 2014) with probability p over embeddings and the encoder hidden states.

We use early stopping to prevent overfitting. A portion of the development set is used as the validation set. After each epoch, performance on validation set is calculated. Initially the model is trained on e_1 epochs. If the highest performance on validation set is obtained within e_2 recent epochs, the model is further trained for e_2 epochs. This goes on until performance on validation set stops improving.

Single layer LSTMs were used as encoders and decoders to reduce number of parameters. Optimal size of embeddings and the number of hidden units in LSTMs were determined based on the performance of the model on a subset of languages in development set.

The values for hyperparameters p, e_1, e_2, embedding size and hidden units of LSTM are given in Table 1.

We used PyTorch for implementing the network. The code for the system is available at `https://github.com/abhishek0318/conll-sigmorphon-2018`.

3.3 Submissions

We made a total of two submissions. For the first submission, we trained only one system for each language and data resource setting pair. We used ensembling technique for the second submission. We trained 5, 3 and 1 system(s) for each language

	System 1	System 2	Baseline
low	49.79%	**52.60%**	38.20%
medium	82.90%	**84.19%**	61.78%
high	94.43%	**94.43%**	75.30%

Table 2: Average accuracy of the system on the test set over all the languages for low, medium and high resource settings respectively.

in low, medium and high data resource settings respectively. Their predictions were combined using hard voting.

4 Results

Average accuracy of the system over all the languages in a data resource setting is presented in Table 2.

Our best performing system outperforms the baseline by very large margins - 14.21%, 22.41% and 19.13% for the low, medium and high resource settings respcctively.

We observe that using ensembling technique (in the second submission) gives a boost of few percentage points in the accuracy over the first submission, where ensembling is not used.

5 Ablation Studies

In this section, we investigate how difference system design choices influenced the performance of the system. As reasonable performances were obtained for medium and high resource settings in previous editions of the shared task, we focus our attention to the low resource setting and compare models on this setting.

5.1 Pointer Generator Network

We examine the performance gain obtained by using Pointer-Generator Network, the essence of our system. We compare the performance of a simple attention based neural encoder-decoder model with and without using ideas from Pointer-Generator Network.

Consider the architecture proposed by Kann and Schütze (2016) for the task of morphological inflection. The architecture is based on simple attention based encoder-decoder model. The source sequence s_i consists of the characters of the lemma followed by the tags.

We include ideas from Pointer-Generator Network into this model. At each time step, the decoder calculates generation probability p_{gen} (See et al., 2017). The network uses the computed attention distribution to determine which character from the lemma it should copy. Because there is only a single encoder, the attention distribution is over both the lemma and the tags. The tags therefore have some attention over them. To use Equation 12, we must normalise the attention weights of the characters, so that we have a new attention distribution over the set of characters.

$$P(c) = p_{gen}P_{vocab}(c) + (1 - p_{gen})\frac{\sum_{i:s_i=c} a_i^t}{\sum_{i:s_i \in C} a_i^t} \tag{15}$$

We use modified form of Equation 12 as shown above to calculate $P(c)$. Here C is the set of characters.

For the same hyperparameters, the architecture used in Kann and Schütze (2016) gives 21.99% average accuracy as compared to the architecture including ideas from Pointer-Generator Network, which gives 44.02% average accuracy tested on development set over all the languages for low resource setting. Thus using Pointer Generator Network increases the performance of the system tremendously for low resource setting.

5.2 Separate Encoder for Tags

We investigate the benefit of using a separate encoder for the tags, instead of encoding them using a same encoder as in Kann and Schütze (2016).

Consider the neural network architecture with two separate encoders for the lemma and the tags. At each timestep while decoding, attention distribution is computed over the lemma. The last hidden state of the tag encoder is used as the representation of the set of tags. It along with the context vector of the lemma is fed to the decoder at each time step. We compare the performance of this architecture, to the architecture described in Section 5.1 (which uses single encoder for the lemma and tags and Pointer-Generator Network). The architecture with a single encoder obtains 44.02% average accuracy, while the one with two separate encoders achieves 48.18% average accuracy tested on the development set for low resource setting.

A possible explanation for the difference in the performance is that the lemma and the tags are completely separate entities and a single encoder can't encode them correctly. We were motivated to represent the tags using embeddings as embeddings have more representational power compared to zeros and ones in case of one hot encoding. As

the number of tags vary for each example, using LSTM to encode them seemed apt. Note that the representation obtained using this approach is not order invariant. Using order invariant representations (Vinyals et al., 2016; Zaheer et al., 2017) is left as future work.

5.3 Attention over Tags

We inspect whether using attention over the sequence of tags as compared to using a fixed vector representation gives better results. We consider the architecture introduced in Section 5.2. Instead of using last hidden state of the encoder to represent the tags, we use attention over tags too and compare the performance. Note this is same architecture we described in 3.1. Using attention over tags leads to average accuracy of 49.08% as compared to 48.18% on the development set for low resource setting.

This can explained as by using attention mechanism, the model doesn't need to compress the information of all the tags into a single vector. It can attend to a specific tag based on the decoder state.

5.4 Hierarchical Attention

We investigate if using Hierarchical Attention (Libovický and Helcl, 2017) instead of just concatenating the two context vectors for lemma and the tags as done in Equation 8 proves advantageous. Libovický and Helcl (2017) proposed Hierarchical Attention technique for combining the context vectors in case of multiple source sequences.

$$a_h = \sigma(v \tanh(w_{h_l^*}h_l^* + w_{h_{tg}^*}h_{tg}^* + w_s s_t + b)) \tag{16}$$

$$h_t^* = a_h h_{l_t}^* + (1 - a_h)h_{tg_t}^* \tag{17}$$

After computing the individual context vectors, a scalar $a_h \in [0, 1]$ is calculated. This scalar corresponds to how the attention should be divided between the lemma and the tag. The combined context vector is obtained by taking the weighted average, as shown above.

Compared to the concatenating the context vectors (as done in our submission), using hierarchical attention gives worse results (46.60% average accuracy as compared to 49.08% average accuracy on development set for low resource setting). This is possibly because of the increase in number of parameters to learn and the additional non linearities such as sigmoid and $\tanh$ which lead to vanishing gradient problem.

6 Conclusion

In this paper, we described IITBHU–IIITH system for Task 1 of CoNLL–SIGMORPHON 2018 Shared Task. Our system is one of the top performing systems in this edition of the shared task and beats the baseline by large margins. Even though our approach was completely based on neural networks, our system works very well for low resource setting.

We conclude that neural network architectures with explicit copying mechanism (like Pointer-Generator Network) perform well in Morphological Inflection task even on low resource setting.

References

Roee Aharoni and Yoav Goldberg. 2017. Morphological inflection generation with hard monotonic attention. In *Proceedings of the 55th Annual Meeting of the Association for Computational Linguistics, ACL 2017, Vancouver, Canada, July 30 - August 4, Volume 1: Long Papers*, pages 2004–2015.

Malin Ahlberg, Markus Forsberg, and Mans Hulden. 2015. Paradigm classification in supervised learning of morphology. In *NAACL HLT 2015, The 2015 Conference of the North American Chapter of the Association for Computational Linguistics: Human Language Technologies, Denver, Colorado, USA, May 31 - June 5, 2015*, pages 1024–1029.

Dzmitry Bahdanau, Kyunghyun Cho, and Yoshua Bengio. 2014. Neural machine translation by jointly learning to align and translate. *CoRR*, abs/1409.0473.

Toms Bergmanis, Katharina Kann, Hinrich Schütze, and Sharon Goldwater. 2017. Training data augmentation for low-resource morphological inflection. In *Proceedings of the CoNLL SIGMORPHON 2017 Shared Task: Universal Morphological Reinflection*, pages 31–39, Vancouver. Association for Computational Linguistics.

Kyunghyun Cho, Bart van Merrienboer, Çaglar Gülçehre, Dzmitry Bahdanau, Fethi Bougares, Holger Schwenk, and Yoshua Bengio. 2014. Learning phrase representations using RNN encoder-decoder for statistical machine translation. In *Proceedings of the 2014 Conference on Empirical Methods in Natural Language Processing, EMNLP 2014, October 25-29, 2014, Doha, Qatar, A meeting of SIGDAT, a Special Interest Group of the ACL*, pages 1724–1734.

Ryan Cotterell, Christo Kirov, John Sylak-Glassman, Géraldine Walther, Ekaterina Vylomova, Arya D. McCarthy, Katharina Kann, Sebastian Mielke, Garrett Nicolai, Miikka Silfverberg, David Yarowsky, Jason Eisner, and Mans Hulden. 2018. The CoNLL–SIGMORPHON 2018 shared task: Universal morphological reinflection. In *Proceedings of the CoNLL–SIGMORPHON 2018 Shared Task: Universal Morphological Reinflection*, Brussels, Belgium. Association for Computational Linguistics.

Greg Durrett and John DeNero. 2013. Supervised learning of complete morphological paradigms. In *Human Language Technologies: Conference of the North American Chapter of the Association of Computational Linguistics, Proceedings, June 9-14, 2013, Westin Peachtree Plaza Hotel, Atlanta, Georgia, USA*, pages 1185–1195.

Manaal Faruqui, Yulia Tsvetkov, Graham Neubig, and Chris Dyer. 2016. Morphological inflection generation using character sequence to sequence learning. In *NAACL HLT 2016, The 2016 Conference of the North American Chapter of the Association for Computational Linguistics: Human Language Technologies, San Diego California, USA, June 12-17, 2016*, pages 634–643.

Mans Hulden, Markus Forsberg, and Malin Ahlberg. 2014. Semi-supervised learning of morphological paradigms and lexicons. In *Proceedings of the 14th Conference of the European Chapter of the Association for Computational Linguistics, EACL 2014, April 26-30, 2014, Gothenburg, Sweden*, pages 569–578.

Katharina Kann and Hinrich Schütze. 2016. MED: the LMU system for the SIGMORPHON 2016 shared task on morphological reinflection. In *Proceedings of the 14th SIGMORPHON Workshop on Computational Research in Phonetics, Phonology, and Morphology, Berlin, Germany, August 11, 2016*, pages 62–70.

Katharina Kann and Hinrich Schütze. 2017. The lmu system for the conll-sigmorphon 2017 shared task on universal morphological reinflection. In *Proceedings of the CoNLL SIGMORPHON 2017 Shared Task: Universal Morphological Reinflection*, pages 40–48, Vancouver. Association for Computational Linguistics.

Diederik P. Kingma and Jimmy Ba. 2014. Adam: A method for stochastic optimization. *CoRR*, abs/1412.6980.

Jindrich Libovický and Jindrich Helcl. 2017. Attention strategies for multi-source sequence-to-sequence learning. In *Proceedings of the 55th Annual Meeting of the Association for Computational Linguistics, ACL 2017, Vancouver, Canada, July 30 - August 4, Volume 2: Short Papers*, pages 196–202.

Peter Makarov, Tatiana Ruzsics, and Simon Clematide. 2017. Align and copy: UZH at SIGMORPHON 2017 shared task for morphological reinflection. In *Proceedings of the CoNLL SIGMORPHON 2017 Shared Task: Universal Morphological Reinflection, Vancouver, BC, Canada, August 3-4, 2017*, pages 49–57.

Einat Minkov, Kristina Toutanova, and Hisami Suzuki. 2007. Generating complex morphology for machine translation. In *ACL 2007, Proceedings of the 45th Annual Meeting of the Association for Computational Linguistics, June 23-30, 2007, Prague, Czech Republic*.

Garrett Nicolai, Colin Cherry, and Grzegorz Kondrak. 2015. Inflection generation as discriminative string transduction. In *NAACL HLT 2015, The 2015 Conference of the North American Chapter of the Association for Computational Linguistics: Human Language Technologies, Denver, Colorado, USA, May 31 - June 5, 2015*, pages 922–931.

Garrett Nicolai, Bradley Hauer, Mohammad Motallebi, Saeed Najafi, and Grzegorz Kondrak. 2017. If you can't beat them, join them: the university of alberta system description. In *Proceedings of the CoNLL SIGMORPHON 2017 Shared Task: Universal Morphological Reinflection*, pages 79–84, Vancouver. Association for Computational Linguistics.

Abigail See, Peter J. Liu, and Christopher D. Manning. 2017. Get to the point: Summarization with pointer-generator networks. In *Proceedings of the 55th Annual Meeting of the Association for Computational Linguistics, ACL 2017, Vancouver, Canada, July 30 - August 4, Volume 1: Long Papers*, pages 1073–1083.

Miikka Silfverberg, Adam Wiemerslage, Ling Liu, and Lingshuang Jack Mao. 2017. Data augmentation for morphological reinflection. In *Proceedings of the CoNLL SIGMORPHON 2017 Shared Task: Universal Morphological Reinflection*, pages 90–99, Vancouver. Association for Computational Linguistics.

Nitish Srivastava, Geoffrey E. Hinton, Alex Krizhevsky, Ilya Sutskever, and Ruslan Salakhutdinov. 2014. Dropout: a simple way to prevent neural networks from overfitting. *Journal of Machine Learning Research*, 15(1):1929–1958.

Ilya Sutskever, Oriol Vinyals, and Quoc V. Le. 2014. Sequence to sequence learning with neural networks. In *Advances in Neural Information Processing Systems 27: Annual Conference on Neural Information Processing Systems 2014, December 8-13 2014, Montreal, Quebec, Canada*, pages 3104–3112.

Oriol Vinyals, Samy Bengio, and Manjunath Kudlur. 2016. Order matters: Sequence to sequence for sets. In *International Conference on Learning Representations (ICLR)*.

Manzil Zaheer, Satwik Kottur, Siamak Ravanbakhsh, Barnabás Póczos, Ruslan R. Salakhutdinov, and Alexander J. Smola. 2017. Deep sets. In *Advances in Neural Information Processing Systems 30: Annual Conference on Neural Information Processing Systems 2017, 4-9 December 2017, Long Beach, CA, USA*, pages 3394–3404.

Chunting Zhou and Graham Neubig. 2017. Morphological inflection generation with multi-space variational encoder-decoders. In *Proceedings of the CoNLL SIGMORPHON 2017 Shared Task: Universal Morphological Reinflection*, pages 58–65, Vancouver. Association for Computational Linguistics.

Tübingen-Oslo system at SIGMORPHON shared task on morphological inflection. A multi-tasking multilingual sequence to sequence model.

Taraka Rama
Department of Informatics
University of Oslo
Oslo, Norway
tarakark@ifi.uio.no

Çağrı Çöltekin
Department of Linguistics
University of Tübingen
Tübingen, Germany
ccoltekin@sfs.uni-tuebingen.de

Abstract

In this paper, we describe our three submissions to the inflection track of SIGMORPHON shared task. We experimented with three models: namely, sequence to sequence model (popularly known as seq2seq), seq2seq model with data augmentation, and a multilingual multi-tasking seq2seq model that is multilingual in nature. Our results with the multilingual model are below the baseline in the case of both high and medium datasets.

1 Introduction

Morphological inflection is the task of predicting the target inflected form from a lemma and a bundle of inflectional features. For instance, given the Norwegian lemma *hus* "house" and the morphological features N, DEF, PL the task is to predict *husene* "houses".

The SIGMORPHON shared task for 2018 (Cotterell et al., 2018) provided three data scenarios consisting of high (10000), medium (1000), and low (100) examples. This paper described the three systems that we submitted to the inflection track in the SIGMORPHON shared task. All our models are based on encoder-decoder model introduced by Faruqui et al. (2016) for the morphological inflection task. We trained our models on all the data sizes and tested on the test datasets provided by the organizers.

2 Background

The morphological (re)inflection task has been studied mainly in last two SIGMORPHON shared tasks (Cotterell et al., 2016, 2017). Most of the morphological inflection models are variants of sequence to sequence models applied by Faruqui et al. (2016) to morphological reinflection.

The input to the model is the source word prepended with relevant morphological tags, the output of the model is the target word for the inflection task. For re-inflection task, the input includes the target tags as well. The success of the system seems to depend highly on 'training data enhancement'. For different tracks (with different restrictions on data used) of the 2016 shared task, Kann and Schütze (2016) developed new techniques to increase the number of training instances. The methods used mostly work well for re-inflection task, since the re-inflection task is symmetric, and one can invert the source and target forms. In the subsequent year's shared task for 2017 (Cotterell et al., 2017), multiple authors explored new data enhancement techniques (Kann and Schütze, 2017; Bergmanis et al., 2017; Silfverberg et al., 2017) to improve the performance of the seq2seq models in medium and low resource scenarios. The work presented in this paper is based on the work of the simple encoder-decoder system of Faruqui et al. (2016).

3 Models

In this section, we describe the three different models and the feature representations used in our experiments.

Morphological features In this paper, we enumerated all the possible features in Unimorph (Kirov et al., 2018) and encoded the feature bundle as multi-hot feature vector. We experimented with both one-hot feature vectors and multi-hot feature vectors. In our development experiments, we found that multi-hot feature vectors have lower dimension than one-hot feature vectors and yielded similar results.

Seq2seq-baseline This model consists of two parts: bidirectional encoder and decoder. In this model, each character is represented as a one-hot vector whereas the morphological features are rep-

Proceedings of the CoNLL–SIGMORPHON 2018 Shared Task: Universal Morphological Reinflection, pages 112–115,
Brussels, Belgium, October 31, 2018. ©2018 Association for Computational Linguistics

resented as multi-hot feature bundle. The encoder consists of LSTM cells that transform a sequence into a continuous vector. The final time step's hidden state and the cell state are used to initialize the decoder LSTM network. The decoder LSTM network predicts a character at each time step by passing the output of the decoder LSTM through a softmax layer. The output of the softmax layer is a predicted character that is input along with the multi-hot morphological feature vector to the next timestep. We intended this model to be the baseline model in our experiments.

Augment-Seq2seq This model is a variation of the baseline encoder-decoder model where the training data is augmented with random strings generated with weights proportional to the character probabilities. This model is similar to the data augmentation model of Silfverberg et al. (2017) who generate new training instances by randomly sampling characters from unigram distributions. In our model, we generate a training instance of the same length as the original training instance. We also experimented with

Seq2seq-MTL-global In this model, we train a single encoder-decoder model which is trained to perform both language identification and language modeling as auxiliary tasks apart from generating the target inflection. The encoder LSTM is trained to predict the next character in the source word at each time step. The final hidden state of the encoder is trained to predict the language of the example. This model differs from the other seq2seq models in that the model is multilingual (or global) and attempts to predict target inflections for all the languages in the test dataset. The seq2seq-mtl-global model is similar to the model of Kann et al. (2018) and Bergmanis et al. (2017) who train their attention enhanced encoder-decoder model using an auxiliary autoencoder objective. In contrast, our model uses both prediction of subsequent character and language prediction as auxiliary tasks.

3.1 Experimental settings

We trained our models at all the three resource settings: high, medium, and low. In all our experiments, the maximum length of both source and target strings are fixed to 30 and padded with zeroes at the end. Both the encoder and decoder LSTM units consisted of 256 hidden units. All the models were trained with Adam (Kingma and Ba, 2014)

with minibatches of size 32 or 128 depending on the size of the data; and, used a early-stop with a patience of 5 to prevent overfitting.

4 Results

Participating in the competition with less than three weeks at hand, we did not have much time to explore the hyperparameter settings required to tune our models. In our development experiments, we found that the baseline seq2seq model performed the best among the tested models. We observed similar results with the test dataset also. We present the average accuracies of all the models at high and medium datasets in table 1. Our results are lower than the baseline system. We also present the top-5 and the bottom-5 languages' accuracies of the three models on high and medium data sizes in table 2. We did not present the results for low sized datasets since all the models had accuracies lower than 5%. Both the seq2seq and augmented-seq2seq systems performed the worst on languages such as Zulu, Swahili, and Basque. On the other hand, the MTL system seemed to perform worse on the languages that have close orthography and substantial amount of borrowing such as Hindi, Urdu, and Persian.

Data size	Seq2seq	Augment-seq2seq	Seq2seq-MTL-global
High	63.048	56.598	49.521
Medium	30.979	29.722	20.973

Table 1: Average accuracies for high and medium datasets with three different models.

5 Conclusion

In conclusion, our global multi-tasking model requires more effort to improve the results for languages with low accuracies. As part of future work, we plan to work on incorporating embeddings and attention which are part of the winning systems from the shared tasks of 2016 and 2017. We observed that the multi-tasking model's auxiliary objective was easier to achieve than the main objective. Therefore, we need to explore ways to regularize the network, for instance, by weighing the individual loss components. Finally, the output softmax layer of the decoder has to be made sensitive to the language of the example in the training data to prevent softmax from yielding low values due to the high dimension of the target of the softmax.

		Seq2seq		Augment-Seq2seq		Seq2seq-MTL-global
High	Adyghe	97.4	Crimean-Tatar	92	Crimean-Tatar	95
	Bashkir	97.1	Bashkir	90.9	Kabardian	94
	Crimean-Tatar	97	Friulian	89	Classical-Syriac	94
	Tatar	97	Adyghe	88.2	Tatar	93
	Yiddish	94	Azeri	88	Bashkir	91.6
	Navajo	12.4	Albanian	10.2	Swahili	4
	Khaling	8.5	Quechua	9.7	Persian	3.7
	Basque	6.2	Basque	9.6	Hindi	2.5
	Swahili	5	Swahili	5	Zulu	2.4
	Zulu	2.7	Zulu	2.5	Arabic	0.1
Medium	Kabardian	81	Turkmen	82	Classical-Syriac	90
	Haida	78	Kabardian	79	Kabardian	75
	Neapolitan	78	Classical-Syriac	71	Turkmen	66
	Kashubian	74	Friulian	66	Khakas	66
	Greenlandic	70	Neapolitan	65	Uzbek	66
	Basque	1.4	Quechua	1.9	Swahili	1
	Zulu	1.2	Russian	1.8	Hindi	0.8
	Swahili	1	Italian	1.5	Navajo	0.8
	Finnish	0.2	Zulu	1.5	Zulu	0.8
	Kazakh	0	Finnish	1.2	Arabic	0

Table 2: Top-5 and bottom-5 languages at which the three models perform the best and worse for high and medium datasets.

Acknowledgments

The authors thank Ryan Cotterell and the rest of the organizers for the encouragement to participate in the shared task when participating on a short notice. The first author is supported by BIGMED project (a NRC Lighthouse grant) which is gratefully acknowledged. Some of the experiments reported in this paper are run on a Titan Xp donated by the NVIDIA Corporation.

References

Toms Bergmanis, Katharina Kann, Hinrich Schütze, and Sharon Goldwater. 2017. Training data augmentation for low-resource morphological inflection. In *Proceedings of the CoNLL SIGMORPHON 2017 Shared Task: Universal Morphological Reinflection*, pages 31–39, Vancouver. Association for Computational Linguistics.

Ryan Cotterell, Christo Kirov, John Sylak-Glassman, Géraldine Walther, Ekaterina Vylomova, Arya D. McCarthy, Katharina Kann, Sebastian Mielke, Garrett Nicolai, Miikka Silfverberg, David Yarowsky, Jason Eisner, and Mans Hulden. 2018. The CoNLL–SIGMORPHON 2018 shared task: Universal morphological reinflection. In *Proceedings of the CoNLL–SIGMORPHON 2018 Shared Task: Universal Morphological Reinflection*, Brussels, Belgium. Association for Computational Linguistics.

Ryan Cotterell, Christo Kirov, John Sylak-Glassman, Géraldine Walther, Ekaterina Vylomova, Patrick Xia, Manaal Faruqui, Sandra Kübler, David Yarowsky, Jason Eisner, and Mans Hulden. 2017. Conll-sigmorphon 2017 shared task: Universal morphological reinflection in 52 languages. In *Proceedings of the CoNLL SIGMORPHON 2017 Shared Task: Universal Morphological Reinflection*, pages 1–30, Vancouver. Association for Computational Linguistics.

Ryan Cotterell, Christo Kirov, John Sylak-Glassman, David Yarowsky, Jason Eisner, and Mans Hulden. 2016. The SIGMORPHON 2016 shared task—morphological reinflection. In *Proceedings of the 14th Annual SIGMORPHON Workshop on Computational Research in Phonetics, Phonology, and Morphology*, pages 20–22. Association for Computational Linguistics.

Manaal Faruqui, Yulia Tsvetkov, Graham Neubig, and Chris Dyer. 2016. Morphological inflection generation using character sequence to sequence learning. In *Proceedings of the 2016 Conference of the North American Chapter of the Association for Computational Linguistics: Human Language Technologies,* pages 634–643, San Diego, California. Association for Computational Linguistics.

Katharina Kann, Johannes Bjerva, Isabelle Augenstein, Barbara Plank, and Anders Søgaard. 2018. Character-level supervision for low-resource pos tagging. In *Proceedings of the Workshop on Deep Learning Approaches for Low-Resource NLP*, pages 1–11. Association for Computational Linguistics.

Katharina Kann and Hinrich Schütze. 2017. The lmu system for the conll-sigmorphon 2017 shared task on universal morphological reinflection. In *Proceedings of the CoNLL SIGMORPHON 2017 Shared Task: Universal Morphological Reinflection*, pages 40–48, Vancouver. Association for Computational Linguistics.

Katharina Kann and Hinrich Schütze. 2016. MED: The LMU system for the SIGMORPHON 2016 shared task on morphological reinflection. In *Proceedings of the 14th Annual SIGMORPHON Workshop on Computational Research in Phonetics, Phonology, and Morphology*, pages 62–70. Association for Computational Linguistics.

Diederik P Kingma and Jimmy Ba. 2014. Adam: A method for stochastic optimization. *arXiv preprint arXiv:1412.6980*.

Christo Kirov, Ryan Cotterell, John Sylak-Glassman, Géraldine Walther, Ekaterina Vylomova, Patrick Xia, Manaal Faruqui, Sebastian Mielke, Arya D. McCarthy, Sandra Kübler, David Yarowsky, Jason Eisner, and Mans Hulden. 2018. UniMorph 2.0: Universal Morphology. In *Proceedings of the Eleventh International Conference on Language Resources and Evaluation (LREC 2018)*, Miyazaki, Japan. European Language Resources Association (ELRA).

Miikka Silfverberg, Adam Wiemerslage, Ling Liu, and Lingshuang Jack Mao. 2017. Data augmentation for morphological reinflection. In *Proceedings of the CoNLL SIGMORPHON 2017 Shared Task: Universal Morphological Reinflection*, pages 90–99, Vancouver. Association for Computational Linguistics.

Combining Neural and Non-Neural Methods
for Low-Resource Morphological Reinflection

Saeed Najafi, Bradley Hauer, Rashed Rubby Riyadh, Leyuan Yu, Grzegorz Kondrak
Department of Computing Science
University of Alberta, Edmonton, Canada
`{snajafi,bmhauer,riyadh,leyuan,gkondrak}@ualberta.ca`

Abstract

We describe our systems and results in the type-level low-resource setting of the CoNLL–SIGMORPHON 2018 Shared Task on Universal Morphological Reinflection. We test non-neural transduction models, as well as more recent neural methods. We also investigate the effect of leveraging unannotated corpora to improve the performance of selected methods. Our best system obtains the highest accuracy on 34 out of 103 languages.

1 Introduction

In this system paper, we discuss our submissions to the CoNLL–SIGMORPHON 2018 Shared Task on Universal Morphological Reinflection (Cotterell et al., 2018). We focus on the sub-task of type-level inflection under the low-resource scenario, in which the training data is limited to 100 labelled examples. Because of the sheer number of tested languages, we attempted no language-specific modifications. The results demonstrate that our non-neural transduction models perform better on average than our neural models. However, combining neural and non-neural models yields the highest accuracy.

In addition to standard submissions, we test novel methods of leveraging additional monolingual corpora, from which we derive target language models and/or word lists. We show that substantial gains in accuracy can be obtained in the way. Again, a combination of neural and non-neural systems produces the best non-standard results.

The paper has the following structure. In Section 2, we describe four standard systems, as well as our weighted-voting method of combining them. Our two non-standard systems and their linear combination are introduced in Section 3. Section 4 discusses the results.

2 Standard Systems

In this section, we briefly describe the four individual standard systems that we experimented with, followed by our voting method for combining them.

2.1 BASELINE (UA-01)

The shared task organizers have provided a baseline system for the type-level sub-task.[1] For each training instance, the baseline system aligns the input and output forms, and uses leading and trailing null alignments to identify prefix and suffix boundaries. Thus, the input and output are each divided into a prefix, stem, and suffix, with the prefix and suffix possibly being empty. The pairs of aligned characters from the suffix, and optionally a trailing substring of the stem, are recorded as suffixing rules for the morphological tag of the instance in question. Prefixing rules are identified in an analogous way. In this way, a series of inflection rules are generated from aligned training pairs for each morphological tag attested in the training data.

To perform reinflection on an unseen instance, the longest applicable suffixing rule for the given tag is selected and applied, as is the most frequent prefixing rule. Since some languages tend to prefer prefixing over suffixing, a heuristic is used to detect which of the two types of affixation is predominant. If a preference for prefixing is detected, all input and output strings for that language are reversed. During development, we found that the output files produced by the BASELINE system for these languages had the lemmas reversed; we rectified this issue for our experiments and submissions.

---

[1] https://github.com/sigmorphon/conll2018/tree/master/task1/baseline

116

Proceedings of the CoNLL–SIGMORPHON 2018 Shared Task: Universal Morphological Reinflection, pages 116–120,
Brussels, Belgium, October 31, 2018. ©2018 Association for Computational Linguistics

2.2 HAEM (UA-02)

The hard attention model over edit actions
(HAEM) of Makarov et al. (2017) performed very
well in the low-resource setting of the 2017 edition of the shared task. We use the implementation
made available by the authors.[2] The method learns
a neural state-transition model with hard monotonic attention. It produces sequences of insertion
and deletion operations on the lemma that trans-
duce it into the appropriate inflected form. The
system that achieved the top results in the 2017
shared task was an ensemble of up to 15 different
models, each trained with multiple seeds. Because
of time constraints, and the difficulties with using
the implementation, we derive only a single transition inflector model for each language, eschewing
the complex ensemble procedures described in the
original paper.

The process of compiling and running the provided code was non-trivial. In particular, libraries
required by the provided code had been supplanted
by newer versions, which lacked backwards com-
patibility. Since the versions used in 2017 are no
longer readily available, we had to adapt the code
to the new versions. Further modifications were
necessary to account for the different format of
the test data this year. Even with these modifications, the code failed to run properly on several
languages, resulting in 0% accuracy.

2.3 DIRECTL+ (UA-03)

We perform string transduction with a modified
version[3] of DIRECTL+, a tool originally designed
for grapheme-to-phoneme conversion (Jiampojamarn et al., 2008). DIRECTL+ is a feature-
rich, discriminative character string transducer
that searches for a model-optimal sequence of
character transformation rules for its input. The
core of the engine is a dynamic programming algorithm capable of transducing many consecutive
characters in a single operation. Using a structured
version of the MIRA algorithm (McDonald et al.,
2005), training attempts to assign weights to each
feature so that its linear model separates the gold-
standard derivation from all others in its search
space. We perform source-target pair alignment
with a modified version[4] of the M2M aligner (Jiampojamarn et al., 2007), which applies the EM to

[2]https://gitlab.cl.uzh.ch/makarov/sigmorphon2017
[3]https://github.com/GarrettNicolai/DTL
[4]https://github.com/GarrettNicolai/m2m

M2M-aligner		
source side	target side	maximum tag
{1-2}	{1-2}	{2-4}
DIRECTL+		
n-gram	context size	joint m-gram
{1-5}	{3-11}	{1-10}

Table 1: The tuning ranges for hyper-parameters.

maximize the conditional likelihood of its aligned
source and target pairs.

We apply the tag splitting and particle handling
techniques described in our 2017 system paper
Nicolai et al. (2017). In particular, we split the
tags into subtags, and append them at both the beginning and end of the lemma. We decided not
apply any subtag reordering techniques this year,
due to the large number of languages.

We tune hyper-parameters for each language using grid search. Table 1 specifies the tuning ranges
for both the aligner and the transducer. The list of
the actual hyper-parameter settings for each language is available on request.

2.4 AC-RNN (UA-04)

AC-RNN is our novel implementation of the
encoder-decoder RNN model, which is specialized to the sequence-labelling task, and trains with
an Actor-Critic reinforcement-learning objective
(Najafi et al., 2018a). The implementation is further modified to incorporate soft-general attention
mechanism, and adapted to the task of morphological reinflection.[5] In an initial experiment, we val-
idated AC-RNN using the high-resource French
dataset from the 2017 shared task, obtaining the
test accuracy of 89.7%, compared to 89.5% of the
best-performing 2017 ensemble system.

2.5 Standard Combination (UA-05)

In our development experiments, we observed that
no system described in this section strictly dominates the others in terms of accuracy on every language; rather, different systems perform well on
different languages. Furthermore, we often found
instances where incorrect predictions were made
by the top-performing system for the language in
question, but the correct output was produced by
other systems. These observations motivated our
attempt to combine the strengths of the four systems.

[5]https://gitlab.com/SaeedNajafi/ac-morph

Our standard combination approach is based on *weighted voting*. The top prediction from each of the four individual systems[6] is assigned a score equal to the system's accuracy on the development set for that language. The prediction with the highest total score is returned.

This system favors predictions from the top-performing system on a given language, while allowing errors to be corrected when other systems agree on a different prediction. If one system achieves an accuracy greater than the sum of the accuracies of all other systems, it dominates the voting, and the output of the combination is identical to the output of that system. This scenario occurred for only seven languages.

3 Non-standard Systems

Large monolingual raw text corpora, which are freely available for a wide variety of languages, offer the possibility of improving the accuracy of transduction models trained on small amounts of source-target pairs. Many of the target forms are observed in raw text corpora. In addition, character-level language models derived from monolingual corpora can reduce the number of output forms that violate the phonotactic constraints of a language. Target language modelling is particularly important in low-data scenarios, where the limited transduction models often produce many ill-formed output candidates. In this section, we describe the sources of the text corpora, and two novel methods that attempt to leverage the additional information.

3.1 Additional Data

The monolingual corpora come from one of two sources. The UniMorph project (Kirov et al., 2018) contains corpora for 46 out of 103 languages.[7] For 42 languages that are not represented in Unimorph, we instead use the target side of the high-resource training data in this shared task. For the 15 remaining languages that lack either of these resources, we simply back off to the standard version of each system. Note that we use only the target-side forms of the high-resource training data (if applicable), so that there is no overlap between the training and testing sets.

The principal use of the additional data is to construct a list of all word types, with counts, into a *target word list*. The idea is to bias the system predictions towards forms that are actually observed in a monolingual corpus. In this shared task, our word list sizes vary between 115 for Arabic and 22,371 for Slovene.

The second use of the unannotated corpora is to derive a target character-level n-gram language model. For this purpose, we employ the CMU language modeling toolkit.[8]

3.2 DTLM (UA-06)

Nicolai et al. (2018) present DTLM, a new system that combines discriminative transduction with character and word language models derived from large unannotated corpora. DTLM is an extension of DIRECTL+ (Section 2.3), whose target language modeling is limited to a set of binary n-gram features, which are based exclusively on the target sequences from the parallel training data. DTLM avoids the error propagation problem that is inherent in pipeline approaches by incorporating the language-model features directly into the transducer.

In addition, DTLM bolsters the quality of transduction by employing a novel alignment method, which is referred to as precision alignment. The idea is to allow null substrings on the source side during the alignment of the training data, and then apply a separate aggregation algorithm to merge them with adjoining non-empty substrings. This alignment method results in substantially higher transduction accuracy.[9]

3.3 AC-RNN with Word Lists (UA-07)

We also indirectly leverage the target word lists (ignoring the counts) in the AC-RNN model (Section 2.4). The neural network is trained with each of these external words as both input and output. We pre-train AC-RNN with this copying procedure for 50 epochs. (Bergmanis et al. (2017) use a similar technique with randomly-generated sequences.) We then fine-tune the model on the actual low-resource dataset. This approach is helpful in a several different ways: it biases the network towards copying input characters in the output, guides the attention parameters towards learning a monotonic alignment, and improves the randomly

---

[6]We had no access to additional top-n predictions from the BASELINE and HAEM systems.

[7]https://unimorph.github.io

[8]http://www.speech.cs.cmu.edu/SLM/toolkit.html

[9]DTLM was also succesfully used in the NEWS 2018 shared task on transliteration (Najafi et al., 2018b).

Method	Dev	Test
Standard		
BASELINE	39.3	38.2
HAEM	40.5	39.2
DIRECTL+	47.2	44.8
AC-RNN	21.4	21.3
Combination	**52.5**	**50.5**
Non-Standard		
AC-RNN + WL	38.7	38.0
DTLM	51.4	49.7
Combination	**54.4**	**53.2**

Table 2: The average accuracy across all languages.

	None	+LM	+LM +WL
High-Resource	38.6	42.6	*28.6*
Unimorph	38.6	45.4	49.7

Table 3: The average accuracy of DTLM on the development sets of 46 languages with additional data.

initialized character embeddings by pre-training them on external data.

We also experimented with two different ideas to re-rank predictions of AC-RNN. The first idea was to train a separate RNN-based language model to re-score predictions. The second idea was to learn a reverse model that would generate the input lemma from the inflected form and tag, for the purpose of re-scoring the n-best lists of AC-RNN. Unfortunately, neither of these approaches outperformed the copying procedure outlined in the previous paragraph.

3.4 Non-standard Combination (UA-08)

We take advantage of the ability of both DTLM and AC-RNN to produce n-best lists of predictions by combining the lists via a linear combination of their confidence scores. The scores from each model are normalized, and the linear coefficients are tuned separately for each language on the provided development sets. The top scoring output for each input instance is returned.

4 Results

Table 2 shows the average accuracy over 103 languages for our eight submitted systems in the low-resource setting. The ranking of the systems is the same for both the development and test sets.[10] The best performing individual standard system is DIRECTL+, followed by HAEM, BASELINE, and AC-RNN. We conclude that 100 training instances are insufficient for the soft-attention based neural models like AC-RNN. Moreover, we were not able to replicate the superior results of HAEM reported in the 2017 shared task, which we attribute to the reasons outlined in Section 2.2. Our

weighted-voting combination of all four systems substantially improves over each individual system. In the development experiments, we observed that all individual systems, including AC-RNN, contributed to the accuracy of the combination system.

Among the non-standard systems, the DTLM model easily outperforms DIRECTL+. The copy pre-training approach on the target word lists almost doubles the accuracy of AC-RNN, but it is not sufficient to even reach the BASELINE. Nevertheless, the linear combination of the two non-standard systems is clearly the best of our submissions, obtaining the highest accuracy on 34 languages in the shared task.

In order to shed light on the effect of additional data on the DTLM results, we ran experiments on 46 languages that have both the Unimorph and high-resource data (Table 3). It is clear that incorporating a target language model from either data source improves the overall accuracy. The results also suggest that the Unimorph corpora are better for the purpose of deriving the language models than the high-resource training data. The addition of the target word lists from Unimorph further improves the results. However, the word lists from the high-resource data are detrimental. Since there is no overlap between the training and development data, there are no useful targets in the word lists to help guide the model outputs.

5 Conclusion

We described the details of the systems that we tested on 103 languages in the low-resource setting of the shared task. In particular, we experimented with combining diverse systems, applying reinforcement learning to neural models, and leveraging target corpora for reinflection. Our results suggest that these techniques lead to improvements in accuracy with respect to the base systems. We hope that this report will serve as a useful reference for future experiments involving the datasets from this shared task.

---

[10]Detailed results on all languages are available on request.

Acknowledgements

We thank Garrett Nicolai for the assistance with DTLM. We thank the shared task organizers for preparing a large number of datasets, and smoothly executing the evaluation process. This research was supported by the Natural Sciences and Engineering Research Council of Canada, Alberta Innovates, and Alberta Advanced Education.

References

Toms Bergmanis, Katharina Kann, Hinrich Schütze, and Sharon Goldwater. 2017. Training data augmentation for low-resource morphological inflection. In *Proceedings of the CoNLL SIGMORPHON 2017 Shared Task: Universal Morphological Reinflection*, pages 31–39, Vancouver. Association for Computational Linguistics.

Ryan Cotterell, Christo Kirov, John Sylak-Glassman, Géraldine Walther, Ekaterina Vylomova, Arya D. McCarthy, Katharina Kann, Sebastian Mielke, Garrett Nicolai, Miikka Silfverberg, David Yarowsky, Jason Eisner, and Mans Hulden. 2018. The CoNLL–SIGMORPHON 2018 shared task: Universal morphological reinflection. In *Proceedings of the CoNLL–SIGMORPHON 2018 Shared Task: Universal Morphological Reinflection*, Brussels, Belgium. Association for Computational Linguistics.

Sittichai Jiampojamarn, Colin Cherry, and Grzegorz Kondrak. 2008. Joint processing and discriminative training for letter-to-phoneme conversion. *Proceedings of ACL-08: HLT*, pages 905–913.

Sittichai Jiampojamarn, Grzegorz Kondrak, and Tarek Sherif. 2007. Applying many-to-many alignments and hidden markov models to letter-to-phoneme conversion. In *NAACL-HLT*, pages 372–379.

Christo Kirov, Ryan Cotterell, John Sylak-Glassman, Graldine Walther, Ekaterina Vylomova, Patrick Xia, Manaal Faruqui, Sebastian Mielke, Arya D. McCarthy, Sandra Kbler, David Yarowsky, Jason Eisner, and Mans Hulden. 2018. UniMorph 2.0: Universal Morphology. In *Proceedings of the Eleventh International Conference on Language Resources and Evaluation (LREC 2018)*, Miyazaki, Japan. European Language Resources Association (ELRA).

Peter Makarov, Tatiana Ruzsics, and Simon Clematide. 2017. Align and copy: Uzh at sigmorphon 2017 shared task for morphological reinflection. In *Proceedings of the CoNLL SIGMORPHON 2017 Shared Task: Universal Morphological Reinflection*, pages 49–57. Association for Computational Linguistics.

Ryan McDonald, Koby Crammer, and Fernando Pereira. 2005. Online large-margin training of dependency parsers. In *Proceedings of the 43rd Annual Meeting of the Association for Computational Linguistics (ACL'05)*, pages 91–98. Association for Computational Linguistics.

Saeed Najafi, Colin Cherry, and Grzegorz Kondrak. 2018a. Sequence labeling and transduction with output-adjusted actor-critic training of RNNs. In preparation.

Saeed Najafi, Bradley Hauer, Rashed Rubby Riyadh, Leyuan Yu, and Grzegorz Kondrak. 2018b. Comparison of assorted models for transliteration. In *Proceedings of the Seventh Named Entities Workshop*, pages 84–88. Association for Computational Linguistics.

Garrett Nicolai, Bradley Hauer, Mohammad Motallebi, Saeed Najafi, and Grzegorz Kondrak. 2017. If you can't beat them, join them: the university of alberta system description. *Proceedings of the CoNLL SIGMORPHON 2017 Shared Task: Universal Morphological Reinflection*, pages 79–84.

Garrett Nicolai, Saeed Najafi, and Grzegorz Kondrak. 2018. String transduction with target language models and insertion handling. In *Proceedings of the 15th SIGMORPHON Workshop on Computational Research in Phonetics, Phonology, and Morphology*, Brussels, Belgium.

BME-HAS System for CoNLL–SIGMORPHON 2018 Shared Task: Universal Morphological Reinflection

Judit Ács

Department of Automation and Applied Informatics
Budapest University of Technology and Economics
and
Institute for Computer Science and Control
Hungarian Academy of Sciences
`judit@sch.bme.hu`

Abstract

This paper presents an encoder-decoder neural network based solution for both subtasks of the CoNLL–SIGMORPHON 2018 Shared Task: Universal Morphological Reinflection. All of our models are sequence-to-sequence neural networks with multiple encoders and a single decoder.

1   Introduction

Morphological inflection is the task of inflecting a lemma given either a target form or some contextual information. Morphology has traditionally been solved by finite state transducers (FST) that employ a large number of handcrafted rules. The discrete nature of such processes makes it difficult to directly translate transducers into neural networks and to effectively train them using back-propagation. There have been various attempts to replace parts of the FST paradigm with neural networks (Aharoni and Goldberg, 2016).

SIGMORPHON first organized a shared task on morphological inflection in 2016 (Cotterell et al., 2016) which involved both inflection (inflect a word given its lemma) and reinflection (inflect a word given another inflected form of the same lemma). The winning solution (Kann and Schütze, 2016) used a character sequence-to-sequence network with Bahdanau's attention (Bahdanau et al., 2015). In the second edition of the shared task (Cotterell et al., 2017) most teams used similar settings.

2   Task formulation

In this section we briefly describe the objective of the task and provide examples for each subtask. A more comprehensive explanation is available on the shared task's website[1] and in task description paper (Cotterell et al., 2018).

---

[1] https://sigmorphon.github.io/sharedtasks/2018/

2.1   Task1: Type-level inflection

Inflection aims to find an inflected word given its lemma and a set of morphological tags in Uni-Morph MSD(Kirov et al., 2018). A few examples are shown below (the second column is the target):

```
release      releasing      V;V.PTCP;PRS
deodourize   deodourize     V;NFIN
outdance     outdancing     V;V.PTCP;PRS
misrepute    misrepute      V;NFIN
vanquish     vanquished     V;PST
resterilize  resterilizes   V;3;SG;PRS
```

The shared task features over 100 languages and 10 additional surprise language were released before the submission deadline. Most languages had three data settings: high (10 000 samples), medium (1 000 samples) and low (100 samples), except some low-resource languages that did not have enough samples for high or medium settings. Each language had a development set of 1 000 or less samples.

2.2   Task2: Inflection in context

Task2 is a cloze task. We were given a sentence with a number of missing word forms (usually 1 or 2) and our task is to inflect the word given its lemma and context. Task2 two had two tracks: in Track1 all the lemmas and morphosyntactic description are given in the sentence context (the morphosyntactic description of the covered word is covered too), and in Track2 only the word forms of the context are given. Below are examples from Track1:

```
Les        le          DET;DEF;FEM;PL
compagnies             compagnie      N;FEM;PL
aériennes              aérien   ADJ;FEM;PL
à          à           ADP
bas        bas         ADJ;MASC;SG
coût       coût        N;MASC;SG
ne         ne          ADV;NEG
_          connaître              _
pas        pas         ADV;NEG
la         le          DET;DEF;FEM;SG
crise      crise       N;FEM;SG
.          .           PUNCT
```


Proceedings of the CoNLL–SIGMORPHON 2018 Shared Task: Universal Morphological Reinflection, pages 121–126,
Brussels, Belgium, October 31, 2018. ©2018 Association for Computational Linguistics

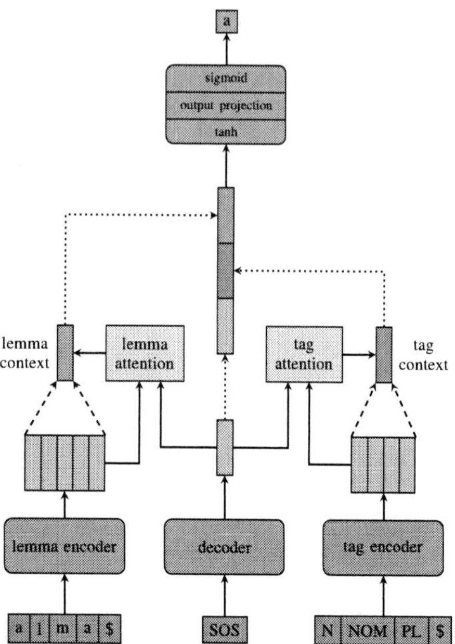

Figure 1: Two-headed attention model used for Task1. The figure illustrates the first timestep of decoding. The output of this step is fed back to the decoder in the next timestep. Modules are colored gray, attention heads yellow, inputs are purple, outputs are teal and encoder output matrices are salmon. Dotted arrows represent copy operations and dashed arrows represent attention summaries. The color scheme is borrowed from `colorbrewer2.org`

and the same sentence for Track2:

```
Les          _       _
compagnies   _       _
aériennes    _       _       _
à            _       _
bas          _       _
coût         _       _
ne           _       _
_          connaître        _
pas          _       _
la           _       _
crise        _       _
.            _       _
```

Both examples are taken from the development sets. The training sets have no covered words, and we generated training examples by covering a single word at a time, and using the rest as its sentence context.

Task2 also featured low, medium and high resource settings with roughly 1 000, 10 000 and 100 000 tokens respectively.

3 Task1 model: two-headed attention

In this section we describe our system for Task 1: Type-level inflection. We explain our experimental setup and the random hyperparameter search, and finally we list three slightly different submissions and their results.

3.1 Two-headed attention seq2seq

Inflection can be formulated as a mapping of two sequences, namely a lemma and a sequence of tags, to one sequence, the inflected word form. The lemma and the inflected word forms are character sequences that usually share a common alphabet while the tags are a sequence of language-specific morphological codes. Figure 1 illustrates our architecture. We use separate encoders for the lemma and the morphological tags and a single decoder. Both encoders employ character/tag embeddings and bidirectional LSTMs, where the outputs are summed over the two directions. The two encoders' hidden states are then linearly projected to the decoder's hidden dimension and used to initialize the decoder's hidden state. This allows using different hidden dimensions in each module. Decoding is done in an autoregressive fashion, one character at a time. At each timestep the decoder reads a single character: *SOS (start-of-sequence)* at first, the ground truth during training (*teacher forcing*) and the previous output during inference. The decoder uses a character level embedding, which may or may not be shared with the lemma encoder (c.f. 3.2), then it passes the embedded symbol to a unidirectional LSTM. Its output is used by two attention modules, hence the name *two-headed attention*, to compute a context vector using Luong's attention (Luong et al., 2015). The lemma and tag context vectors are concatenated with the decoder output, then passed through a *tanh*, an output projection and finally a sigmoid layer which produces a distribution over the character vocabulary of the language. Greedy decoding is used.

3.2 Experimental setup

All experiments were implemented in Python 3.6 and PyTorch 0.4. We used three different Debian servers, two with NVIDIA GTX TITAN GPUs (12GB) and one with a GTX 980 (4GB). We created our own experiment framework that allows running and logging a large number of experiments. The framework is available on Github[2] and the configurations and scripts used for this shared task are available in a separate repository[3]. The latter repository contains all best configurations including the random seeds (we generate the random seeds at the beginning of each experiments, then save them for reproducibility).

All experiments shared a number of configuration options while the others were randomly optimized. We list the ones we fixed here and the others in 3.3. Each experiment used a batch size of 128 for both training and evaluation except the ones on the Kurmanji language because the development dataset contained very long sequences and we had to reduce the batch size to 16 to fit into memory (12GB). We used the Adam optimizer with learning rate 0.001 and we stopped each experiment when the development loss did not decrease on average in the last 5 epochs compared to the previous 5 epochs. We ran at least 20 epochs before stopping even if the early stopping condition was satisfied to avoid early overfitting, which happened in about 10% of the experiments. We also set a hard upper limit for the number of epochs (200) but this was reached only two times out of 1 886 experiments. The average number of epochs before reaching the early stopping condition was 51 and only 2.7% of experiments ran for more than 100 epochs. After each epoch, we saved the model if its development loss was lower than the previous minimum. We used cross entropy as the loss function.

3.3 Random parameter search

Our initial experiments suggested that the model is very sensitive to random initialization and the same configuration can result in models with very different performance. This is probably due to the limited training data even in *high* setting and the large number of parameters of the model. We chose three languages, Breton, Latin and Lithuanian, and ran a large number of experiments with random configuration on them. The reason these were chosen is that the development accuracy on these were in the mid-ranges among all the language during our initial experiments. The following random experiments were all run on the *high* training sets. Common parameters (c.f. 3.2) were loaded from a base configuration and some param-

Table 1: Parameter ranges

Parameter	Values
dropout	0.1, 0.3, 0.4, 0.6
share vocab	true, false
inflected embedding size	10, 20, 30, 50
inflected hidden size	128, 256, 512, 1024
inflected num layers	1, 2
lemma embedding size	10, 20, 30, 50
lemma hidden size	128, 256, 512, 1024
lemma num layers	1, 2, 3, 4
tag embedding size	5, 10, 20
tag hidden size	64, 128, 256
tag num layers	1, 2, 3, 4

eters were overriden with a value uniformly sampled from a predefined set. The range of values are listed in Table 1. Both encoders (lemma and tag) and the decoder (listed as *inflected*) have three varying parameters: the size of the embedding, the number of hidden LSTM cells and the number of LSTM layers. We also varied the dropout rate for both the embedding and the LSTMs and the whether to share the vocabulary and the embedding among the lemma and the decoder or not.

The running time of an experiment is dependent on the average length of the input sequences and the size of the vocabulary. It turns out that these vary greatly among the languages in the dataset. As listed in Table 2 Breton is much "smaller" in both alphabet and sequence length than Lithuanian or Latin and this was evident from the difference in average running time.

Table 3 summarizes the results of our random parameter search. Since the average running time of different language experiments is very different, we ended up running many more Breton experiments in roughly the same time. The standard deviation of results is quite large, especially for Breton, which we attribute to the small alphabet, the short sequences and the small number of lemmas (44) as opposed to Latin (6517) or Lithuanian (1443).

We observed that models with the same parameters often result in very different word accuracy. To test this, we took the best performing configuration for each language and trained 20 models (by language) with identical parameters but different random seeds. Table 4 shows that identical pa-

---

[2]https://github.com/juditacs/deep-morphology
[3]https://github.com/juditacs/sigmorphon2018

Table 2: Dataset statistics.	Breton	Latin	Lithuanian
alphabet size	27	55	58
inflected maxlen	14	23	32
inflected types	1790	9896	9463
lemma maxlen	11	19	28
lemma types	44	6517	1443
tag types	20	33	34
tags maxlen	9	7	6

Table 2: Dataset statistics.

Table 3: Summary of the parameter search. The running time is given in minutes.

		Breton	Latin	Lithuanian
experiments		1033	610	243
dev acc	mean	70.92	62.32	80.25
	max	93.00	78.90	88.40
	std	28.70	11.30	8.37
time	mean	0.83	5.42	8.61

rameters can result in models with very different performance.

3.4 Submission

We took the 5 highest scoring model for each language and trained a model with those parameters for each language and each data size, thus training 15 models per dataset. Our first submission is simply the model with the highest development word accuracy. The second submission is the result of majority voting by all 15 models. The third one is the same as the first one but we changed the evaluation batch size from 128 to 16. This results fewer pad symbols on average. Table 5 lists the mean performance of each submission.

Table 4: Accuracy statistics of 20 models trained with the same parameters but different random seed.

		Breton	Latin	Lithuanian
train acc	mean	96.29	92.58	96.69
	std	1.39	3.21	2.25
	min	94.30	84.57	90.51
	max	99.04	97.14	99.08
dev acc	mean	87.35	74.73	86.95
	std	2.41	3.17	2.32
	min	84.00	69.00	81.80
	max	92.00	79.10	90.60

Table 5: The mean accuracy of our Task1 submissions.

Subm	Data size	Accuracy	Ranking
#1	High	93.884884	7
	Medium	67.430392	8
	Low	3.742718	22
#2	High	**94.662791**	**3**
	Medium	67.258824	10
	Low	2.429126	25
#3	High	93.973256	6
	Medium	67.357843	9
	Low	3.634951	23

4 Task2: Inflection in Context

In this section we describe our system for Task2 - Track1, then explain how the model for Track2 differs from the model for Track1.

The development datasets for Task2 have two versions: covered and uncovered. An example is provided in 2.2.

Figure 2 illustrates the model at a single timestep (decoding one character). The model has several inputs (colored purple):

target lemma The lemma of the target word. The inflected form of this lemma is the expected output.

left/right token context The other (inflected) tokens in the sentence. Left context refers to the tokens preceding the covered token and right context refers to the ones succeeding it.

left/right lemma context The lemmas of the preceding and succeeding tokens.

left/right tag context The corresponding tags of the preceding and succeeding tokens.

previously decoded symbol Start-of-sequence at the first timestep, then the last symbol produced by greedy decoding.

The left and right contexts are encoded separately in the following way. Each token and lemma are encoded by a bidirectional character LSTM, preceded by a character embedding, and the tag sequence of the corresponding token are encoded by a separate biLSTM and tag embedding. The lemma and the token share their alphabet and our experiments showed that sharing the encoder results in a slight improvement in accuracy. By taking the last output of each of the three encoders,

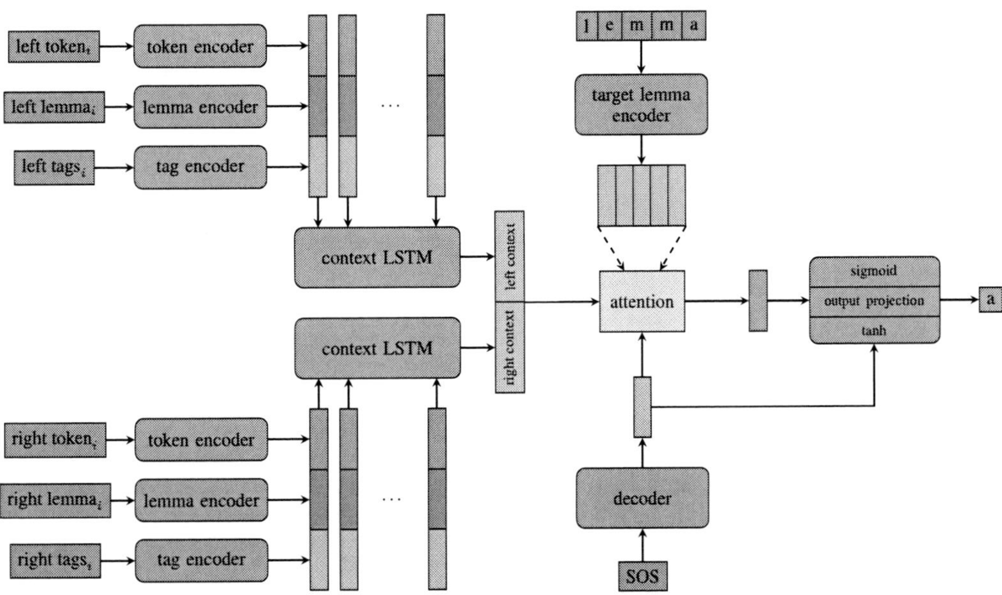

Figure 2: Task2 architecture. The figure illustrates the first timestep of decoding. The output of this step is fed back to the decoder in the next timestep. The target lemma encoder's hidden state is used to initialize the decoder hidden state (not pictured for the sake of clarity). The same coloring scheme is used as in 1.

we acquire three fixed dimensional vector representation for each token. We concatenate these and use another biLSTM (context LSTM) to create a single vector representation of the left/right context. The context LSTM is shared by the left and the right context. The target lemma is encoded by the same encoder as the other lemmas and inflected tokens and the output is used by the attention mechanism. The last hidden state of the encoder is used to initialize the hidden state of the decoder. Decoding is similar to the autoregressive process used in Task1 but there is only one attention mechanism and it attends to the target lemma encoder outputs. Attention weights are computed using the concatenation of the decoder output at a single timestep and the left and right context vectors. The output of the attention module is concatenated with the decoder output, passed through a *tanh* and an output projection and finally a softmax layer outputs a distribution over the character alphabet of the language. Similarly to our Task1 model, the ground truth is fed to the decoder at training time and the greedily decoded character at inference time. The cross entropy of the output distributions and the ground truth is used as a loss function.

Our model for Track2 is very similar to the model for Track1, except the left and right lemma and tag encoders are missing and the context vectors are derived only from the left and right tokens.

4.1 Experimental setup

Since our experiments for Task2 were significantly slower than the ones for Task1, we were unable to run extensive parameter search. We did perform a smaller version of the same random search using the parameter ranges listed in Table 6. We chose the French dataset with medium setting, which is about 10 000 tokens. The average length of one experiment was 100 minutes and we were able to run 38 experiments. We ran the best configuration of the 38 on each language and each data size at least once. Since our parameter search was very limited, we also varied the parameters manually and tried other combinations. The exact configurations are available on the GitHub repository. All experiments were run on NVIDIA GTX TITAN X GPUs (12GB), since they did not fit into the memory of the smaller cards (4GB).

Task2 uses a subset of the parameters that Task1 uses, so we were able to train the "same" configuration emerged as the best one during the limited hyperparameter search. We also tried using 2 layers instead of 1 layer in every encoder and decoder. Unfortunately time constraints did not allow running more experiments.

Table 6: Predefined parameter ranges used for Task2 parameter search.

Parameter	Values
batch size	8, 16, 32, 64
dropout	0.0, 0.2
early stopping window	5, 10
char embedding size	30, 40, 50
context hidden size	64, 128, 256
context num layers	1, 2
decoder num layers	1
tag embedding size	10, 20, 30
tag num layers	1, 2
word hidden size	64, 128, 256
word num layers	1, 2

Table 7: Task2 results.

	Track1			Track2		
	high	med	low	high	med	low
de	73.21	56.83	30.64	64.61	52.17	27.81
en	76.23	66.77	61.33	69.89	64.05	56.90
es	56.10	42.50	29.17	41.65	32.12	27.77
fi	53.75	22.11	10.29	30.24	17.15	8.89
fr	67.21	51.12	26.27	45.42	23.63	9.57
ru	67.67	38.76	21.59	56.73	33.73	19.68
sv	65.64	41.91	26.06	54.26	34.89	22.34

4.2 Submission and results

For both Track1 and Track2 we only submitted one system, the output of the highest scoring model on the development dataset. In both tracks, we finished in 2nd place. Table 7 lists our detailed results.

5 Conclusion

We presented our submissions for the CoNLL–SIGMORPHON 2018 Shared Task: Universal Morphological Reinflection. We employed variations of sequence-to-sequence or encoder-decoder networks with Luong attention. Our experiments for Task1 suggest that at the current data size, the model is very sensitive to random initialization, so we used an ensemble of many systems, which placed 2nd of all teams in the high data setting. We also placed 2nd in both tracks of Task2. Our code and configuration files including the random seeds are available on Github.

References

Roee Aharoni and Yoav Goldberg. 2016. Morphological inflection generation with hard monotonic attention. *arXiv preprint arXiv:1611.01487*.

Dzmitry Bahdanau, Kyunghyun Cho, and Yoshua Bengio. 2015. Neural machine translation by jointly learning to align and translate. In *International Conference on Learning Representations (ICLR 2015)*.

Ryan Cotterell, Christo Kirov, John Sylak-Glassman, Géraldine Walther, Ekaterina Vylomova, Arya D. McCarthy, Katharina Kann, Sebastian Mielke, Garrett Nicolai, Miikka Silfverberg, David Yarowsky, Jason Eisner, and Mans Hulden. 2018. The CoNLL–SIGMORPHON 2018 shared task: Universal morphological reinflection. In *Proceedings of the CoNLL–SIGMORPHON 2018 Shared Task: Universal Morphological Reinflection*, Brussels, Belgium. Association for Computational Linguistics.

Ryan Cotterell, Christo Kirov, John Sylak-Glassman, Géraldine Walther, Ekaterina Vylomova, Patrick Xia, Manaal Faruqui, Sandra Kübler, David Yarowsky, Jason Eisner, and Mans Hulden. 2017. The CoNLL-SIGMORPHON 2017 shared task: Universal morphological reinflection in 52 languages. In *Proceedings of the CoNLL-SIGMORPHON 2017 Shared Task: Universal Morphological Reinflection*, Vancouver, Canada. Association for Computational Linguistics.

Ryan Cotterell, Christo Kirov, John Sylak-Glassman, David Yarowsky, Jason Eisner, and Mans Hulden. 2016. The SIGMORPHON 2016 shared task— morphological reinflection. In *Proceedings of the 2016 Meeting of SIGMORPHON*, Berlin, Germany. Association for Computational Linguistics.

Katharina Kann and Hinrich Schütze. 2016. MED: The LMU system for the SIGMORPHON 2016 shared task on morphological reinflection. *ACL 2016*, page 62.

Christo Kirov, Ryan Cotterell, John Sylak-Glassman, Géraldine Walther, Ekaterina Vylomova, Patrick Xia, Manaal Faruqui, Sebastian Mielke, Arya D. McCarthy, Sandra Kübler, David Yarowsky, Jason Eisner, and Mans Hulden. 2018. UniMorph 2.0: Universal Morphology. In *Proceedings of the Eleventh International Conference on Language Resources and Evaluation (LREC 2018)*, Miyazaki, Japan. European Language Resources Association (ELRA).

Thang Luong, Hieu Pham, and Christopher D. Manning. 2015. Effective approaches to attention-based neural machine translation. In *Proceedings of the 2015 Conference on Empirical Methods in Natural Language Processing*, pages 1412–1421. Association for Computational Linguistics.

Author Index